D1594811

Monographs of the
Hebrew Union College
Number 15

———

Baraita de-Melekhet
ha-Mishkan:

A Critical Edition
with
Introduction and Translation

Monographs of the Hebrew Union College

1. Lewis M. Barth, *An Analysis of Vatican 30*

2. Samson H. Levey, *The Messiah: An Aramaic Interpretation*

3. Ben Zion Wacholder, *Eupolemus: A Study of Judaeo-Greek Literature*

4. Richard Victor Bergren, *The Prophets and the Law*

5. Benny Kraut, *From Reform Judaism to Ethical Culture: The Religious Evolution of Felix Adler*

6. David B. Ruderman, *The World of a Renaissance Jew: The Life and Thought of Abraham ben Mordecai Farissol*

7. Alan Mendelson, *Secular Education in Philo of Alexandria*

8. Ben Zion Wacholder, *The Dawn of Qumran: The Sectarian Torah and the Teacher of Righteousness*

9. Stephen M. Passamaneck, *The Traditional Jewish Law of Sale: Shulḥan Arukh, Ḥoshen Mishpat, Chapters 189-240*

10. Yael S. Feldman, *Modernism and Cultural Transfer: Gabriel Preil and the Tradition of Jewish Literary Bilingualism*

11. Raphael Jospe, *Torah and Sophia: The Life and Thought of Shem Tov ibn Falaquera*

12. Richard Kalmin, *The Redaction of the Babylonian Talmud: Amoraic or Saboraic?*

13. Shuly Rubin Schwartz, *The Emergence of Jewish Scholarship in America: The Publication of the Jewish Encyclopedia*

14. John C. Reeves, *Jewish Lore in Manichaean Cosmogony: Studies in the Book of Giants Traditions*

15. Robert Kirschner, *Baraita de-Melekhet ha-Mishkan: A Critical Edition with Introduction and Translation*

Baraita de-Melekhet ha-Mishkan

A Critical Edition
with
Introduction and Translation

Robert Kirschner

Hebrew Union College Press
Cincinnati

ⒸCopyright 1992 by the Hebrew Union College Press
Hebrew Union College – Jewish Institute of Religion

LIBRARY OF CONGRESS CATALOGING-IN-PUBLICATION DATA

Baraita de-melekhet ha-mishkan: a critical edition with
introduction and translation / Robert Kirschner
  p. cm.– (Monographs of the Hebrew Union College; no.
15) Includes bibliographical references and index.
ISBN 0-87820-414-8 (hardcover: alk. paper)
1. Tabernacle–Early works to 1800. 2. Baraita de-melekhet ha-
mishkan–Criticism, Textual. I. Kirschner, Robert (Robert S.)
II. Baraita de-melekhet ha-mishkan. English. 1992. III.
Series
BM507.5.E6E5 1992   90-27783
96.1'263–dc20   CIP

Printed on acid-free paper
Manufactured in the United States of America
Distributed by Behrman House, Inc.
235 Watchung Avenue, West Orange, NJ 07052

Contents

Acknowledgments

A project of this kind is not possible without the assistance of many people and institutions.

For permission to consult or photograph manuscripts and editions for this study, I wish to thank the Jewish National University Library, Jerusalem; Bayerische Staatsbibliothek, Munich; Bibliothèque Nationale, Paris; Biblioteca Palatina, Parma; Bodleian Library, Oxford; British Library, London; Cambridge University Library; Dropsie College Library, Philadelphia; Hebrew Union College Library, Cincinnati; and the Jewish Theological Seminary Library, New York City. Personal thanks are owed to Benjamin Richler of the Institute for Microfilmed Hebrew Manuscripts and Shulamith Berger and Lili Kahan of the JTS Library for their kind cooperation.

For guidance on technical questions of paleography and codicology, I am indebted to Malachi Beit-Arie and the Hebrew Paleography Project. For an introduction to statistical techniques of textual criticism, I wish to thank James Joyce of San Francisco and John Dawson of the Literary and Linguistic Computing Center at Cambridge University.

The arduous task of producing a technical typescript in Hebrew and English was accomplished with singular skill and care by Ila Cherney, Muriel Cohn, and Bonnie Gallaty. At Hebrew Union College, Michael Meyer, Chairman of the Publications Committee, and Barbara Selya, Assistant to the Committee, contributed invaluable advice and expertise to the preparation of this book, and Richard Sarason kindly checked the Hebrew text before the manuscript was typeset. I also wish to thank Allan Satin for his work on the index.

In the course of research, I benefited greatly from consultation on various aspects of this work with Jacob Sussman, the late Ephraim Urbach, Chaim Milikowsky, Menachem Kahana, Amos Funkenstein, Lewis Barth, Michael Signer, and Norman Cohen, who first called my attention to Baraita de-Melekhet ha-Mishkan. To each of them I offer this expression of appreciation.

A special word of thanks is owed to three scholars: Marc Bregman, whose generous assistance and guidance were crucial to this project; Stefan C. Reif of the Taylor-Schechter Genizah Research Unit at Cambridge University, whose time and hospitality were graciously provided; and Ben Zion Wacholder, who kindly devoted many hours helping me to analyze the parallel passages discussed in chapter 3 of this study.

Among my teachers at the University of California at Berkeley, I wish particularly to acknowledge my debt to the late Baruch Bokser; and also to Peter Brown, David Winston, David Daube, and Eliezer Segal. Above all, I am grateful to Jacob Milgrom, whose erudition I can scarcely emulate and whose many kindnesses I cannot hope to repay.

To my wife Reesa and to our children, Nili, Jesse, Talia, and Eva, for their love and forbearance, the greatest of all debts is owed. Whatever the merit of this labor, it is theirs too.

Abbreviations

Ant.	Antiquitates Judaicae
Ar.	Arakhin
ARN	Avot de-R. Nathan
AZ	Avodah Zarah
b.	Babylonian Talmud (Bavli); *ben* (son of)
Bar.	Baruch
BB	Bava Batra
B.C.E.	before the common era
Bez.	Bezah
BH	Biblical Hebrew
BM	Bava Mezia
BMM	Baraita de-Melekhet ha-Mishkan
BQ	Bava Qamma
c.	century
ca.	circa
Cant.	Canticles (Song of Songs)
Cant. R.	Canticles Rabbah
C.E.	common era
ch.	chapter(s)
Chr.	Chronicles
col.	column
Deut.	Deuteronomy
Eccl.	Ecclesiastes
Eccl. R.	Ecclesiastes Rabbah
ed.	edition
EJ	*Encyclopedia Judaica*, 16 vols. (Jerusalem, 1971)
Er.	Eruvin
ET	Wilhelm Bacher, *Die Exegetische Terminologie der Jüdischen Traditionsliteratur* (repr. Darmstadt, 1965)

Ex.	Exodus
Ex. R.	Exodus Rabbah
Ezek.	Ezekiel
f(f).	folio(s)
Gen.	Genesis
Gen. R.	Genesis Rabbah
Ḥag.	Ḥagigah
Ḥal.	Ḥallah
Heb.	Hebrews
Her.	Quis Rerum Divinarum Heres Sit
Hor.	Horayot
HTR	*Harvard Theological Review*
HUCA	*Hebrew Union College Annual*
Ḥul.	Ḥullin
Is.	Isaiah
JBL	*Journal of Biblical Literature*
JJS	*Journal of Jewish Studies*
Josh.	Joshua
JPS	Jewish Publication Society (translation)
JQR	*Jewish Quarterly Review*
Kel.	Kelim
Ket.	Ketuvot
Ki.	Kings
Kil.	Kila'im
LA	Legum Allegoriarum
Lev.	Leviticus
M.	Mishnah
Macc.	Maccabees
Meg.	Megillah
Mek.	Mekhilta
Men.	Menaḥot
MH	Mishnaic Hebrew
MHB	Mishnaic Hebrew (Babylonian)
MHP	Mishnaic Hebrew (Palestinian)
Mid.	Middot
Mos.	De Vita Mosis
MQ	Mo'ed Qatan
MS(S)	manuscript(s)
Num.	Numbers
Num. R.	Numbers Rabbah

PAAJR	*Proceedings of the American Academy for Jewish Research*
Pes.	Pesaḥim
PRK	Pesiqta de-Rav Kahana
Ps.	Psalms
QE	Quaestiones et Solutiones in Exodum
Qid.	Qiddushin
R.	Rabbi, Rav
RH	Rosh Hashanah
Sam.	Samuel
Sanh.	Sanhedrin
Shab.	Shabbat
Sheq.	Sheqalim
Som.	De Somniis
Sot.	Sotah
Suk.	Sukkah
T.	Tosefta
Ta'an.	Ta'anit
TM	C. Y. Kosovsky, *Thesaurus Mishnae*, 4 vols. (Jerusalem, 1960)
T-S	Taylor-Schechter (Genizah Collection)
TSifra	B. Kosovsky, *Thesaurus Sifra*, 4 vols. (Jerusalem, 1967-69)
TSifre	B. Kosovsky, *Thesaurus Sifre*, 5 vols. (Jerusalem, 1971-74)
TT	Wilhelm Bacher, *Tradition und Tradenten in den Schulen Palästinas und Babyloniens* (repr. Berlin, 1966)
Uq.	Uqẓin
v(v).	verse(s)
y.	Yerushalmi (Palestinian Talmud)
Yev.	Yevamot
YK	Yom Kippur
Zev.	Zevaḥim

Chapter 1

Description, Structure, Genre

According to the priestly source of the Pentateuch, the central phenomenon of holiness is the desert tabernacle. Its architectonic design (Ex. 25-27, 30, 31), technical execution (Ex. 35-40), disassembly and transportation (Num. 3-4) are described in searching detail. Its inventory of furniture and utensils is catalogued and recapitulated (Ex. 30:26-30; 31:7- 11; 35:11-19; 39:33-41; 40:2-5, 18-33, etc.). The construction[1] of the tabernacle (*melekhet ha-mishkan*) is the Israelites' first response to the theophany at Sinai; its completion marks a new beginning in time (Ex. 40:17).[2] The prototype was drafted by God himself (Ex. 25:9,40; 26:30; 27:8). From Sinai the Israelites carried the tabernacle through the wilderness to the land of Canaan, where various reports place it at Gilgal (Josh. 4:9, 5:10), Shiloh (Josh. 18:1, 19:51), Gibeon (1 Chr. 21:29, 2 Chr. 1:3-6), and finally Jerusalem (2 Sam. 7:6). Although the biblical data are contradictory, it is possible that the tabernacle was in use until David's time (2 Sam. 7:6). Its final destination is not certain, nor is its ultimate fate.[3]

The Temple built by Solomon (1 Ki. 6-7) reflects the tabernacle model.[4] The sanctuary described in the first section (col. 3-13) of the Temple Scroll seems to have been especially influenced by the wilderness shrine.[5] The fragments of Eupolemus (ca. 160 B.C.E.) devoted to descriptions of the Jerusalem Temple allude in certain details to the tabernacle traditions of the Pentateuch.[6] Josephus too dwells at length on the account of the tabernacle (Ant. 3:7). Clearly the Sinaitic blueprint exerted a lasting hold on the ancient Jewish imagination.

In the absence of artifactual evidence, the scriptural record of the tabernacle is its sole witness. However, the tabernacle texts are often difficult to understand owing to various contradictions, improbabili-

1

ties, lacunae, and a highly technical vocabulary. Unlike other types of scriptural literature, the tabernacle description is removed from the context of human relationship. It depicts the dwelling place of Israel's deity with a flatness of language that evokes distance from human experience.[7]

Exegesis of the tabernacle account begins with Philo of Alexandria (Mos. II: 71-148; cf. QE 2:51-124). In the Greek tradition of allegorical exegesis, Philo sees the tabernacle as an archetype of the universe, that physical entity most nearly approximating the divine abode. The cosmic symbolism of the tabernacle is detected in every detail and dimension: the ark represents the incorporeal world; the cherubim signify the creative and regent powers; the lampstand symbolizes heaven and the lamps the planets. Philo notes that the length of the curtain, 28 cubits, is equal to the sum of its factors ($1 + 2 + 4 + 7 + 14 = 28$), a cubic number ($1 \times 4 \times 7$; $2 \times 2 \times 7$) composed of consecutive units from one to seven ($1 + 2 + 3 + 4 + 5 + 6 + 7 = 28$).[8] The prototype tabernacle and furniture shown to Moses on the mountain are designated by Philo as *paradeigmata*. Out of pity, God constructed the tabernacle as a symbol of truth and a copy of wisdom. He stamped the invisible forms on the mind of Moses so that the prophet could see with his soul. Moses then conveyed the patterns to Bezalel, who followed them as if tracing shadows.[9] In the Wisdom of Solomon, the work of an Alexandrian Jew more or less contemporary with Philo, the tabernacle is likewise described as a terrestrial copy of an eternal archetype (9:8). David Winston notes that the Greek *mimēma*, "copy," the term used by both Hellenistic writers in reference to the tabernacle, is a *vox Platonica* meant to emphasize by contrast the greater reality of the heavenly form.[10]

In apocalyptic literature the image of a celestial sanctuary is especially pronounced, although it is the Temple rather than the tabernacle that is the paradigm.[11] At least one passage (2 Bar. 4:5), however, specifies the tabernacle and its vessels among the divine prefigurations of what will be revealed in Paradise. Later exegetes tend also to ignore or even to deny the concrete existence of the tabernacle. Typical of patristic exegesis in this respect is the view of the early Church father Origen (*De Principiis* IV:2, ca. 225 C.E.). He writes that the tabernacle description is completely figurative:[12]

> When we read of the equipment of the tabernacle, we hold it as certain
> that the things described therein are figures of some hidden realities,
> but to attach them to their appropriate meanings and to bring to light

and discuss each separate detail is, I think, a very difficult, not to say impossible task. However, as I said, it does not escape even the common intellect that the description is full of mysteries.

There is no sustained or consecutive exegesis of the tabernacle description in the major tannaitic, amoraic, or geonic compendia now extant.[13] Scattered throughout the literature, however, are a variety of remarks and explanations, especially in the later midrashic collections. The Platonic notion of an earthly counterpart for a celestial archetype is well attested, although most frequently with respect to the Temple (e.g. Mek. *be-Shallah* 10; y. Ber. 4:5, 8c) and to Jerusalem (e.g. b. Ḥag. 12b, b. Ta'an. 5a).[14] The heavenly Temple was either contemplated (Gen. R. 1:4) or created (Sifre Deut. 37; b. Pes. 54a; b. Ned. 39b) before the world existed. One holy of holies is located exactly opposite the other (Mek. *be-Shallah* 10; cf. Cant. R. 3:10). The two Temples are only eighteen vertical miles apart (Gen. R. 69:17). The tabernacle, while less frequently invoked in this respect, is also understood to replicate a divine model. According to a tradition found in two slightly different amoraic recensions (PRK 1:3; Cant. R. 3:11), Moses was shown the pattern of the tabernacle, composed of four colors of fire, during a heavenly ascent.

> R. Abun said: It may be compared to a king who had a beautiful image. He said to his servant: Make me one like this. He replied: My Lord the king, how can I make one like this? He said to him: You with your colors and I with my glory.... R. Berakhiah in the name of R. Bezalel: It may be compared to a king who showed himself to his servant in a beautiful garment of jewels and said to him: Make me one like this. He replied: My Lord the king, how can I make one like this? So did the Holy One, blessed be He, say to Moses: Make me a tabernacle. (Cant. R. 3:11)

Likewise the individual components of the tabernacle correspond to celestial paradigms:

> It is not written there (Ex. 26:15), "He stood up the (planks of) acacia wood" but rather "They are standing," as they are stationed in the heavenly host. (Cant. R. 3:11)

> As the seraphim stand above, so shall the (planks of) acacia wood stand below. As there are stars above, so shall there be clasps (e.g. Ex. 26:6) below. (PRK 1:3)[15]

The vessels, too, are replicas. An ark of fire, a table of fire, and a lampstand of fire came down from heaven, and Moses reproduced them (b. Men. 29a). The lampstand posed special difficulty,[16] requiring the assistance of an angel. The completion of the tabernacle and its vessels registered on a cosmic scale: "Until the tabernacle was set up, the earth trembled; once it was set up, the earth was firmly established" (PRK 1:4).

Aside from cosmological speculations, amoraic literature occasionally derives more homiletical lessons from the tabernacle description. For example, a tradition attributed to R. Johanan associates the ark with the distinction of learning; thus in the verse (Ex. 25:10), "They shall make an ark of acacia wood," the plural indicates that a scholar's living expense should be provided by the community. So also with respect to Ex. 25:11, "Overlay it with gold inside and out," Raba said: "One whose inside is not like his outside cannot be a scholar" (b. Yoma 72b).[17] Elsewhere, commenting on the biblical description of the tabernacle cherubim "facing one another" (Ex. 25:20), the gemara concludes that the two visages were actually turned sideways, the same posture that a disciple must assume when taking leave of his master (b. BB 99a).

More copious and fanciful interpretations of the tabernacle account are found in later rabbinic literature, including, e.g., Tanhuma, Tanhuma Buber, Pirke de-R. Eliezer, Ex. R., Num. R., Pesiqta Rabbati, Genesis Rabbati, Midrash Konen, and Midrash Tadshe.[18] Many of these elaborations reflect the early Hellenistic stratum of cosmology and arithmology. For instance, the order of the tabernacle's construction corresponds to the order of the world's creation (Ex. R. 34:2, 35:6; Num. R. 12:13). The ark is an image of the celestial throne (Tanhuma *Vayaqhel* 7).[19] The two tablets of the Law correspond to the heaven and the earth, the curtain to the firmament, the lampstand to the sun and the moon (Tanhuma *Pequde* 2; Num. R. 12:13). The dimensions of the altar, 5 x 5 x 3 cubits, correspond to the five commandments on each of the tablets and the three deliverers (Moses, Aaron, Miriam) sent by God to Egypt (Tanhuma *Terumah* 10). The two wings of the cherubim correspond to the two names of God; the measure of the wingspan to the number of letters in the Hebrew alphabet (Midrash Tadshe 2).

Homiletical deductions also multiply. Israel's history of subjection is implicit in the tabernacle building materials: the gold signifies Babylon; the silver, Persia; the bronze, Greece; the tanned ram skins, Rome (Tanhuma *Terumah* 7). The bronze altar corresponds to the human body, the golden altar to the soul: as both altars served a divine purpose in the tabernacle, so both body and soul should be devoted to God (Midrash Tadshe 11). Although Scripture seems to say that Moses set up the tabernacle (e.g. Ex. 40:18), it was the Holy Spirit that rested upon him; the tabernacle erected itself (Tanḥuma Buber *Pequde* 8; Ex. R. 52:4).

In contrast to the aggadic stream of interpretation in rabbinic sources, early and late, there are substantial passages in tannaitic and amoraic sources that treat the tabernacle and its vessels as concrete historical objects. Often these traditions are cited in the context of descriptions of the Solomonic and Herodian Temples. Chapter 3 of the Introduction discusses these passages in some detail.[20] The aggregate indicates that, beside the rabbinic tendency to interpret the tabernacle symbolically, there was also considerable interest in its physical reality.

Baraita de-Melekhet ha-Mishkan (BMM) is the only systematic rabbinic exegesis of the tabernacle account to emerge from late antiquity or the Middle Ages.[21] In contrast to Philo, the Church fathers, and the aggadic midrashim, BMM treats the tabernacle and its furnishings as realia susceptible of measurement and objective description. Of specific concern to BMM are the technology of construction, the calculation of measurements, and the delineation of architectural forms. BMM also describes the physical setting of the desert tabernacle among the Israelite tribes and the procedures for its disassembly and transportation.

In published editions and most MSS, BMM is divided into fourteen chapters. A brief summary of their contents follows: Ch. 1) contributions[22] for the maintenance of the priesthood and the building of the tabernacle; dimensions of the tabernacle; configuration of the planks, bars, posts, tenons, sockets, and rings. Ch. 2) dimensions, arrangement, fabrication, and attachment of the linen curtains and Ch. 3) of the goat's hair curtains and the two outer covers of the tabernacle. Ch. 4) description and comparison of the veil and the screen; enumeration of sancta in the adytum; arrangement of the furnishings in the shrine and the distances among them. Ch. 5) dimensions and assembly of the enclosure. Ch. 6) dimensions of the ark; placement of the tablets and Torah scroll; excursus on the history and contents of the ark. Ch. 7) manufacture of the ark and ark cover; placement of the ark within the adytum; protrusion of the carrying poles; excursus on the fate of the ark; differing features of the Solomonic and Herodian Temples. Ch. 8) dimensions of the table and arrangement of the showbread; relationship of the Mosaic table to the Solomonic tables. Ch. 9) design and manufacture of the lampstand and lamps; reference to the two silver trumpets (Num. 10:2). Ch. 10) further technical description of the lampstand; digression on syntactical difficulty of a pertinent biblical verse; relationship of Mosaic lampstand to Solomonic lampstands; procedures for kindling and extinguishing lamps. Ch. 11) dimensions, features, and relative proportions of the various altars. Ch. 12) the Mosaic laver, the ten Solomonic lavers, and the cast iron tank (lit. "sea") of Solomon's Temple; calculations of the tank's cubic volume and description of its appearance; addendum enumerating the officers of the Temple (M. Sheq. 5:1-2).[23] Ch. 13) guard duties of the Levites; geographical distribution of the encampment; levitical procedures for dismantling and transporting the tabernacle; system of breaking and moving camp. Ch. 14) description of the divine pillar of cloud; the locus of the divine voice within the tabernacle.

Each of the fourteen chapters of BMM is structured around the pertinent set of biblical prescriptions. The cumulative result is virtually a verse by verse exegesis of the tabernacle texts, although not necessarily in their scriptural sequence. For example, within the first four chapters of BMM, Ex. 26 is cited as follows: ch. 1 = vv. 19, 24, 28, 29, 32, 33; ch. 2 = vv. 1, 2, 3, 4, 6; ch. 3 = vv. 7, 8, 9, 10, 11, 12, 14; ch. 4 = vv. 35, 36. The exposition of Ex. 25 is distributed over five chapters: ch. 6 = v. 10; ch. 7 = vv. 11, 15, 21; ch. 8 = vv. 23, 25, 26; ch. 9 = v. 31; ch. 10 = vv. 32, 33, 34, 40. Obviously the exegesis is organized according to subject rather than according to sequence of the biblical text.

Arrangement by subject is characteristic of the Mishnah and the Tosefta. Unlike them, BMM is prone to cite Scripture in the manner of the halakhic midrashim. Yet unlike the halakhic midrashim, BMM does not follow the order of Scripture in its exposition. This divergence from, or perhaps convergence of, distinct rabbinic genres is a unique characteristic of BMM. It helps to explain the variety of names for the work attested in medieval citations: *mishnah, baraita, pirqe,* or without generic classification, e.g. Melekhet ha-Mishkan, Ma'aseh Mishkan.[24] Leopold Zunz, the pioneer of modern rabbinic scholarship, identifies the rhetoric and terminology of BMM with the genre of midrash.[25] Its last two chapters in particular are comprised largely of *midrash aggadah.*

By some definitions advanced by contemporary scholarship, BMM may indeed be regarded as midrash. Geza Vermes argues that the function of midrash is to solve problems within the biblical texts by explaining contradictions and providing missing details.[26] Gary Porton defines midrash as a type of literature that stands in direct relationship to a canonical text and either cites it or alludes to it.[27] More stringently, David Weiss Halivni confines the classification of midrash to direct quotation of biblical chapter and verse.[28] Each of these definitions of midrash clearly applies to BMM.

On the other hand, most scholars discern in the genre of midrash a purpose transcending mere exegesis. Vermes, for instance, has also written of midrash as "applied exegesis," concerned less with the evident meaning of the text than with the discovery of fundamental truths. "Applied exegesis" utilizes Scripture to solve problems having little or nothing to do with the text itself.[29] In a similar vein, Renée Bloch describes "adaptation to the present" as a fundamental criterion of midrash: "If midrashic exegesis consists primarily in an attentive study of the texts, it does not stop there. Its aim is not purely theoretical. Its goal is primarily practical: to define the lessons for faith and for the religious way of life contained in the biblical text."[30] B. Childs has suggested that "the heart of the midrashic method" is the connection between the biblical text and a new situation.[31] None of these criteria of midrash are satisfied by BMM.

Nor do the recognized forms of midrashic composition apply to BMM. The major expositional midrashim (e.g. Sifra, Sifre, Mekhilta, Genesis Rabbah, Lamentations Rabbah) interpret the texts, in whole or in substantial part, of discrete books of Scripture. Individual sections may be imported from other sources, but relationship is imposed upon them by the order of the biblical text. They are organized by verse, not by topic. Homiletical midrashim (e.g. Leviticus Rabbah, Deuteronomy Rabbah, the Pesiqtot) constitute a different form of literary expression: collections of independent theological essays informed by a nexus of assorted biblical verses from throughout the canon. In homiletical midrashim, the order of the text at hand is not the point of reference but the point of departure. In its systematic attention to the tabernacle texts, BMM may be compared to expositional midrash. In its form of topical composition, emancipated from the scriptural text sequence, it may be compared to homiletical midrash. But even if BMM is considered a form of midrash, it is a unique one.

To identify BMM as a mishnah is also justifiable in certain respects. Like the Mishnah of Judah ha-Nasi, BMM is organized according to topic. Formally, both works are independent of scriptural sequence. Both relate their dicta in repetitive formulary patterns. BMM bears particular resemblance to those Mishnah tractates that rehearse in their own words what is already prescribed in Scripture, e.g., the cultic tractates of Seder Qodoshim and much of Seder Tohorot. As Jacob Neusner has shown, these tractates elaborate upon the scriptural data but are completely dependent upon it.[32] For its part, BMM is largely a restatement of the tabernacle description in the Pentateuch. Its elaborations are usually matters of detail or comparison, and its digressions are often dictated by mnemonic or redactional associations. The Mishnah's concern for matters of definition, classification, and specification is also characteristic of BMM.

Yet again, the generic correspondence between the two is problematic. *Mishnayyot* are primarily statements of law. Their language is apodictic rather than exegetical; their concerns are halakhic rather than descriptive. BMM constantly adverts to Scripture; *mishnayyot* rarely. Although it has been described as a messianic[33] or even fantastic[34] document, the Mishnah still addresses the contemporary life of Israel in its land. BMM is an architectural treatise irrelevant to contemporary time or place.

Falling somewhere between the categories of midrash and mishnah, BMM may be viewed as a conflation of forms. In the perennial debate over the chronological priority of midrash or mishnah, it has been assumed that the two genres are distinct: midrash, inquiry into the biblical text to determine laws and applications; and mishnah, autonomous statements of law arranged by topic. Weiss Halivni, however, suggests that mishnah is actually "abridged midrash," i.e. midrash eviscerated of its scriptural justification. Only by restoring biblical citations, he argues, do we "make sense of the ellipticalness, the sudden interruptions, the awkward contextual arrangements that are so common in the Mishnah." The Mishnah "was not composed *de novo* but was excerpted from earlier sources, from Midrash." Weiss Halivni maintains that the mishnah form was short-lived; subsequent rabbinic generations reverted to explicit scriptural justification. Those pericopae that begin with an assertion and proceed to the verse that supports it, introducing Scripture with the formula "as it says," are designated by Weiss Halivni as "mishnaic midrash."[35] Granting the ambiguity of this term with respect to the history of rabbinic literature, it is quite apt to describe BMM.

If BMM may be imperfectly defined as "mishnaic midrash" in form, nonetheless it is most frequently called a baraita. It is to this phenomenon of rabbinic literature that we now turn. In its widest sense, baraita denotes an ancient tradition or collection of traditions not included in the Mishnah of Judah ha-Nasi. In the Babylonian Talmud,[36] the term is often used to emphasize a tannaitic dissent from the canonical Mishnah. Tannaitic baraitot originated in the land of Israel and were collected in the centers of learning in Babylonia. Various traditions and halakhot ascribed to the Tannaim circulated outside the framework of the gemara and were drawn upon for comparative or critical purposes. They are attested not only in the Talmuds but in the Tosefta and the halakhic midrashim. Numerous collections of baraitot are presumed to have existed in amoraic times, though only remnants have survived.[37] Abraham Weiss theorizes that these were not haphazard compilations but codified works similar in form, if not in scope, to Mishnah and Tosefta.[38] Hanoch Albeck maintains that a similar process occurred with the collection of midrashic interpretations: early exegetical traditions, already compiled and arranged in fixed form, served as sources for the extant, more ramified midrashim.[39]

Multiple versions and disputed attributions make it very difficult to isolate the materials utilized by the Amoraim. The sages themselves were not always familiar with one another's baraitot (e.g. b. Shab. 115b) and occasionally questioned the accuracy or authenticity of a received tradition (e.g. b. Pes. 99b-100a). What is more, the stratum of baraitot is not necessarily coextensive with tannaitic collections. Traditions ascribed to Tannaim in one Talmud are ascribed to Amoraim in the other.[40] A baraita is often glossed or modified by a later tradent. Albeck shows that some baraitot originate entirely with Amoraim, having no tannaitic basis whatsoever.[41] In short, to identify a rabbinic pericope or collection as a baraita is hardly to narrow its definition.

Other than the Mishnah, it is not certain that the surviving tannaitic corpora were even known to the Amoraim. Some baraitot in the Tosefta, in the halakhic midrashim, and in BMM have parallels in the Talmuds; others do not. The Talmuds often fail to cite sources found in our collections which would seem decisive to their discussions. While the Babylonian Talmud mentions Tosefta, Sifra, and Sifre by name, it is highly doubtful that the titles refer to our versions. Albeck maintains that neither Talmud knew of our halakhic midrashim or of our Tosefta. He brings copious evidence for this contention: not only do the Amoraim fail to cite these works, but they do cite affinitive and disparate tannaitic traditions covering

similar ground. One can only deduce that the Amoraim were oblivi-
ous to the existence of our collections.[42] On the other hand, J. N.
Epstein points out that the Amoraim also fail to cite vast sections
of the Mishnah which were certainly in their possession. If certain
baraitot from the Tosefta or halakhic midrashim are not cited at all
or occur in different versions, this merely demonstrates that the
Amoraim knew the collections in earlier recensions.[43] In sum, as
with the definition of baraitot, so with the extant collections: our
knowledge of their origins and descent is hampered by the fluidity
of the literary tradition during the tannaitic and amoraic eras.

This fluidity is felt not only in content but in form. Evaluating
baraitot on the basis of attributions and formal characteristics is a
difficult enterprise. The consensual mode of its transmission tends
to homogenize rabbinic language; the requirements of redaction
often impose semantic conformity. Attributions, too, are just as
likely to have been assigned by a subsequent editor as by a contemporary witness.[44] David Hoffmann's classic distinction between the
schools of R. Ishmael and R. Akiba on the basis of attributions, hermeneutic principles, and exegetical terminology[45] continues to
inform research of the halakhic midrashim. But the studies of
Albeck in particular show Hoffmann's division to be more relative
than absolute. For instance, the term מגיד, allegedly unique to the
school of R. Ishmael (Mekhilta, Sifre Numbers, Midrash Tannaim),
is attested many times in Sifre Deuteronomy and Mekhilta de-R.
Simeon b. Yoḥai, two of the works attributed by Hoffmann to R.
Akiba's school. יכול, allegedly unique to Akiba (e.g. Sifra) is found
also in Mekhilta and Sifre Numbers. שומע אני, allegedly unique to
Ishmael, is found also in Mekhilta de-R. Simeon. להוציא, allegedly
unique to Ishmael, is found also in Sifra and Sifre Deuteronomy.
Such examples can be multiplied.[46] Albeck's conclusion is inescapa-
ble: any distinctions that may have originally obtained between the
terminologies of the two schools have been blurred by subsequent
redactors. These editors combined earlier traditions with later ones,
recasting the language and disguising the seams. Likewise the
tannaitic traditions cited in the Talmuds, although drawn from the
same sources as the halakhic midrashim, exhibit a terminology of
their own imposed by a different set of redactors.[47]

The assimilation of tannaitic language extends also to the identification of the Tannaim themselves. While some sages are identified
with the school of R. Ishmael and others with the school of R. Akiba,

some are identified with both schools and bring the traditions of one to the other.[48] Epstein locates a discrete source in Sifre Numbers (*pisqa'ot* 78-106, 131, 134-41) that includes six sages who belong to Ishmael's school and eleven who do not.[49] Mekhilta de-R. Simeon cites Ishmaelian and Akiban names.[50] Epstein also assembles component parts of Sifra and Sifre Deuteronomy that appear to be wholesale transpositions from the school of R. Ishmael, including explicit citations of Ishmaelian Tannaim. Epstein considers all of these to be later editorial or scribal accretions. His proof for this judgment is that Ishmaelian traditions or tendencies are obviously out of place in Akiban compositions.[51] But this is an exercise in circular reasoning: separate terminologies are authenticated by the texts, and the texts are authentic when the terminologies are separate. Albeck arrives at a more rigorous deduction. Rather than dividing the halakhic midrashim into two schools, he divides them into two redactions of the same aggregate of sources. The respective terminologies are influenced at least as much by the proclivities of the redactor as by the schools of opinion with which they have been identified.[52] In fact, Porton concludes that the exegetical practices attributed to Ishmael are "at earliest, an Amoraic construction."[53]

All of these phenomena—the amplitude of the baraita literature, the permeability of tannaitic and amoraic sources, the coalescence of terminologies and attributions—complicate any attempt to determine with certainty the date, provenance, authorship, or editorial development of BMM. As with all such rabbinic documents, systematic evaluation must begin with the text itself: its linguistic characteristics, vocabulary, exegetical terminology, and identification of tradents.

Notes to Chapter One

DESCRIPTION, STRUCTURE, GENRE

1. A more exact term might be "project" or "skilled labor"; see Jacob Milgrom, *Studies in Cultic Theology and Terminology* (Leiden, 1983), 18-46, who differentiates between מלאכה, an enterprise calling for skill and workmanship, and עבודה, signifying raw manual labor. מלאכה may also denote the finished product, approximating the idea of manufacture.

2. Cf. b. Shab. 87b.

3. Various traditions report that the planks, hooks, bars, pillars, and sockets of the tent of meeting were deposited beneath the crypts of the Solomonic Temple (e.g. b. Sot. 9a); the anointing oil (Ex. 30:31), the jar of manna (Ex. 16:33-34), and the staff of Aaron (Num. 17:23-25) were hidden by Josiah (e.g. T. Sot. 13:1, y. Sot. 8:3, 22c, b. Hor. 23a, and cf. BMM 4:3-5); the ark went into exile in Babylonia, or was hidden in the Temple chamber of the woodshed, or was buried, possibly forever (e.g. b. Yoma 53b-54a, and cf. BMM 7:21-27). Earlier traditions are attested in the Apocrypha and Pseudepigrapha: the prophet Jeremiah concealed the tent, ark, and incense altar in a cave on Mount Nebo and then sealed off the entrance so that no one could find it (2 Macc. 2:4-8); at the pronouncement of an angel, the tabernacle vessels were swallowed up by the earth (e.g. 2 Bar. 6:7-9); Jeremiah seized the ark with its contents and caused it to be swallowed up in a rock, upon which he engraved with his finger the divine Name, over which a cloud hovers; but no one knows the place and no one can read the name (Lives of the Prophets 2:11-17).

4. The correspondence between the tabernacle as depicted in P and Solomon's Temple as described in 1 Ki. and 2 Chr. is evident, e.g., from the sancta that appear in both: the ark, altars, table(s), lampstand(s), and laver(s). Both sources also describe corollary structures of outer court and inner sanctum and gradations from copper or bronze to gold. These and other similarities have led some scholars to see the tabernacle as a retrojection, i.e., a mythic precursor of the Temple. This argument is criticized by Menahem Haran, *Temples and Temple Service in Ancient Israel*

(Oxford, 1978), 189-204. Establishing the harmony and continuity between the tabernacle and the Solomonic Temple is a major preoccupation of BMM; see especially BMM ch. 8, 10, 12.

5. See Yigael Yadin, *Megillat ha-Miqdash* (Jerusalem, 1979), 1:139, cf.1:141, 146; Ben Zion Wacholder, *The Dawn of Qumran* (Cincinnati, 1983), 210. However, the Temple Scroll reproduces the furniture of the tabernacle, not the architecture. See the discussion in ch. 4 of our Introduction.

6. For example, Eupolemus' description of the base of the laver(s) in the Solomonic Temple is influenced by Ex. 30:17-21 rather than by 1 Ki. 7:27-39; see Ben Zion Wacholder, *Eupolemus: A Study of Judaeo-Greek Literature* (Cincinnati, 1974), 190-93.

7. Cf. Baruch A. Levine, "The Descriptive Tabernacle Texts of the Pentateuch," *Journal of the American Oriental Society* 85 (1965): 307-18; Carol L. Meyers, *The Tabernacle Menorah*, American Schools of Oriental Research Dissertation Series no. 2 (Missoula, 1976), 1-2.

8. QE II:87. Cf. H. R. Moehring, "Moses and Pythagoras: Arithmology as an Exegetical Tool in Philo," Studia Biblica I, *Journal for the Study of the Old Testament* Suppl. Series II (1979): 205-8.

9. Her. 112, Mos. 2:74-76, Som. I:206, LA III:102. That Bezalel saw only shadows is deduced from the translation of his name, "in the shadow of God." Cf. b. Ber. 55a.

10. David Winston, *The Wisdom of Solomon*, Anchor Bible v. 43 (New York, 1979), 203 f.

11. E.g. 1 Enoch 14:16-20, 90:28-29; 2 Bar. 4:1-3; Testament of Levi 3:4-6. Cf. Heb. 8:2,5.

12. *On First Principles*, tr. G. W. Butterworth (repr. Gloucester, 1973), 273.

13. Although substantial sections of y. Sheq. and b. Men., e.g., are devoted to details of the tabernacle account; see ch. 3 of the Introduction.

14. See E. E. Urbach, "Lower Jerusalem and Upper Jerusalem," *Jerusalem Through the Generations* (Hebrew), (Jerusalem, 1969).

15. Cf. BMM 2:10-11 and parallels.

16. Cf. BMM 10:23-24; Sifre Num. *be-Ha'alotkha* 61; b. Men. 29a.

17. Cf. Philo, QE 2:54.

18. For a thorough collection of citations, see L. Ginzberg, *Legends of the Jews* (repr. Philadelphia, 1968), 3:148-66, 6:316-48; for an attempt to formulate them, A. Aptowitzer, "The Heavenly Temple according to the Aggadah" (Hebrew), *Tarbiz* 2 (1931): 137-53, 257-87. Both of these mention earlier traditions as well. Aptowitzer's discussion is flawed by the premise that rabbinic sources centuries and even millennia removed from one another can be uniformly credited and evaluated as a single systematic statement.

19. There is probably scriptural warrant for this association: cf. 1 Sam. 4:4, 6:2; 2 Sam. 22:11; Ps. 68:5,34.

20. A complete collection of baraitot from the Babylonian Talmud concerning the tabernacle description of Ex. 25-27 f. is provided by E. Z. Melamed, *Midreshe Halakhah shel ha-Tannaim be-Talmud Bavli* (Jerusalem, [2]1988), 147-51.

21. Since the seventeenth century other rabbinic treatises on the tabernacle have appeared, including Joseph Shalit Richietti, *Ḥokhmat ha-Mishkan* (Mantua, 1676); Immanuel Hai Ricchi, *Ma'aseh Ḥoshev* (Venice, 1716); A. Z. Deglin, *Miqdash Aharon* (repr. Vilna, 1896).

22. "Contributions" = תרומות. For the origin and cultic significance of the term, see Jacob Milgrom, *Studies in Cultic Theology and Terminology* (Leiden, 1983), 159-62, 171-72. For our English translation, we have retained "heave-offerings" as the widely accepted term.

23. M. Sheq. 5:1-2 is attested in only two MSS, A and G[1] (see explanation of sigla below, pp. 149-50). However, in our judgment they are also the two most important witnesses to the text of BMM; see below, ch. 5-6.

24. BMM is designated as *mishnah* by Rashi (R. Solomon b. Isaac, 1040-1105, France), e.g. Ex. 26:25, and by Ramban (R. Moses b. Naḥman, 1194-1270, Spain), e.g. Ex. 25:12; as *baraita* by Ramban, e.g. Ex. 25:39, and by Tosafot (ca. 12th-14th centuries, France), e.g. b. Shab. 22b s.v. וכי; as *pirqe* by Yalqut ha-Makhiri (ca. 14th century, Spain?), Is. 60:1; and without generic classification by Rashi, e.g. Ex. 26:26, and Arukh (11th century, Italy) s.v. סן.

25. L. Zunz/H. Albeck, *Ha-Derashot be-Yisrael* (Jerusalem, [3]1974), 43.

26. Geza Vermes, "Bible and Midrash: Early Old Testament Exegesis," *Cambridge History of the Bible*, ed. P. Ackroyd/C. Evans (Cambridge, 1970), 1:202.

27. Gary Porton, "Defining Midrash," *The Study of Ancient Judaism I: Midrash, Mishnah, Siddur*, ed. J. Neusner (New York, 1981), 62.

28. David Weiss Halivni, *Midrash, Mishnah, and Gemara* (Cambridge, MA/London, 1986), 17.

29. Geza Vermes, *Post-Biblical Jewish Studies* (Leiden, 1975), 62.

30. Renée Bloch, "Midrash," tr. M. H. Callaway, *Approaches to Ancient Judaism: Theory and Practice*, ed. W. S. Green, Brown Judaic Studies 1 (Missoula, 1978), 32.

31. Cited by Porton, op.cit. 59.

32. See, e.g., Jacob Neusner, "Scripture and Tradition in Judaism," *Approaches to Ancient Judaism* v. 2, ed. W. S. Green, Brown Judaic Studies 9 (Chico, 1980), 187-90.

33. E.g. Ben Zion Wacholder, *Messianism and Mishnah* (Cincinnati, 1979). See the discussion in ch. 4 of the Introduction.

34. E.g. Jacob Neusner, *Judaism: The Evidence of the Mishnah* (Chicago/

London, 1981), 75; cf. *Method and Meaning in Ancient Judaism*, Brown Judaic Studies 10 (Missoula, 1979), 139-40.

35. Weiss Halivni, op.cit. 52-53, 34 respectively.

36. In the Palestinian Talmud the term baraita is attested only once, y. Ned. 3:3, 50d. Baraitot are most frequently cited without specification; see E. Z. Melamed, *Mavo le-Sifrut ha-Talmud* (Jerusalem, 1977), 80.

37. So David Hoffman, *Zur Einleitung in die halachischen Midraschim* (Berlin, 1887), 2-3; I. H. Weiss, *Dor Dor ve-Dorshav* v. 3 (Vilna, 1911), 204, 217; Abraham Weiss, *Al ha-Yeẓirah ha-Sifrutit shel ha-Amoraim* (New York, 1962), 172.

38. Abraham Weiss, ibid. 168.

39. Hanoch Albeck, *Mavo la-Talmudim* (Tel Aviv, 1969), 87-88. Judith Hauptman, "Development of the Talmudic Sugya by Amoraic and Post-Amoraic Amplification of a Tannaitic Proto-Sugya," *HUCA* 58 (1987): 227-50, argues for the presence of a similar phenomenon in the Babylonian Talmud: a tannaitic substratum, consisting of intact literary units, into which amoraic data were later inserted in response to the baraitot.

40. For examples see Melamed, *Mavo le-Sifrut ha-Talmud* 81, 407-12.

41. Albeck, op.cit. 47-50.

42. Hanoch Albeck, *Meḥqarim be-Baraita ve-Tosefta* (Jerusalem, 1969), 89-138; *Mavo la- Talmudim*, 102-43. Benjamin DeVries, "The Problem of the Relationship of the Two Talmuds to the Tosefta" (Hebrew), *Tarbiẓ* 28 (1959): 158-70, criticizes Albeck's evidence as an argument from silence.

43. J. N. Epstein, *Mevo'ot le-Sifrut ha-Tannaim* (Tel Aviv, 1957), 241-62 regarding Tosefta; 545-47, 609-15, 663-66 regarding the halakhic midrashim.

44. We take up this issue in ch. 2 of the Introduction.

45. David Hoffmann, *Zur Einleitung in die halachischen Midraschim* (Berlin, 1887).

46. Albeck, *Mavo la-Talmudim*, 93-102; E. Z. Melamed, *Midreshe Halakhah shel ha-Tannaim be-Talmud Bavli* (Jerusalem, ²1988), 34-36.

47. Albeck, ibid. 101. Cf. idem, *Untersuchungen über die halakischen Midraschim* (Berlin, 1927), 84 ff.

48. For examples see E. Z. Melamed, *Mavo le-Sifrut ha-Talmud*, 11-12.

49. J. N. Epstein, op.cit. 597-98.

50. Ibid. 739.

51. Ibid. 682-702.

52. See Albeck, *Mavo la-Talmudim*, 143, and the summary of his conclusions in Moshe D. Herr, "Midreshei Halakhah," *EJ* 11:1522-23.

53. Gary Porton, *The Traditions of Rabbi Ishmael* (Leiden, 1976-82), II:7; cf. III: 2 f.

Chapter 2

Language, Terminology, Tradents

Before proceeding to describe and evaluate the linguistic features of BMM, it is necessary to explain the formulation of reliable criteria for such an assessment. After setting forth the various methodological approaches, we seek to apply them to BMM.

To evaluate the language of a rabbinic text poses formidable difficulties: the shortage (or absence) of reliable MSS; the vagaries and distortions of scribal transmission and geographic diffusion; the lack of adequate scientific grammars, comprehensive dictionaries, or concordances.[1] The most fundamental difficulty, however, is the self-referential character of rabbinic language. Amoraic literature, for instance, frequently speaks tannaitic Hebrew; geonic literature speaks amoraic and tannaitic Hebrew; medieval rabbinic texts speak all three; and every rabbinic language speaks the biblical tongue. While chronological development between biblical and mishnaic Hebrew is evident,[2] subsequent stratification is complex. As Moshe Goshen-Gottestein has argued, rabbinic Hebrew cannot be forced into a procrustean bed of sequential development.[3] Owing to its tendency toward linguistic consolidation, a diachronic model may not be possible. Hybrid forms are already characteristic of the earliest strata, and the problem intensifies in later centuries with the introduction of Palestinian and Babylonian dialects, evident in Aramaic but less visible in Hebrew. No longer a spoken language, mishnaic Hebrew was gradually overlaid with linguistic features of later periods that overlap in time and often coincide in form. By the Middle Ages, the original strata of rabbinic Hebrew are obscured: Goshen-Gottestein contends that medieval Hebrew cannot be isolated chronologically.[4]

Despite these obstacles, much progress has been made toward the recovery of the original language of the Tannaim and the subsequent stages of its development. The discovery of important MSS (e.g. the Kaufmann and Parma MSS of the Mishnah) and fragments of the Cairo Genizah have provided a more reliable basis for linguistic research. The lexicographical studies of such scholars as J. N. Epstein and Saul Lieberman have opened new frontiers in the study of the historical evolution of rabbinic language.[5] Knowledge of cognate languages has also expanded in modern scholarship. Building upon these foundations, E. Y. Kutscher and his students have pioneered the effort to identify and periodize mishnaic Hebrew.

Kutscher divides mishnaic Hebrew (MH) into two periods: the MH of the Tannaim (MH[1]) when it was still a spoken language (until ca. 200 C.E.), and that of the Amoraim (MH[2]) when MH was no longer spoken (ca. 200-500 C.E.). These categories admit of further refinement into regional dialects: the MH of the Tannaim as transmitted in Palestine (MH[1]P) as distinct from Babylonia (MH[1]B), and likewise the MH of the Amoraim of Palestine (MH[2]P) as distinct from Babylonia (MH[2]B).[6] Each of these subdivisions, Kutscher maintains, has its own characteristics, although they cannot always be delineated with assurance. For instance, since MH was never a spoken language in Babylonia, it is at once more prone to the influence of biblical Hebrew (BH) and less prone to the phonological changes wrought by Aramaic spoken dialect. Kutscher provides numerous examples of this phenomenon.[7] The possibility of distinguishing among mechanical errors, hypercorrections, and variant traditions in later MSS is greatly enhanced if there are prior linguistic criteria of evaluation. However, Kutscher concedes that even the best MSS rarely permit certain differentiation between Palestinian and Babylonian provenance, nor the isolation of MH from the influence of BH. Extant MSS of Tosefta, Sifre, and Mekhilta, for example, reflect mixed origin and linguistic tendency.[8]

Kutscher's enterprise has been significantly advanced by two of his students, Michael Sokoloff and Menaḥem Moreshet. On the basis of the text of Gen. R. according to MS Vat. 30, Sokoloff distinguishes between MH[1] and MH[2] by comparing declensions, conjugations, orthography, and proper names.[9] He finds both chronological and regional variations, concluding that the place of origin can be as decisive as the date. The influence of Galilean Aramaic on MH[2] is clearly perceptible. MH[2]P is also inclined to biblical locutions, suggesting that by then it was a purely literary language no longer governed by contemporary speech. Sokoloff acknowledges, however, that the recovery of MH¹ is complicated by several intrinsic difficulties. First of all, the composition of the Talmuds and midrashim may have been separated from the time of their redaction by the same chronological divide separating MH¹ from MH². Second, as Kutscher noted, the subsequent influence on MH¹ of BH and MH² is not easily calculated. Finally, MH²P is certain to have influenced the later Palestinian scribal version of MH¹P.

Moreshet has undertaken a series of studies seeking to differentiate MH¹ from MH² in tannaitic and amoraic collections, particularly the Babylonian Talmud.[10] He assumes that the Hebrew baraitot in the Talmuds are, for the most part, authentic tannaitic traditions. But given the date of redaction some three centuries after the Tannaim, he contends that the Amoraim have left their impress on the antecedent language. Comparing the talmudic baraitot to parallel texts from the Tosefta and halakhic midrashim, Moreshet identifies lexical differences, Aramaisms, resurrected biblical verbs, "new" verbs, morphological modifications, and editorial interpolations, all pointing to the influence of a later period and perhaps also to the impact of oral transmission.[11] These changes follow a linguistic pattern that cannot be attributed merely to scribal errors or variants. Corroboration for this conclusion lies in the congruence of baraitot with parallels in the Palestinian Talmud, where common regional origin left the Hebrew more or less intact.[12] Moreshet also finds that the revived biblical verbs or otherwise unattested "new" verbs in MH²B are found mainly in the statements of Babylonian Amoraim, although there are some parallels in the Palestinian Talmud that might be explained by contact between the two rabbinic communities. Moreshet does not deny that some versions of Babylonian baraitot may accurately reflect the usage of the Tannaim. But on the preponderance of evidence, he recommends a separate linguistic classification.[13] Having located some ninety new and revived verbs found in MH² but not MH¹, Moreshet conjectures that so pronounced a pattern would likely apply to the noun as well.[14] Notwithstanding the absence of linguistically decisive MSS such as MS Vat. 30 utilized by Sokoloff, Moreshet claims to have isolated the strata of MH¹B and MH²B.[15]

To test this methodology, Moreshet has taken a rabbinic text of disputed origin, Mishnat R. Eliezer (also called Midrash of Thirty-Two Rules, Midrash Agur),[16] and sought to determine its date by lexical analysis, particularly by comparison to the "new" verbs identified in previous studies.[17] The results indicate that Mishnat R. Eliezer cannot be assigned to the tannaitic era. This is demonstrated by the presence of numerous verbs and several nouns that are not attested until MH[2]. Mishnat R. Eliezer intersperses Babylonian and Palestinian versions of baraitot. It employs biblical lexemes and morphemes that had disappeared from MH[1] but were revived in MH[2]B. Finally, it includes linguistic usages with no parallels in tannaitic or sometimes even in amoraic literature. The study of Mishnat R. Eliezer leads Moreshet to conclude that linguistic analysis can distinguish the various strata of MH.

Coextensive with the attempt to recover the diachronic development of MH has been the effort to differentiate its synchronic forms, particularly with respect to Babylonian as distinct from Palestinian traditions. In his preparation of a critical edition of Mishnah Avodah Zarah,[18] David Rosenthal has detected separate Palestinian and Babylonian branches of readings. His criteria for differentiation include additions, deletions, consistent word substitutions, distinctive orthography and grammar, morphology, and syntax. He also considers the readings and elaborations of the Mishnah in the two Talmuds as a source of "internal" comparison. On a broader if less exacting scale, Abba Bendavid has sought to identify discrete Palestinian and Babylonian dialects.[19] He proposes that the MH of Lod, Sepphoris, and Tiberias can be distinguished from that of Nehardea, Pumbedita, and Sura, notwithstanding mutual contacts and shared idioms. Babylonian Hebrew is characterized as an artificial literary language inclined to greater ornamentation and rhetorical expression. Palestinian Hebrew is idiomatic, succinct, elliptical, and often truncated. Bendavid derives this contrast of attributes from an impressionistic comparison of various pericopae and whole *sugyot* but also seeks to differentiate the two dialects by their respective vocabularies, orthographies, and loanwords.[20]

Scholars have also labored to detect the border between the late antique and medieval transmission of MH. Although the isolation of a discrete medieval stratum is problematic, certain linguistic characteristics have been identified. Bendavid, for example, describes medieval MH as increasingly artificial, ornate, and biblicized in vocabulary and grammar (e.g. Pirke de-R. Eliezer, Tanna de-ve Eliyyahu, Tanḥuma). Not only form but content can reveal medieval origins: when MH texts assume knowledge of amoraic discussions, this is a likely sign of a later date.[21] Medieval MH passages may be paraphrases or translations from Aramaic, a process that often leaves a visible linguistic trail. Assimilations of tannaitic and amoraic idioms and exegetical terminology are also characteristic of medieval MH.[22] The influence of vernacular languages, especially Arabic,[23] may be registered in MH lexemes and morphemes. Finally, the influence of the Babylonian Talmud becomes more and more pervasive the further MH is removed in time from its origins.[24]

This is particularly evident in the unique textual history of Palestinian Talmud tractate Sheqalim (y. Sheq.). Because it has no Babylonian counterpart, it was appended to Mishnah Sheq. in the geonic era[25] and was already included in editions of the Babylonian Talmud before the Palestinian Talmud was published. Thus there were two versions of the same tractate, one of which had long been subjected to and altered by its displaced context, and the other inevitably affected by it. By a systematic comparison of MSS, Genizah fragments, and medieval testimonia, Jacob Sussman has sought to isolate the original text (version A) from its Babylonian revision (version B).[26] He places special emphasis on linguistically distinct readings attested by more than one witness but does not rule out other variants, obvious scribal errors, or interpolations. The separation of the two branches of y. Sheq. text tradition is of critical importance for assessing parallel rabbinic texts of uncertain origin.

Yet to be discussed is the possibility of periodization based upon exegetical terminology, i.e., citation formulae and hermeneutical idioms. The historical and philological classification of these terms has been a long-standing project of rabbinic text scholarship.[27] Fixed terminologies and attributive formulae are unique to various tannaitic and amoraic sources. However, as discussed in chapter 1 of the Introduction, these conventions may be the product of redaction rather than composition. Later hands may impose uniformity upon an inherited text. While this possibility calls synchronic distinctions into question (e.g. the "schools" of R. Akiba and R. Ishmael), it does not prevent diachronic analysis. Tannaitic and amoraic terminologies differ most obviously between Hebrew and Aramaic; other usages also tend to follow consistent formulary patterns.[28] Exegetical terminology is therefore a significant criterion of rabbinic text periodization.

Finally, we consider the most venerable of all methods of dating rabbinic documents: tradent attributions. This method assumes that words ascribed to various sages were actually theirs; that

unattributed traditions in the same document were contemporaneous with named tradents; and that redaction, if it was not simultane-
ous with composition, left ascriptions of authority intact. Thus any
work containing tannaitic attributions only is presumed to be
tannaitic; once Amoraim are included, the work is ascribed to them
unless later authorities are mentioned. However, as we discuss below
in chapter 4 of the Introduction, each of these assumptions is doubtful. In light of pseudepigraphic tendencies in late antique and post-
talmudic literature, tradent attributions may be viewed as a way of
conferring authority rather than identifying it. Statements ascribed
to a certain sage may not have originated with him but with disciples
or later interpreters. Moreover, the uniform rhetorical patterns in
which many attributions are cast[29] suggest that redaction is effec-
tively the act of authorship that may include the assignment of attributions. On the other hand, attestations from parallel sources or ver-
ifications by other criteria may corroborate the accuracy of tradent
attributions in a given work. If it is too credulous to suppose that
all views assigned to a sage actually originated with him, it does not
follow that all attributions are, *ipso facto*, spurious. The classification of tradents is one criterion for evaluating and dating rabbinic
texts, but only in conjunction with more reliable tests of
authenticity.

Having described the scope of methodologies by which rabbinic
Hebrew can be stratified and dated, we now seek to evaluate the language of BMM. For our analysis we rely upon the base text of the
present edition, a transcription of MS Oxford 370.11 (ca. 13th century). A description of this MS and our reasons for choosing it are
described in chapters 5-6 of the Introduction. Citations from BMM
are listed by chapter and line number (ch.:line). Variant readings
from other witnesses may be compared by consulting the critical
apparatus at the text location indicated.

BMM is written in the language of the Tannaim (MH). It remains
to be demonstrated whether the Hebrew is authentically tannaitic
(MH[1]), amoraic (MH[2]) or post-talmudic; and, if possible, whether it
is of Palestinian (MHP) or Babylonian (MHB) provenance. While
Kutscher laid the foundation for this taxonomy, we must turn to
Sokoloff and Moreshet for systematic demonstrations. In his study
of Gen. R., MS Vat. 30,[30] Sokoloff shows that MH[2]P is distinguished
from MH[1]P by the influence of Galilean Aramaic and a propensity

for biblical locutions. With respect to the latter, BMM is uniquely difficult to evaluate: the biblical description of the tabernacle is so prominent in citation, vocabulary, and syntax that the extent of "biblicization" is hard to gauge. Regarding the influence of Aramaic, however, the verdict is more decisive. Sokoloff lists numerous lexical and morphological examples of MH²P. None of them are attested in BMM.

On a much wider scale of comparison, Moreshet's research produces the same result.[31] His description of MH² in the Talmuds identifies new (or previously unattested) verbs, modified verbs, revived (viz., absent from MH¹) biblical verbs, and interpolations in parallel sources. Of the multitude of lexemes classified by Moreshet as MH², not one is found in BMM. Where MH² substitutes for MH¹ verbs, BMM attests the latter: e.g. הסתכל (MH¹, BMM 14:11) vs. צפה (MH²);[32] ממלא (MH¹, BMM 14:3) vs. מדלה or מביא (MH²).[33] Nor have we found in BMM any other signs of conscious language transfer identified by Moreshet, e.g. changes in morphemes, *hapax legomena*, altered usages, or new forms and connotations from familiar verbs. In his study of the superficially tannaitic Mishnat R. Eliezer, Moreshet demonstrates its post-talmudic origin by identifying over a hundred MH² lexemes, including new verbs, revived biblical verbs, loanwords, proper names, archaisms, neologisms, etc.[34] None of these examples can be found in BMM. In those cases where exact vocabulary coincides, BMM attests the MH¹ form exclusively, eg.: (ש)משוקע (MH¹, BMM 1:27) vs. (נ)שקע(ו) (MH²); שזור (MH¹, BMM 2:4,6) vs. משוזר (MH²); דד(י) (MH¹, BMM 7:17) vs. שד (MH²); (ש)זרחה (MH¹, BMM 14:11) vs. מזריח את (MH²).[35] In sum, to the extent that Sokoloff and Moreshet have separated MH¹ from MH², the language of BMM is uniformly MH¹.

While the lexical features of BMM are common to the Mishnah, Tosefta, and halakhic midrashim, the uniquely technical subject matter requires a specialized vocabulary. Not all of the architectural or mathematical nomenclature is clear, owing in part to MS defects and in part to limited modern knowledge of ancient technology. As G. B. Sarfatti points out in his study of ancient and medieval Hebrew scientific literature, the mathematical terminology of BMM is more abstract than concrete.[36] A lack of linguistic precision for geometrical concepts is characteristic of biblical and ancient rabbinic literature, and it is often felt in BMM. For instance, BMM has no vocabulary for such fundamental geometrical figures as point, line, center, or diameter. With respect to measurement, BMM attests a greater lexical repertoire. It includes terms of biblical metrology from both the tabernacle account (e.g. טפח, אמה) and elsewhere (e.g. סאה, ככר, כור, אצבע), as well as the later vocabulary of the rabbis for linear (e.g. מיל), surface (e.g. בית סאתים) and cubic (e.g. מקוה) measure. Attempts have been made to calculate the values of these measures by comparison with excavated buildings and vessels or by correlation with Greek and Roman equivalents, but the results are highly speculative.[37] More is known about internal ratios (e.g. 1 אמה = 6 טפח = 24 אצבע), but absolute values are based on conjecture.

Still greater lexical difficulty is posed by details of workmanship, metallurgy, and structural design. The architectonic description of the lampstand (ch. 9-10), for instance, employs biblical terms (e.g. גביע, ירך, קנה, פרח, כפתור) and rabbinic locutions (e.g. כוסות אלכסנדריים, תפוחים הבירותיים (?)) that are obscure. The vocabulary of ancient metallurgy in chapter 9 (e.g. זהב באה ככר, זהב טהור, זהב מקשה) refers to processes that are unknown to us. The text of BMM occasionally resorts to similes (e.g. כמין קורה, 7:17; כשני דדי אשה, 2:10-11; ככוכבים ברקיע, 10:1) that underscore the difficulty of conveying iconographic forms in the medium of language.

Once exposed to the Arabic nomenclature of Hellenistic science, rabbinic Hebrew developed a greater capacity for mathematical description, calculation, and abstraction. This language is not found in rabbinic literature until the treatise Mishnat ha-Middot (ca. tenth c. ?),[38] concerning the calculation of the dimensions of plane and solid geometric figures and including a description of the tabernacle. This account attests Arabic loanwords, syntax, and methods of computation that clearly indicate its medieval origin. For instance, as Sarfatti explains:[39]

> The author introduced a new subdivision of the cubit based on sexagesimal fractions, a system largely employed by the Babylonians, Greeks and Arabs for calculations of quantities smaller than the unity; nevertheless, in accordance with his tendency to express himself in mishnaic Hebrew, he called the first sub-unit *se'ora*, a name that he found in the Mishna to signify a certain size. He was compelled to invent this sub-division ... because in ancient mathematics, until the Middle Ages, it was usually preferred to express quantities smaller than the unity by sub-units of measures rather than by arithmetical fractions.

None of these innovations, linguistic or conceptual, are attested in BMM. Nor have we found any of the other signs of medieval origin discussed earlier in this chapter, e.g. paraphrastic citation, interpolated parallels, hypercorrection, anachronism, vernacular influence, etc. Thus the specialized vocabulary of BMM, no less than its more common lexical features, corroborates its assignment to MH[1].

Further confirmation of this judgment may be found in Sussman's study of y. Sheq.,[40] where two distinct branches of readings are disclosed: version A, the earlier, more pristine text, and version B, the later Babylonian recension. Presumably rabbinic works that cite or match version A are of earlier origin than those that rely upon version B. In the case of BMM, this correspondence can be tested, since these are a number of parallels to y. Sheq. (see ch. 3 below). If BMM indeed belongs to the MH[1] stratum, its citations of y. Sheq. should conform to version A. The following table lists specific parallels between BMM (left column, by chapter and line number) and y. Sheq. (right column, by page, column, and line number of *editio princeps*, Venice 1522/23) according to Sussman's identification of y. Sheq. versions A and B:

Ch.: line	*BMM*	*VERSION B*	*VERSION A*	*Y. SHEQ.* *page, column: line*
1) 6:11	ורחבן שלשה	ורחבו/ן ששה	ורחבו/ן שלשה[41]	49d: 17, 22, 31, 35
2) 6:18	ר' יהוד' בן לקיש	ר' יהודה ב"ר אילעי	ר' יודה בן לקיש	49c: 26, 32, 34
3) —	ח'	ח'	מהלכין	49c: 26
4) 7:2	נתן של עץ בתוך של זהב ונתן של זהב בתוך של עץ	נתן של זהב בשל עץ ושל עץ בשל זהב	נתן של עץ בשל זהב ושל זהב בשל עץ[42]	49d: 39
5) 10:14	והייתה יתירה דינר זהב	ח'	והיתה יתירה דינר זהב	50b: 17
6) 10:31	הם כולם זהב של שלמה	הוא כאילו זהבו של שלמה	הן כילו זהבו של שלמה	50b: 14

Of the six parallels adduced, BMM corresponds to y. Sheq. version A in four of them (parallels 1, 2, 4, 5) and to version B in one (parallel 3). Concerning parallel 6, BMM is closer to version A and attests a variant reading (see apparatus at BMM 10:31) that matches. Granting the limited sample of comparative data and the conjectural content of Sussman's classification, BMM appears to rely on the earlier text of y. Sheq.

Is it possible to determine whether BMM is of Babylonian or Palestinian provenance? Of the studies we have considered, only Bendavid's analysis[43] provides a sufficient basis for comparison to BMM. The following table lists those of Bendavid's dialect examples that are attested in BMM. The citations, listed by chapter and line number, are illustrative, not exhaustive.

	Palestinian Hebrew	*Babylonian Hebrew*	*BMM (ch.: line)*
1)	דינר	זוז	דינר 10:14
2)	פרסוף	פרצוף	פרצוף 4:17
3)	על גבי	לגבי	על גבי 4:2, 10:33
4)	מיכן ומיכן	אילך ואילך	אילך ואילך 10:17,18, 19
			מכאן ומכאן 1:13, 6:4
5)	אי/אין אתה/את	אינך	אין אתה 5:2, 5:13
6)	הרי הוא אומר	והלא כבר נאמר	הרי הוא אומר 11:10, 12:8-9
			והלא כבר נאמר 8:11
7)	...מעשה ש	...מעשה ו	מעשה ו... 10:14
8)	...ללמד ש	הא למדת	הא למדת 4:11, 5:10, 7:18
			ללמד ש... 5:17, 5:28
9)	למעלן/למטן	למעלה/למטה	למעלה 3:14, 11:16
			למטה 10:2, 11:14
			ולמעלן 11:17, 18
			ולמטן 11:17, 18
10)	יוסה	יוסי	יוסה 1:8, 5:27, 11:6
			יוסי 3:10
11)	כאיזה צד	כיצד	כיצד 1:8, 2:1, 5:4
12)	יודה	יהודה	יהודה 6:9, 8:2, 13:37

Of the twelve examples of Hebrew distinctions, four (2,7,11,12) reflect Babylonian usage, three (1,3,5) reflect Palestinian usage, and five (4,6,8,9,10) reflect both. If this verdict were not already mixed, even those cases of alleged Palestinian or Babylonian precedence in BMM are belied by variant readings in the MSS. Although our sample is limited, it suggests that Bendavid's binary model of dialects is either untenable in general or unprovable in the case of BMM. Possibly the original Palestinian or Babylonian dialect distinctions were obscured in the course of scribal transmission; possibly they were already fused in the archetype. Either way, Bendavid's analysis brings us no closer to ascertaining the provenance of BMM.

Next we turn to the exegetical terminology and attributive formulae of BMM. Here the linguistic data are both more abundant and more decisive. The following table is arranged alphabetically (excluding the prefixes 'ו and 'ש). Each occurrence of a locution is listed by chapter and line number (ch.:line). To provide a more global picture of parallel passages in the Mishnah, Tosefta, and halakhic midrashim, the table refers the reader to concordances rather than to individual citations: Wilhelm Bacher, *Die exegetische Terminologie der jüdischen Traditionsliteratur* (abbreviated ET, vol., page); or when not attested there, C. Y. Kosovsky, *Thesaurus Mishnae* (TM, vol., page); B. Kosovsky, *Thesaurus Sifra* (TSifra, vol., page), *Thesaurus Sifre* Numbers and Deuteronomy (TSifre, vol., page).[44]

Parallels	*BMM (ch.: line)*	*Exegetical Terminology*
ET 1:109	9:5, 9:8	אחר שריבה הכתוב מיעט
ET 1:7	7:15, 7:16, 12:6, 12:7	אי אפשר לומר
TM 1:159-160	10:7, 12:20	(ו) אילו הן
ET 1:68-69	5:2, 5:13, 5:15	אין אתה יודע
ET 1:199-200	1:17, 1:32, 5:16-17, 7:3-4, 12:3	(ש) אין תלמוד לומר... ומה ת״ל
TM 1:118	1:29	אינו כן אלא
ET 1:68-69	11:6	איני יודע
(M. RH 2:9)	5:28	אלא ללמד
ET 1:6	8:17, 10:27, 12:12 (twice)	(ו) אם תאמר
ET 1:6	7:10	אמרת
TM 1:252-255	7:8, 8:15, 10:25	(ו) אעפי ש...

Source	References	Term
TM 2:476	3:14, 8:6, 10:32, 11:5	דברי...
TM 2:551-552=		דברי... שהיה [...] אומ'
שהיה אומ'	2:4-7, 4:16-17	
(Sifra ed. Weiss 9:4, 56A =		(דברי... שהיה... או')
ET 1:77	7:16-17, 12:8	הא כיצד
ET 1:29	4:11, 4:23, 4:26, 5:10, 5:24, 5:26, 7:18	הא למדת
ET 1:6	5:3	הוי אומ'
ET 1:42, 77	8:11, 8:18, 10:28	(ו) הלא
ET 1:46-48	1:23, 6:3, 6:10, 12:10	הרי
ET 1:6	11:10, 12:8-9	הרי הוא אומ'
ET 1:72	9:4	יכול
ET 1:6, 77	7:15-16, 7:16, 8:11, 12:6, 12:7	(ש) כבר נאמ'
TM 3:928; TSifre 3:995-996	7:13, 13:18, 14:1	כיון ש...
ET 1:77	1:8, 1:22, 1:34, 2:1, 5:4, 7:1, 10:1, 10:31, 13:1	כיצד
ET 1:116	4:16	כל מקום ש...
TM 3:971	6:22, 6:23	(ו) כן הוא או' ב...
ET 1:6, 30	5:23 (5:13 = 'כשנא'[45])	כשהוא או'
TM 3:937; TSifra 3:1013-1014	1:28-29, 4:9, 4:11-12, 4:13-14, 5:11-12, 7:11-12, 7:19-20, 12:31-32	כשם ש... כך...
ET 1:74-75	9:5, 9:7	(ו) להוציא
ET 1:15, 93	1:20 (11:8 = ונאמ' להלן)	(ו) להלן הוא אומ'
ET 1:96	5:17, 5:28	ללמד
ET 1:94-95	10:5, 12:14	למדנו
TM 4:1446	7:14	לפיכך
ET 1:180	9:4, 9:7	לרבות
ET 1:30-32	10:24	מגיד
ET 1:170; ET 1:105	9:13	(ו) מה אני מקיים
TM 1:251-252	5:3-4, 11:11	מה... אף
ET 1:15	11:8-9	מה האמור להלן... אף האמור כאן
TSifre 3:1009-1011	5:14	מה... כך

ET 1:199-200	8:18-19, 12:15	(ו) מה ת"ל... אלא
ET 1:199-200	10:28, 11:6-7	(ו) מה ת"ל
ET 1:41	14:15	מהיכן
ET 1:15	11:7	מופנה להקיש לדון ממנו גזירה שוה
ET 1:74-75	9:6, 9:9	(ו) מוציא אני
ET 1:76	8:3	מכאן אמרו
ET 1:76	5:29-30, 10:35	מכאן היה... או'
ET 1:31-32, 96	7:4	מלמד ש...
ET 1:192	11:6	ממשמע
ET 1:6, 106	7:12	מניין אתה או'
TM 3:1141	7:17, 7:18, 7:19, 12:11, 12:13, 12:14, 13:34	(ו) מניין ש...
TM 3: 1426-1427	10:14	מעשה ו...
TSifre 5:1722	9:5, 9:8	מרבה אני
ET 1:15	11:7-8	נאמ' כאן... ונאמ' להלן
ET 1:115	10:23	נמצאת או'
ET 1:72	9:3	שומע אני
ET 1:199-200	9:3, 9:4	ת"ל

Without exception, every exegetical or attributive term in BMM is attested in either the Mishnah, Tosefta, or halakhic midrashim. However, the aggregate yields no support for a classification by vocabulary adhering to R. Akiba's or R. Ishmael's "school." On the contrary, the dichotomous terminologies proposed by Hoffmann[46] are found side by side in BMM. Those terms characteristic of the Akiban midrashim (viz., Sifra, Sifre Deuteronomy, Mekhilta de-R. Simeon) are amply attested in BMM, e.g.: מה תלמוד לומר (8:18-19, 10:28, 11:6-7, 12:15); יכול (9:4); מלמד ש... (7:4); לרבות (9:4, 9:7); אחר (9:5, 9:8). Ishmaelian terminology also occurs, e.g.: מופנה להקיש לדון ממנו גזרה (9:5, 9:7); להוציא (10:24); מגיד (9:3); שומע אני שוה (11:7). BMM also includes a term (אמרת, 7:10) attributed to the unique usage of Sifre Zuta. Chapter 9 of BMM includes a section particularly thick with exegetical language; it too is split almost evenly between Akiban and Ishmaelian terms. The rest of the exegetical terminology in BMM, including its most frequent expressions (e.g. כיצד, nine citations; כשם ש... כך..., seven; מניין ש..., seven) is common to all of the extant tannaitic corpora.

The same uniformity of tannaitic usage appears in attributions to named tradents. Only Tannaim are mentioned in BMM. All but three of them are mentioned in the Mishnah, all but one are mentioned in the Tosefta, and every one of them is mentioned in the halakhic midrashim. Except for chapter 12, every chapter names at least one tradent. The following table groups the tradents named in BMM according to three chronological strata designated by the respective geographical centers of tannaitic activity: Yavneh (ca. 70-130 C.E.); Usha (ca. 135-170); and Beth Shearim (ca. 170-200). Each name is followed by its citation(s) in BMM, listed by chapter and line (ch.:line). Those of uncertain date are enclosed in brackets.

Tradents

BMM	(ch.:line)
Yavneh	
Eliezer (b. Hyrcanus)	7:24
Simeon b. Azzai	14:17
[disciple(s) of R. Ishmael]	14:18
Usha	
Simeon b. Yoḥai	14:8
Nehemiah	1:18, 2:4, 3:14, 4:16
Judah (b. Ilai)	1:20, 3:14, 6:9, 6:26, 8:2, 8:13, 13:37
Meir	6:3, 8:6, 11:5
Jose (b. Ḥalafta)	1:8, 3:10, 5:27, 11:6
Joshua b. Qorḥa	9:12
Abba Saul	8:9
Nathan	10:35, 14:16
Isi b. Aqavya	10:13
[Isi b. Judah]	10:6
Beth Shearim	
Rabbi (Judah I)	1:1, 7:25, 10:33
Jose b. Judah	5:30
Judah b. Laqish	6:18, 7:22
[Ḥakhamim]	2:5, 7:23, 10:33

There are a total of thirty-seven attributions, five of uncertain date. Of these five, three cite *ḥakhamim*; one cites a disciple or disciples of R. Ishmael, presumably either Yavnean or Ushan; and one cites Isi b. Judah, a Tanna of uncertain identity but most likely from the period of Usha.[47] Of the remaining thirty-two attributions, twenty-four derive from the Ushan period, six from Beth Shearim, and two from Yavneh. Even when conflicting attributions attested in the MSS are taken into account, there can be no doubt that the vast majority of attributions in BMM cite Tannaim from the mid-second century.

As in the case of BMM's exegetical terminology, so also its tradents are divided between the schools of Akiba and Ishmael. Isi b. Aqavyah, for example, is mentioned ten times in Mekhilta/Sifre Numbers and not once in Akiban midrashim; Nathan is mentioned some one hundred times in Mekhilta/Sifre Numbers and only three times in Akiban midrashim. On the other hand, most of the other tradents (e.g. Judah, Jose, Simeon, Nehemiah) are associated with the school of Akiba.

BMM includes several tradents (e.g. Abba Saul, Isi b. Aqavya, Joshua b. Qorḥa, Judah b. Laqish) who are infrequently mentioned in the tannaitic corpora. Of this group, Judah b. Laqish is the only one mentioned more than once in BMM, yet curiously he is the least attested elsewhere (Mishnah = 0, Tosefta = 4, Mekhilta = 1, Sifra = 1). ישמעאל ר' של תלמידיו (some MSS = תלמידו) does not appear in the Mishnah, Tosefta, or halakhic midrashim. The same grammatical form is attested once in connection with Judah ha-Nasi: ר' תלמידיו (Mek. *be-Shallaḥ* 4:1). However, an expression similar to של תלמידו ישמעאל ר' is found several times: ישמעאל ר' מתלמידי אחד (Mek. *Mishpatim* 4, 10; *Vayaqhel* 1; Sifre Num. 107).

On those occasions when BMM reports conflicting opinions among the Tannaim, the named tradents in controversy align with the dispute patterns attested in the Mishnah, Tosefta, and halakhic midrashim. The next table lists the tannaitic controversies in BMM by tradent pairs or aggregates. Each controversy is cited by chapter and line (ch.:line). For parallel passages from the Mishnah and Tosefta, the table refers the reader to the concordance of Wilhelm Bacher, *Tradition und Tradenten in den Schulen Palästinas und Babyloniens* (abbreviated TT) by page number.[48]

Controversies

	BMM ch:line	Parallels
Nehemiah/Judah	1:18-21; 3:13-16	TT 136
Meir/Judah	6:3-15	TT 134-135,144
Meir/Judah (+ Abba Saul)	8:2-11	
Meir/Jose	11:4-12	TT 135,144
Nehemiah/Ḥakhamim	2:3-7	TT 154
Meir/Ḥakhamim	10:31-34	TT 151-152
Eliezer/Rabbi/Judah		TT 149-150
b.Laqish/Ḥakhamim	7:22-27	(=Eliezer/Ḥakhamim)
Simeon b. Azzai/Disciple(s)	14:16-19	
of Ishmael/Nathan		

Of the nine tannaitic controversies in BMM, six are reported by tradent pairs, and each of these is attested in the Mishnah and Tosefta. Of the remaining three, one adds Abba Saul to an attested pair, Meir/Judah; one adds Rabbi and Judah b. Laqish to an attested pair, Eliezer/Ḥakhamim; and one is unique, Simeon b. Azzai/Disciple(s) of Ishmael/Nathan.

To summarize, the attribution of opinions in BMM, the names of tradents, and the pairs or aggregates of opinions in controversy are all consistent with the patterns of the Mishnah, Tosefta, and halakhic midrashim. Were we to rely upon the names of tradents for a chronological determination of BMM's origin, the preponderance of Ushan Tannaim together with six attributions to the circle of Judah ha-Nasi would suggest the third or fourth century C.E. as the earliest possible date. As we have pointed out, tradent attributions cannot be credulously accepted. But in the case of BMM there are other, more compelling indications of tannaitic origin.

BMM is composed entirely in MH[1], whether of Babylonian or Palestinian provenance. MH[2], as described by Sokoloff and Moreshet, is entirely absent from BMM, nor is there any trace of medieval influence. Of the six passages in BMM that parallel y. Sheq., all but one match the early text identified by Sussman. With respect to exegetical terminology, every single example is consistent with the usage of tannaitic Hebrew. The foregoing analysis of the language of BMM leads us to conclude that it is a collection of authentic tannaitic traditions.

Notes to Chapter Two

LANGUAGE, TERMINOLOGY, TRADENTS

1. Those now in use are based on published editions of rabbinic works rather than on MSS, limiting their value for linguistic research.

2. But even this development can be difficult to trace. The slow emergence of tannaitic Hebrew as an independent language produced a literary form that bridged the biblical and mishnaic periods and often obscured their distinguishing features. See Shraga Abramson, "Biblical Hebrew in Mishnaic Hebrew" (Hebrew), in *Meḥqarim be-Lashon*, ed. M. Bar-Asher (Jerusalem, 1985), 211-42, who argues that the well-known talmudic assertion (b. AZ 58b, b. Ḥul. 137b) לשון תורה לעצמה לשון חכמים לעצמן does not mean that the sages failed to recognize the fundamental adhesion of rabbinic to biblical Hebrew. Cf. J. N. Epstein, *Mavo le-Nusaḥ ha-Mishnah* (Jerusalem, 1949), 282-83.

3. Moshe Goshen-Gottestein, "Corpus, Genre and the Unity of Hebrew" (Hebrew), *Meḥqarim be-Lashon*, ed. M. Bar-Asher (Jerusalem, 1985), 57-73.

4. Ibid. 67-68.

5. E. Y. Kutscher estimates that nearly one-fourth of the Hebrew and Aramaic lexemes contained in rabbinic literature now require re-examination; see his "The Present State of Research into Mishnaic Hebrew and its Tasks" (Hebrew), *Erkhe ha-Milon he-Ḥadash le-Sifrut Ḥazal* v. 1, ed. E. Y. Kutscher, Bar Ilan Univ. (Ramat Gan, 1972), 3-28.

6. E. Y. Kutscher, "Mittelhebräisch und Jüdisch-Aramäisch in neuen Köhler-Baumgartner Hebräische Worforschung," *Festschrift W. Baumgartner* (Leiden, 1967), 158-75 = Supplements to *Vetus Testamentum* 16.

7. E. Y. Kutscher, "Some Problems of the Lexicography of Mishnaic Hebrew and its Comparison with Biblical Hebrew" (Hebrew), *Erkhe ha-Milon he-Ḥadash le-Sifrut Ḥazal* v. 1, op.cit. 29-105.

8. Ibid. 47-49, 52.

9. Michael Sokoloff, "The Hebrew of Genesis Rabbah according to MS Vatican 30" (Hebrew), *Leshonenu* 33 (1979): 25-42, 135-49, 270-79 = *Qovez*

Ma'amarim be-Leshon Ḥazal, ed. M. Bar-Asher (Jerusalem, 1982), 257-301.

10. Menaḥem Moreshet, "The Language of the Baraitot in the Babylonian Talmud is not MH¹" (Hebrew), *Sefer Zikkaron le-Ḥanokh Yalon*, ed. E. Y. Kutscher et al (Ramat Gan, 1974), 275-314; "New and Revived Verbs in the Baraitot of the Babylonian Talmud" (Hebrew), *Erkhe ha-Milon* v. 1, 117-62; "Further Studies of the Language of the Hebrew Baraitot in the Babylonian and Palestinian Talmuds" (Hebrew), ibid. v. 2, ed. M. Z. Kaddari (Ramat Gan, 1974), 31-73; *Leqsiqon ha-Po'al* (Ramat Gan, 1980).

11. This finding is anticipated by J. N. Epstein, *Mevo'ot le-Sifrut ha-Tannaim* (Tel Aviv, 1957), 245-46.

12. Moreshet, "The Language of the Baraitot..." op.cit. He concedes that there are occasional and even significant variants between baraitot in the Palestinian Talmud and parallel tannaitic texts but contends that these can be explained by other factors that do not negate his thesis: Moreshet, "Further Studies..." op.cit.

13. Moreshet, "New and Revived Verbs..." op.cit.

14. Ibid. 160.

15. A simpler but less rigorous classification of talmudic baraitot has been suggested by Ze'ev ben-Ḥayyim, "On the Chronology of an Article in the Historical Dictionary" (Hebrew), *Proceedings of the Fifth World Congress of Jewish Studies* 5 (1973): 3-11. For historical purposes he would divide them into three categories: those that match tannaitic sources; those that parallel tannaitic sources but differ in language and style; and those that are otherwise unattested. This may not produce a verifiable chronological sequence, but it does furnish a taxonomy by which MH might be evaluated.

16. For a summary of the scholarly debate concerning the origins of this work, see Moshe Zucker, "Toward the Solution of the Problem of the Thirty-Two Hermeneutic Rules and Mishnat R. Eliezer" (Hebrew), *PAAJR* 23 (1954): Hebrew pagination 1-39. Zucker concludes that the work can be dated no earlier than the tenth century, since he detects use of the commentary on Sefer Yeẓirah written by Saadia Gaon in 931. Moreshet (see the following note) proposes a *terminus a quo* in the seventh or eighth century.

17. Menaḥem Moreshet, "The Language of Mishnat R. Eliezer" (Hebrew), *Annual of Bar Ilan University Studies in Judaica and the Humanities* (Hebrew) v. 11, ed. M. Z. Kaddari et al (Ramat Gan, 1973), 182-223.

18. David Rosenthal, *Mishna Aboda Zara: A Critical Edition with Introduction* (Hebrew), 2 vols. (Jerusalem, 1980).

19. Abba Bendavid, *Leshon Miqra u-Leshon Ḥakhamim*, 2 vols. (Tel Aviv, 1967-71), 1:171-222.

20. Moreshet criticizes Bendavid's classification for failing to distinguish

between MH[1] and MH[2] or between tannaitic and amoraic sources: "The Language of the Baraitot..." op.cit. 277 n. 8.

21. Bendavid, *Leshon Miqra u-Leshon Hakhamim*, 1:236 ff.

22. See, e.g., Samuel Morell, "Sources of Halakhot Pesuqot: A Formal Analysis" (Hebrew), *PAAJR* 49 (1982): Hebrew pagination 41-95 at 80 f.

23. For a summary and brief lexicon of Hebrew under Arabic influence, see E. Goldenberg, "Medieval Hebrew," *EJ* 16:1607-42 at 1626-33. Cf. Zucker, op.cit. 35-39, who furnishes three conclusive examples of Arabic influence on Mishnat R. Eliezer, belying the late origin of a work written in tannaitic style.

24. On this phenomenon see, e.g., Y. M. Ta-Shema, "The Library of the Sages of Ashkenaz of the Eleventh and Twelfth Centuries" (Hebrew), *Kiryat Sefer* 60 (1985): 298-309; but note the objections of Ch. Milikowsky in *Kiryat Sefer* 62 (1987): 169-70.

25. B. M. Bokser, "An Annotated Bibliographical Guide to the Study of the Palestinian Talmud, *Aufstieg und Niedergang der Römischen Welt* II:19:2 (Berlin/New York, 1979), 139-256 at 151.

26. Jacob Sussman, "Masoret Limmud u-Masoret Nusah shel ha-Talmud ha-Yerushalmi," *Mehqarim ba-Sifrut ha-Talmudit*, Israel Academy of Sciences and Humanities (Jerusalem, 1983), 12-76.

27. Systematic descriptions may be found, e.g., in M. Higger, *Ozar ha-Baraitot*, 10 vols. (New York, 1938-48); J. N. Epstein, *Mavo le-Nusah ha-Mishnah* (Tel Aviv, ²1964); H. Albeck *Mehqarim be-Baraita ve-Tosefta* (Jerusalem, 1969).

28. See, e.g., B. DeVries, *Mehqarim be-Sifrut ha-Talmud* (Jerusalem, 1968), 200-214; H. Albeck, *Mavo la-Talmudim* (Tel Aviv, 1969), 561-64; more recently, M. Chernick, *Le-Heqer ha-Middot*, Hermeneutical Studies in Talmudic and Midrashic Literatures (Tel Aviv, 1984); N. Goldstein, "On Some Midrashic Conjunctive Terms" (Hebrew), *PAAJR* 49 (1982): Hebrew pagination 1-7.

29. Jacob Neusner has abstracted and classified these patterns in many of his studies, e.g. *A History of the Mishnaic Law of Purities*, 22 vols. (Leiden, 1974-77), 3:192-236, 5:131-48, 8:108-21, 10:93-109. For an analysis of rhetorical patterns in halakhic midrash, see, e.g., W. S. Towner, *The Rabbinic Enumeration of Scriptural Examples* (Leiden, 1973).

30. See above, n. 9.

31. See above, nn. 10, 17.

32. Moreshet, "Further Studies..." op.cit. 48.

33. Ibid. 37-40, 51-52.

34. Moreshet, "The Language of Mishnat R. Eliezer," op.cit. 197-219.

35. Ibid. 208, 213, 204 n. 102, 209 respectively.

36. Gad B. Sarfatti, *Mathematical Terminology in Hebrew Scientific Literature of the Middle Ages* (Hebrew; Jerusalem, 1968), 36-37.

37. See, e.g., the table of talmudic metrology in W. M. Feldman, *Rabbinical Mathematics and Astronomy* (New York, ³1978), 222-23.

38. See below, ch. 4, n. 4. Cf. Sarfatti, op.cit.; B. Spain, "Mathematics," *EJ* 11:1121-24.

39. G. B. Sarfatti, "Some Remarks About the Prague Manuscript of Mishnat ha-Middot," *HUCA* 45 (1974): 197-204 at 202.

40. See above, n. 26.

41. This reading is from the unrevised Codex Leiden Scal. 3 on which the Venice ed. is based. Sussman identifies this text as version A; see appendix 2 of his study, op.cit. 66 n. 168; 73.

42. See previous note.

43. See above, n. 19.

44. Wilhelm Bacher, *Die exegetische Terminologie der jüdischen Traditionsliteratur*, 2 vols. (repr. Darmstadt, 1965); C. Y. Kosovsky, *Thesaurus Mishnae*, 4 vols. (Jerusalem, 1960); B. Kosovsky, *Thesaurus Sifra*, 4 vols. (Jerusalem, 1967-69); idem, *Thesaurus Sifre*, 5 vols. (Jerusalem, 1971-74).

45. כשנא' is an error in our base text; other MSS have כשהוא או' or שנ'.

46. David Hoffmann, *Zur Einleitung in die halachischen Midraschim* (Berlin, 1887); see the discussion in ch. 1 of our Introduction.

47. According to b. Pes. 113b, Isi b. Judah is identical to Joseph of Huẓal, Joseph the Babylonian, Isi b. Gur Aryeh, Isi b. Gamaliel, Isi b. Mahalalel, and Isi b. Aqavya. Other passages in both Talmuds and in the halakhic midrashim give other identifications; see J. N. Epstein, *Mevo'ot le-Sifrut ha-Tannaim* (Tel Aviv, 1957), 571.

48. Wilhelm Bacher, *Tradition und Tradenten in den Schulen Palästinas und Babyloniens* (repr. Berlin, 1966).

Chapter 3

Parallel Passages and Medieval Citations

I. PARALLEL PASSAGES

Fully one-third of the text of BMM is found in parallel passages in the Mishnah, Tosefta, Sifre Numbers, and the Talmuds.[1] By the term parallel we concede the difficulty of establishing the priority of one passage or the other. The presence of identical or very similar passages in disparate works may be explained by any number of theories. If only two passages are involved, one may depend upon the other, both may draw upon a third, or each may have developed separately under more distant influence. It is also possible that editors, glossators, or copyists have interpolated or conflated passages from other sources. When the number of parallels is greater than two, the possibilities multiply exponentially. Even when a particular passage is proven to be primary or secondary, it is hardly conclusive for the work as a whole, since many rabbinic compositions are compendia of circulating traditions.

To determine the relationship of parallels within a rabbinic work or within the literature as a whole, one must examine both the immediate context and the more global traits of the composition at hand. If no obvious seams are visible at the location of a given passage, this may be as easily explained by adroit redaction as by intrinsic continuity. One must evaluate the passage for consonance with the formal attributes of the work as a whole: its structure, order, proportion, exegetical repertoire, etc. Should a rabbinic work evidence the qualities of a distinctive composition rather than a compendium, individual passages need also to be tested for consistency with the prevailing program and point of view. Such labors have occupied generations of investigation and debate. Given the vagaries of rab-

37

binic literary formulation, transmission, and redaction, the question
of priority among parallel passages is often insoluble.

A major purpose of the present study is to clarify the relationship
of BMM to the various strata of tannaitic and amoraic literature.
While the evidence from parallels cannot always be decisive, in the
present case it is particularly important. Following are two tables.
Table 1 lists the location of tannaitic and amoraic parallels by
sequence in BMM (by chapter and line). Table 2 lists the parallels
by source.

Table 1

BMM (ch.:line)   *Parallels*

1:18-21	b. Shab. 98b
2:3-7	y. Sheq. 8:4, 51b
2:10-11	y. Meg. 1:14, 72c-d; b. Shab. 98b-99a; PRK 1:3
4:3-5	T. YK 3:7; T.Sot. 13:1; y. Sheq. 6:1, 49c = y. Sot. 8:3, 22c; b. Hor. 12a = b. Yoma 52a = b.Ker. 5b; ARN A 41
4:4-5	T. Kel. BQ 1:7
4:15-17	y. Sheq. 8:4, 51b; b. Yoma 72b
4:16-17	T. Sheq. 3:14
4:18-19	y. Sheq. 6:4, 50b
5:29-31	b. Er. 23b
6:1-17, 26-27	b. BB 14a
6:1-22	y. Sheq. 6:1, 49c, 49d
6:1-24	y. Sot. 8:3, 22c-d
6:18-22	T. Sot. 7:18; Sifre Num. *be-ha'alotkha* 82
7:1-6	y. Sheq. 6:1, 49d = y. Sot. 8:3, 22d
7:12-19	T. YK 3:7
7:15-17	y. Sheq. 6:1, 49c; b. Yoma 54a; b. Men. 98a-b
7:21-27	T. Sheq. 2:18; y. Sheq. 6:1, 49c
8:3-11	M. Men. 11:5
8:15-20	T. Men. 11:9; y. Sheq. 6:4, 50a; b. Men. 99a
9:3-4	Sifre Num. *be-ha'alotkha* 61
9:4-14	b. Men. 88b
9:9-12	b. Men 28a
10:6-7	b. Yoma 52a-b

10:6-14	y. AZ 2:7, 41c-d
10:13-14	y. Sheq. 6:4, 50b; b, Men. 29a
10:15-23	b. Men. 28b
10:25-31	T. Men. 11:10; y. Sheq. 6:4, 50b; b. Men. 99a
10:35-36	Sifre Num. *be-ha'alotkha* 59; b. Men. 98b
11:4-12	b. Zev. 59b-60a
11:12-13	M. Mid. 3:1
11:12-16	b. Zev. 10b, 53a
12:4-8	T. Kel. BM 5:2
12:6-15	y. Er. 1:5, 19a
12:20-27	M. Sheq. 5:1-2
13:18-19	y. Er. 5:1, 22c
13:31-32	y. Er. 5:1, 22c
14:3-8	Sifre Num. *be-ha'alotkha* 83

Table 2

Parallels	BMM (ch.:line)
Mishnah	
Sheq. 5:1-2	12:20-27
Men. 11:5	8:3-11
Mid. 3:1	11:12-13
Tosefta	
Sheq. 2:18	7:21-27
3:14	4:16-17
YK 3:7	4:3-5; 7:12-19
Sot. 7:18	6:18-22
13:1	4:3-5
Men. 11:9	8:15-20
11:10	10:25-31
Kel. BQ 1:7	4:4-5
Kel. BM 5:2	12:4-8
Sifre Numbers	
be-ha'alotkha 59	10:35-36
61	9:3-4
82	6:18-22
83	14:3-8

Yerushalmi

Sheq. 6:1, 49c-d	4:3-5; 6:1-22; 7:1-6, 15-17, 21-27
6:4, 50a-b	4:18-19; 8:15-20; 10:13-14, 25-31
8:4, 51b	2:3-7; 4:15-17
Er. 1:5, 19a	12:6-15
5:1, 22c	13:18-19, 31-32
Meg. 1:14, 72c-d	2:10-11
Sot. 8:3, 22c-d	4:3-5; 6:1-24; 7:1-6
AZ 2:7, 41c-d	10:6-14

Bavli

Shab. 98b-99a	1:18-21; 2:10-11
Er. 23b	5:29-31
Yoma 52a	4:3-5
52a-b	10:6-7
54a	7:15-17
72b	4:15-17
BB 14a	6:1-7, 26-27
Hor. 12a	4:3-5
Zev. 10b	11:12-14
53a	11:14-16
59b-60a	11:4-12
Men. 28a	9:9-12
28b	10:15-23
29a	10:13-14
88b	9:4-14
98a-b	7:15-17; 10:35-36
99a	8:15-17; 10:25-27
Ker. 5b	4:3-5

Table 1 shows that of the fourteen chapters of BMM, only one (ch. 3, concerning the outer covers of the tabernacle) attests no parallels in extant tannaitic or amoraic sources. This is probably not significant: chapter 3 is only half the length of the average BMM chapter, and the want of parallels is just as likely a matter of chance. Chapters 1, 5 and 13 contain few passages preserved elsewhere. At the other extreme, virtually every line of chapters 6 and 10 is attested in other sources. No evident pattern emerges from this breakdown: chapters 4, 6, 7, 8, 9, 10, 11, 12 contain both tannaitic and amoraic parallels; chapters 2, 4, 6, 7, 8, 10 include passages found in both Talmuds;

Tosefta parallels are found in chapters 4, 6, 7, 8, 10, 12; Sifre Numbers in chapters 6, 9, 10, 14; Mishnah in chapters 8, 11, 12. In short, while fully informed by these parallel sources, the internal structure of BMM evinces no special affinities with any one of them.

Table 2 reverses the perspective, showing the diffusion of BMM passages among parallel sources. Among the tannaitic documents, the parallels in Sifre Numbers are fragmentary; two of the three in the Mishnah comprise finished units of discourse; and those in the Tosefta are the most numerous, some comprehending entire pericopae. With respect to the Talmuds, although the parallels in the Bavli are more widely dispersed, those in the Yerushalmi are nearly twice as extensive. One *sugya* (y. Sheq. 6:1 = Sot. 8:2) parallels an entire chapter (6) of BMM. Of all the parallel sources, Yerushalmi displays the most pronounced relationship to materials in BMM.

We now turn to a closer look at individual passages. An exhaustive analysis of each of them is beyond the scope of the present study. Rather we seek to examine, across both tannaitic and amoraic strata, a sufficient number and representative variety of parallels to clarify BMM's place in the rabbinic corpus. Our inquiry proceeds according to the sequence of Table 2: Mishnah, Tosefta, Sifre Numbers, Yerushalmi and Bavli.

Mishnah

M. Sheq. 5:12 (= BMM 12:20-27) is absent from all witnesses to the text of BMM except for one MS and a corroborating fragment from the Cairo Genizah. However, this MS is, in our judgment, the best extant witness to the complete text of BMM (see Introduction ch. 5) and constitutes the *codex optimus* of the present edition. The passage is an appendix to the description in BMM chapter 12 of the lavers and cast iron tank of the Solomonic Temple. It lists the officers of the Herodian Temple and their corresponding duties, subjects extraneous to the rest of BMM. Since there is no evident mechanical or mnemonic linkage with the adjacent text, the presence of M. Sheq. 5:1-2 in BMM is anomalous. Only the first half of 5:2 is included, giving further evidence of haphazard transmission. On the other hand, BMM's version of the Mishnah text provides a more pristine reading than the printed editions.[2]

M. Men. 11:5 (= BMM 8:3-11) is introduced by the citation formula מכאן אמרו, indicating that the redactor had the Mishnah before him. The correspondence of wording and spelling, while not identical, is close enough to show that BMM knows the Mishnah in its canonical form. The one significant disparity between the two versions is found in the teaching attributed to Abba Saul and the rejoinder. The Mishnah's version comprises a more logical sequence: Abba Saul's statement שם היו נותנין שני בזכי לבונה שללחם הפנים is challenged by the citation of a contradictory verse (Lev. 24:7), which Abba Saul refutes with another citation (Num. 2:20). In BMM, the statement by Abba Saul is different: נותן ארכה כנגד ארכו של שלחן ורחבה כנגד רחבו של שלחן referring to the arrangement of the loaves on the table rather than to the presence of frankincense. The subsequent citation (Lev. 24:7), which appears in the Mishnah as a contradiction of Abba Saul, is brought by BMM as a validation; conversely, the second citation (Num. 2:20), which appears in the Mishnah as a validation of Abba Saul, is brought by BMM as a contradiction. The problem with BMM's version is that Abba Saul's statement concerning the arrangement of the loaves does not match the Lev. 24:7 proof text concerning the frankincense. Likewise the second citation (Num. 2:20), proving that the preposition על has the force of "beside," has no bearing on Abba Saul's statement as BMM reports it. Thus BMM appears to have garbled the last part of Men. 11:5, which is clearly the prior text. Some MSS of BMM attest a reading closer, but still not identical, to the Mishnah.[3]

Unlike Sheq. 5:1-2, Men. 11:5 does not appear as an addendum to the text of BMM. It is fully integrated into the structure and content of chapter 8. R. Judah is the unifying tradent: his statements appear immediately before and after the Mishnah quotation as well as within it.

M. Mid. 3:1 concludes with a description of the red line that encircled the altar to indicate the locus for the upper and lower sprinkling of blood. This account includes the sentence וחוט שלסקרא חוגרו באמצע להבדיל בין הדמים העליונים לדמים התחתונים, which is also found at BMM 11:12-13. The parallel is exact, although no citation terminology is attested in the MSS of BMM. Despite the many similarities in language and content between BMM and M. Mid., this one sentence constitutes the only parallel between the two. This may be explained in part by BMM's focus on the Solomonic Temple and M. Middot's on the Herodian. Still, given the consonance of subject matter, i.e. details and measurements of the holy precincts and their component parts, it is noteworthy that these two treatises do not overlap. Commenting on the parallels between M. Mid. and M. Tamid, Albeck suggests the possibility of a common source for the two tractates.[4] It is possible that BMM too draws upon such an antecedent source, utilizing other traditions pertinent to its subject of the tabernacle. In any case, in their extant form, M. Mid. and BMM are completely independent.

Tosefta

T. Sheq. 2:18 and BMM 7:21-27 are both concerned with the fate of the ark of the covenant. The texts differ in sequence and attributions. BMM begins with the rhetorical phrase היכן ארון נתון and then relates the respective opinions of R. Judah b. Laqish, the sages, R. Eliezer, and Rabbi. With the exception of the sages, each tradent furnishes a scriptural proof text. In the Tosefta's version, there is no introductory phrase, and only three opinions (Eliezer, Simeon, Judah b. Laqish) are reported, each with a proof text. The opinions and scriptural citations of Eliezer and Judah b. Laqish are the same in both versions. But Simeon's statement is absent from BMM, and the statements of both Rabbi and the sages are absent from Tosefta. In this case BMM and Tosefta appear to be drawing from common sources. BMM's discussion is more complete.

T. Sheq. 3:14 and BMM 4:15-17 (cf. y. Sheq. 8:4, 51b; b. Yoma 72b) ascribe to R. Nehemiah a tradition concerning the distinction between מעשה חשב and מעשה רקם. BMM's citation terminology suggests a quotation from a known source: דברי ר'...שהיה אומ'. However, BMM is probably not citing the Tosefta as we have it, since its hermeneutical formula כל מקום שנ' is unique. In T. Sheq. 3:14, R. Nehemiah's statement is part of a larger pericope, introduced by דבר אחר and concluding with a scriptural citation (Ex. 26:33) concerning the folding of the veil. Tosefta's contextual integration of the R. Nehemiah tradition within a larger unit of discourse, together with BMM's explicit citation terminology, indicate that BMM is citing selectively from a fuller tannaitic discussion of the veil and its workmanship (cf. y. Sheq. 8:4, 51b = BMM 2:3-7, 4:15-17, treated below).

T. YK 3:7[5] and BMM 7:12-19 contain parallel descriptions of the protrusion of the two carrying poles of the ark from the Holy of Holies. BMM's account is preceded by a description of the placement and external appearance of the ark; T. YK 3:7 (cf. T. Sot. 13:1) commences with a list of the contents of the Holy of Holies, found

elsewhere with some differences in BMM (4:3-5).[6] As in the parallels
of T. Sheq. 2:18 = BMM 7:21-27 and T. Sheq. 3:14 = BMM 4:15-17,
BMM introduces its account with a rhetorical expression (in this
case, מניין אתה או') absent from Tosefta. T. YK. 3:7, T. Sot. 13:1 and
BMM 7:12-19 all cite 1 Ki. 8:8/2 Chr. 5:9 to prove that the carrying
poles reached the veil of the Holy of Holies. BMM states further that
for this reason the doors could not be closed. T. YK. 3:7 and BMM
both point out the apparent discrepancy in 1 Ki. 8:8/2 Chr. 5:9
between ויראו and ולא יראו. T. YK. 3:7 employs the exegetical formula
יכול...ת"ל; BMM has a more involved construction: אי איפשר לומ'...
בולטים בפרכת ונראין. BMM's resolution, שכבר נאמ' (ב' פעמים)...הא כיצד
כשני דדי אשה, attested also in y. Sheq. 6:1, 49c, b. Yoma 54a, and b.
Men. 98a-b, is absent from Tosefta, which instead gives a truncated
reading, והיו נראין מתוכה. Tosefta's proof text, Cant. 1:13, includes the
phrase בין שדי ילין, but the connection to the phrase כשני דדי אשה is
missing. Of the two parallel texts, BMM 7:12-19 provides a more
symmetrical exegesis and a more cohesive formulation than T. YK
3:7.

BMM chapter 6, attested virtually in full in the Yerushalmi, also
includes a parallel with Tosefta (Sot. 7:18 = BMM 6:18-22) concerning a tradition that there were two arks in the wilderness, one which
remained in the Israelite encampment and one which went forth to
battle. In the two witnesses to the Tosefta text (MS Vienna and MS
Erfurt) published by Lieberman, as well as in the MSS of BMM,
there are contradictory versions of this tradition, viz. which ark contained the Torah scroll and which contained the tablets.[7] Both BMM
and Tosefta cite the same tradent (R. Judah b. Laqish) and the same
scriptural texts (Num. 10:33, 14:44), but BMM expands the discussion (6:22-27) with the repeated phrase וכן הוא או' introducing a succession of citations (1 Sam. 14:18, 2 Sam. 11:11, 1 Sam. 4:4) on the
same subject. Once again BMM provides a more sustained
discourse.

T. Men. 11:9 and BMM 8:15-20 pertain to the ten tables fashioned
by Solomon for the Temple and the one table in the wilderness tabernacle. Tosefta's concern is to specify the Temple utensils and furniture. Men. 11:9 is in the midst of a catalogue describing the table
props (11:6), rods (11:7), ark staves (11:8), and lampstands (11:10 =
BMM 10:25-27). Tosefta accepts the primacy of the Mosaic table as
a given datum, despite its absence from 2 Chr. 4:8. 1 Ki. 7:48 is
cited as corroboration: by its singular referent עליו, it excludes the

Solomonic tables. BMM too notes that 2 Chr. 4:8 fails to mention the Mosaic table and proposes an exegetical proof (ואם תאמר...והלא אלא...ת"ל...ומה...) to reconcile the contradiction. However, Tosefta's proof, 1 Ki. 7:48, is not brought by BMM;[8] instead 2 Chr. 4:19 is cited although it includes the plural עליהם, again deleting the Mosaic table. One MS[9] of BMM includes, immediately before this citation, the statement of R. Eliezer b. Shammua that the bread of display was set on all the tables (b. Men. 99a).[10] This would explain the citation of 2 Chr. 4:19 but does not furnish scriptural justification for BMM 8:17-20. We conclude that the text of BMM here is defective, despite the near unanimity of text witnesses. Nonetheless, BMM's argument seeks a verdict that Tosefta already assumes. Thus in this parallel, BMM appears to be a prior text.

Such is also the case with the parallel T. Men. 11:10 = BMM 10:25-31. Men. 11:10 gives the same formulation for the Solomonic lampstands that 11:9 gives for the tables: there were ten (2 Chr. 4:7), but only the tabernacle lampstand was kindled (2 Chr. 13:11). BMM describes the contradiction and resolves it, while Tosefta takes the resolution for granted. In structure and terminology, BMM's exegetical proof here is virtually identical to 8:15-20 concerning the tables. In form and content T. Men. 11:9/11:10 and BMM 8:15-20/10:25-31 are matched sets. However, in the case of BMM the two passages are not adjacent, since the subjects of the table and the lampstand occupy separate chapters.

Both T. Kel. BQ 1:7 and BMM 4:4-5 mention that the high priest entered the Holy of Holies four times on the Day of Atonement. In Tosefta this tradition is attributed to Abba Saul; in BMM it is reported anonymously. The contexts of the two versions differ. In Tosefta, Abba Saul wishes to establish the degrees of sanctity of the Temple's inner chambers. Entry to the Holy of Holies is more frequent than to the upper chamber; this is proved by the high priest's four annual visits. In BMM the parallel text follows upon a list of articles stored inside the tabernacle adytum (= T. YK 3:7). Its inclusion here may be explained by either a mnemonic association (שם היה, 4:3; שם היה, 4:4-5) or the adjacent reference to the (vestments of the) high priest. Either way it is irrelevant to the context or concerns of BMM.

T. Kel. BM 5:2 and BMM 12:4-8 describe the liquid capacity of the "sea" or cast iron tank fashioned by Solomon. Tosefta attributes the description to R. Jose; in BMM there is no attribution. The two versions are parallel in structure, but their quotations of Scripture differ slightly in number and sequence: Tosefta cites 2 Chr. 4:5 and 1 Ki. 7:26; BMM cites 1 Ki. 7:23, 1 Ki. 7:26, 2 Chr. 4:5. Exegetical usage also varies slightly: Tosefta = הוא אומר...במקום אחר הוא אומר...; אמור מעתה BMM = שנ'...ואו'...הא כיצד. More important than these divergences in attribution, citation, and terminology is the difference in context between the two passages. T. Kelim's subject is the susceptibility of various utensils to uncleanness. Mention of Solomon's tank is occasioned by a reference to liquid measure in the preceding pericope (T. Kel. BM 5:1); otherwise it is extrinsic to Tosefta's discussion. In BMM, however, the description of Solomon's tank is integral both to the immediate context and to the work as a whole. A primary theme of BMM is the harmonization of the Mosaic tabernacle and the Solomonic Temple: the same conciliation is sought with respect to the tables (ch. 8), the lampstands (ch. 10), and the lavers (ch. 12). The last comparison leads directly to the description of Solomon's tank, emphasized by BMM as a departure (שלמה הוסיף) from the tabernacle model. Because BMM 12:4-8 is intrinsic to the design of this chapter and to the argument advanced in other chapters of BMM, it is highly unlikely that it is derived from another source. In this instance, Tosefta's text appears to be derivative.

Sifre Numbers

As mentioned above, the parallels between BMM and Sifre Numbers are fragmentary. Sifre 59 (ed. Horovitz p. 57, line 6) and BMM 10:35-36 are virtually identical except that BMM adds a scriptural citation (Num. 8:2). Both are occasioned by references to the middle lamp of the lampstand. Both employ citation terminology, מיכן/מכאן היה (ר' נתן) אומר, that suggests the quotation of a known source. However, the other parallel to this passage, at b. Men. 98b, places מכאן within R. Nathan's statement rather than before it. The three parallels corroborate a common tradition, but there is no evidence of priority.

In the parallel Sifre 61 (ed. Horovitz p. 59, lines 3-5) = BMM 9:3-4 we find a textual situation analogous to T. Men. 11:9/11:10 = BMM 8:15-20/10:25-31. That is, BMM argues for a resolution that Sifre already assumes. The subject here is the construction of the lampstand. Sifre interprets the phrase עד ירכה עד פרחה (Num. 8:14) to include as hammered work of gold both base and petal. Sifre then cites Ex. 25:31 to include the cups and calyxes as well as to prove that the entire lampstand was fashioned from one ingot of gold. BMM 9:1-9 arrives at the same conclusions but only after furnishing an elaborate exegetical proof. According to Ex. 25:31, the lampstand was made of pure gold and of one piece. Among the requisite components of the lampstand the verse mentions the base, shaft, cups, calyxes, and petals. BMM points out that the lamps themselves are not mentioned. If the entire lampstand is made of gold, then the lamps must be of gold; but if Scripture's omission of the lamps means that they were not of gold, then perhaps the other ornaments were not of gold either. Next BMM considers whether the lamps were gold and the ornaments were not; or whether the lamps were fashioned as part of the lampstand and the ornaments were not; or whether the tongs and fire pans (Ex. 25:38) were also included or not. Each of these questions is resolved by recourse to the hermeneutical rule אחר שריבה הכתוב מיעט. Sifre reports only the decision of inclusion (ריבוי); BMM discusses a series of ריבוי and מיעוט propositions. BMM 9:1-9 comprises a self-contained rhetorical unit of which the parallel with Sifre (= 9:3-4) is only a part. Sifre appears to cite selectively from a tradition fully explained in BMM.

Sifre 82 (ed. Horovitz p. 78, lines 5-7) parallels BMM 6:18-22 and T. Sot. 7:18 (see above, p. 44). In BMM and Tosefta, R. Judah b. Laqish is the tradent; Sifre's version is anonymous. The discussion, concerning the contents of the ark, is generated by Num. 10:33. This verse is cited by Sifre (as the lemma) and BMM (as the proof text) but is absent from Tosefta, which instead presents supplementary citations. This suggests that the Num. 10:33 tradition is assumed by Tosefta. For its part Sifre comments only on the ark of the encampment, but its reproduction of the phrase זה שיצא עמהם indicates that it too is acquainted with the tradition of two arks. Sifre's text is corrupt: זה שיצא עמהם במחנה should read either זה שהיה עמהם במחנה or זה שיצא עמהם למלחמה, as both BMM and Tosefta attest.[11]

Sifre 83 (ed. Horovitz p. 79, lines 9-12) provides the only tannaitic or amoraic parallel to materials in BMM chapter 14, and the parallel is only approximate. Both describe the seven clouds of glory that accompanied Israel in the wilderness. Sifre's version is more laconic: ארבעה מארבע רוחותם ואחד מלמעלה ואחד מלמטה ואחד מלפניהם compared to BMM's אחד מימין ואחד משמאל אחד מלפניהם ואחד מאחריהם ואחד למעלה מהם וענן שכינה ביניהם ואחד נוסע לפניהם. There are also differences in vocabulary, e.g. מנמיכו (Sifre) vs. משפיל (BMM); מכה (Sifre) vs. הורג (BMM).

Furthermore, Sifre reports a series of dissenting opinions giving alternate numbers: fourteen clouds (R. Judah), four (R. Josiah), and two (Rabbi). None of these three opinions is mentioned in BMM. Sifre's phrase מיכן אמרו at the beginning of the pericope (ed. Horovitz p. 79, line 6) indicates reliance on a known source. In this parallel both Sifre and BMM appear to be drawing on a common source. Only one of them (or neither) is quoting with exactitude, however, since there are so many differences in detail.

Yerushalmi

Y. Sheq. 6:1, 49c-d (cf. y. Sot. 8:3, 22c-d) parallels almost all of BMM chapter 6 and nearly half of chapter 7. At times the correspondence of language is exact; more often similarities are dispersed among other baraitot and Aramaic elaborations. The order of materials is completely different. The Yerushalmi arranges the parallel traditions in the following sequence: the fate of the ark (BMM 7:21-27); protrusion of the carrying poles (BMM 7:15-19); the two arks (BMM 6:18-22); contents of the Holy of Holies (BMM 4:3-4); further exposition on the fate of the ark (BMM 7:21-27); dimensions of the ark and the tablets (BMM 6:1-16; cf. y. Sot. 8:3, 22c-d); and the manufacture of the ark (BMM 7:1-6).

In several places it appears that BMM preserves the antecedent text. For example, the opinion that the ark cubit measured six handbreadths, attributed by BMM 6:3 to R. Meir, is attributed by y. Sot. 8:3, 22c to R. Joḥanan, who then identifies the original source as Meir: מאן תנא אמה של ששה טפחי' רבי מאיר. Later in the same Yerushalmi passage, the contrary opinion that the ark cubit measured five handbreadths, attributed by BMM 6:9 to R. Judah, is attributed to R. Simeon b. Laqish, who then identifies the original Tanna: מאן תנא אמה של חמשה טפחים רבי יהודה. The opinion that the tablets in the ark measured six by three cubits, attributed by BMM 6:11 to R. Judah, is already assumed by y. Sot. 8:3, 22c before Judah is identified as its source. Furthermore, traditions reported anonymously by BMM 7:1-6 are attributed to Palestinian Amoraim (R. Ḥanina, R. Simeon b. Laqish) by y. Sheq. 6:1, 49d = y. Sot. 8:3, 22d. The same Yerushalmi passage adds explanatory glosses (e.g. לשילוט; להביא בין נסר לנסר) absent from BMM yet retains only the latter half of BMM's exegetical pair שאין ת"ל...ומה ת"ל. Similarly, ...אי איפשר לומ'

שכבר נאמ' (BMM 7:15-16 = T. YK 3:7) is rendered by y. Sheq. 6:1, 49c in Aramaic, כתיב...ואת אמר.

An internal contradiction of note between y. Sheq. 6:1, 49d and y. Sot. 8:3, 22c concerns the dimensions of the tablets in the ark: the former reports four times that they were square, six by six cubits; the latter specifies the dimensions as six by three, an opinion corroborated by BMM 6:11. The agreement of BMM and y. Sot. against y. Sheq. does not settle the matter, however; b. BB 14a agrees with y. Sheq. with respect to length and width and attributes this opinion to both R. Meir and R. Judah. Yet b. BB 14a reports a third dimension: ארכן ששה ורחבן ששה ועביין שלשה. Neither BMM nor Yerushalmi attests this description.

Y. Sheq. 6:4, 50 a-b contains traditions paralleled in three different chapters of BMM. Sheq. 6:4, 50b and BMM 4:18-19 are virtually identical readings concerning the location of the incense altar. In the Yerushalmi the parallel is only part of a baraita that also describes the location of the table: השלחן היה נתון מחצי הבית ולפנים משוך מן הכותל כשתי אמות כלפי הצפון ומנורה כנגדו בדרום. BMM does not include this information; at 4:17-18 we find only וקני המנורה היו מכוונים כנגד רחבו של שלחן הזהב. Thus the baraita that the Yerushalmi is quoting (והא תני) is not BMM, at least not in its present form.

At y. Sheq. 6:4, 50a we also find parallels to BMM 8:15-20 = T. Men. 11:9 (regarding the Solomonic and Mosaic tables) and BMM 10:25-31 = T. Men. 11:10 (regarding the lampstands). However, the exegetical proofs are more carefully stated in Yerushalmi. Seeking to show the primacy of the Mosaic table, BMM asserts that a table placed by the south wall of the shrine would be פסול. Only Yerushalmi, however, cites the verse (Ex. 26:35) that proves it. Likewise BMM 10:28 asserts that a lampstand to the north would be פסול but omits the scriptural justification (Ex. 26:35) found in Yerushalmi. In both discussions, BMM states the conclusion (אעפ"י שעשה שלמה..., 8:15, 10:25-26) before advancing the argument; Yerushalmi's sequence allows the discussion to generate the verdict (אף על פי כן לא היה...). However, aside from these structural differences, the parallels between BMM and Yerushalmi correspond.

Y. Sheq. 6:4, 50b = BMM 10:13-14 (cf. b. Men. 29a) constitutes a brief parallel concerning the smelting of gold for the lampstand. Different tradents are cited: BMM has Isi b. Aqavya; Yerushalmi has R. Jose b. Judah. Several references in both Talmuds suggest that these two names refer to the same person.[12] BMM's version appears

after an extraneous discourse (10:6-13) attributed to another tradent
identified with these two, Isi b. Judah. The parallel tradition may
appear in BMM owing to the association of tradents or to the details
of the lampstand's manufacture at the outset of the chapter (10:1-6).
Either way, BMM's version lacks continuity with the preceding and
ensuing discussions. In the Yerushalmi, on the other hand, this tradition is related as part of a comparison between the smelting procedures of Solomon and Moses. Where BMM's version is elliptical
(מעשה והייתה...), Yerushalmi is more expansive (מעשה במנורת זהב שעשה
משה במדבר והייתה...) and adds a concluding phrase, ולא חסרה כלום,
absent from BMM.

Y. Sheq. 8:4, 51b = BMM 2:3-7, 4:15-17 concerns the tapestry
work of the curtains and veil. BMM 2:3-7 relates three linked traditions, the first two attributed to R. Nehemiah, the third to the sages.
Yerushalmi begins with the third tradition followed by the second,
each in abbreviated form and without attribution. Next Yerushalmi
includes a baraita absent from BMM. Each of the tannaitic statements in Yerushalmi is concluded with a computation, the last two
in Aramaic. As noted above in connection with T. Sheq. 3:14, BMM
introduces the second tradition of R. Nehemiah with דברי ר'...שהיה
אומ', terminology which suggests a quotation from a known source.
BMM is not quoting Yerushalmi, however, since its version of the
text is more complete and fully integrated. Nor does the reverse
seem likely, since Yerushalmi includes a baraita absent from BMM.
The most plausible explanation is the existence of a common source
from which each draws selectively. BMM gives the fuller account,
including attributions; Yerushalmi conveys the traditions in more
cursory form but adds the numerical sums.

Similarly BMM 4:15-17 (cf. T. Sheq. 3:14) ascribes to R. Nehemiah a tradition concerning the distinction between מעשה חשב and
מעשה רקם. The pericope is introduced by the scriptural description
of the veil (Ex. 26:36), and the same quotation terminology is used,
דברי ר'...שהיה או'. In Yerushalmi only R. Nehemiah's conclusion is
mentioned, without attribution or scriptural citation. Yerushalmi
appears to summarize what BMM explains.

Y. Er. 1:5, 19a includes a passage that reports the same information as BMM 12:6-15. However, neither wording nor sequence corresponds. Yerushalmi begins with the geometric shape and liquid
volume of Solomon's "sea" and then proceeds to compare liquid and
dry measure. BMM discusses these two subjects in the reverse order.

There can be little question that BMM preserves the primary text in the present parallel, since, as argued above with respect to T. Kel. BM 5:2 = BMM 12:4-8, the comparison of the Solomonic Temple to the wilderness tabernacle is integral to BMM chapter 12 and to the work as a whole. The same baraita is transmitted by Yerushalmi in different language.

Y. Er. 5:1, 22c includes a tradition concerning the Israelite procession in the wilderness, some of which is found at BMM 13:18-19, 31-32. The components of this tradition are separated in BMM by a self-contained unit (13:20-31) describing the priestly and tribal procedures for breaking camp. In Yerushalmi the parallel passage is preceded by a brief reference to the duties of the Merarites and Kohathites, which are addressed in different language and greater detail at BMM 13:1-10. Again we find some of the same information related in different words, e.g. כיצד היו (Yerushalmi) vs. כיון היו (BMM); נוסעין vs. מהלכין. Elsewhere there are discrepancies between the two versions. In BMM the simile כקורה refers to the pillar of cloud; in Yerushalmi it refers to the Israelites. In BMM the כקורה material is anonymous; in Yerushalmi it is attributed to R. Ḥama b. Ḥanina as part of a dispute with R. Hoshaya. With respect to BMM 13:31-32, once again Yerushalmi attests different language: כשם שהיו חונין כך היו נוסעין (BMM) vs. מה בחנייתן...אף בנסיעתן (Yerushalmi). Yerushalmi's amoraic attribution in this parallel suggests a later development of the BMM text.

This relationship is also evident in y. Meg. 1:14, 72c-d = BMM 2:10-11, a brief parallel describing the appearance of the hooks and loops inside the tabernacle. What is reported anonymously in BMM (and in identical language at b. Shab. 98b-99a) is attributed by Yerushalmi to R. Jose b. R. Bun, a late Palestinian Amora. Moreover, while BMM introduces its comments by citing the pertinent biblical text (Ex. 26:6), Yerushalmi generalizes, קרסיו קרשיו בריחיו ועמודיו ואדניו, a sign of editorial summary.

Y. AZ 2:7, 41c-d = BMM 10:6-14 (cf. b. Yoma 52a-b) consists of a list of problematic verses of the Pentateuch which is attributed by BMM to Isi b. Judah and by Yerushalmi via R. Ḥunya to R. Ḥama b. Uqba. The two versions differ in the sequence of citations; the MSS of BMM and of Bavli also vary in this regard.[13] In BMM the passage is obviously generated by the adjacent mention (10:4-5) of Ex. 25:34, one of the five verses classified by the phrase אין להם הכרעה. Yerushalmi does not attest this phrase but names the same five verses. The entire pericope is irrelevant to BMM's subject. Its presence here is a purely mnemonic or mechanical transfer of material associated with Ex. 25:34.

Bavli

B. Shab. 98b = BMM 1:18-21 describes the dimensions of the tabernacle boards. Two opinions are reported. BMM attributes the first to R. Nehemiah and the second to R. Judah; in the Bavli the attributions are reversed, conforming to chronological Mishnah usage by listing Judah first. The first opinion is identical in both versions. The second opinion, although its content is the same in both passages, diverges in form. Bavli's rhetorical expression is more elaborate, viz. the construction כשם ש...כך. BMM's compressed wording, מלמטן ומלמעלן עובײן, suggests a summary rather than a formulary statement.

BMM 5:29-31 attributes to R. Jose b. Judah a tradition comparing measures of enclosed area to the size of the tabernacle enclosure. The passage is introduced by the explicit citation formula מכאן היה ר'...או', but the source of the quotation is not extant. In terminology, the closest parallel to this passage is found at b. Er. 23b, where the locutions קרפף שהוא (יותר מ) בית (BMM 5:31) and מטלטלין בתוכה סעתים (BMM 5:30) are both found. However, in the Bavli the two are separated by an intervening discussion in Aramaic. The same vocabulary of surface measure is familiar to both passages; otherwise they are unrelated.

B. Yoma 54a and Men. 98a-b include passages parallel to BMM 7:15-19 = T. YK 3:7 = y. Sheq. 6:1, 49c, discussed above. At Yoma 54a, Bavli gives a condensed statement of the problem posed by the apparent internal contradiction in 1 Ki. 8:8/ 2 Chr. 5:9. In place of the אי איפשר...שכבר נאמ' construction in BMM or the יכול...ת"ל sequence in Tosefta, Bavli has merely הא כיצד. However, both Yoma 54a and Men. 98a include a baraita also found in Tosefta but missing from BMM which raises the question of whether the protruding carrying poles of the ark might have perforated the veil. Both Bavli passages attest with BMM the simile כשני דדי אשה missing from Tosefta, but they corroborate Tosefta's scriptural citation (Cant. 1:13) missing from BMM. This combination of identical and variant details suggests a common source or sources for this group of parallels. Tosefta's reading is inferior to both BMM's and Bavli's, but between the latter two there is no clear evidence of priority.

B. Yoma 72b and BMM 4:15-17 both attribute to R. Nehemiah a tradition distinguishing between חושב and רוקם. The information in the two passages is very similar, but the language and sequence differ entirely. The BMM passage commences with a description of the veil as מעשה רוקם. This generates R. Nehemiah's statement, which is introduced by the citation formula דברי ר'...שהיה או'. However, it is not likely that BMM is citing Bavli, since its version attests different wording and reverse clauses: BMM = כל מקום שנ' מעשה חשב שתי רוקם מעשה מחט לפיכך פרצוף פרצוף אחד; Bavli = פרצופות מעשה רקם פרצוף אחד חושב מעשה אורג לפיכך שני פרצופות. The reversal of clauses and Bavli's addition of bridging language (לפיכך) might be a function of oral or redactional transmission, but the vocabulary (מחט, אורג) missing from BMM indicates that in this instance neither passage relies directly upon the other.

B. BB 14a = BMM 6:1-7, 26-27 has already been mentioned above in conjunction with the Yerushalmi parallels to BMM chapter 6. Again we find like content but disparate language, e.g.: מכאן (BMM) vs. לכותל זה (Bavli); גובהו vs. קומתו. There are also content discrepancies. Bavli includes a discussion applying the hermeneutic principle מיעוט אחר מיעוט that is absent from BMM. As mentioned above, Bavli describes the tablets in three dimensions, where BMM and Yerushalmi give only two. Bavli also furnishes an explanation for the extra space in the ark reserved for the Torah scroll, נכנס ויוצא כשהוא דחוק, which is not attested in BMM; the latter in turn has a statement concerning the scroll, לא היה נתון אלא מן הצד (BMM 6:16), that is missing from Bavli. Yet BMM and Bavli do coincide in sequence as distinct from the Yerushalmi parallels. All of the parallels in this group attest a common tradition, but the number of disparities rules out the possibility of mutual reliance.

B. Zev. 59b-60a and BMM 11:4-12 present a controversy concerning the dimensions of the altar of burnt-offering. In BMM the disputants are R. Jose and R. Meir; in Bavli, R. Jose and R. Judah. BMM introduces the controversy with an anonymous statement disclosing the altar's length and width and citing Ex. 38:1. In contrast, Bavli's quotation of the baraita (דתניא)[14] begins with a statement ascribed to R. Judah (absent from BMM) reporting the height of the altar. Bavli also includes another statement of R. Judah, אפשר כהן עומד ע"ג המזבח ועבודה בידו וכל העם רואין אותו מבחוץ,[15] which is more simply stated at BMM 11:10 in the name of R. Meir: נמצא גבוה מן הקלעים. Both versions include the same גזרה שוה, but only BMM introduces it with a specification of the hermeneutic principle, מופנה להקיש לדון

ממנו גזרה שוה, the only time this terminology occurs in the entire work. Moreover, BMM compares the height of the altar to the width; Bavli compares the height to the length. As in nearly every other parallel between BMM and Bavli, there are variants in language, e.g. כדבריך (BMM) vs. אפשר (Bavli); כשנים vs. פי שנים. In short, the two passages are similar enough to be considered parallels but divergent enough to discourage any notion of mutual relationship.

B. Men. 28a and BMM 9:11-14 discuss the talent of gold from which the lampstand was forged. Exactly the same information is conveyed by both passages, but in reverse order: BMM begins with the example of the lampstand ornaments and then deduces a general principle, כשהיא באה משל זהב באה ככר וכשאינה באה זהב אינה באה ככר; Bavli begins with a more compressed statement of the principle, באה זהב באה ככר אינה באה זהב אינה באה ככר and then proceeds to the example of the lampstand ornaments, compressing BMM's text in the same way. The only lexical difference between the two passages is the use of טעונה (BMM) vs. באה (Bavli). Given the mirror image of the two passages and the fuller version in BMM, it is plausible that Bavli is citing (דתניא) a baraita as found in BMM.

B. Men. 28b = BMM 10:15-23 describes the dimensions and configuration of the lampstand. Much of the parallel material is identical in language and content, but there are several discrepancies. Following the depiction of each pair of lampstand shafts, Bavli includes a phrase which does not appear in BMM, ונמשכין ועולין כנגד גובהה של מנורה. In one instance Bavli specifies a measure of one handbreadth where BMM specifies two.[16] In another, Bavli gives a more meticulous description of the ornaments, ג' גביעין וכפתור ופרח, compared to גביעין כפתורין ופרחין in BMM (10:19-20).[17] BMM includes a scriptural citation (Ex. 25:33) absent from Bavli. Otherwise, unlike most of the parallels between BMM and Bavli, these two passages are remarkably similar. There is no sign of priority.

B. Men. 88b = BMM 9:4-14 concerns whether the lampstand ornaments and utensils are implied in the prescription of Ex. 25:31, as discussed above. Bavli attributes to R. Nehemiah views stated anonymously in BMM. Regarding the series of רבוי and מיעוט propositions in BMM, Bavli relates only the רבוי half of the argument and only with respect to the lamps, tongs, and firepans, deleting the various ornaments. Both passages cite R. Joshua b. Qorḥa, but their versions of his opinion are different: according to Bavli, he excludes the tongs, fire pans, and lamps from the talent of gold; at BMM 9:13, only the lamps are mentioned. Between its quotations of baraitot Bavli inserts a few Aramaic locutions to clarify the argument. Although drawing upon the same traditions as BMM and relating them in similar sequence, Bavli's discussion is structured as a set of tannaitic disputes bearing little resemblance to BMM chapter 9.

Summary

The foregoing analysis of tannaitic and amoraic parallels to BMM corroborates our conclusions in chapter 2 of the Introduction concerning the tannaitic origin of BMM. BMM appears to know the canonical Mishnah (e.g. Sheq. 5:1-2, Men. 11:5) and possibly its sources pertaining to Temple traditions (Mid. 3:1). But while the Mishnah certainly antedates BMM, the same cannot be said of either Tosefta or Sifre Numbers. In fact, two passages in Tosefta (Men. 11:9-10, Kel. BM 5:2) appear to derive from materials in BMM, and one (Sheq. 2:18) appears to draw on a source common to BMM. In most of the parallels (e.g. Sheq. 2:18, YK 3:7, Sot. 7:18), BMM preserves a more cohesive and complete text, although this may be attributed to the more piecemeal composition of Tosefta. A similar relationship obtains between BMM and Sifre Numbers. Sifre 61 appears to derive from the passage at BMM 9:1-9; Sifre 59, 82, and 83 all appear to draw on sources common to BMM. The evidence from Tosefta and Sifre Numbers indicates that the parallel materials in BMM are at least contemporaneous and possibly earlier.

Regarding the numerous parallel passages in the Yerushalmi, several (e.g. Er. 1:5, 19a; Er. 5:1, 22c; Meg. 1:12, 72c) reflect the later development of materials in BMM. Others (e.g. Sheq. 8:2, 51b) suggest reliance upon a common tannaitic source. In two passages at Sheq. 6:3, 50a-b, Yerushalmi furnishes the superior text, but there is no evidence that BMM relies upon these or any other readings from Yerushalmi. With respect to parallels in the Bavli, the results of our analysis are not as clear. In only one passage (Men. 28a) does the priority of BMM's text seem likely. Otherwise the relationship between the two works is clouded by equally plausible disparities in language, attribution, and detail. Even the most dissimilar parallels (e.g. Er. 23b, BB 14a, Zev. 59b-60a, Men. 88b) clearly draw upon traditions common to both works. In at least two cases (Shab. 98b-99a, Men. 28b), Bavli and BMM appear to cite the identical source. However, there is little to indicate that one ever cites the other or even knows the other.

At the outset of the chapter, we noted the difficulty of determining the provenance of parallel passages. Yet the consistent pattern that emerges from the comparisons leaves little doubt that BMM is a tannaitic composition that originated in the era between the Mishnah and the Talmuds.

II. MEDIEVAL CITATIONS

The earliest certain quotation of BMM is found in the oldest extant commentary on the Mishnah, Perush ha-Geonim le-Seder Tohorot, traditionally attributed to Hai b. Sherira Gaon (939-1038) but probably not written by him.[18] This work is a compilation of geonic textual and lexical notes confined to Seder Tohorot. It is a primary source for the first talmudic dictionaries and later Mishnah commentaries. Simha Assaf has sought to attribute the work to Saadia Gaon (882-942), especially given Saadia's propensity for linguistic annotations.[19] J. N. Epstein, however, points out that Saadia wrote all of his commentaries in Arabic, while Perush ha-Geonim is composed in Hebrew.[20] Epstein fixes the date of the Perush toward the end of the ninth century and identifies the author as a Sura gaon contemporary with either Saadia or Nahshon b. Zadok (gaon of Sura, 871-79).

Epstein detects two quotations from BMM in Perush ha-Geonim: at Kel. 10:6 and 25:1. The first of these, however, is highly speculative; Epstein reconstructs the source on the basis of a fuller citation in a later work, the Arukh. Moreover, the wording of the Perush at Kel. 10:6 (s.v. בסינין) is not attested in any of the MSS of BMM. The second citation (Kel. 25:1), however, is certain: כדאמר ביריעות ועושה בה ד' תוברין ותולה אתה באונקלי. The MSS of BMM (4:2) corroborate virtually the exact wording. Perush ha-Geonim does not cite BMM by name, but this is not unusual: the author often fails to identify quotations from the Palestinian Talmud and never mentions some of his other sources, e.g. Genesis Rabbah.[21]

BMM is cited twice in the Arukh of Nathan b. Yehiel of Rome (1035- ca.1110), a lexicon of talmudic and midrashic literature completed in 1101. The Arukh draws extensively from Perush ha-Geonim, inserting whole entries word for word but often failing to acknowledge the source.[22] One of the two citations is a direct quo-

tation from Perush ha-Geonim (s.v. תבר = Perush Kel. 25:1). The
other citation (s.v. סך) also quotes Perush ha-Geonim (Kel. 10:6) and
goes on to identify BMM by name: במעשה משכן הסינין יוצאין מן הקרשים.
This is the only citation of BMM by the title מעשה משכן.[23] The quotation is found in some MSS of BMM (chapter 1) but not in others.
The MS chosen as the base text of the present edition fails to attest
it.[24]

By far the most extensive citation of BMM in any medieval work
is found in Sefer ve-Hizhir (probably identical to Midrash
Hashkem[25]), a compendium of halakhic and aggadic traditions
derived from the She'eltot of R. Aḥa, Halakhot Gedolot, and to a
lesser extent, Tanḥuma. Like the She'eltot, ve-Hizhir is arranged
according to the annual cycle of Scripture readings. Zunz assigns ve-
Hizhir to the tenth century; it is already quoted in the eleventh.
Zunz conjectures that the work was composed in the south of
Europe, but more recently Simḥa Assaf has argued that it was written
in Palestine. The author is unknown.[26]

The first twelve of BMM's fourteen chapters are recorded in full
in ve-Hizhir. They are included in the critical apparatus of our edition and are described in chapter 5 of the Introduction together with
the other surviving witnesses to the text. The absence of chapters
13-14 from ve-Hizhir has led some scholars to speculate that these
two chapters were not part of the original text of BMM. This view
cannot be accepted, as we demonstrate below, pp. 68-69.

In his commentary on the Pentateuch, Rashi (R. Solomon b. Isaac,
France, 1040-1105) cites BMM by name five times: at Ex. 25:35,
26:25, 26:26, and at Num. 4:32 and 9:18. In his edition of Rashi's
commentary, C. D. Chavel identifies three additional citations without attribution (Ex. 27:10, 29:42, Num. 10:2) as quotations from
BMM;[27] only Num. 10:2, however, coincides with the MSS of BMM.
Rashi's explicit designations of BMM are as follows:

1) Ex. 25:35   כך שנינו במלאכת המשכן
2) Ex. 26:25   כך שנויה משנת מעשה סדר קרשים במלאכת המשכן
3) Ex. 26:26   כך היא מפורשת במלאכת המשכן
4) Num. 4:32   כמו ששנויה במלאכת המשכן
5) Num. 9:18   שנינו במלאכת המשכן

Two of these citations (Ex. 25:35, 26:25), as well as the
unattributed Num. 10:2, include direct quotations of BMM: Ex.
25:35 = BMM 10:15-21; Ex. 26:25 = BMM 1:12-15; Num. 10:2 =
BMM 13:32-33. The other three (Ex. 26:26, Num. 4:32, 9:18) are

written in either paraphrastic or summary form. For instance, Rashi's comment at Num. 9:18 is a conflation of BMM and Sifre Num. 84 and includes a word (מתקפל) unattested by any MS of BMM.

A Yemenite MS of Rashi's commentary, published in 1981 by M. R. Lehmann,[28] attests a unique version of the BMM citation at Num. 4:32: כמו ששנויה במכלתא במלאכת המשכן. The proximity of במכלתא and במלאכת suggests a simple metathesis, although the editor does not indicate a scribal mark of error or erasure.[29] For this to be a reference to the Mekhilta, the citation should properly have the spelling במכילתא rather than במכלתא. The possibility that BMM was originally part of the Mekhilta has been suggested by Epstein;[30] see below, p. 71.

Ramban (R. Moses b. Naḥman, Spain, 1194-1270) cites BMM by name at seven locations in his commentary on the Pentateuch:

1) Ex. 25:12		ובמשנת המשכן שנו
2) Ex. 25:39		בברייתא של מלאכת המשכן שנויה
3) Ex. 26:17 (citing Rashi)		בברייתא של מלאכת המשכן מצאתי
4) Ex. 26:24		ומצאתי בברייתא של מלאכת המשכן
5) Num. 4:32 (citing Rashi)		ולא מצאתי במשנת מלאכת המשכן
6) Num. 10:6		וכך היא שנויה בברייתא של מלאכת המשכן
7) Num. 10:17		בברייתא של מלאכת המשכן ראיתי

When referring to BMM, Ramban uses the terms ברייתא and משנה interchangeably. Virtually all of his citations are direct quotations of BMM: Ex. 25:12 = BMM 7:6-7; Ex. 25:39 = BMM 9:1-14; Ex. 26:17 = BMM 1 (attested in some MSS but missing from our base text); Ex. 26:24 = BMM 1:15-18; Num. 4:32 = BMM 5:10-12, 13:4-5; Num. 10:17 = BMM 13:20-28. Only at Num. 10:6 does Ramban refer to BMM in summary form and there only in contradistinction to a disputing opinion from Sifre Numbers (63). Unlike Rashi, Ramban quotes BMM at length and distinguishes clearly between citation and interpolation.

Tosafot (ca. 12th-14th centuries, France), a repository of novellae and interpretations of the Babylonian Talmud, includes four mentions of BMM:

1) Shab. 22b, s.v. וכי		כדאמרינן בברייתא דמלאכת המשכן
2) Shab. 98b, s.v. תנא		פליגא אברייתא דמלאכת המשכן
3) Yoma 72a, s.v. כתיב (end)		ואע״ג דבברייתא דמלאכת המשכן תניא
4) Men. 86b, s.v. מחוץ		כדאיתא בברייתא דמלאכת המשכן

At both Shab. 22b and Men. 86b, Tosafot cites BMM 14:11-12, although the two brief quotations are not identical and neither corresponds precisely to any MS of BMM. At Yoma 72a, however, an exact quotation of BMM 6:6-8 is found. Tosafot's comment at Shab. 98b is a summary of BMM 1:24-28 rather than a quotation.

The collection of Tosafot to tractate Yoma identified in printed editions as Tosafot Yeshanim and attributed to R. Meir b. Barukh of Rothenburg (Germany, ca. 1215-93)[31] includes one mention of BMM at Yoma 6a, s.v. מביתו = מבריכת המשכן דמלאכת בבריית דתניא. However, the citation that follows is not attested in any MS of BMM: שכל שבעת ימי המילואים היה משה מעמיד המשכן ומפרקו. Meir Friedmann (Ish-Shalom) notes that the passage is found in Sifra, Mekhilta de-Millu'im (ed. Weiss 42d), suggesting the possibility that this unique section of (or addendum to) Sifra was originally part of BMM.[32] We discuss this theory in chapter 4 of the Introduction.

Midrash ha-Gadol, a thirteenth or fourteenth century Yemenite compendium of midrashim on the Pentateuch attributed to R. David b. R. Amram Edeni, was first recognized in the nineteenth century as an important source of tannaitic traditions otherwise wanting or unknown. Major portions of such works as Mekhilta de-R. Simeon b. Yoḥai (ed. Epstein-Melamed) and Sifre Zuta (ed. Horovitz) have been reconstructed from attestations in Midrash ha-Gadol. However, these readings cannot always be trusted owing to the author's freedom of citation and tendency to assimilate texts. Except in rare instances, he does not identify his sources and often fails to indicate when he is quoting one. He may abbreviate or expand a passage, change the wording or transpose the sequence. Concerning Sifre Zuta, for example, Saul Lieberman observes that Midrash ha-Gadol often begins and concludes with the text but interposes quotations from Maimonides.[33] J. N. Epstein describes the same editorial license with respect to Midrash ha-Gadol's quotations of the Mekhilta: the author revises the text to accord with the Babylonian Talmud, combines it with passages from Sifre, and formulates it on the basis of Maimonides.[34] He also tends to delete dissenting opinions and controversies and to intersperse discrete materials. Just within Midrash ha-Gadol's quotations of Mekhilta de-R. Simeon b. Yoḥai, E. Z. Melamed identifies passages from the Mishnah, Tosefta, Mekhilta (de-R. Ishmael), Sifre, Bereshit Rabbah, Midrash Tehillim, Tanḥuma, the Pesiqtot, and the Babylonian Talmud, among others.[35]

Consequently, readings from antecedent rabbinic works in Midrash ha-Gadol must be considered suspect in terms of textual integrity and accuracy. Mordecai Margulies, in the introduction to his edition of Midrash ha-Gadol to Exodus, argues that the author's liberties with sources do not extend to changing the actual wording of a citation.[36] Lieberman, too, notes that, at least with respect to difficult or unusual words in Sifre Zuta, Midrash ha-Gadol refrains from altering the received text.[37] On the other hand, in Midrash ha-Gadol to Numbers, Z. M. Rabinowitz finds that the author does change passages of the Yerushalmi, emending them to conform to Babylonian language, usage, and attributions.[38]

Because of Midrash ha-Gadol's composite character and its author's omission of source citations, the origin of various passages is a matter of conjecture. In an article published in 1954,[39] Aaron Greenbaum claims that a MS (which he does not identify) of Midrash ha-Gadol to Exodus contains copious quotations of BMM. Admitting that some are doubtful and others alloyed with talmudic texts, Greenbaum lists twenty-one quotations of which he is certain: twelve from BMM chapter 1, four from chapter 2, and one each from chapters 3, 4, 6, 8, 9.[40]

Unfortunately, Greenbaum's identification of BMM passages does not always depend upon correspondence of language or content. For example, he cites the following passage from Midrash ha-Gadol (no specific reference to book or verse is given): ר' אומר משכן שעשה משה רביע מה שעשה שלמה שעשה משה שלשים ארכו ועשר אמות רחבו ושעשה שלמה ששים אמות ארכו ועשר רחבו (צ"ל עשרים) הוי רביע מה שעשה שלמה. This passage, Greenbaum maintains, is a certain quotation of BMM 4:9-11 (ed. Friedmann, p. 27):[41] וכשם שהיו מונחים באהל מועד כך היו מונחים בבית עולמים אלא שאהל מועד ארכו שלשים אמה ורחבו עשר אמות ובית עולמים ארכו ששים ורחבו עשרים אמה הא למדת שאהל מועד רביע של בית עולמים. Although congruent information is conveyed in the two passages, the language is far too divergent to suggest a direct quotation, let alone to establish it with certainty. In fact, although several witnesses to the text of BMM have come to light since Friedmann's edition (1908), many of Greenbaum's "certain" citations of BMM remain unattested in any source.

Our own study of Midrash ha-Gadol yields corroborated quotations of BMM 1:1-35; 2:3-6; 3:12-16; 6:3-16; 8:3-11; 10:6-13, 31-34; 11:4-12 which are included in the critical apparatus of our edition. The location of these passages in Midrash ha-Gadol (Genesis and

Exodus, ed. Margulies; Leviticus, ed. Steinsaltz; Numbers, ed. Rabinowitz)[42] and the textual criteria for their identification are given in chapter 5 of the Introduction.

Yalqut Shimoni, a midrashic anthology attributed to Simeon ha-Darshan (ca. 13th century, Germany), is the largest extant collection of rabbinic traditions arranged according to the Bible. The Yalqut assembles passages from more than fifty halakhic and aggadic works, including some (e.g. Yelammedenu, Midrash Tadshe) for which it is the only extant source. The author sometimes names his sources, but the references that have come down to us are often incorrect. Like Midrash ha-Gadol, Yalqut Shimoni abridges, interpolates, glosses, and combines statements from independent sources. From his study of passages from Sifre Zuta, Lieberman concludes that the author of the Yalqut is liable to change vocabulary, simplify usage, and delete difficult words that have no bearing on his subject.[43]

In his compilation of sources cited by Yalqut Shimoni,[44] Arthur Hyman identifies passages from BMM chapters 1, 2, 3, 4, 5, 7, 9, 10, 11, 12, 13, 14 of the Friedmann edition. Comparison of these passages to extant MSS of BMM discloses a striking correspondence to MS Oxford 151 (described in chapter 5 of the Introduction). Following is a brief sample of unique readings common to Yalqut Shimoni[45] (*Terumah*) and MS Oxford 151 against all other witnesses:

BMM	*Yalqut Shimoni/ MS Oxford 151*	*Base Text*
1:8	—	ארכו
7:6	בארון	—
7:14	דלתי	דלתות
7:15	ויראו	ולא יראו
7:22	נגנז	נתון
7:24	בכל	לככל

Further evidence of the Yalqut's correspondence to MS Oxford 151 is an addition to the text of BMM following the citation of 2 Chr. 35:3 at BMM 7:26, as reported in our critical apparatus. Other than these two witnesses, no other MS or secondary reading attests this passage.

The concurrence of MS Oxford 151 and Yalqut Shimoni renders the latter a superfluous witness to the text of BMM. Therefore its readings are not included in our edition.

Yalqut ha-Makhiri, attributed to Makhir b. Abba Mari (ca. 14th century), is an anthology of talmudic and midrashic traditions of which portions on various books of the Prophets and Hagiographa have survived. This collection includes quotations of tannaitic literature. As a rule, the author identifies sources and is quite scrupulous about literal citations. However, his quotations are sometimes wanting from existing editions. In Yalqut ha-Makhiri to Isaiah (ed. Spira),[46] at Is. 60:1 there is a single reference to BMM by the otherwise unattested title פרקי מלאכת המשכן. It is followed by a quotation of BMM 14:8-15. The quotation corresponds to several extant MSS of BMM with some variants.[47]

To summarize, BMM is quoted in extant works of rabbinic literature beginning in the tenth century. That it had achieved its present form by this date is proven by the text of Sefer ve-Hizhir, which records the first twelve of BMM's fourteen chapters. Although secondary attestation of chapters 13 and 14 is not found until quotations in Tosafot and Yalqut Shimoni (12th-14th centuries), fragments from the Cairo Genizah (described in ch. 5 of the Introduction and transcribed in Appendix A) testify that chapters 13 and 14 were included in BMM as early as the tenth century, when Sefer ve-Hizhir first appeared.

Granting that the origin and geographical diffusion of rabbinic compendia are often uncertain, it is evident from the array of citations that MSS of BMM circulated among Oriental, Sephardic, and Ashkenazic Jewry. Most of the extensive citations are found in Oriental and Sephardic works, e.g. Arukh (Italy), Sefer ve-Hizhir (Palestine or Provence), Ramban (Spain), Midrash ha- Gadol (Yemen), and Yalqut ha-Makhiri (Spain).[48]

Notes to Chapter Three

PARALLEL PASSAGES AND MEDIEVAL CITATIONS

1. We have used the following MSS and editions: Mishnah = *Faksimile-Ausgabe des Mischnacodex Kaufmann A 50*, ed. G. Beer (repr. Jerusalem, 1969); Tosefta = *Tosephta* ed. M. S. Zuckermandel (repr. Jerusalem, 1965) except, where noted, *The Tosefta according to Codex Vienna with Variants from Codex Erfurt, Geniza MSS and Editio Princeps*, ed. S. Lieberman (New York, 1955-73); Sifre Numbers = *Siphre ad Numeros adjecto Siphre zutta*, ed. H. S. Horovitz (Jerusalem, 1966); Palestinian Talmud (Yerushalmi) = *Talmud Yerushalmi Codex Leiden Scal. 3* (Jerusalem, 1971); Babylonian Talmud (Bavli) = *Talmud Bavli* (New York, 1969) = repr. of Romm ed. (Vilna, 1895) except, where noted, *Diqduqe Soferim: Variae Lectionis in Mishnam et in Talmud Babylonicum*, ed. R. Rabbinovicz (repr. New York, 1976).

2. See J. N. Epstein, *Mavo le-Nusaḥ ha-Mishnah* (Tel Aviv, ²1964), 944; *Mevo'ot le-Sifrut ha-Tannaim* (Tel Aviv, 1957), 25-26; *Mevo'ot le-Sifrut ha-Amoraim* (Jerusalem, 1962), 527. The reading of BMM 12:20-27 concurs with the pristine text of the Mishnah.

3. See the collation of variants in our critical apparatus at BMM 8:9-11.

4. *Shishah Sidre Mishnah*, ed. H. Albeck, *Qodoshim* (Jerusalem / Tel Aviv, 1959), 291, 314.

5. In the Lieberman edition of Tosefta, T. YK 3:7 = 2:15.

6. The version of this list in BMM (4:3-5) includes ובגדי כהנים ובגדי כהן גדול, missing from Tosefta; T. YK. 3:7 (cf. T. Sot. 13:1) includes וארגז שהשיבו בו פלשתים דורון ליי' אלהי ישראל, missing from BMM. Cf. other parallels: b. Hor. 12a = b. Yoma 52a = b. Ker. 5b; ARN A 41, ed. Schechter 67a.

7. The disparate readings are discussed by Saul Lieberman, *Tosefta ki-Feshutah: A Comprehensive Commentary on the Tosefta* (New York, 1955), 8:686.

8. Although it appears in one MS; see apparatus at BMM 10:20.

9. See apparatus at BMM 10:20.

10. At T. Men. 11:10, this tradition is attributed to R. Jose b. R. Judah. There R. Eleazar b. Shammua suggests a proof for the primacy of the Mosaic table that does rely on 2 Chr. 4:19, namely that the plural referent עליהם includes both the "great table of gold" inside the Great Hall and the table on the porch at the entrance of the Temple where the discarded bread was left. This tradition would explain BMM's citation of 2 Chr. 4:19, but there is no trace of it in the MSS.

11. Among the *variae lectionis* at Sifre Num. 82, ed. Horovitz (Jerusalem, ²1966), p. 78, line 5, there is one attestation of במלחמה in place of במחנה, matching Tosefta's reading.

12. See Introduction, ch. 2 n. 47; cf. b. Men. 29a. Louis Ginzberg, "Baraita on the Erection of the Tabernacle," *Jewish Encyclopedia* (New York/London, 1903-6), 2:517, incorrectly identifies the statement of Isi b. Aqavya as a late interpolation because it is wanting from MS Munich Cod. Hebr. 95. As our discussion of this MS demonstrates (see below, Introduction ch. 5), it is plagued by numerous omissions and scribal errors. BMM 10:13-14 is attested in several antecedent and more reliable witnesses. Its absence from MS Munich is evidence of a faulty MS, not of a late interpolation.

13. See the apparatus at BMM 10:6-14. For various readings among Bavli MSS, see *Diqduqe Soferim* v. 1, *Yoma* p. 28.

14. The Bavli's specific citation terminology (תניא, ת״ר, תנן, etc.) does not seem to be a criterion for identifying or classifying baraitot, as E. Z. Melamed has shown with respect to Bavli parallels to the halakhic midrashim: *Midreshe Halakhah shel ha-Tannaim be-Talmud Bavli* (Jerusalem, ²1988), 4-15. Nor does the Bavli's mode of quotation differentiate between passages found in the halakhic midrashim and those found in other baraitot; see 15-19, 79-80.

15. Some Bavli MSS do not attest this reading in full, but none resembles BMM; see *Diqduqe Soferim* v. 2, *Zevaḥim* p. 24.

16. One MS of BMM also specifies one handbreadth; see apparatus at BMM 10:18 s.v. וטפחיים.

17. According to *Diqduqe Soferim* v. 2, *Menaḥot* p. 15, the version of b. Men. 28b found in MS Munich 95 lacks the specification of three, thus agreeing with the text of BMM and several other witnesses; see the note of Rabbinovicz, ad loc.

18. Louis Ginzberg, *Geonica* (repr. New York, 1968), 1:172, argues against the attribution to Hai Gaon. In the introduction to his edition of Perush ha-Geonim (Jerusalem / Tel Aviv, 1982), Hebrew pagination 73-82, J. N. Epstein demonstrates the authorial unity of the work but notes that it includes later additions. He is inclined to attribute it to a Sura gaon other than Saadia; see infra.

19. Simḥa Assaf, *Tequfat ha-Geonim ve-Sifrutah* (Jerusalem, 1976), 144-46.

20. Epstein, *Perush ha-Geonim*, Hebrew pagination 36.

21. Ibid. Hebrew pagination 64. Among other unattributed sources in Perush ha-Geonim identified by Epstein are passages from Targum Onqelos, the Palestinian Talmud (some passages), and Halakhot Gedolot.

22. Ibid. Hebrew pagination 117.

23. Earlier editions of Arukh mistakenly have כמעשה in place of במעשה; see *Arukh Completum*, ed. A. Kohut, 8 vols. (Vienna, [2]1926), 4:80 n. 11. This error is already noted by Solomon Buber, *Yeriot Shlomo* (Warsaw, 1896), 15, who suggests further that the correct reading might be במשנת משכן.

24. The quotation is missing from the following witnesses (see pp. 149-50 for sigla identifications): MSS A, B, P; eds. H, V. It is attested with some variations in MSS G[2], M, L, E, and ed. D.

25. Arguments for the identity of the two works are advanced, e.g., by Julius Theodor, "Midrash Haggadah," *Jewish Encyclopedia* (New York/London 1903-6), 8:563-64; A. N. Z. Roth, "A Fragment from Midrash ve-Hizhir" (Hebrew), *Talpiyyot* 7 (1958): 89-98. In the introduction to the first volume of his edition of Sefer ve-Hizhir (Leipzig, 1873), vi-xiii, I. M. Freimann maintains that Midrash Hashkem is a separate composition.

26. Freimann, ibid. xiii-xiv, attributes Sefer ve-Hizhir to Ḥefeẓ Alluf (ca. 10th century), a view rejected by Theodor, op.cit. 8:564; by Ginzberg, *Geonica* 1:88; and by Assaf, *Tequfat ha-Geonim ve-Sifrutah* 162-63.

27. *Perushe Rashi al ha-Torah*, ed. C. D. Chavel (Jerusalem, [3]1983), 283 (attributing Rashi Ex. 27:10 to BMM ch. 5); 296 (Ex. 29:42 = BMM 14), 433 (Num. 10:2 = BMM 13). Rashi's method of citing sources is inconsistent: he may identify them in detail, in general, or not at all; he may excerpt them, allude to them, or paraphrase them. See, e.g., E. Z. Melamed, *Midreshe Halakhah shel ha-Tannaim be-Talmud Bavli* (Jerusalem, [2]1988), 60-64 regarding Rashi's citation of halakhic midrashim in his commentary on the Bavli; Yoel Florsheim, *Rashi la-Miqra be-Ferusho la-Talmud* v. 2 (Jerusalem, 1981); more generally, Yonah Fraenkel, *Darko shel Rashi be-Ferusho la-Talmud ha-Bavli* (Jerusalem, 1975).

28. *Perush Rashi al ha-Torah*, ed. M. R. Lehmann (New York, 1981).

29. Ibid. Hebrew pagination 113; cf. introd. 39.

30. J. N. Epstein, *Mevo'ot le-Sifrut ha-Tannaim* (Tel Aviv, 1957), 549.

31. The ascription of the Tosafot in Yoma to Meir of Rothenburg is accepted by Irving Agus, "Meir b. Baruch of Rothenburg," *EJ* 11:1252.

32. *Baraita de-Melekhet ha-Mishkan*, ed. M. Friedmann (Vienna, 1908), introd. 5.

33. Saul Lieberman, *Siphre Zutta* (New York, 1968), 79.

34. J. N. Epstein, op.cit. 632-33.

35. *Mekhilta D'Rabbi Sim'on b. Jochai*, ed. J. N. Epstein/E. Z. Melamed (Jerusalem, 1955), Hebrew pagination 55-56.

36. *Midrash ha-Gadol* Exodus, ed. M. Margulies (Jerusaelm, 1983), 6 n.
37. Lieberman, *Siphre Zutta* 79.
38. *Midrash ha-Gadol* Numbers, ed. Z. M. Rabinowitz (Jerusalem, 1983), 11. The citation technique of Midrash ha-Gadol has been a particular concern of modern editors of rabbinic texts. In addition to the sources cited above, see David Hoffmann, introd., *Mekilta de-R. Simeon b. Yoḥai* (Frankfurt, 1905), viii-ix; E. Z. Melamed, introd., *Mekilta D'Rabbi Sim'on b. Jochai* (Jerusalem, 1955), 53-56; H. S. Horovitz, introd., *Siphre ad Numeros adjecto Siphre zutta* (Jerusalem, 1966), xix-xx.
39. Aaron Greenbaum, "Baraita de-Melekhet ha-Mishkan within a Manuscript of Midrash ha-Gadol" (Hebrew), *Sura* 1 (1954): 490-513.
40. Greenbaum also maintains that there are sure to be other citations of BMM scattered throughout Midrash ha-Gadol. Our own investigation produced several; see the discussion of Midrash ha-Gadol in ch. 5 of the Introduction.
41. Greenbaum's exclusive reliance on the Friedmann ed. of BMM constitutes a problem in its own right. Friedmann's text is eclectic, including editorial transpositions unattested in any MS (see our discussion of the Friedmann ed. in ch. 5). To utilize the Friedmann text to corroborate quotations of BMM in Midrash ha-Gadol is to compare one composite to another.
42. *Midrash ha-Gadol.* Genesis: ed. M. Margulies (Jerusalem, 1975); Exodus: ed. M. Margulies (Jerusalem, 1983); Leviticus: ed. A. Steinsaltz (Jerusalem, 1976); Numbers: ed. Z. M. Rabinowitz (Jerusalem, 1983).
43. Lieberman, *Siphre Zutta* 79. For a description and specific examples of citation technique in Yalqut Shimoni, see E. Z. Melamed, *Midreshe Halakhah shel ha-Tannaim be-Talmud Bavli* (Jerusalem, ²1988), 68-70.
44. Arthur Hyman, *Meqorot Yalqut Shimoni*, 2 vols. (Jerusalem, 1965), 1:743, 2:542; cf. Zunz/Albeck, *Ha-Derashot be-Yisrael* (Jerusalem, ³1974), 268 n. 14.
45. *Yalqut Shimoni* Exodus v. 2, ed. A. Hyman/Y. Shiloni (Jerusalem, 1980). This edition is based on MS Oxford Bodleian 2637.
46. *Yalqut ha-Makhiri* Isaiah, ed. J. Z. K. Spira (repr. Jerusalem, 1964), 241.
47. In the introductory notes to his edition of Yalqut ha-Makhiri, xxix, Spira describes this passage as משונה קצת.
48. In this chapter we list the most important medieval citations of BMM; our references are not exhaustive. Zunz/Albeck, *Ha-Derashot*, 268 n. 14 also mentions Sefer ha-Yashar 286 (ca. 13th century). Solomon Buber, *Yeriot Sholomo* (Warsaw, 1896) 15, adds Meiri, Shab. 98a (13th century) and Sefer Kaftor va-Feraḥ 1 (Estori ha-Parḥi, 14th century). Chaim M. Horowitz, *Tosefata Attiqata* v. 1 (Frankfurt am Main, 1889), 16, adds (without foundation) Maimonides, Mishneh Torah, *Bet ha-Beḥirah* 3:6, 4:1.

Chapter 4

Origin, Date, Significance

Other than the pioneering edition published by Meir Friedmann (Ish Shalom) in 1908, BMM has been largely ignored by modern scholarship. While cited occasionally in biblical researches for the purpose of clarifying details of the tabernacle's construction,[1] BMM as a text has received little critical attention. However, several theories of its origin and date have been advanced over the last century.

Leopold Zunz, the first scientific scholar of rabbinic literature, classified BMM with Seder Olam as a specialized baraita abstracted from the major compilations on account of its lack of halakhic or aggadic application. He characterizes its language as typical of the early midrashim but considers it of later date than the Mekhilta or the Baraita of Thirty-two Rules. Zunz also makes the observation that the final chapter of BMM is entirely aggadic, but he does not suggest that it is a later addition.[2]

In 1889 Chaim Meir Horowitz proposed another theory of BMM's origin. Noting that tractate Middot is one of the few in the Mishnah lacking a companion in the Tosefta, Horowitz argues that BMM, together with the Baraita of Forty-nine Rules, constitutes the missing Tosefta.[3] He tries to prove this by showing that the Baraita of Forty-nine Rules, known to us only from quotations in medieval sources,[4] parallels material in BMM. His examples of correspondence, however, are forced. For instance, he cites Rashi's mention of a Mishnah of Forty-nine Rules at b. Suk. 8a. But the quotation or paraphrase that follows does not correspond to any extant passage in BMM. The only phrase that does attest a parallel in BMM (although in only three MSS[5]), מכדי כמה מרובע יתר על העיגול רביע, is Rashi's lemma from the gemara of Suk. 8a. In his gloss on Rashi, R. Joshua Boaz (Mesoret ha-Shas) notes that the same phrase is already found at M. Oholot 12:6, שהמרובע יתר על העגול רביע (an exact parallel to the three

MSS of BMM). Horowitz cites another occurrence of the Suk. 8a
phrase at b. BB 27a, attributed by Tosafot (s.v. כמה) to both the
Baraita of Forty-nine Rules and tractate Eruvin. Given the multiple
attestations of this phrase, Horowitz's allegation of a unique correspondence between the lost Baraita of Forty-nine Rules and BMM
cannot be sustained.

Two other examples are offered by Horowitz: Rashi to Ex. 26:5,[6]
corresponding to BMM chapter 2, and Rashi to Ex. 27, corresponding to BMM chapter 11. At Ex. 26:5, Rashi concludes his commentary with זו מצאתי בברייתא דמסכת מדות, but it cannot be determined if
the foregoing text is a quotation, paraphrase, or summary, nor is it
clear where it commences. In any case, the text of Rashi to Ex. 26:5,
while addressing subject matter discussed in BMM chapter 2, has no
parallel in any extant witness to BMM. With respect to Ex. 27,
Rashi's commentary never mentions the Baraita (or Mishnah) of
Forty-nine Rules.[7]

By describing the Baraita of Forty-nine Rules as נוסחא אחרת
ומשונה מהברייתא דמלאכת המשכן, Horowitz concedes the disparities
between the two texts. He compares the discrepancies to those
between versions A and B of Avot de-R. Nathan (ed. Schechter),[8]
but as we have seen, even the few citations he brings fail to support
his contention. Horowitz's theory of correspondence between BMM
and the Baraita of Forty-nine Rules is actually based on the subjects
addressed rather than on the texts attested. Were similar subject
matter the criterion of adducing origin, a better case could be made
for BMM's relationship to parts of Mishnah, Tosefta, Sifre Numbers, or the Talmuds, where authentic parallels are found.

Horowitz fixes a date for BMM contemporaneous with the
Mekhilta, which it either antedates or supplements to complete the
portions wanting (Ex. 25-30, 35-40).[9] He bases this date not only on
the text of BMM but on its presence in a medieval MS[10] which also
includes Mishnah tractates Sheqalim, Arakhin, Me'ilah, Tamid,
Middot, and extracanonical tractates Kallah, Semahot, and
Soferim.[11] He also discerns significance in the placement of the text
of BMM at the head of MS Munich, the earliest complete MS of the
Babylonian Talmud (see below, ch. 5). Horowitz seems to believe
that the decision of a medieval copyist to include or exclude a given
rabbinic work is proof of its date of origin. However, medieval codices often include works of widely divergent date and provenance.[12]

In 1898 Eleazar Gruenhut published BMM chapters 13-14
together with a commentary in which he seeks to prove that these

two chapters are a late addition to the text.[13] His evidence is the absence of chapters 13-14 from the recension of BMM found in Sefer ve-Hizhir. He also invokes the opinion of Zunz concerning the aggadic character of BMM's conclusion; he does not mention that Zunz speaks only of the last chapter, not the last two. Gruenhut hypothesizes that chapters 13 and 14 were added to BMM shortly after the appearance of Sefer ve-Hizhir, since Rashi already quotes from them. He concludes that the two chapters were originally part of the Baraita of Forty-nine Rules; unlike Horowitz, however, he does not claim that this is true of BMM as a whole. On the contrary, he detects in chapters 13-14 distinctive language unlike chapters 1-12, so that each of the two components must have arisen from a separate source. Presumably the two were combined owing to their shared subject, although Gruenhut does not state this explicitly. For further proof he brings a quotation of chapters 13-14 from Yalqut Shimoni which follows after a mention of the Baraita of Forty-nine Rules. He admits that the passage in question is not identified by the Yalqut but claims that it must derive from the same source.

Gruenhut's argument may be refuted on a number of counts. First of all, he fails to take account of the internal structure of Sefer ve-Hizhir itself. In the introduction to the second volume of his edition of Sefer ve-Hizhir,[14] I. M. Freimann points out that the contents of each portion are enunciated in the opening scriptural verse. The first verse of *Tezavveh* (Ex. 27:20) concerns the oil for lighting the lampstand of the tabernacle. Sefer ve-Hizhir proceeds to discuss the location of the lampstand within the shrine (ed. Freimann v. 1, pp. 161-62). The quotation of BMM chapters 1-12 follows, obviously occasioned by the adjacent discussion. When BMM departs (ch. 13-14) from its description of the tabernacle, Sefer ve-Hizhir returns to its own place of departure, Ex. 27:20. In its own context and arrangement, Sefer ve-Hizhir's omission of chapters 13-14 is perfectly coherent and necessary.[15] Gruenhut must also account for quotations of BMM chapters 13-14 in Yalqut Shimoni. He is reduced to the assertion that the Yalqut cites a later recension of BMM that combined two unrelated sources, although he never explains how or why this took place, whether before Sefer ve-Hizhir or after. Finally, Gruenhut's claim that Sefer ve-Hizhir's omission of BMM chapters 13 and 14 proves that they are a late addendum is most decisively contradicted by the unanimity of MS witnesses, the earliest of which are as old as Sefer ve-Hizhir.

Meir Friedmann (Ish Shalom), a magisterial rabbinic scholar whose editions of such works as Sifre Numbers and Deuteronomy (1864), Mekhilta (1870), and Pesiqta Rabbati (1880) set new standards of erudition and analytical rigor, published an edition of BMM in 1908, the year of his death. This edition is discussed below in chapter 5. It includes a brief introduction in which Friedmann sets forth his conclusions concerning the origins of BMM. He begins by identifying portions of the Pentateuch deleted from the halakhic midrashim because of their non-halakhic character: the tabernacle construction, the priestly vestments, the inauguration of the priests, and the Israelite encampment. Friedmann maintains that these portions too were elucidated by the Tannaim in such works as BMM and Mekhilta de-Millu'im, the latter now included in Sifra but clearly a separate composition.[16] He notes that a quotation of Mekhilta de-Millu'im (ed. Weiss 42d) is attributed by Tosafot Yeshanim (b. Yoma 6a, s.v. מביתו) to BMM. From this anomaly he concludes that in the author's MS Mekhilta de-Millu'im was part of BMM. Under the influence of the affinitive description of priestly duties in Lev. 6-8, Mekhilta de-Millu'im was eventually transferred to Sifra.

However, Friedmann cannot account for the absence from BMM (save 4:12-13) of any discussion of the priestly vestments (Ex. 28, 39), since many baraitot concerning them are found in the Talmud (e.g. b. Yoma 71a, b. Suk. 5a, b. Sot. 36a-b, b. Zev. 88a-b). On the basis of a reference in the seventeenth century book *Ḥokhmat ha-Mishkan*,[17] he suggests that BMM must have once included a description of the priestly vestments that, in the course of transfer with Mekhilta de-Millu'im to Sifra, was unaccountably lost. Friedmann fixes the date of BMM after the Mishnah, since R. Judah ha-Nasi is mentioned, but before the Talmuds, since no Amoraim are named in the text. While conceding that some critics might demand more compelling proof of this early date, Friedmann insists that there can be no doubt: כאן נמצא וכאן היה.[18] Yet aside from the exclusively tannaitic attributions, Friedmann's introduction presents no further evidence of BMM's antiquity.

The date of origin proposed by Friedmann has been accepted by most scholars. Louis Ginzberg also assumes that BMM was available to the Amoraim in fixed form.[19] However, he is inclined to favor the theory of Horowitz and Gruenhut that the last two chapters were constituents of the Baraita of Forty-nine Rules, a view rejected by Friedmann.[20] In his compilation of baraitot found in the Talmuds,

Michael Higger attributes a number of them to BMM. He also assumes that BMM is the source of certain passages in Sifre Numbers.[21] J. N. Epstein maintains that although they are not included in our Mekhilta, the chapters of Exodus describing the tabernacle were certainly studied by the school of R. Ishmael and must have comprised a special baraita approximating (מעין) our BMM.[22] Saul Lieberman, in a passing reference quoted by Yigael Yadin in his edition of the Temple Scroll, identifies BMM as "a source from the era of the Tannaim."[23] This verdict is also accepted by Y. D. Grintz, who assumes that amoraic parallels are extracts from BMM.[24] In the introduction to his study of halakhic midrashim quoted in the Babylonian Talmud, E. Z. Melamed lists BMM among them.[25]

On the other hand, Benjamin DeVries ascribes BMM to the period subsequent to the development of the tannaitic corpora and minor talmudic tractates.[26] Ben Zion Wacholder suggests a distinction between the age of the component materials of BMM and the date of their redaction. He characterizes BMM as "a rabbinic text of uncertain date which appears to be an early medieval collection of second century A.D. tannaitic statements."[27] While Wacholder does not proceed beyond this comment, elsewhere he advances a similar theory with respect to the Mekhilta, which he describes as a post-talmudic midrash compiled from both tannaitic and amoraic sources.[28]

As noted in chapter 2 of the Introduction, the possibility that BMM is not an authentic tannaitic composition but a later fabrication must be considered. The same is true of any rabbinic work of ancient attribution whose existence cannot be independently corroborated until the Middle Ages. For instance, the first references to Sifre as a midrashic commentary on Scripture are not found until such geonic works as Seder Tannaim ve-Amoraim and Iggeret Rav Sherira Gaon.[29] The appellation Mekhilta as the title of a work does not appear until the tenth century.[30] The first explicit reference to Genesis Rabbah is found in Halakhot Gedolot, dating from the same period.[31] Avot de-R. Nathan is first mentioned by R. Nissim Gaon and the Arukh.[32] Like these compositions, BMM is not cited until the geonic era.

Two factors make it necessary to regard the antiquity of such works with circumspection. The first is the scarcity of surviving MSS from the early centuries of the common era. As Malachi Beit-Arie has observed, there is an almost total gap of some eight centuries between the oldest extant MSS (the Dead Sea Scrolls) and the earliest dated Hebrew codex (894/5 C.E.).[33] Works dating from the tannaitic era do not surface in writing until the geonic era at the earliest, and by then only secondary quotations may survive. The second reason to suspect claims of literary antiquity is the well-attested phenomena of pseudepigraphy and archaism in ancient and medieval Hebrew literature. To lend credibility and authenticity to their work, writers would adopt an older style and vocabulary, feigning obsolete terminology in order to validate the claim of antiquity.

Pseudepigraphy is not forgery in the modern sense; it is a claim to authoritative tradition rather than to literary origins.[34] Pseudonymity can also be a consequence of anonymity: a mistaken attribution of a work whose original author is unknown. In Hebrew literature, pseudonymity is found as early as the Bible, e.g. the Deuteronomic legislation ascribed to Moses; the Psalms ascribed to David; and Proverbs and Ecclesiastes ascribed to Solomon. Ecstatic and oracular identification with revered figures from antiquity is an essential characteristic of apocalyptic literature. Since divine inspiration was declared to have ceased centuries before, these works claimed to predate the closure of the prophetic canon. The apocalyptic authors saw themselves as the latest conduit of an inspired stream of tradition. Their pseudonymity was a claim not only to antiquity but to revelation.[35]

Whether a similar dynamic applies to later rabbinic literature has not, to our knowledge, been proven. A pseudepigraphical pattern is certainly evident in various works of Hekhalot literature; and the Zohar, composed in the late thirteenth century, claims the authorship of a second century sage and his circle. Apart from the mystical and esoteric tradition, however, archaism and fictive attribution are not often as obvious. Until recently, historical scholarship of the talmudic and geonic eras has assumed the accuracy of attributions to tannaitic sages, but this credulity must now be questioned.[36] In the juristic and midrashic corpora, the consensual, composite mode of expression tends to blur individual identities and uniqueness of expression. The organizing principle is not authorship but Scripture or subject. Unattributed traditions are accorded equal (or greater) standing. This form of composition lends to these documents a collective, even transcendent quality.[37] Adding to the difficulty of authorial verification is the diffusion of the evidence. The legal dicta and exegetical remarks attributed to various sages, as well as the episodic narratives purporting to describe events in their careers, are dispersed throughout the literature in documents of assorted form and provenance. Given the chronological and generic disparities among these works, the task of verifying individual authors is probably hopeless.[38]

Nor is archaism easily identified or isolated. Archaized Hebrew is already evident in the Dead Sea Scrolls, where the imitation of biblical Hebrew vocabulary is conspicuous.[39] Literary convention came to require that baraitot and heavenly messages, among other texts, always appear in Hebrew.[40] Baruch Bokser has aptly suggested that rabbinic literary activity as a whole parallels the pseudepigraphic genre of rewritten Scripture, which revises as well as interprets the original biblical text.[41] Imitation and replication of antecedent language frame the rabbinic mode of discourse. Eventually the term "baraita" came to designate any aggregate of traditions that originated or was claimed to have originated in tannaitic times.[42] The diachronic dimension of rabbinic literature is often disguised, further complicating determinations of date and authorship.

Rabbinic compositions of indeterminate origin continue to generate debate among modern scholars. That some works are pseudepigraphic (e.g. Pirke de-R. Eliezer, Tanna de-ve Eliyyahu) is no longer doubted, although even these may contain earlier, otherwise unattested traditions. But other works such as Avot de-R. Nathan and tractate Semaḥot, like BMM, are composed strictly in the language and style of the Tannaim. There is nothing obvious within these texts to indicate a later date, even if one is inclined to suspect it.[43] One may also need to distinguish between the age of the component materials and the time of their redaction: as finished works, they may not have achieved their present form until the Middle Ages. For documents of this kind, any effort to fix time and place of origin or to verify authorship is open to doubt.

Notwithstanding these reservations, our conclusions in this study support the estimate of Friedmann that BMM is a tannaitic work originating in the third or fourth century. We base this conjecture on internal characteristics of structure and genre (Introduction, ch. 1); language, vocabulary, exegetical terminology, textual attributions, and dispute patterns (ch. 2); and external confirmations in parallel passages across both tannaitic and amoraic strata (ch. 3). Medieval citations (ch. 3) confirm that by the tenth century BMM closely approximated its present form, as MSS and fragments from the Cairo Genizah attest (ch. 5). It is certainly possible, as Wacholder suggests, that BMM is a collection of authentic tannaitic traditions that was not compiled until the geonic era when it is first mentioned. But if this were so, one would expect some sign of pseudepigraphy or archaized language, and our analysis has detected none. One would also expect greater reliance upon the Babylonian Talmud, whose influence by medieval times was ubiquitous. Yet as we have seen (ch. 3), BMM differs from the Bavli in both form and substance far more often than it conforms.

Nor can we accept the view of Horowitz and Gruenhut that the last two chapters of BMM are a late addition to the text. This allegation is contradicted not only by the earliest MSS and medieval citations but by the very passages adduced in its support.

Concerning the alleged relationship of BMM to the lost Baraita of Forty-nine Rules or to Sifra Mekhilta de-Millu'im, we find insufficient evidence for either possibility. Horowitz's analogy between BMM and the Baraita of Forty-nine Rules on the one hand and versions A and B of Avot de-R. Nathan on the other is nullified by the want of an extant text. Friedmann's case for a link between BMM and Mekhilta de-Millu'im, while more substantive, is still dubious. He maintains that since both works are non-halakhic in character, they were likely to have been associated in the rabbinic Torah curriculum. However, the only evidence he can offer is a brief quotation of Mekhilta de-Millu'im attributed by Tosafot Yeshanim (13th century) to BMM. Since there is no trace of this or any other passage from Mekhilta de-Millu'im in the attested text of BMM, it seems at least as probable that Tosafot Yeshanim's source citation is wrong. Moreover, if the affinitive account of Lev. 6-8 explains why Mekhilta de-Millu'im was transferred to Sifra, it does not explain why it was struck from BMM. In light of the uncertain evidence, a theory of original linkage between BMM and Sifra Mekhilta de-Millu'im must be regarded as unproven.

It remains to consider the significance of BMM in the context of tannaitic literature and in light of the rabbinic enterprise as a whole. Defining the purpose of an ancient literary composition is often a hypothetical exercise; in the case of BMM, it is necessarily so. We have before us a rabbinic work that is formally, topically, and generically anomalous. It is neither mishnah nor midrash, neither halakhah nor aggadah, neither "Akiban" nor "Ishmaelian." Fully one-third of its pericopae are attested in tannaitic and amoraic parallels, yet its composition is self-referential, distinctive, and internally cohesive. It betrays no sign of its contemporary situation or place of origin. Its primary agendum is exegetical, but its principle of organization is taxonomic. It is at once an exercise in scriptural induction and in descriptive deduction. There is nothing quite like it, to our knowledge, in rabbinic literature.

While it does not explain every anomaly, the most plausible theory of origin is still the one advanced by Friedmann: that BMM was originally a constituent of the Mekhilta or an earlier form of tannaitic midrash on Exodus. The extant halakhic midrashim comprise the closest analogue to BMM in language, structure, and exegetical purpose. Like BMM, they engage the scriptural text but often depart from it in extended expositions. The Mekhilta as we have it covers Ex. 12:1-23:19, then skips to 31:12-17 and concludes with 35:1-3. Sifre Numbers, with which several BMM passages coincide, is also fragmentary, treating Num. 5-12, 15, 18-19, 25:1-13, 26:52-31:24, 35:9-34. That none of the extant halakhic midrashim is comprehensive suggests that some parts are lost or displaced. Moreover, it should be noted that the term "halakhic" is really a misnomer for these midrashim: more than half of the Mekhilta and Sifre Deuteronomy, for instance, consists of non-legal exposition on narrative passages. The scriptural account of the tabernacle, of course, is neither legal nor narrative; but as Epstein points out, this does not mean that it was not also subjected to exegesis.[44] On the other hand, owing in part to the unique and self-contained nature of the tabernacle description, it is certainly possible that a tannaitic elaboration developed separately. Steven Fraade has proposed such a thesis for the tannaitic midrashim as a whole: the missing sections of commentary are not necessarily lost; rather they are lacunae from earlier commentaries arranged according to other principles of organization. This earlier stratum of traditions did not follow scriptural order, so that commentary may not have been available for all parts of the Pentateuch when the tannaitic midrashim were compiled.[45] This thesis could explain BMM as a discrete source which, because of its exceptional subject matter, was not assimilated into the larger compendia. It survived as a separate aggregate of tannaitic traditions that eventually achieved its redacted form.

Further evidence for the association of BMM with tannaitic scriptural exegesis lies at the very beginning of the work (1:1-6), a catalogue of the various *terumot*, "heave-offerings." This exordium precedes the systematic description of the tabernacle. The scriptural account begins with Ex. 25:2, the commandment to offer *terumah*. Although the scriptural order is different from that found in BMM, both begin with the *terumot*. In fact, the presence of BMM 1:1-6 is impossible to explain unless it serves as the formal link to the Pentateuch lection (*Parashat Terumah*)[46] and the point of departure for BMM. This may reflect the structure of "pre-existing" materials inferred by Fraade or a redactional connection to the scriptural text. Either way, it evinces a specific relationship to a section of the Pentateuch that is not addressed elsewhere in the tannaitic corpora.

Locating BMM in the stream of rabbinic exegesis tells us that it was part of a larger intellectual project. Yet BMM constitutes more than a scriptural commentary: it is an architectural treatise, a technical description of divine artifacts. It seeks to portray the dwelling place of God and to imagine, beyond the aniconic scriptural account, the unspecified details of its construction. Given the extent of biblical elaboration and repetition concerning the tabernacle and its furniture, it is evident that the significance of these objects transcends their literal function.[47] In seeking to reduce sacred archetypes to material description, BMM often verges on abstraction.[48] However, although the subject of BMM is the tabernacle, it also addresses many features and details of the Solomonic and Herodian Temples. Here there is a more historical basis for discussion, greater acquaintance with realia, and fuller corroboration from other sources. BMM may be viewed in the succession of Temple descriptions embracing biblical (e.g. 1 Kings, 2 Chronicles, Ezekiel), Hellenistic (e.g. Eupolemus, Josephus), sectarian (e.g. the Temple Scroll), and rabbinic (e.g. M. Middot) literatures.

The Temple Scroll is of particular interest to us because of its fusion of tabernacle and Temple models. Both for content and style (including God addressing Moses), the author adverts to the Exodus tabernacle account, although he appears to be less concerned than BMM with architectural design and more concerned with issues of purity and impurity.[49] The Temple Scroll's recurring prescription of gilded furnishings relies upon the precedent of the tabernacle vessels. Its effort to harmonize divergent biblical prescriptions, e.g. between Ex. 30:18 and 1 Ki. 7:39 concerning the laver and the "sea" of Solomon, mirrors a major theme of BMM.[50] Yigael Yadin proposes that the entire structure of the Temple Scroll sanctuary description is explained by the evident discrepancy between Ex. 25-27, in which the fabrication of the vessels precedes the tabernacle, and Ex. 36-38, where the order is reversed. Because the Temple Scroll wishes to begin by describing the Temple building before enumerating its contents, the author starts with the edifice, as in Ex. 36-38, but then breaks off to accommodate the Ex. 25-27 vessel sequence before returning to the Temple courts in the order shared by both accounts.[51] Lawrence Schiffman suggests another characteristic of the Temple Scroll that invites comparison to BMM:[52]

> While (the author) tends toward scriptural order, he maintains in the macrostructure, as he did in the microstructure, the desire to associate material that somehow is related by subject. This is especially true in his tendency to organize sacrificial law around his descriptions of the relevant Temple furniture and equipment needed for the performance of the rituals. Our author seems to be torn between the midrashic and mishnaic modes of organization.

For the present purpose, however, we seek to link the Temple Scroll to BMM only with respect to the importance that both accord, in differing degrees, to the desert tabernacle.

BMM may also be contrasted to the archaeological, iconographic, and other non-literary renderings of the tabernacle and its vessels that have survived from late antiquity. The lampstand in particular is a common motif of Jewish ornamental art from as early as the first century B.C.E. It is depicted on reliefs, capitals, lintels, tombstones, and synagogue mosaic pavements.[53] The golden table is sometimes shown beside it; in one case the two are depicted on reverse sides of a Hasmonean coin.[54] The relief panel of the triumphal Arch of Titus shows the lampstand, the table, and the trumpets. With the destruction of the Temple, writes Rachel Hachlili, "a need for a concrete visual image becomes strongly felt" in Jewish synagogue and funerary art. Representations of the Temple, its architecture, ritual, and ceremony became more prevalent. The lampstand and other vessels and utensils comprised "a unified design of Jewish symbols" that came to be associated with Judaism.[55] The wall murals of the synagogue at Dura-Europos in eastern Syria (ca. 245 C.E.) prove that Jewish pictorial art existed by this time, but no iconographic MSS from late antiquity have been discovered. The oldest known Jewish MSS containing drawings of the tabernacle and its vessels date from tenth and eleventh century Egypt. A Karaite Bible from Cairo (930 C.E.) includes stylized drawings of the tabernacle (or Temple), the lampstand, ark, altar(s), laver, and various utensils. The prominence of geometric patterns and vegetal motifs reflects obvious Muslim influence.[56] Thirteenth century Spanish Hebrew Bible MSS were routinely adorned with preliminary folios portraying the tabernacle and Temple vessels, some apparently influenced by Maimonidean as well as biblical prescriptions.[57] It has been suggested that these medieval depictions may have late antique Jewish origins in illuminated MSS now lost or in traditions reflected by surviving mosaic pavements (e.g. Beth Alpha, sixth century).[58] But the evidence available at present does not establish a historic continuity. In any event, the iconographic tradition of tabernacle or Temple representation and the literary descriptions of BMM reflect neither mutual knowledge nor relationship.[59]

Within the corpus of late antique rabbinic literature, as we have emphasized, BMM appears to be unique. But there are two other works that bear a generic resemblance: Megillat Ta'anit (ca. first century C.E.) and Seder Olam (ca. second century). Both of these works also stand apart from the attested mainstream of rabbinic literature. Like BMM, each addresses matters of documentary or antiquarian record. In the introduction to his critical edition of Seder Olam, Chaim Milikowsky describes this work as unique: "All other rabbinic texts, whether halakhic or aggadic, are 'projective,' that is to say, their subject matter is projected into their own age and made relevant." But the concern of Seder Olam "can be described as antiquarian, and its major purpose is historical rather than didactic. Of no other rabbinic work can this be said."[60] However, Milikowsky has since modified this judgment by acknowledging the similarity of BMM.[61] Megillat Ta'anit has also been likened to Seder Olam as a genre of historical chronicle[62] but is probably closer to the literary tradition of the scribal list represented in biblical (e.g. 1 Chr. 1-9), sectarian (e.g. the Temple Scroll), tannaitic (e.g. M. Shab. 7:2, M. Qid. 4:1), and post-talmudic (e.g. Seder Tannaim ve-Amoraim) literatures. The concerns of Megillat Ta'anit are governed by the perennial cycle of the year: days of the month are noted but not years, suggesting a less historical and more calendrical conception and purpose.[63]

Whether or not the ancient rabbis wrote "history" or even thought "historically" is a question of some moment for the evaluation of BMM. Certainly historiographic accounts are rare in rabbinic literature. From scattered passages, B. Dinur has sought to extract the fol-

lowing categories of historical data: 1) direct historiography, a chronological record of events; 2) chronicles of events generating halakhic
decisions, among which he classifies Megillat Ta'anit; 3)
"historiographic halakhah," describing laws and customs that are either
contemporary or anticipated to take effect in the future, e.g. the praxis
of the Temple cult reported in the Mishnah.[64] But Dinur's examples
are meager and his premise doubtful.[65] Even in the writings of helle-
nized Jews, systematic records of events are often subordinated to apol-
ogetic purposes (e.g. Josephus) or transcendent concerns (e.g. Philo of
Alexandria).[66] Arnaldo Momigliano concludes that "the Jews who survived the destruction of the Temple without passing over to the Roman
side apparently ceased to write history."[67]

Yet even if there is no rabbinic parallel to the works of Herodotus
or Tacitus, there are other forms of historical record from late antiquity to which Megillat Ta'anit, Seder Olam, and BMM may be compared. In both Greek and Latin literature, aspects of the ancient past
were examined in monographs designated generically as *archaiologia*
(= Latin *antiquitates*). Some of these works were devoted to religious
subjects, e.g. Plutarch on the Delphic oracle, or Lucian on the Syrian
goddess. At the turn of the common era, notes Momigliano, numerous erudite Greek works were devoted to the preservation of cere-
monies that were becoming obsolete. Although many such works are
presumed to be lost, antiquarian records of Etruscan, Persian, Egyp-
tian, and Greek cults are widely attested in extant sources.[68] If rabbinic historiography cannot be said to exist, this does not mean that
there was no impulse to preserve the past. The genre of *archaiologia*
seems particularly appropriate to BMM. Although it is a part of the
exegetical project of the sages, BMM is also an archival document.[69]
It is both descriptive and prescriptive, at once a matter of record
and a blueprint for implementation. As Yosef Haim Yerushalmi has
observed, the sages salvaged what was relevant to them and to the
ongoing religious and communal life of the Jewish people. They did
not (to our knowledge) compose a consecutive history of the period
of the Second Temple and its destruction, but they meticulously
recorded the details of the Temple service. "The relevant past... was
clearly the remote past. What had happened long ago had determined what had occurred since, and even provided the fundamental
explanations for what was still transpiring."[70] In this regard, BMM
is distinct from either the calendar of Megillat Ta'anit or the
chronography of Seder Olam. It more closely resembles the catalogue

of Temple rites in the Mishnah and Tosefta. It is a historical description of a metahistorical phenomenon.

The intellectual premise of BMM, like that of virtually all rabbinic literature, is that biblical rather than contemporary experience is the sovereign reality of Israel. Like the Mishnah, which is written as if the Temple still stood, BMM describes the ancient tabernacle as if its dimensions still mattered. While granting that the ark of the covenant had disappeared (BMM 7:21-27), BMM never mentions that the tabernacle had too. The Israelite camp in the desert is described (BMM 13-14) as if the sages were there to see it. Severed from its physical referent, BMM reconstitutes it in words. The tabernacle is transformed from a shrine to a treatise without acknowledging any change or loss.

This assertion of continuity, perhaps even identity, with the past may be explained in part by the Temple's destruction in 70 C.E. and the crushing defeat of subsequent Jewish revolts. The effects were catastrophic. Both the power of Israel's God and the certainty of Israel's election were in doubt. The divine covenant appeared to be sundered. Atonement could not be won upon the broken altars. The response of the Mishnah, as Jacob Neusner has written, was to proceed as if nothing had changed:[71]

> Israel had originally become Israel and sustained its perpetual vocation through its living on the holy Land and organizing all aspects of its holy life in relationship to the conduct of the holy Temple, eating like priests and farming in accord with the cultic taboos and obsessions with order and form, dividing up time between profane and holy in relationship to the cult's calendar and temporal division of its own rites. Now Israel remained Israel, loyal to its calling, through continuing to live in the mirror and under the aspect of the same cult.

In its preoccupation with the yet more distant Israelite past, its close adhesion to Scripture, its obliviousness to contemporary time and place, BMM appears also to be a willful denial of Israel's disaster. The ordered, immutable quality of the tabernacle description may have functioned as a kind of counterweight to the disorder of Jewish life in defeat and dispersion. The eternal designs revealed by God were beyond the reach of any conqueror. Divine patterns that were not visible in subjection were still visible in Scripture, where each vessel is designed and fabricated to perfection. To concentrate on such matters is to escape from harsh realities and perhaps also to transcend them.

It is also possible that the description of the past was intended to be a vision of the future. As the eschatological Temples of Ezekiel and the Temple Scroll evoke pre- exilic models, so BMM may reflect not only a historical tradition but a messianic one.[72] By projecting backward to Israel's first sanctuary, BMM carries forward the promise of its restoration. By describing the vessels as they once appeared, BMM in effect prescribes how they are to appear again. The axial significance of the tabernacle is not confined to its career in the wilderness. It is a paradigm of divine proximity. It conjures up an age when Israel had access to God. BMM is a magnification of the ideal past that devalues the present but not the future. As Baruch Bokser has suggested, distress at the Temple's loss was replaced by the desire to supersede it:[73]

> Paradoxically, such a decrease in the significance of the physical Temple in the lives of Jews may be correlated with the rise in apocalyptic and imaginary messianic speculation . . . The Temple in the abstract was thus honored and venerated; it was something from the past and, hopefully, of the not too distant future. The further, though, it receded from contemporary reality and experience, the more imagination took over in thinking about it.

BMM is not an explicit exercise in messianic speculation, yet its preoccupation with the details of tabernacle construction suggests a messianic perspective. Rarely is the perspective as evident as at BMM 11:18-20, where it is said that the dimensions of the tabernacle altar of burnt-offering will be identical in the world to come. More often, if it is present, it is found in such imagery as that of the concluding chapters (BMM 13-14) describing the seven clouds of glory and the exact location of God's voice.

Although such hypotheses must be advanced with trepidation, an upsurge in messianic speculation may well have been occasioned by the brief reign (361-63 C.E.) of the Roman emperor Julian, who proclaimed his intention to rebuild the Temple in Jerusalem. While this initiative received considerable notice in contemporary Latin sources, it is not mentioned explicitly in extant rabbinic literature. Whether or not the sages approved of Julian's project,[74] it is likely that they felt its impact. Like Julian, they were involved in the struggle to resist Christianity after the conversion of Constantine. The effects of Christian competition and Jewish national catastrophe tended to reinforce each other: as long as the Temple was in ruins, the Church could claim to be the true Israel; should the Temple be rebuilt, the claim could be denied. While we are poorly informed of Jewish reactions to Julian's plan, Christian sources testify to the magnitude of the controversy. Ephraem, a Syrian, reported that the Jews of Nisibis "were seized by a frenzied enthusiasm, sounded the ram's horn and rejoiced."[75] Church historian Rufinus of Aquileia wrote that the Jews thought "one of the prophets had returned; they began to taunt us as if the time of their kingdom had returned, to threaten us sharply and to treat us with great insolence."[76] The Cappadocian Church father Gregory of Nazianzus claimed that Jews, wishing to "restore the authority of the ancient tradition," actually donated money and jewelry to assist in rebuilding the Temple.[77] In Antioch a generation later, John Chrysostom was still complaining about Jews "boasting that they will get their city back again."[78] According to the pagan historian Ammianus Marcellinus, work on the reconstruction actually commenced but was suspended by an outbreak of fire near the foundations of the Temple.[79] Notwithstanding the likelihood of exaggeration or polemic in each of these accounts, there can be little doubt that the renewed emphasis on the Temple deepened the conflict between Christians and Jews. Whether it also generated a wave of messianic anticipation among the Jews at large or among the rabbis in particular is admittedly unprovable; certainly the extant rabbinic writings do not report it. Moreover, BMM is more concerned with the tabernacle than the Temple, so that any connection with Julian's project is oblique.[80] Still, given the time of origin that we have deduced from the internal characteristics of BMM, it is at least possible that its composition coincided with the religious contention and anticipation of the fourth century.

Ultimately BMM must be appreciated from its own angle of vision: as an attempt to apprehend divinity through the medium of Scripture. Here we are referring to the rabbinic regard of Scripture as the constitutive and generative element of religious life, divinely revealed *in toto* and *in parvo*. The artifactual tabernacle was lost, but its image inhered in Scripture: both declared the glory of God. For the rabbis, to enhance comprehension and precision through exegesis was not merely philology but worship, a form of divine communion.[81] God's nearness, if no longer palpable, might still be felt through the conduit of theonomous language. If the design and construction of the tabernacle exposed the presence of God, then intellection on the subject, even without the object, might have the same result. BMM engages in conjecture beyond the realm of practice or possibility. But because of its foundation in divine revelation, it is as urgent as any rabbinic document. At b. Ḥul. 66b, the Amoraim ask why Scripture includes a certain passage of no apparent utility. "R. Abbahu said: So it was taught in the school of R. Ishmael: 'To magnify and glorify (His) teaching'" (Is. 42:21).[82] At the time of its composition and redaction, BMM had no prospect of practical application. Yet in the rabbinic universe, this had no bearing on its transcendent purpose.

Notes to Chapter Four

ORIGIN, DATE, SIGNIFICANCE

1. E.g. G. B. Sarfatti, "The Tables of the Covenant as a Symbol for Judaism" (Hebrew), *Tarbiz* 29:4 (1960): 370-93; M. Haran, "The Priestly Image of the Tabernacle," *HUCA* 36 (1965): 191-226; D. Sperber, "The History of the Menorah," *JJS* 16:3-4 (1965): 135-59; E. Weisenberg, "Problems Regarding the Ark of the Covenant" (Hebrew), *Essays Presented to Chief Rabbi Israel Brodie*, ed. H. J. Zimmels et al, Hebrew vol. (London, 1967), 107-28.

2. L. Zunz/H. Albeck, *Ha-Derashot be-Yisrael* (Jerusalem, ³1974), 42-43.

3. Chaim M. Horowitz, *Tosefata Attiqata* v. 1 (Frankfurt am Main, 1889), 7-11.

4. E.g. Rashi, Ibn Ezra, Asher b. Yeḥiel, Tosafot, Yalqut Shimoni; bibliographical references are collected by Louis Ginzberg, "Baraita of the Forty-Nine Rules," *Jewish Encyclopedia* (New York/London, 1903-6), 2:517-18. Ginzberg rejects the theory, first proposed by Moritz Steinschneider, *Mishnat ha-Middot, die Erste Geometrische Schrift in Hebräischer Sprache* (Berlin, 1864), that the Baraita of Forty- nine Rules and Mishnat ha-Middot are one and the same. The Steinschneider theory generated a series of related hypotheses. Horowitz, e.g., argues that BMM, Mishnat ha-Middot, and the Baraita of Forty-nine Rules all comprise parts of the (missing) Tosefta to M. Middot. Solomon Gandz, "Mishnat ha-Middot," *PAAJR* 4 (1933): 1-12, maintains that there were two versions of Mishnat ha-Middot: a geometry treatise (ch. 1-5) of medieval origin bearing the impress of Arabic science; and a "midrashic" one (ch. 6 onward) identical or similar to BMM and antecedent to the Mishnah itself. Gandz bases this conjecture on a Genizah fragment in the Bodleian Library (MS Heb. c. 18) which includes part of a sixth chapter of Mishnat ha-Middot that he considers similar to sections of BMM. Subsequently Alexander Scheiber, "The Prague Manuscript of Mishnat ha-Middot," *HUCA* 45 (1974): 191-96, published part of a manuscript attesting the last portion of chapter 6.

Our comparison of BMM to both fragments of Mishnat ha-Middot chapter 6 (viz. MS Heb. c. 18, MS Prague 259) yields insufficient textual evidence to identify the two works. Neither structure, sequence nor pericopae correspond, and the vocabulary of Mishnat ha-Middot differs from BMM as often as it coincides. For two compositions to be devoted (in the case of Mishnat ha-Middot, only in part) to the same scriptural subject is hardly improbable. We conclude with Ginzberg that Mishnat ha-Middot is a separate work from BMM. Nor do we identify BMM with the (lost) Baraita of Forty-nine Rules, as we explain below.

5. MSS M, L, E (for identification of sigla, see pp. 149-50), BMM 12:13, apparatus.

6. Mistakenly cited by Horowitz as Ex. 26:4.

7. At Ex. 27:5 there is a mention of Mishnah tractate Middot that Horowitz has apparently confused with Mishnat ha-Middot.

8. *Aboth de Rabbi Nathan*, ed. S. Schechter (Vienna, 1887).

9. The theory that BMM is an addition to the Mekhilta is also suggested by Nehemiah Brüll, *Central-Anzeiger für jüdische Literatur* (Frankfurt am Main, 1891), 32. A conjecture that it was originally part of Mekhilta de-R. Simeon b. Yoḥai is advanced by Israel Lewy, *Ein Wort über die Mekilta des R. Simon* (Breslau, 1889), 3.

10. Horowitz lists Oppenheim no. 502 folio, no. 429 quarto, no. 157 octavo. The last of these apparently refers to MS Opp. 726 (Ol. 157), Neubauer 370.11, which is described below in ch. 5 and constitutes the base text of the present edition.

11. See below, pp. 97-98.

12. A typical example is MS Munich Cod. Hebr. 95 itself. Aside from BMM and the Babylonian Talmud, this codex includes Seder Olam, Seder Tannaim ve-Amoraim, Taqqanot of R. Gershom, and assorted document forms. These texts span a millennium. See M. Steinschneider, *Die Hebräischen Handschriften der K. Hof-und Staatsbibliothek in München* (Munich, 1895), 60.

13. Eleazar Gruenhut, *Sefer ha-Liqqutim* v. 2 (Jerusalem, 1898).

14. *Sefer ve-Hizhir*, ed. I. M. Freimann, v. 2 (Warsaw, 1880), unpaginated introd.

15. Further evidence for this deduction is the similarly selective citation by Sefer ve-Hizhir, *Ki tissa*, ed. Freimann, v. 1 (Leipzig, 1873), English pagination 201-26, of y. Sheqalim. Ch. 1-6 are cited in full while ch. 7-8, devoted to unrelated subjects, are deleted. See Jacob Sussman, "Masoret Limmud u-Masoret Nusaḥ shel ha-Talmud ha-Yerushalmi," *Meḥqarim ba-Sifrut ha-Talmudit*, Israel Academy of Sciences and Humanities (Jerusalem, 1983), 12-76 at 19 n. 46.

16. The anomalous character of Mekhilta de-Millu'im is discussed by David Hoffmann, *Zur Einleitung in die halachischen Midraschim* (Berlin,

1887), who suggests (p. 30) that portions of it may be taken from Seder Olam; cf. Hanoch Albeck, *Untersuchungen über die halakischen Midraschim* (Berlin, 1927), 82-84. J. N. Epstein, *Mevo'ot le-Sifrut ha-Tannaim* (Tel Aviv, 1957), 640-42, 690-97 and *Mevo'ot le-Sifrut ha-Amoraim* (Jerusalem, 1962), 641, 698, isolates Mekhilta de-Millu'im on the basis of Ishmaelian terminology that he considers foreign to the text of Sifra proper. However, as we have argued in ch. 1 of the Introduction, redactional distinctions based on an assumed Ishmaelian-Akiban polarity are hazardous, if not untenable. Furthermore, Abraham Goldberg, "The Duplicate Interpretations of Mekhilta de-Millu'im" (Hebrew), *Sinai* 89 (1981): 115-18, shows that Epstein based his judgment on the truncated fragment of Mekhilta de-Millu'im attested in MS Rome Codex Assemani 66; even this fragment, Goldberg maintains, contains mixed terminology. Goldberg theorizes that Mekhilta de-Millu'im is a conflation of two exegeses, both elaborating upon the ordination of Aaron and his sons, the second intended to counteract the negativity of the first. In the course of redaction or scribal transmission, confusion of the two strands led to the fragmentary attestations of the witnesses. Further disturbance of this text is evident from MS Codex Assemani 66, where Sifra's usual division into chapters and verses is absent; see Gideon Haneman, "On the Linguistic Tradition of the Written Text in the Sifra MS" (Hebrew), *Sefer Zikkaron le-Ḥanokh Yalon*, Bar Ilan University (Ramat Gan, 1974), 84-98.

17. By R. Joseph Shalit Richietti (Mantua, 1676).

18. In a footnote to this statement, *Baraita de-Melekhet ha-Mishkan* (Vienna, 1908), introd. 7 n. 1, Friedmann defends himself against the charge of claiming false antiquity for works of uncertain origin. Such a debate had already been prompted by his claim (*Nispaḥim le-Seder Eliyyahu Zuta*, Vienna, 1904) that parts of Tanna de-ve Eliyyahu were to be dated as early as the third century; see Max Kadushin, *The Theology of Seder Eliahu* (New York, 1932), 6-12. An argument against Friedmann's position and in favor of a ninth century date is advanced by Friedmann's former student A. Aptowitzer, "Seder Elia," *Jewish Studies in Memory of George A. Kohut* (New York, 1935), 5-39. Apparently Friedmann anticipated that his assignment of an early date to BMM would also be challenged.

19. Louis Ginzberg, "Baraita on the Erection of the Tabernacle," *Jewish Encyclopedia* (New York/London, 1903-6), 2:517.

20. *Baraita de-Melekhet ha-Mishkan*, ed. Friedmann (Vienna, 1908), introd. 3; cf. 89.

21. *Oẓar ha-Baraitot*, 10 vols. (New York, 1938-48), 6:381-83. According to Higger, the following baraitot cited in the Bavli are already found in or should be attributed to BMM: 1) Shab. 98b-99a (= y. Meg. 1:12, 72c; Exodus R. 35 end); 2) Shab. 99a; 3) Yoma 71b (cf. Sifra *Ẓav* 2, ed. Weiss 29d; Zev. 18b); 4) Men. 98b. Regarding the baraitot that he attributes to

Sifre Num. (e.g. Men. 28a-b), Higger writes (p. 381) that they originate with BMM.

22. J. N. Epstein, *Mevo'ot le-Sifrut ha-Tannaim* (Tel Aviv, 1957), 549. BMM is described similarly by Menaḥem Moreshet, *Leqsiqon ha-Po'al she-nitḥadesh be-leshon ha-Tannaim* (Ramat Gan, 1980), 29.

23. Yigael Yadin, *Megillat ha-Miqdash* (Jerusalem, 1977), 2:21 col. B. Cf. Saul Lieberman, *Hellenism in Jewish Palestine* (New York, 1950), 174 n. 93, who approves Friedmann's assignment of tannaitic origin but adds that the date of final compilation is unknown.

24. Y. D. Grintz, "Baraita de-Melekhet ha-Mishkan," *EJ* 4:193-94.

25. E. Z. Melamed, *Midreshe Halakhah shel ha-Tannaim be-Talmud Bavli* (Jerusalem, ²1988) 4, as follows: Mekhilta de-R. Ishmael, Torat Kohanim (Sifra), Sifre Num., Sifre Deut., Mekhilta de-R. Simeon b. Yoḥai, Sifre Zuta, Midrash Tannaim to Deut., Baraita de-Melekhet ha-Mishkan.

26. Benjamin DeVries, *Mavo Kelali la-Sifrut ha-Talmudit* (Tel Aviv, 1966), 81. DeVries offers no proof for his assertion.

27. Ben Zion Wacholder, *Eupolemus: A Study of Judaeo-Greek Literature* (Cincinnati, 1974), 199.

28. Ben Zion Wacholder, "The Date of the Mekhilta de-Rabbi Ishmael," *HUCA* 39 (1968): 117-44, contra Jacob Z. Lauterbach, *Mekhilta de-Rabbi Ishmael*, 3 vols. (Philadelphia, 1933-35), I:xix-xxiii.

29. See Steven D. Fraade, "Sifre Deuteronomy 26: How Conscious the Composition?" *HUCA* 54 (1983): 245-301 at 297-98.

30. Louis Finkelstein, "The Mekhilta and Its Text," *PAAJR* 5 (1933-34): 547-48.

31. Moshe D. Herr, "Genesis Rabbah," EJ 7:400.

32. See Solomon Schechter, *Aboth de Rabbi Nathan*, tr. J. Goldin, (New Haven, 1955), xxii n. 18 where Goldin relates that Saul Lieberman called his attention to an earlier quotation of ARN (version B, ch. 19) in the She'eltot (ed. Berlin, pt. 3, p. 212).

33. Malachi Beit-Arie, *Hebrew Codicology* (Jerusalem, 1981), 9-11.

34. There is a considerable literature explaining the phenomenon of ancient and medieval pseudonymity and pseudepigraphy. Major studies of note include W. Speyer, *Die literarische Fälschung im Altertum* (Munich, 1971); N. Brox. ed., *Pseudepigraphie in der heidnischen und jüdisch-christlichen Antike* (Darmstadt, 1977); D. G. Meade, *Pseudonymity and Canon* (Grand Rapids, 1987); more generally, A. Taylor and F. Mosher, *The Bibliographical History of Anonyma and Pseudonyma* (Chicago, 1951). On the distinction between pseudepigraphy and forgery, see esp. N. Brox, "Zum Problemstand in der Erforschung der Altchristlichen Pseudepigraphie," *Kairos*, n.s. 15 (1973): 10-23; B. M. Metzger, "Literary Forgeries and Canonical Pseudepigrapha," *JBL* 91 (1972): 3-24.

35. D. S. Russell, *The Method and Message of Jewish Apocalyptic* (London, 1964), 127-39.

36. The leading critic of presumptive reliance on tradent attribution has been Jacob Neusner, e.g.: *Reading and Believing: Ancient Judaism and Contemporary Gullibility* (Atlanta, 1986). For a less polemical approach, see two essays by Neusner's student William Scott Green: "What's in a Name? The Problematic of Rabbinic 'Biography,'" *Approaches to Ancient Judaism* I, ed. W. S. Green, Brown Judaic Studies 1 (Missoula, 1978), 77-96; "Context and Meaning in Rabbinic 'Biography,'" *Approaches to Ancient Judaism* II, ed. W. S. Green, Brown Judaic Studies 9 (Chico, 1980), 97-111.

37. W. S. Green, "What's in a Name?" 88.

38. See David Kraemer, "On the Reliability of Attributions in the Babylonian Talmud," *HUCA* 60 (1989): 175-90, who seeks to date and authenticate attributed amoraic traditions by identifying characteristic literary patterns. He concludes (at 186) that, even if this technique is viable, it permits at most stratification by generation but not the ascription of individual authorship.

39. E. Y. Kutscher, *A History of the Hebrew Language*, ed. R. Kutscher (Jerusalem/Leiden, 1982), 102; E. Qimron, "The Language of the Temple Scroll" (Hebrew), *Leshonenu* 42 (1978): 83-98; G. Brin, "Remarks on the Language of the Temple Scroll" (Hebrew), *Leshonenu* 43 (1979): 20-28.

40. E. Margaliyot, "Hebrew and Aramaic in Talmud and Midrash" (Hebrew), *Leshonenu* 27-28 (1963-64): 20-33. See also Louis Jacobs, "Are There Fictitious Baraitot in the Babylonian Talmud?" *HUCA* 42 (1971): 185-96; idem, "How Much of the Babylonian Talmud is Pseudepigraphic?" *JJS* 28 (1977): 46-59, who argues that the Talmud's redactors consciously engaged in what amounts to literary fiction, inventing Hebrew baraitot for the purpose of invoking tannaitic authority or providing a contrived argument.

41. Baruch M. Bokser, *Post-Mishnaic Judaism in Transition*, Brown Judaic Studies 17 (Chico, 1980), 448.

42. Ben Zion Wacholder, "The Date of the Mekhilta de-Rabbi Ishmael," *HUCA* 39 (1968): 117-44 at 134. Wacholder cites (at 144) the comment of Sherira Gaon (ca. 906-1006): "When we now find texts of baraitot we do not rely upon them, and they are not studied, because we do not know whether or not they are authentic, except those of R. Ḥiyya only, which are read by scholars. There are other baraitot, which they call minor . . . but they are not to be used as halakhic sources."

43. On this aspect of ARN, see L. Finkelstein, *Mavo le-Massekhtot Avot ve-Avot de-R. Nathan* (New York, 1950); J. Goldin, *The Fathers According to R. Nathan* (New Haven, 1955), introd. On Semaḥot see D. Zlotnick, *The Tractate "Mourning" (Semaḥot)* (New Haven, 1966), introd. These examples are emblematic, not exhaustive. On the modern enterprise of dating or even identifying tannaitic collections, the scholarly literature is extensive. A useful bibliography is provided by Fraade, "Sifre Deuteronomy 26," op.cit. 296-97.

44. See the references above, n. 22.

45. Fraade, op.cit. 254-57 esp. n. 21.

46. *Parashat Terumah* commences with Ex. 25:1 whether according to the annual or to the so- called "triennial" cycle of Pentateuch lections attested from late antiquity; see Jacob Mann, *The Bible as Read and Preached in the Old Synagogue* v. 1 (repr. New York, 1971), 481 ff.; prolegomena by B. Z. Wacholder, appendix 1, LI, LXV.

47. Cf. Carol Meyers, *The Tabernacle Menorah*, AASOR Dissertation Series 2 (Missoula, 1976), 4-11.

48. Even in the case of a more historical (as opposed to metahistorical) subject, the difficulty of reifying the physical appearance of a vanished architectural structure is reflected in the writings of Pliny the Elder (23-79 C.E.), who seeks to describe the extinct Mausoleum of Halikarnassos; see Spiro Kostof, *A History of Architecture* (New York/Oxford, 1985), 5-7.

49. See B. Z. Wacholder, *The Dawn of Qumran* (Cincinnati, 1983), 9-16.

50. See Yigael Yadin, *The Temple Scroll* (New York, 1985), 127-28; cf. BMM 8, 10, 12.

51. Yadin, ibid. 117-19.

52. Lawrence Schiffman, "The Temple Scroll in Literary and Philological Perspective," *Approaches to Ancient Judaism* v. 2, ed. W. S. Green, Brown Judaic Studies 9 (Chico, 1980), 143-58 at 153.

53. Rachel Hachlili, *Ancient Jewish Art and Archaeology in the Land of Israel*, Handbuch der Orientalistik VII (Leiden, 1988), 238 f.

54. Ibid. 251.

55. Ibid. 285, 401-2.

56. Mendel Metzger, "Quelques caractères iconographiques et ornamentaux de deux manuscrits hébraïques du Xe siècle," *Cahiers de civilisation médiévale* 1 (1958): 205-13.

57. Joseph Gutmann, "The Messianic Temple in Spanish Medieval Hebrew Manuscripts," *The Temple of Solomon: Archaeological Fact and Medieval Tradition in Christian, Islamic and Jewish Art*, ed. J. Gutmann (Missoula, 1976), 125-45; cf. Thérèse Metzger, "Les objets du culte, le sanctuaire du désert et le Temple de Jérusalem dans les bibles hébraïques médiévales enluminées," *Bulletin of the John Rylands Library* 52 (1970): 397-436.

58. C. Roth, "Jewish Antecedents of Christian Art," *Journal of the Warburg and Courtauld Institutes* 16 (1953): 37 ff.

59. In early Christian and Byzantine art there is also a significant record of figurative representation of the tabernacle and its vessels. They are usually depicted either as schematic frontispiece images without human figures or in miniatures showing scenes of the priestly service; see Joachim Gaehde, "Carolingian Interpretations of an Early Christian Picture Cycle,"

Frühmittelalterliche Studien 8 (1974): 351-84, including a full bibliography at 359-60 n. 41. The Codex Amiatinus, a monastic work dating from the seventh century, contains a diagrammatic illustration of the tabernacle according to the specifications of Ex. 25 ff., including the lampstand, table, altars, and ark, each object clearly labeled in Latin. The configuration of the Israelite tribes surrounding the tabernacle is also delineated. Stanley Ferber, "The Temple of Solomon in Early Christian and Byzantine Art," *The Temple of Solomon*, op.cit. 21-43, concludes that the Codex Amiatinus is dependent upon a prototype of Alexandrian Jewish origin, dating from the second or first centuries B.C.E. However, other than presuming the influence of apocryphal literature, he offers no substantiation for this claim. By the ninth century, Christian tabernacle images are found in typological and doctrinal contexts. In a Carolingian miniature, for example, the tabernacle tent and veil are covered with crosses and the entire design is a cruciform structure; see Gaehde, 358-65.

60. Chaim Milikowsky, *Seder Olam: A Rabbinic Chronography*, 2 vols. (Ph.D. diss., Yale Univ., 1981), 4-5.

61. Chaim Milikowsky, "Seder Olam and Jewish Chronography in the Hellenistic and Roman Periods," *PAAJR* 52 (1985): 121 n. 10.

62. Yekutiel Neubauer, *Halakhah u-Midrash Halakhah* (Jerusalem, 1948), 1-3; but cf. I. H. Weiss, *Dor Dor ve-Dorshav* v.3 (Vilna, 1911), 225, who defends the appellation of *aggadah* to these two works.

63. This is the argument of Meir Bar-Ilan, "The Character and Origin of Megillat Ta'anit" (Hebrew), *Sinai* 98 (1986): 114-37.

64. B. Dinur, "An Investigation of the Historiographic Fragments in Talmudic Literature" (Hebrew), *Proceedings of the Fifth World Congress of Jewish Studies* (Jerusalem, 1972), 137-46.

65. See the criticism of Dinur by Y. H. Yerushalmi, *Zakhor: Jewish History and Jewish Memory* (Seattle, 1982), 20-21: ". . . The attempts by some modern scholars to find traces of historiography in the Talmudic period reflect a misplaced projection of their own concerns upon a reluctant past." See also 112 n. 27.

66. See, e.g., H. W. Attridge, "Josephus and His Works," *Compendia Rerum Iudicarum ad Novum Testamentum* v. 2, ed. M. E. Stone (Philadelphia, 1984), 185-232.

67. Arnaldo Momigliano, *On Pagans, Jews and Christians* (Middletown, 1987), 131.

68. Ibid. 11-16.

69. Jonathan Z. Smith, *Map Is Not Territory: Studies in the History of Religions* (Leiden, 1978), 70, defines the archival enterprise as a scribal science of *Listenwissenschaft*: "It depends upon catalogues and classification; it progresses by establishing precedents, by observing patterns, similarities and conjunctions, and by noting their repetitions." The scribes "developed

complex hermeneutic and exegetical techniques to bridge the gap between paradigm and particular instance, between past and present." In several respects Smith's phenomenological description aptly characterizes BMM.

70. Y. H. Yerushalmi, *Zakhor*, op.cit. 25, 34.

71. Jacob Neusner, *Judaism: The Evidence of the Mishnah* (Chicago/London, 1981), 77.

72. This is the view of Ben Zion Wacholder with respect to the Mishnah, which he describes as a work of "messianic historicism" that "makes no sense except under the supposition of Jerusalem's central shrine in all its glory": *Messianism and Mishnah* (Cincinnati, 1979), 39, 23 respectively.

73. B. M. Bokser, "Rabbinic Responses to Catastrophe: From Continuity to Discontinuity," *PAAJR* 50 (1983): 37-61 at 58-59. Cf. Yonah Fraenkel, *Iyyunim be-Olamo ha-Ruḥani shel Sippur ha-Aggadah* (Tel Aviv, 1981), 120-37; R. Kirschner, "Apocalyptic and Rabbinic Responses to the Destruction of 70," *HTR* 78 (1985): 27-46.

74. Saul Lieberman, "The Martyrs of Caesarea," *JQR* n.s. 36 (1945-46): 239-53, concludes that the rabbis opposed the restoration of the Temple by a Roman emperor. His evidence is scarce: reconstructing a passage from Eccl. R. 10:10, he derives the locution "disgrace of Julian" which he takes to refer to the shame Israel would suffer were the Temple to be rebuilt by pagan hands. Michael Avi-Yonah, *The Jews under Roman and Byzantine Rule* (repr. Jerusalem, 1984), 197-98, deduces a contrary (although no more certain) interpretation from such passages as y. Ma'aser Sheni 5:2, 56a: "R. Aḥa said: The Temple will be built before the reign of the house of David," and y. Ta'an. 2:1, 65a, where it is said that the absence of certain sacred objects from the Second Temple did not invalidate its sanctity, implying that a Third Temple with still fewer sancta might also be valid.

75. *Contra Iulianum* 1:16, 2:7 cited in R. L. Wilken, *John Chrysostom and the Jews* (Berkeley/Los Angeles/London, 1983), 145.

76. *Hist. eccl.* 10:38, ibid.

77. *Oratio* 5:3, 5:5, ibid.

78. *Adversus Iudaeos* 7:1, ibid.; see Wilken's discussion, 146-53.

79. *Res Gestae* 23, 1:2-3; *Greek and Latin Authors on Jews and Judaism* v. 2, ed. M. Stern (Jerusalem, 1980), no. 507, 607-9.

80. Although, on the other hand, the resuscitation of the tabernacle ideal might be perceived as a rejection of an imperial Temple in Jerusalem.

81. While BMM does not verge on the esoteric or mystical, it may be compared in this respect to Shi'ur Qomah, a Hekhalot tradition that records the dimensions of the godhead, seeking to reduce supernal forms to an imaginary scale. Unlike BMM, Shi'ur Qomah is not a sincere or scripturally based attempt to calculate and verify measurements; rather it conjures a vision of God beyond the descriptive limits of language or number. Shi'ur

Qomah is further distinguished from BMM by its theosophical content, apparently inspired by theurgic rather than exegetical concerns. See Martin S. Cohen, *The Shi'ur Qomah* (Lanham, 1983).

82. On the imperative of Torah study regardless of practical application, see David Weiss Halivni, *Midrash, Mishnah and Gemara* (Cambridge/London, 1986), 106-10. Cf. b. Sanh. 71a (and parallels) regarding the biblical punishment of the defiant son (Deut. 21:18-21): "There never has been such a defiant son and there never will be. Why then was the law written? Study it and receive reward."

Chapter 5

Manuscripts and Editions

The present critical edition of BMM is based on the investigation of all available MSS as catalogued by the Institute of Microfilmed Hebrew Manuscripts of the Jewish National and University Library in Jerusalem, supplemented by the entries in *Sefer ha-Meqorot*, a list of MSS and fragments compiled for use in the Historical Dictionary Project of Israel's Academy of the Hebrew Language.[1] In addition we utilize witnesses as yet uncatalogued: fragments published by Simon Hopkins in *A Miscellany of Literary Pieces from the Cambridge Genizah Collections*,[2] and another fragment from the Cambridge Genizah collection discovered by the present writer in July, 1984. In the absence of a colophon or other confirmation of date and provenance, our paleographical observations rely upon the expertise of Malachi Beit-Arie of the Hebrew Paleography Project, to whom we render grateful acknowledgment. All Genizah fragments held in the Cambridge University Library, as well as the two complete MSS of BMM held in Oxford University's Bodleian Library, have been transcribed from the original documents. Otherwise transcriptions have been taken from microfilm photocopies by permission of the various libraries in whose possession the MSS are found.[3]

Our edition of BMM includes two collateral sources, for which we rely on published editions: citations from Midrash ha-Gadol Genesis and Exodus (ed. Margulies), Leviticus (ed. Steinsaltz), and Numbers (ed. Rabinowitz);[4] and the quotation of BMM chapters 1-12 in Sefer ve-Hizhir (ed. Freimann),[5] part of which is supplemented by a MS fragment discovered since the edition was published.[6] Finally, all known published editions of BMM have been consulted, and the *editio princeps* (Venice 1602) has been incorporated into the critical apparatus.

The following two tables list the MSS (Table 1) and printed editions or collateral sources (Table 2) utilized in the present edition and the portions of BMM attested. MSS and editions are listed by their respective sigla in the Introduction (English letters) and apparatus (Hebrew letters). Portions of BMM are listed by chapter and line number (ch.:line).

Table 1

Sigla		MS	BMM (ch.:line)
A	א	Oxford Bodleian 370.11	1-14 (complete)
B	ב	Oxford Bodleian 151.3	1-14 (complete[7])
G[1]	ג[1]	Genizah Taylor-Schechter A45.24, K21.20, F11.32	1:4-11, 17-35; 5:2-20, 26-31; 6:1-14; 8:11-20; 9:1-3, 11-15; 10:1-11, 20-37; 11:1, 9-24; 12:1-3, 10-27; 13:1-2, 8-31, 34-37; 14:1-16
G[2]	ג[2]	Genizah Dropsie 83, Adler 2940, Taylor-Schechter K21.82	1:1-16; 3:12-16; 4:1-6, 14-26; 5:1-3; 6:1-27; 7:1-31; 8:1-20; 9:1-15; 10:1-3; 14:18-19
L	ל	Jewish Theological Seminary L899a.24	1-14 (complete)
M	מ	Munich Bayerische Staatsbibliothek Cod. Hebr. 95	1-14 (complete)
E	ע	Epstein 31.11 (now lost[8])	1:1-35; 2:2-3, 14-15; 3:1-13; 4:4-13, 19-26; 5:1-4, 15-29; 6:3-27; 7:1-4, 10-31; 8:1-9, 18-21; 9:3-7, 10-15; 10:1-14, 23-37; 11:5-24; 12:1-19; 13:2-6, 17-21, 32-37; 14:6-18

P	פ	Paris Bibliothèque Nationale 353.5	1:1-28, 31-35; 2:1-7, 10-13; 3:1-13; 4:1-26; 5:1-2, 18-22, 28-31; 6:1-27; 7:1-17, 22-31; 8:1-20; 9:1, 14-15; 10:25-35; 11:1-24; 12:1-19; 13:1-37; 14:1-16
R	ר	Parma Biblioteca Palatina 2198	14:2-20
V²	²ו	Sopron (Oedenburg) Hungary 2	1:1-4:24

Table 2

Sigla		Edition	BMM (ch.:line)
D	ר	Venice 1602 (*editio princeps*[9])	1-14 (complete)
H	ה	Midrash ha-Gadol: Genesis and Exodus (ed. Margulies), Leviticus (ed. Steinsaltz), Numbers (ed. Rabinowitz)	1:1-35; 2:3-6; 3:12-16; 6:3-16; 8:3-11; 10:6-13, 31-34; 11:4-12
H²	²ה	Midrash ha-Gadol: Leviticus (ed. Steinsaltz)	8:3-11
V	ו	Sefer ve-Hizhir (ed. Freimann)	1-12

We now proceed to descriptions of the individual witnesses according to the order of Tables 1 and 2. After that we discuss the MSS and editions that we exclude from the critical apparatus and our reasons for doing so. All references to BMM (ch.:line) in the ensuing discussion refer to variants cited at that location in the apparatus.

MSS

MS A א *Oxford Bodleian 370.11*
MS A is described by A. Neubauer in the *Catalogue of the Hebrew Manuscripts in the Bodleian Library*.[10] It consists of 231 folios (vel-

lum) of which BMM occupies ff. 203-6. There is no colophon.
Neubauer characterizes the script as German rabbinic. Beit-Arie
agrees that the hand is Ashkenazic and assigns it a date of approxi-
mately the thirteenth century.

MS A is divided into fourteen chapters, all but the first signified
by פרק and number. On the frontispiece a list of contents appears in
the following order, two corrected by another hand in the margin:
(1) מסכת קינים (crossed out); (2) תמיד; (3) אבות (crossed out; in margin
= מידות); (4) מעילה; (5) מעילה (crossed out; in margin = ומעילה); (6)
עירכין (7); כלה (8); שמחות (9); ופרוש משקלים (10); ומסכת שקלים (11);
הלכות עבודה וחיי עולם (12); מ"ס סופרים (13); ברייתא מלאכת המשכן. The
last page (206b) concludes in a larger hand, סליקא ברייתא דמלאכת
המשכן. The MS preserves numerous unique readings, which may be
compared to the other witnesses by consulting the apparatus at the
text location noted, e.g.: מלמטן עובײן, BMM 1:19-20; שהיה אומר, 2:4;
אורך, 2:15; לגג, 3:8; היו למעלה, 3:14; הוי אומר, 5:3; ללמד, 5:17; יוסה, 5:27;
שלשה, 6:11; הארון, 7:25; ושני טפחים, 8:5; החיצון, 11:21.

The scribe of MS A is a careful copyist consistent in orthography
(with the exception of *matres lectionis*), abbreviations and
supralinear punctuation. To justify the left margin, he will sometimes abbreviate a word or dilate a letter, but his usual practice is
to fill in leftover space with as many letters of the word as will fit
and then write the complete word at the beginning of the next line.[11]
Copying mistakes are marked by a horizontal line above defective
words or letters; one correction appears in the margin, possibly
added by a later hand. Despite the evident quality of the transcription, however, there are some scribal errors, including a few
dittographies (e.g. 4:22; at the beginning of a new page, 11:17; at the
beginning of a new line, 13:4), haplographies (e.g. 10:21), misquota-
tions of Scripture (e.g. 7:19 vs. both 1 Ki. 8:8 and 2 Chr. 5:9) and a
homoeoteleuton (12:11-12).

MS A has a propensity for brevity and compression, e.g. לוחות (MS
A) vs. לוחות הברית (other MSS), 6:26; שהכניסו הכהנים vs. שהכניסו הארון;
אחד אילך ואחד vs. אילך ואילך, 7:20; כנפי הכרובים vs. כנפיהם, 7:13; את הארון,
כמין קורה vs. כקורה, 11:2; ועשית מזבח מקטר הקטרת vs. מזבח, 10:17; אילך
13:19. The MS usually deletes the accusative particle את (e.g. מעמיד
הקרשים, 1:9-10; נותן הקונטסין, 5:6) but sometimes includes it (e.g. 9:7,
14:7).[12] The scribe is more prone to defective than *plene* spelling,
(e.g. רקם, חשב, נחשת, שמנה) but occasionally includes *matres lectionis*
(e.g. הפרוכת, וגובהו) and in at least one case gives both spellings on
the same line (השלחן...השולחן, 4:25).

MS A constitutes the *codex optimus* (i.e. base text) of the present edition. The reasons for this choice are discussed in chapter 6 of the Introduction.

MS B ב *Oxford Bodleian 151.3*

MS B is also described by Neubauer in the Bodleian catalogue.[13] It consists of 431 folios (vellum); the lower margins of many leaves are damaged and some letters and words are illegible. BMM occupies ff. 155-59. Neubauer incorrectly lists the first to the middle of the fourth chapters wanting; this text is found in full on f. 156 a-b. Neubauer's error is explained by the disorder of the folios: f. 155 = chapters 4-7 (our siglum B[1] ב[1]); f. 156 = chapters 1- 4; f. 157 = a second copy of chapters 4-7 (our siglum B[2] ב[2]); f. 158 = chapters 7-11; f. 159 = chapters 11-14. The colophon reports that the MS was copied by Yeḥozedeq b. Elḥanan for R. Aaron b. Eliezer; 151.1 (= Pesiqta de-R. Kahana) was finished in 1291. Neubauer describes the script as Greek rabbinic.

According to Beit-Arie, however, MS B is not an original part of the codex. He identifies the script as fourteenth century Ashkenazic and discerns three different hands: (1) f. 155; (2) f. 156; (3) ff. 157-158. F. 157b occupies only three-fourths of the page, the scribe halting in the middle of a line. Since ff. 157a and 155a begin with the same word, and ff. 157b and 155b end at the same place, it seems obvious that 157 (B[2]) copied 155 (B[1]). However, B[2] sometimes departs from B[1] in ways that cannot be explained by copying errors, e.g. at BMM 6:18-19 where B[2] attests a passage absent from B[1]. This is certain evidence of contamination, since the scribe of B[2] had more than one exemplar before him.

MS B is divided into thirteen chapters, combining BMM chapters 4-5. The end of each chapter is indicated by סליק פרק or סליק פרקין, followed by פרק and number for the ensuing chapter, all in enlarged script. There are several notations and corrections in the margins and an extensive interpolation at chapter 8 (=BMM ch. 9). A marginal correction of a dropped line on f. 159a is written in a later cursive hand.

None of the three hands who contributed to MS B is painstaking or particularly consistent. The second of the three (f. 156) is prone to frequent mistakes (e.g. והיה וחברן [MS B] vs. והיה מחברן, BMM 2:9; היה כופל vs. היה סורח, 3:11; וכסה vs. מכסה, 3:13; אומת vs. אמות, 4:1) although many errors are committed by the other hands as well (e.g. לאהל vs. למשכן, 5:12; משה vs. בצלאל, 10:1). Words are often shortened

even when they do not occur at the end of a line (e.g. הבתי vs. הבתים,
12:9). There are dittographies (e.g. at 2:7) and haplographies (e.g. at
3:15). In one case a question mark appears by a doubtful reading
(? קרפין = קרפף, 5:30).

Despite its sometimes inferior transcription, MS B attests a number of variants and interpolations that are not scribal errors but evidence of a unique source, e.g. at 2:7, 10:17, 10:31, and 13:18.[14] There
is also virtually certain evidence that one of the exemplars of MS B
was MS A: at BMM 1:32, MS B crosses out three misplaced words,
כיצד היה עושה, which appear in MS A (f. 203a) in the same horizontal
position on the line immediately below. The most obvious explanation is an eye-skip by the scribe, who then noted his error and corrected it. Either the scribe had MS A before him or a MS identical
to it.

MS G¹ ᵍ Genizah Taylor-Schechter A45.24, K21.20, F11.32
These fragments from the Cairo Genizah are described in part by
Simon Hopkins in *A Miscellany of Literary Pieces from the Cambridge Genizah Collections*, a catalogue of texts in the Taylor-
Schechter (T-S) collection (Old Series, Box A45).[15] Although originally sorted in different boxes, these three fragments are among
thirteen containing portions of folios belonging to the same MS. The
fragments of T-S A45.24 are vellum, severely mutilated; the size of
the most intact leaf measures 21.8 cm. with a written space of 18 x
15 cm. BMM occupies the following folios of A45.24: 6(1) recto and
verso; 6(2) recto and verso; 7 and 8 recto and verso; 9 recto.

BMM also appears on the recto and verso of T-S K21.20 and F11.32.
Although Hopkins lists these fragments as part of the same MS, he does
not describe them, and they are not photographed in the catalogue. Our
own measurement of K21.20 = 13.5 x 7.5 cm. Sixteen lines are preserved on the recto and eighteen on the verso, which is stained in the
lower left corner. The top margin is visible on both sides. Our measurement of F11.32 = 16.5 x 9.5 cm. with a written space of 14 x 7 cm.
The text is well-preserved, twenty-one lines recto and verso. The lower
right quadrant on the recto is stained.

The three fragments are written in a square Oriental hand. Beit-
Arie fixes their date in the tenth century. This estimate is based not
only on paleographical criteria, which are still tentative,[16] but on
codicological data. Beit-Arie's Hebrew Paleography Project has
shown that apart from a few codices, mostly of biblical texts, all

existing Oriental MSS copied after 1005 are written on paper.[17] In the present case, the combination of an Oriental hand and a vellum MS indicates a *terminus ante quem* of the tenth century, making this set of fragments (MS G[1]) the oldest extant witness to the text of BMM.

Because of its signal importance to the history of our text, MS G[1] (=T-S A45.24 ff. 6-9, K21.20, F11.32) is transcribed in full in Appendix A. Although the scope of the fragments furnishes a limited sample of scribal characteristics and variants, it is evident that MS G[1] attests a superior text. Paleography and orthography are meticulous; abbreviations are confined to numbers; with a few exceptions at the end of a line (e.g. A45.24, 6(2) verso, line 8), only frequent terms like 'שנ, 'אומ, 'וג, and 'ר, are shortened. There is even an isolated Tiberian vowel point (A45.24, 7 verso, line 1). The scribe occasionally forms ligatures combining 'א and 'ל.[18] Number transcription is not always consistent; for instance, at A45.24, 6(2) recto, some numbers are written as words (lines 7, 9, 10) and others as letters (lines 8, 11). In another instance, the scribe uses two different abbreviations for the number five on the same line (K21.20 recto, line 8). An unusual characteristic, to our knowledge, is the scribe's use of ה"י instead of ט"ו for the number fifteen (e.g. A45.24, 7 verso, line 10).

Chapters are concluded with פירקא סליק or סליק spaced from the body of text. A feature unique to MS G[1] is a title heading for some (apparently not all) chapters, spaced from the text and marked with dots over each letter. There are three examples preserved in the fragments: הַמְּנוֹרָה (K21.20 verso, line 7) beginning BMM chapter 10; כִּיּוֹר (F11.32 verso, line 19) beginning chapter 12; and שִׁימוּשׁ הַמִּשְׁכָּן (A45.24, 6(2) recto, line 6) between 1:7 and 1:8 of the present edition, indicating that in MS G[1], BMM 1:1-7 constituted a prologue set off from the first chapter.

MS G[2] ג Genizah Dropsie 83, Adler 2940, Taylor-Schechter K21.82
Dropsie 83 is included by B. Halper in the Dropsie College Library's *Descriptive Catalogue of Genizah Fragments in Philadelphia*[19] and was published by Louis Ginzberg in 1928 together with a brief introduction and annotation.[20] It consists of two paper leaves measuring 27.9 x 19 cm. Halper describes them as badly damaged, but from the photographs it appears that they are in far better condition than the other two fragments of MS G[2]. There are twenty-seven lines to a page written in semi-cursive script.

Adler 2940, according to our examination of photographs, is a paper leaf with twenty-five lines visible on the recto (2940.1) and twenty-three lines on the verso, which does not fill the page since it marks the end of the last chapter. Adler 2940.1 measures 21.5 x 18.2 cm. with a visible written space of 17 x 12 cm. The left, right, and bottom margins are visible; the paper is holed and badly rubbed with the last five lines at the right margin wanting. Adler 2940.2 = 21.5 x 17.5 cm. with a written space of 16 x 12 cm. All four margins are visible.

To our knowledge, this study marks the first published identification of Taylor-Schechter K21.82 as a fragment of BMM.[21] It consists of one paper leaf, 20 x 19.5 cm. The left, right, and bottom margins are visible leaving a written space of 14 x 13 cm. on both recto and verso. Nineteen lines are visible on each side. The text is horizontally intact except for the five uppermost lines; the top quarter of the leaf is missing. The upper half is holed and badly rubbed on the verso, some of which is scarcely legible.

Although they are now scattered in three different collections, these fragments appear to belong to one MS. In this case our identification is not as certain as it is for MS G[1], since except for the original T-S K21.82 fragment, we had to rely on photographs of varying magnification. Still, Beit-Arie's inspection of photocopies corroborated with reasonable certainty that the fragments match. If not, they are undoubtedly of similar origin. Beit-Arie classifies the hand of all three fragments as Oriental, dating from the twelfth century.

Except for Dropsie 83, already published by Ginzberg, MS G[2] (= Adler 2940 (.1) (.2), T-S K21.82) is fully transcribed in Appendix A. While corresponding to MS G[1] in many respects (discussed in ch. 6), MS G[2] preserves unique readings, e.g. at BMM 3:11, 4:2, and a long passage concluding BMM (Appendix A, Adler 2940.2, lines 4-19).[22] The scribe designates chapter conclusions by סליק פרקא (K21.82 recto) or סליק פירקא (K21.82 verso) in enlarged script spaced from the text or centered on an open line. Letters with horizontal bars are frequently dilated at the end of lines to justify the left margin. A consistent characteristic of MS G[2] is the assimilation of the genitive של to the following noun. There are some errors in the fragments, e.g. בעצצע (MS G[2]) vs. כאצבע, 1:19; a haplography, 9:14; a homoeoteleuton, 10:3-4. In one case the scribe marks his own mistake with a supralinear correction. Defective spelling predominates over *plene*, but both are attested (e.g. הפרכת, K21.82, recto, line 14; שהפרוכת, K21.82 verso, line 2).

MS L ל Jewish Theological Seminary L899a.24
According to the colophon of the codex, MS L was written by a scribe named Solomon on 6 Tevet 5436 or 5437 (1675 or 1676) from a MS copied or owned by Samuel b. Ḥayyim Vital (1598 – ca. 1678), the noted talmudic authority and kabbalist of Damascus and later of Cairo.[23] BMM occupies ff. 101-3. The title משנת המשכן appears at the upper right margin of f. 101 in a larger hand and centered at the top margin of each page in the same size as the text. Likewise the beginning of each chapter is marked by פרק and number in a larger hand, while the end of each chapter has סליק פירקא in the same size as the text. The script is Oriental cursive in a very cramped hand in which individual letters are often indistinct. There are forty-five to forty-eight lines per page, with ample left and right margins. At the foot of the left margin of each page is a catchword (viz. the first word of the next page).[24]

Notwithstanding its relatively late date, MS L represents a distinct branch of the textual history of BMM. It includes unique scriptural citations (e.g. at BMM 3:2, 14:16-17), attributions (e.g. 10:33), sequences (e.g. 13:15-17), glosses (e.g. 10:4), and pericopae (e.g. 14:12-17). There is also some evidence of influence from the Babylonian Talmud (e.g. 11:8-9).[25] While the difficulty of deciphering the script makes orthographic characterizations hazardous, the scribe's errors are quite rare (e.g. עשרים [MS L] vs. עשר, 5:23; קרקף vs.קרפף, 5:30). However, MS L does contain several dittographies (e.g. 7:14, 10:32) and haplographies (e.g. 3:2-5, 4:9-10), and the scribe is particularly prone to homoeoteleuton (2:5-6; 5:19-20; 7:17-18; 8:5-8).

MS M מ Munich Bayerische Staatsbibliothek Cod. Hebr. 95
MS M was first described by Raphael Rabbinovicz in 1867, catalogued by Moritz Steinschneider in 1895, and published in facsimile by H. L. Strack in 1912.[26] It is the oldest surviving MS containing the entire Babylonian Talmud. Although the last leaf is numbered 576, Rabbinovicz counts a total of 570 leaves, indicating an error in foliation. The MS includes two colophons, both naming the scribe, Solomon b. Samson, and giving the date in 1342. MS M is written on parchment in a semi-cursive Ashkenazic hand, but there is some textual and codicological evidence of French provenance.[27]

BMM appears at the very beginning of the MS (ff. 1a-2b) without a title. The first word, אומר, is a rubrication; apparently the rubricator omitted the preceding ר׳. Although all fourteen chapters of BMM are included in MS M, chapter numeration does not commence until our chapter 2, resulting in a total of thirteen chapters. Each chapter heading, פרק and number, is spaced from the text in a larger hand. There are two columns per page and eighty lines per column. The margins are quite exact, with some letter dilatation but a greater tendency toward abbreviation at the end of the line. Several corrections and interpolations appear in the left, right, and center margins, some in the same hand and some in another.

Unfortunately the scribe was a careless copyist. There are numerous omissions of sentences (e.g. at BMM 1:6; 4:23-24; 6:21-24; 13:31-32), phrases (e.g. 1:17-18; 4:10-11; 7:16-17; 10:15), and words (e.g. 1:18; 7:30; 10:13; 10:15). At BMM 6:14, MS M copies 6:7-14 a second time. The repetition does not appear to be an instance of homoeoteleuton; in any case the scribe was unaware of the meaning, since his repetition produces an incomprehensible text (cf. ככר וככר [MS M] vs. קרש וקרש, 1:24). MS M also attests dittographies (e.g. 11:15) and many spelling errors (e.g. רביעי vs. רביע, 4:11; אמנת vs. אמרת, 7:10; וחפוי vs. וחיפו, 7:20). Occasionally the scribe notes his own errors with supralinear corrections of letters or words in a smaller hand. His scriptural citations are usually shortened, sometimes to one word (e.g. 1:11).

Nonetheless, owing to its complete copy of BMM, certain date, frequent correspondence to G^2 (see ch. 6), and multitude of readings unique among the MSS, MS M is an important, if uneven, witness to our text.

MS E ‎ע‎ *Epstein 31.11 (now lost)*

MS E was first discussed by A. Marx in 1901 and catalogued by A. Z. Schwarz in 1931 with a voluminous description.[28] According to its colophon, it was written at Salonika in 1509. For his edition of BMM published in 1908, Meir Friedmann (Ish Shalom) relied upon transcriptions from MS E by his student A. Aptowitzer,[29] and in his commentary he frequently cites them. In 1926, MS E came into the possession of the Vienna Jewish Community Library. During World War II the library was looted, and although other MSS in the collection have since been located, MS E has disappeared.[30] The only surviving record of its text of BMM (ff. 216-23) are the quotations in Friedmann's commentary, which have been culled and incorporated into the apparatus of the present edition. Aside from the fact that we must rely on a secondary source for MS E, the citations also pose the difficulty of extracting the transcription of the MS from Friedmann's quotation and occasional gloss, summary, or ellipsis. For instance, at BMM 5:22, MS A (our base text) cites Ex. 38:15, ולכתף השנית מזה ומזה לשער החצר וגו'. MS E, according to Friedmann's citation, has ולכתף השנית מזה ומזה לשער החצר וכו'. From the וכו' we cannot tell whether MS E abridges Ex. 38:15 (as MS A does) or Friedmann abridges MS E. When he wishes to indicate that MS E is in error, Friedmann adds his comments or emendations in brackets. However, few obvious scribal errors appear in the quotations; thus we are unable to determine whether the original scribe, Aptowitzer, or Friedmann deserves the credit for the superior quality of the text.

Even with these limitations in mind, the value of this MS is evident. While often corresponding to MS L (see ch. 6), MS E attests several unique attributions (e.g. at BMM 6:18, 7:22), scriptural citations (e.g. 13:34), pericopae (e.g. 8:20, 10:31, 14:10), and many distinctive variants (e.g. 6:15, 7:29, 7:31, 13:2-3; also the computation term הוצא vs. צא in other MSS, e.g. 5:21, 6:11-12, 6:13).

MS P פ *Paris Bibliothèque Nationale 353.5*

MS Paris 353 was first catalogued by H. Zotenberg in 1866 and is quoted by I. M. Freimann in his commentary to Sefer ve-Hizhir (part 1, 1873).[31] The MS is written on paper. Zotenberg assigns its date to the sixteenth century; Beit-Arie estimates the fifteenth, describing the script as Sephardic cursive with some Byzantine and Italian elements. BMM, the last work included in the MS, is found on ff. 100b-112a. There are twenty-five lines of text per page.

The chapter divisions of MS P differ from all other witnesses to the text of BMM. After an introductory paragraph, there are twenty-seven chapters, none corresponding to other MSS or editions. The longest chapter (1) occupies sixty lines of text; the shortest (12) occupies three lines. Each chapter concludes with סליק פרק and number; all but the first begin with פרק and number. Both notations are spaced from the body of text in script of the same size. There are a few supralinear insertions and several corrections in the left margin written in the same hand. The scribe's favored methods of justifying the left margin are to dilate final letters or to elevate them above the line. Words and especially numbers are often abbreviated. On the last folio, two titles are mentioned, the first comprehending the twenty-seven chapters of MS P, the second apparently referring to

MS P's quotation of b. Men. 94a-95b (discussed below): סליקא לה
ברייתא דמשכנא ופרקהא כ"ז חזק ונתחזק נשלם פירקא דמשכנא דמנחות הצור
ינהלינו על מי מנוחות.

Our study of MS P concludes that it is a separate recension
entirely, which includes much of the attested BMM text but adds,
drops, glosses and transforms at will. Interpolations are so frequent
and extensive that they could not be accommodated in our critical
apparatus; instead they are collected in Appendix B where they are
listed according to their point of departure from the text of BMM
(by chapter, line, and word). Where MS P follows or parallels the
text of BMM, or where its additions are not too unwieldy, it is incorporated into the apparatus.

The first paragraph of MS P consists of M. Men. 11:1 and b. Men.
94a (from שתי הלחם to איתמר לחם הפנים). The second paragraph commences the first chapter (although no chapter heading is given),
beginning with תניא and proceeding with BMM 1:1. At the bottom
of f. 105b, corresponding to BMM 8:11 (see Appendix B), the scribe
indents and centers the following line: מיכאן ואילך סופה דבריית דלעיל
עד סוף פרק ט, after which he returns to b. Men. 94a from the exact
place he left off in the first paragraph of the MS. Ff. 106a-107a repli-
cates b. Men. 94b-95b. The MS then returns to the text of BMM
(8:15); for some reason, the bottom half of this page (f. 107b) is
blank.

There are other lengthy interpolations in MS P, including one at
the beginning of BMM chapter 12 (see Appendix B) from which we
have identified passages from or parallels to sources as diverse as
Pesiqta de-R. Kahana, b. RH, b. Sot., Rashi, Tanḥuma, and Ex. R.[32]
An interpolation at BMM 13:21 (see Appendix B) appears to draw
on Targum Yerushalmi;[33] another at 14:14 (see Appendix B) bor-
rows from Midrash Tehillim and Cant. R.[34]

Apart from its propensity for anthology, MS P tends to combine,
paraphrase, or misquote verses of Scripture, e.g. at 11:13 (see
Appendix B), a conflation of Lev. 4:25, 30, 34; or at 13:34 (see apparatus), a misquotation of Num. 9:18. The scribe also commits errors
(e.g. ה' [MS P] vs. ארבע, 1:10; ירמיהו ויאשיהו vs. יאשיהו, 7:25), drops
words (e.g. at 1:9, 1:23), and omits biblical citations (e.g. 6:2) or adds
them (e.g. 14:14). On the other hand, MS P corroborates some readings from the oldest and most reliable witnesses to the text of BMM,
including MSS A, G[1], and G[2]. Despite the obvious contamination
of MS P, among the scribe's exemplars was at least one MS that

attests to our text. We have sought to recover it by selective citation in the critical apparatus, preserving glosses and alternate readings but removing the larger anomalies to Appendix B.

MS R ר *Parma Biblioteca Palatina 2198*

MS R was first catalogued by I. B. DeRossi in 1803, where it is entered as Cod. 540.[35] DeRossi, whose descriptions are not exhaustive, did not identify BMM, listing only five entries. BMM's correct DeRossi number is 540.6. The colophon of MS R does not name the scribe but identifies the city of Ravenna and the date of 1494. The hand is cursive Italian. Only the last page of BMM is preserved consisting of seventeen lines, the first thirteen of which contain BMM 14:2-20. The title בריי' דמלאכת המשכן is mentioned at the end. One word, שכינה, appears in the left margin in the same hand to correct a marked omission on the line.

Although the BMM fragment of MS R is too brief to draw many conclusions about the text it preserves, some scribal characteristics emerge. The scribe tends to shorten words, sometimes to the point of obscurity (e.g. ואח' = ואחד; ביו' = ביום). Our fragment attests a defective spelling, סכה, where all other witnesses have סוכה. There are also several errors, even within our small sample: צרך (MS R) vs. נצרך, 14:9; מדבר vs. מדברת, 14:16; הכפרת vs. הפרכת, 14:16-17. MS R contains no significant unique readings but corroborates the text of the majority of MSS.

MS V² 2ו *Sopron (Oedenburg) Hungary 2*

MS V² is one leaf removed from a non-Hebrew book binding inscribed with the date 1543. It was first published by Miksa Pollak (1868-1944), who in his history of Oedenburg Jewry (published in Hungarian in 1896)[36] mistakenly identified it as a fragment of the Mekhilta. In an article published in 1958,[37] A.N.Z. Roth identified MS V² as a fragment of Sefer ve-Hizhir, part of which contains Sefer ve-Hizhir's quotation of BMM 1:1-4:24.[38] The MS is written in square Ashkenazic characters. There are thirty-five lines on the recto; the citation of BMM begins in the middle of line 16. Lines 16-19 are damaged at the left margin, but otherwise the text is well-preserved. On the verso, however, the first eighteen lines are damaged at the right margin, where there is a notation, only partly legible. There are thirty-eight lines on the verso; the last three, separated by an empty line, do not parallel Sefer ve-Hizhir but do bear some resemblance to MSS G² and M.³⁹ Otherwise, MS V² hews very closely to Freimann's text of Sefer ve-Hizhir (=Ed. V). There are some differences in spelling (e.g. יודה [MS V²] vs. יהודה [Ed. V], BMM 3:14), an occasional variant (e.g. לולאות vs. יריעות, 2:7), a tendency toward fuller scriptural citations (e.g. 1:17, 1:23), and relatively few errors (e.g. לגבהו vs. לרחבו, 3:9).

Editions

Ed. D ד Venice 1602 (editio princeps)
Ed. D was published (together with Mishpete Shevuot, the Hebrew translation of an Arabic work attributed to Hai Gaon) from a MS belonging to Ezra b. Isaac Fano of Mantua and Venice,⁴⁰ a collector and publisher of Hebrew MSS. Technically it is not the *editio princeps*; the first printed edition was published in Safed in 1587 (together with Baraita de-R. Eliezer and other works) by Menaḥem b. Judah DeLonzano, but only the title page of this edition survives.⁴¹ We may properly refer to ed. D as the *editio princeps*, since it is the basis for virtually all subsequent printed editions.

Fano apparently annotated the MS for ed. D, since several references to other rabbinic works appear in parentheses, e.g. b. Shab. (at BMM 2:11), b. Men. and Arukh (10:22), and b. Er. (12:6-7). It is also evident that he had before him several MSS of BMM, since occasionally he includes alternative readings in parentheses (e.g. at 1:14-15, 6:11, 10:31), some of which (e.g. 7:20, 14:16-19) are unattested in any extant source. Of our MSS, ed. D relies to the greatest extent on MS M, although there are many departures from it (e.g. at 2:8, 6:12). Like MS M, ed. D is replete with errors, including many not inherited from MS M, e.g. בין (ed. D) vs. מן, 5:14; עשרים vs. חמשים, 5:24; כחצר vs. בחצר, 5:30; פרכות vs. פרוכות, 7:30; יוסי vs. יוחי, 14:8-9; בטפיח vs. בטפיס, 14:11; עזאי vs. יוחאי, 14:17.

Despite its defects, ed. D is a crucial witness to the text history of BMM. Owing to its multiple sources as well as its influence on subsequent editions, it is included in our critical apparatus.

Ed. H ה Midrash ha-Gadol: Genesis and Exodus (ed. Margulies), Leviticus (ed. Steinzaltz), Numbers (ed. Rabinowitz)
Ed. H² ה² Midrash ha-Gadol: Leviticus (ed. Steinzaltz)
In chapter 3 of the Introduction, we discuss the problem of identifying citations of BMM in Midrash ha-Gadol. Our major criterion for verifying a quotation is a recognizable corroboration by at least one

other witness to the text. Quotations have been located by checking every citation of the Pentateuch in BMM against equivalent citations in Midrash ha-Gadol. Such a method is by no means exhaustive, but it yields a sufficient number of confirmed quotations to suggest the line of descent to which they belong. For the text of Midrash ha-Gadol, we rely upon the editions of Mordecai Margulies (Genesis and Exodus), Adin Steinsaltz (Leviticus), and Zevi Meir Rabinowitz (Numbers), each of which is based on various MSS described in their respective introductions.[42]

Following is a list of each of the quotations of BMM (ch.:line) according to its location in Midrash ha-Gadol:

BMM (ch.:line)	*Midrash ha-Gadol*
1:1-35	Ex. 25:2, 26:16-18, 40:18
2:3-6	Ex. 26:1
3:12-16	Num. 3:25
6:3-16	Ex. 25:10
10:6-13	Gen. 4:7
10:31-34	Lev. 24:4
11:4-12	Num. 3:26

In one instance, Midrash ha-Gadol contains two different quotations of the same BMM passage, requiring a separate siglum:

8:3-11	Ex. 40:23 (=H ה)
	Lev. 24:7 (=H² ²ה)

Ed. V ו Sefer ve-Hizhir (ed. Freimann)

Ed. V was published by I. M. Freimann in two volumes (1873-80)[43] from MS Munich Bayerische Staatsbibliothek Cod. Hebr. 205. This MS is described by Steinschneider as one of the oldest in the Munich collection, although he hazards no date.[44] It is written on parchment and consists of two hundred folios in Ashkenazic script. Sefer ve-Hizhir's quotation of BMM chapters 1-12 appears in the section introduced by Ex. 27:20. Ed. V annotates the text with scriptural references, ellipses to indicate lacunae, and corrections or expansions enclosed in brackets. Readings judged by the editor to be corrupt are enclosed in parentheses. Footnotes refer the reader to the accompanying commentary, in which the editor includes variant readings from MS P.[45]

In some places, ed. V fails to distinguish between MS transcription and editorial emendation. For instance, the editor inserts one correction[46] from which the closing bracket has been deleted, so that there is no way of telling where the emendation ends and the MS resumes. Aside from such errors, there are obvious mistakes in ed. V (e.g. spelling errors at BMM 1:35 and 7:20; a misquotation of Scripture at 7:18; a haplography at 8:8) that are not marked by the editor, leaving it unclear whether they are scribal errors or transcription errors. For the purposes of our critical apparatus, we have recorded ed. V variants according to the original MS readings, including those marked as errors by the editor, and have ignored his bracketed emendations.

The text of BMM in ed. V exhibits a strong affinity to MS B but shares some readings with other MSS against MS B and also attests unique variants, e.g. at 2:7, 8:17, 11:20, 12:8. The interrelationships between ed. V and the various MSS are discussed in chapter 6.

MSS Excluded from the Critical Apparatus

The present edition includes all but four known MSS of BMM, three of which are extant. MS Oxford Bodleian 371.11, MS Oxford Bodleian 372:11, and MS British Library OR 10032 (Gaster 698) are late copies of MS A and therefore of no text-critical value. The fourth, MS Epstein 72, has been lost since the Nazi era.

MS Oxford Bodleian 371.11
This copy of MS A is catalogued by Neubauer.[47] It consists of 194 folios (paper) written in German cursive script. BMM is found on folios 185-87. We consulted this MS as a check against our transcription of MS A and found in the first few lines numerous mistakes, e.g.: ר' יהודה (MS Oxford 371.11) vs. 'ר, BMM 1:1; נעשית vs. ונעשה, 1:6; המשכן vs. משכן, 1:6; יוסי vs. יוסה, 1:8; היו vs. היה, 1:10; ועושים vs. ועושין, 1:13; נחמיא vs. נחמיה, 1:18; במעריב vs. במערב, 1:23, etc. Obviously MS Oxford 371.11 is an inferior transcription of MS A.

MS Oxford Bodleian 372.11
Also catalogued by Neubauer,[48] this copy of MS A consists of 257 folios (paper) written in German cursive characters. BMM appears on folios 219-23. This MS too is plagued by copying errors, e.g. חלה (MS Oxford 372.11) vs. תודה, BMM 1:2; יהא vs. יהו, 1:16; ולמעלן vs. ומלמעלן, 1:19; תשעה vs. שמנה, 1:30; ומקליה vs. ומקלו, 4:4; כהונה vs. כהנים, 4:4, etc.

MS British Library OR 10032 (Gaster 698)

This MS was written by Menashe Grossberg (ca. 1860-?), a Russian rabbinical scholar and copyist of Hebrew MSS. In the first decade of the twentieth century, he settled in London, assisting scholars in Europe by transcribing MSS at the British Museum and the Bodleian Library,[49] where he copied MS A. Grossberg's handwritten title for the MS indicates that he not only copied the MS but sought to compare its readings to MS B. He also added his own notes and comments.

MS Epstein 72

Like MS E (Epstein 31.11), this MS disappeared after the German occupation of Vienna in World War II (see above, p. 104). While quotations of MS E survive in Friedmann's edition of BMM, no record remains of MS Epstein 72 except for the published description by A. Z. Schwarz in his catalogue of the Vienna collection.[50] The MS consisted of seven folios (paper) written in Italian rabbinic script and divided into sixteen chapters, with the title ברייתא ממלאכת המשכן on the last folio.

Both the Institute for Microfilmed Hebrew Manuscripts and *Sefer ha-Meqorot* list one more MS of BMM, Jewish Theological Seminary Rab. 98 (Adler 875), which is numbered but not described in the catalogue of the Adler collection.[51] According to an unpublished catalogue entry written by Judah Brumer and provided for us by the Library of the Jewish Theological Seminary, this MS includes some material from the printed editions of BMM but does not coincide with any of them. It consists of twenty-two leaves (paper) in a cursive Italian hand dated by Brumer to the seventeenth century.

However, our own investigation of a photocopy of this MS revealed that the title listed in the Adler catalogue and assigned by Brumer, מדרש מלאכת המשכן, does not appear in the MS. Nor could we find evidence of textual correspondence to associate this MS with BMM. There are no chapter divisions that approximate those in other witnesses; rather the MS includes the following sequence of headings: 1) הארון (2; המנורה (3; ומלקחיה (4; ומחתותיה (5; מסך (6; הכפורת (7; מזבח העולה (8; החצר (9; השולחן (10; מזבח הקטרת (11; הכיור. Comparison of the text of this MS to BMM shows that it is a separate, if affinitive or even derivative, composition. While we are not able positively to identify it, we conclude that it is not a copy or recognizable version of BMM.

Printed Editions Excluded from the Critical Apparatus

Since the appearance of the *editio princeps* (Venice 1602 = ed. D), published editions of BMM include: Hamburg 1782 (appended to Mishpete Shevuot); Offenbach 1802 (ed. Scheuer); Vilna 1802 (appended to Aggadat Bereshit); A. Jellinek, *Bet ha-Midrash* 3:144-54, Leipzig 1855; Warsaw 1876 (with Aggadat Bereshit); Konitz 1899 (ed. Flesch); Vienna 1908 (ed. Friedmann); J. D. Eisenstein, *Oẓar Midrashim* 2:298-304, New York 1915; Bene Berak 1961 (ed. Kanivsky); Jerusalem 1965 (with Ma'aseh Ḥoshev, ed. Shefer). From a text- critical perspective, most of these editions need not detain us: the Hamburg and Leipzig (Jellinek) editions follow ed. D; the New York (Eisenstein) and Bene Berak editions reproduce Friedmann's text (Vienna 1908); the Vilna, Warsaw, and (with some unexplained exceptions[52]) Jerusalem editions follow Offenbach.[53]

The Konitz edition may also be dismissed, since it is based on MS M, which we have included in the apparatus. However, because Friedmann relied upon it for his readings from MS M, it exercised a considerable influence on his and subsequent editions of BMM. This is unfortunate, for the transcription of MS M by H. Flesch is riddled with errors. In order to correct these corruptions of the MS tradition, we have listed the more flagrant mistakes found in Flesch's published text.[54]

Nor is the Friedmann edition (Vienna, 1908) of text-critical value to us, since except for MS E we have used the same MSS that Friedmann did (MSS A, B, M, P) plus many that were not available to him (MSS G[1], G[2], L, R, V[2], H, H[2]). What is more, Friedmann relied upon secondary transcriptions;[55] in the case of MS M (copied by Flesch) and MS P (quoted intermittently by I. M. Freimann), the evidence available to him was deficient.

Another defect of Friedmann's text of BMM is its eclecticism. As we observe in chapter 6, the pioneering critical editions of rabbinic literature relied on editorial preferences that were rarely explained or even identified. In his introduction to BMM, Friedmann mentions three MS copies at his disposal (MSS A, B, E), and in the course of his commentary he cites quotations of two others (MSS M, P). But nowhere does he explain his criteria for preferring one witness to another or one reading to another. Since the text of MS E is lost except for Friedmann's quotations, we cannot determine to what extent he was guided by it in his choice of sequence, structure, or

wording. Compared to all existing MSS, however, Friedmann's text
is in effect a conflation or a new recension. He often appears to prefer the sequence of the Offenbach edition: e.g., BMM 1:7-8 followed
by 1:22-23, then resuming with 1:8; or 5:1 followed by 5:18-28, then
resuming with 5:2-18 and concluding with 5:28-31. None of our
MSS attests these transpositions.

Friedmann's text is a mixture of readings available to him, chosen
in each case according to his own editorial judgment. By fusing
rather than filtering sources, he creates a new rendition of BMM.
Whatever its other merits, it cannot contribute to our task of text-
criticism. We should note, however, that Friedmann's voluminous
commentary, in which he interprets the text from a multitude of rabbinic sources, cites alternate readings, points out discrepancies, and
compares opinions, is still invaluable.

One printed edition remains to be discussed: Offenbach 1802,
published with references and notes by I. Scheuer of Frankfurt am
Main. On the final page of this edition, Scheuer writes that he has
sought to correct the errors of the *editio princeps* (ed. D) and to clarify difficulties in the text. In the body of the text he encloses proposed deletions in parentheses and additions in brackets. At the foot
of each page he either gives the source of his correction (e.g. a parallel reading) or invokes his own opinion (לע״ד). Friedmann is puzzled
by the fact that, although Scheuer claims to correct the *editio princeps*, the order of his text sometimes departs from it without editorial notice or comment. This leads Friedmann to suspect that
Scheuer had an otherwise unknown MS that he does not
mention.[56]

Our investigation of the Offenbach edition reveals some evidence
for this theory. The text includes a number of unique variants, e.g.:
ואת כל כליה (Offenbach) vs. את כל הכלים האלה שיהיו כליה (ed. D), BMM
9:14; מזבח העולה vs. מזבח הזהב, 10:24; קשוי ושבח vs. קשוי ושכחה,
11:20-21. In several places there are otherwise unattested additions
to the text, e.g.:

at BMM 4:2 (following העמודים) = ונמנו שיהא ממנו של משכן שלישית בשלישית ופורסה
ולפנים עשר אמות וממנו ולחוץ עשרים אמה
at 4:3 following (הפרוכת) = נמצא בית קדשי הקדשים עשר על עשר
at 8:20 (following הפנים) = בלבד משה בשל אלא מסדר היה לא כן פי על אף
שנ' ואת השלחן אשר עליו לחם הפנים רבי יוסי
ברבי יהודה אומר על כולן הי' מסדר

at 10:30 (following וגו') =   לבער בערב בערב רבי יוסי ברבי יהודה אומר
על כולן היה מבעיר שנ' ואת המנורות ונרותיהם
at 12:11 (following סאה) =   שכל מקוה ומקוה מחזיק ארבעים סאה שנ' ורחץ
בשרו במים מים שכל בשרו עולה בהן וכמה הן אמה
על אמה ברום שלש אמות מכאן שערו חכמים שעור
מקוה ארבעים סאה

There are also several transpositions, such as those in BMM chapters 1 and 5 already mentioned in our discussion of the Friedmann edition. The most pronounced MS affinity of the Offenbach edition is to MSS L and E, e.g. הסנין (L, E, 1:14-15); האבנים (L, E, 6:27); עקביא (E, 10:13); הברתיים (E, 10:23); deletion of למדנו שעגול מלמעלה (L, 12:14). However, there are too many exceptions to this concurrence to draw certain conclusions about the text of the Offenbach edition.

Our reason for excluding this edition from the critical apparatus is Scheuer's explicit statement of purpose, viz., to correct the *editio princeps* and to clarify difficulties. Friedmann's suspicion that Scheuer had a unique MS cannot be proven; what is more, we do not understand why such a fact would be concealed. At least as plausible an explanation for the discrepancies between Offenbach and ed. D is Scheuer's own editorial activity. Evidence for this surmise is found among the uncorroborated additions to the Offenbach text cited above, the largest of which are talmudic quotations or paraphrases. The Offenbach addition to BMM 8:20 = y. Sheq. 6:3, 50a; the addition to 10:30 = y. Sheq. 6:3, 50b; the addition to 12:11 = b. Er. 14a-b. While it is certainly possible that Scheuer had a MS of BMM that included these quotations, it is just as likely that he added them himself for his declared purpose of clarification. Likewise the various transpositions and variants cannot be assumed to have been inherited by the editor.

We conclude that Scheuer's claim to have corrected and emended the text of ed. D rules out the Offenbach edition as a credible witness to the authentic text of BMM. Therefore we exclude it from the critical apparatus.

Notes to Chapter Five

MANUSCRIPTS AND EDITIONS

1. *Sefer ha-Meqorot*, Academy of the Hebrew Language (Jerusalem, 1963), pt. 1, p. 54, entry 36. BMM is listed in the chronological category of works prior to 300 C.E., including the Mishnah, Tosefta, and halakhic midrashim.

2. Simon Hopkins, *A Miscellany of Literary Pieces from the Cambridge Genizah Collections: A Catalogue and Selection of Texts in the Taylor-Schechter Collection, Old Series, Box A45* (Cambridge Univ. Library, 1978), 78-91.

3. Grateful acknowledgment is hereby tendered to the Bodleian Library, Oxford (MSS A, B); Cambridge University Library (MSS G^1, G^2); Dropsie College Library, Philadelphia (MS G^2); Jewish Theological Seminary Library, New York City (MSS G^2, L); Bayerische Staatsbibliothek, Munich (MS M); Bibliothèque Nationale, Paris (MS P); Biblioteca Palatina, Parma (MS R).

4. *Midrash ha-Gadol.* Genesis: ed. M. Margulies (Jerusalem, 1975); Exodus: ed. M. Margulies (Jerusalem, 1983); Leviticus: ed. A. Steinsaltz (Jerusalem, 1976); Numbers: ed. Z. M. Rabinowitz (Jerusalem, 1983).

5. *Sefer ve-Hizhir*, ed. I. M. Freimann, v. 1 (Leipzig, 1873), v. 2 (Warsaw, 1880).

6. MS Sopron (Oedenburg) Hungary 2, published by Abraham Naftali Zevi Roth, "A Fragment from Midrash ve-Hizhir" (Hebrew), *Talpiyyot* 7 (1958): 89-98.

7. MS B includes two folios covering the same text but copied by different hands from divergent sources. We assign to these two versions the sigla B^1 and B^2; they are described in detail under the heading of MS B below.

8. The attestations of BMM are from quotations of MS E culled from Meir Friedmann's commentary to his edition of BMM (Vienna, 1908); see below under the description of MS E.

9. Actually the first published work containing BMM appeared in Safed in 1587, but only the title page survives; see below under the description of ed. D.

10. Adolf Neubauer, *Catalogue of the Hebrew Manuscripts in the Bodleian Library and in the College Libraries of Oxford* (Oxford, 1886), 1:80.

11. This was a common method among medieval copyists; see Malachi Beit-Arie, *Hebrew Codicology* (Jerusalem, 1981), 88-89.

12. The deletion of את is characteristic of the Babylonian Talmud; see Abba Bendavid, *Leshon Miqra u-Leshon Ḥakhamim* (Tel Aviv, 1967-71), 1:194.

13. Adolf Neubauer, op.cit. 1:24.

14. We note here a very brief quotation of BMM which in some distinctive ways corresponds to the reading of MS B (BMM 1:12-14): MS Corpus Christi Coll. 165 (Neubauer 2440), f. 152 recto, the first two lines =

ראיתי בברית' דמלאכת המשכן חורץ את הקרש מלמטה רביע מכאן ורביע מכאן והחריץ
חצין באמצע ועודה לן ב' ידות כמין שני חמוקים ומכניסן לתוך שני אדנים כו'.

Of extant MSS of BMM, MS B bears the closest resemblance to this passage, but no witness duplicates it.

15. See above, n. 2.

16. See, e.g., Malachi Beit-Arie, "The Paleography of the Genizah Literary Fragments" (Hebrew), *Cairo Genizah Studies*, ed. M. A. Friedman (Tel Aviv, 1980), 193-99.

17. Beit-Arie, *Hebrew Codicology*, 20.

18. Ligatures are not identified in our transcription (Appendix A) of MS G¹.

19. B. Halper, *Descriptive Catalogue of Genizah Fragments in Philadelphia* (Philadelphia, 1924), 45-46.

20. Louis Ginzberg, *Ginze Schechter*, 3 vols. (repr. New York, 1969), 1:374-83.

21. In July 1984 at the Cambridge University Library, the present writer noticed a pencil notation referring to BMM on the paper folder of the fragment, now sewn to a transparent "Melinex" envelope. Dr. Stefan C. Reif, Director of the Taylor-Schechter Genizah Research Unit, could not identify from the handwriting the writer of the notation, to whom we owe the original identification of T-S K21.82.

22. Among the sources of this passage, we have identified b. Yoma 16a-b = b. Zev. 58b; b. Yoma 36a = b. Zev. 20a; Yalqut Shimoni *Pequde* 418 (ed. Hyman/Shiloni, Ex. v. 2, p. 790).

23. I am indebted to Benjamin Richler of the Institute of Microfilmed Hebrew Manuscripts, Jewish National and University Library, Jerusalem, for the identification of the colophon.

24. See Beit-Arie, *Hebrew Codicology*, 51-59.

25. E.g., at BMM 11:8 MS L has פי שנים (= b. Zev. 59b) against all other witnesses.

26. R. N. Rabbinovicz, *Diqduqe Soferim: Variae Lectionis in Mishnam et in Talmud Babylonicum*, 2 vols. (repr. New York, 1976), introd. 1:9-10; M. Steinschneider, *Die Hebräischen Handschriften der K. Hof-und Staatsbibliothek in München* (Munich, 1895), no. 95, p. 60; H. L. Strack, *Der Babylonische Talmud nach der Münchener Handschrift Cod. Hebr. 95* (Leiden, 1912).

27. On the ascription of Provencal origin to MS Munich 95, see the discussion in Chaim Milikowsky, "Seder Olam: A Rabbinic Chronography," 2 vols. (Ph.D. diss., Yale Univ., 1981), 1:44, 99.

28. Arthur Zacharias Schwarz, *Die Hebräischen Handschriften in Österreich (Ausserhalb der National-bibliothek in Wien)* (Leipzig, 1931), pt. 1, no. 31, pp. 16-17.

29. *Baraita de-Melekhet ha-Mishkan*, ed. M. Friedmann (Vienna, 1908), introd. 3.

30. MSS from the collection that have been located are listed in A. Z. Schwarz/D. S. Loewinger/E. Roth, *Die Hebräischen Handschriften in Österreich* v. 2, American Academy for Jewish Research Texts and Studies 4 (New York, 1973).

31. H. Zotenberg, *Catalogues des Manuscrits Hébreux et Samaritans de la Bibliothèque Impériale* (Paris, 1866), no. 353, pp. 48-49; *Sefer ve-Hizhir* v. 1, ed. I. M. Freimann (Leipzig, 1873). Freimann's commentary, entitled *Anfe Yehudah*, quotes MS P intermittently between pp. 163-96 (Hebrew pagination 82a-98b). There are several errors of either printing or transcription in Freimann's citations, e.g. on p. 167 (Hebrew p. 84a): ממנו (Freimann) vs. הימנה (MS P); הדבור vs. הדביר; מוקף vs. מקיף; מדתן vs. מידתן; on p. 183 (Hebrew p. 92a): וד' vs. וב'.

32. Pesiqta de-R. Kahana *pisqa* 11:10 (ed. Mandelbaum 1:186-87); b. RH 26a; b. Sot. 11b; Rashi Ex. 35:27; Tanḥuma *Pequde* 9; Ex. R. 36:1.

33. Targum Yerushalmi Num. 2:3-25; cf. Louis Ginzberg, *Legends of the Jews* (repr. Philadelphia, 1968), 3:233, 6:82 n. 442.

34. Midrash Tehillim 23:4; Cant. R. 4:11, 12.

35. *MSS. Codices Hebraici Biblioth. I. B. De-Rossi* (Parma, 1803), v. 2, no. 540, pp. 76-77.

36. *A zsidok története Sopronban* (Budapest, 1896).

37. Abraham Naftali Ẓevi Roth, "A Fragment from Midrash ve-Hizhir," 89-98.

38. *Sefer ve-Hizhir* ed. Freimann, v. 1, pp. 163-74, Hebrew pagination 82a-87b.

39. The text of the last three lines of the verso:

ארכן של יריעות שלשים אמה שנ' ארך היריעה האח' שלש' באמ' צא מהן עשר עשר לרחבו
שלמשכן נשתיירו שם עשר אמות מצד זה ועשר אמות מצד זה שהן יורדות ומכסות את
הקרשים וארנים עד שמגיעות לארץ אמה מיכן ואמה מיכן שנ' והאמה מזה והאמ' מזה בעודף.

There is no trace of this passage in Freimann's text (MS Munich 205). Cf. the reading of MS M at BMM 3:6, apparatus, s.v. ועשית קרסי נחשת חמשים.

40. In an early edition of BMM (Offenbach, 1802), the editor (I. Scheuer) mistakenly identified the owner of the MS as Menaḥem Azariah da Fano (1548-1620) which led him to give the incorrect date of the *editio princeps*.

41. The title page reads:

ברייתא דרבי אליעזר בנו של יוסי הגלילי ומדרש אגור וברייתא דמלאכת המשכן ובריתות
אחרות... הוציא אור החכם הנעלה כמה"ר מנחם די לונזאנו יזיי"א נדפס' פה בצפת תוב"ב
בגליל העליון היום יום א' י' אייר שמ"ז לפ"ק.

42. For bibliographical data see above, n. 4.

43. For bibliographical data, see above, n. 5.

44. M. Steinschneider, *Die Hebräischen Handschriften*, no. 205, p. 88.

45. Freimann's quotations of MS P are sometimes in error; see above, n. 31.

46. *Sefer ve-Hizhir*, ed. Freimann, v. 1, pp. 186-87 (Hebrew pagination 93b-94a) = BMM ch. 9.

47. *Catalogue of the Hebrew Manuscripts in the Bodleian Library* 1:80.

48. Ibid.

49. See the biographical entry in *EJ* 7:935-36.

50. A. Z. Schwarz, *Die Hebräische Handschriften in Österreich*, pt. 1, no. 72, p. 47.

51. *Catalogue of Hebrew Manuscripts in the Collection of Elkan Nathan Adler* (Cambridge Univ. Press, 1921), no. 875, p. 10. Adler 2940, described above under MS G², is also listed under the same title, מלאכת המשכן.

52. The Jerusalem, 1965 ed. of BMM (with Ma'aseh Ḥoshev, ed. Shefer) differs from the Offenbach ed. in several respects. The editor completes abbreviated biblical citations and forms paragraphs by his own lights. He also claims, without substantiation, that BMM is divided into *pisqa'ot*. In his notes he cites alternate readings but does not report their sources. Among these readings we have identified variants from MSS A, B, G², E, and ed. D.

53. In the introduction (pp. 1-3) to his edition of BMM, Meir Friedmann discusses the relationships among the Venice, Hamburg, Offenbach, and Vilna editions. The Kanivsky (Bene Berak, 1961) edition utilizes Friedmann's text but does not acknowledge it.

54. Mistakes in the Flesch transcription (Konitz, 1899) of MS M, cited by page and line number (the list is not exhaustive):
מרין (ed. Konitz) vs. מדין (MS M), p. 3:2; קרניו vs. קרש, p. 3:8; עובין omitted, p. 4:8; ועששה vs. וששה, p. 4:10; ואחת added, p. 4:22; בכל vs. כפול, p. 4:27; פורפן vs. שרפן, p. 5:9; וארכה vs. ואמה p. 5:11; יהידה vs. יהודה, p. 6:9; הפסח vs.

הפתח, 7:4, 5; לפתח vs. לפסח, p. 7:6; אחד vs. אחר, p. 7:7; חמש vs. חמוש, p. 7:11; ועמודי' vs. והעמוד, p. 7:17; שהנדע vs. שתדע, p. 7:17; כיון שכתוב vs. כמו שכתב, p. 7:17; למדת vs. למרת, p.8:5; שבין vs. שכין, p. 8:5; חוף vs. קרפף, p. 9:2; שנים p. 8:2; נתון vs. נתנו, p. 9:23; אלא vs. אל, p. 9:23; תצפנו omitted, p. added, p. 9:17; היתה vs. היה, p. 10:12; מקובעות vs. מנובעות, p. 10:13; נעולו vs. ננעלו, p. 10:11; דברות vs. העצים, p. 11:6; בבנין vs. בבית, p. 11:8; ולחם 10:19; ר' vs. ד', p. 11:5; ריה vs. ריוח, p. 11:18; מקשה הפנים ארכו עשרה ורחבו חמשה omitted, p. 11:14; או כמין vs. וכמין, p. 13:2; עז vs. אז, p. 13:8; מזיין vs. וטעונה omitted, p. 12:2; במצקתו vs. במצבתיו, p. 17:3. מזיזן, p. 14:8; יהל vs. מול, p. 14:10;

55. See *Baraita de-Melekhet ha-Mishkan*, ed. Friedmann (Vienna, 1908), introd. 3, where Friedmann thanks the students who copied MSS E, A, and B for him.

56. Ibid. introd. 2.

Chapter 6

Text Criticism and Stemmatic Analysis

Classical philology seeks to recover or reconstruct ancient texts. By following the threads of transmission and sorting through the scribal process that preserved and disseminated a given work, the editor tries to restore the lost original. Since autograph MSS from classical antiquity have not survived, the editor must rely on later MSS and quotations, each of which lies at an unknown number of removes from its ancestor. Text criticism is necessitated by the variable accuracy of such witnesses. The law of information theory holds that mediation always entails contamination; that is, accuracy inevitably suffers in the process of transmission. The task of the text critic is to restore the integrity of the text by reconstructing the history of its transmission and exposing the errors that have corrupted it.

A "scientific" or "critical" edition of an ancient work begins with a systematic collation of text witnesses. The purpose of this process is not only to assemble all relevant texts but to determine their descent. When multiple versions exist, a reasoned choice among them is impossible without knowledge of their relationship to one another. The sum of all the lines of MS descent may be described by the model of a genealogical tree, or stemma. In a closed recension, the descent pattern diverges downward and converges upward; that is, the vertical relationship of the extant MSS infers transcription from a single original. But in an open recension, a scribe has copied from more than one exemplar, preferring first one, then the other, or conflating several at once. This phenomenon of horizontal transmission, or contamination, is fatal to pure stemmatic analysis.

Even in the event of contamination, however, it is possible to distinguish MS "families," i.e. groups of witnesses shown by conjunctive characteristics to belong together as against other witnesses. For instance, suppose a text is preserved in six MSS (A,B,C,D,E,F). One of them (A) stands apart, exhibiting its own peculiar traits; while two (B,C) on the one side and three (D,E,F) on the other resemble each other but differ from the rest. The BC correspondence suggests the existence of a (hypothetical) common ancestor (Y); likewise the DEF correspondence suggests a separate exemplar (Z). Presumably any reading of Y or Z that can be deduced from the respective agreement of BC or DEF is of greater textual authority than a discrepant reading of B,C,D, E,F taken singly. The next step is to compare Y and Z for common agreement, check those results against the unique readings of A, and so to build a theoretical stemma in spite of horizontal variation.

A genealogical series of MSS is not necessarily chronological. Certainly in most cases a late MS will be separated from the original by a larger number of intervening copies and therefore a greater deterioration of accuracy. But depending upon the exemplar(s) at hand, a later scribe may preserve a more pristine reading or a more faithful transcription. Even printed editions may attest readings that could not have been invented by later hands; in such cases the printed version is the only extant witness to a branch of MS descent. Likewise citations of ancient works by later authors may preserve a correct reading that extant MSS have quoted in error. It is also possible that a later variation in transcription may, intentionally or accidentally, restore the reading of an earlier ancestor.

Another canon of text criticism is that MSS must be weighed, not counted.[1] Stemmatic considerations alone are insufficient to determine the quality of a witness. Extant MSS may share unanimous agreement yet still represent only one branch of a more ramified textual history. The value of a MS is gauged not only by external correspondences but by internal tests: orthography, lacunae, corrections, additions, etc. The fidelity of the scribe is at least as crucial as the pedigree of the MS.

The process of scribal transcription is characterized by predictable types of mechanical variation. For instance, when similar words stand adjacent on a line of text, one or the other is liable to be omitted. When similar words or phrases are separated by several lines, the copyist's eye is apt to skip from the first reading to the second, omitting everything in between. Letters or words may be unnecessarily repeated. Transposition errors are also common, including letter reversals, fluctuations in word order, and displaced lines or whole passages. Mechanical errors may also be induced by paleographical similarities, grammatical assimilations, or the influence of the immediate context. Aside from inadvertent miscopying, transcriptions may suffer from losses owing to physical damage to the exemplar: illegible ink, perforations, missing leaves, detached quires, etc.

A separate class of scribal variation may be attributed to the copyist's own volition. Medieval MSS are characterized by deliberate revisions and interpolations. Marginal or interlinear comments are added to the text in the course of transcription. Conflations of variants are commonplace. While in major matters a copyist may follow his exemplar(s), in minor matters of orthography or usage he may follow his own regional custom. He may omit an objectionable passage or alter a difficult reading. When he encounters a text sequence he cannot follow, he may simplify or summarize it. He may notice an error in his exemplar and correct it in his own copy. The revised text may actually be improved, but it is nonetheless a corruption of the exemplar.

Quotations of Scripture are particularly susceptible to scribal variation. Medieval copyists were not likely to verify citations; ancient scrolls were unwieldy, and codices were not as conveniently divided or numbered as are modern books. The scribe was apt to cite from memory, with all the possibilities for error that memory entails. Transcription may also be hampered by different habits of quotation: one scribe's abbreviated citations may be misunderstood or incorrectly expanded by a subsequent copyist. If a quotation is remembered or copied from an ancillary source instead of the exemplar, another factor of scribal variation is added.

Given the difficulty of tracing both the transmission and transcription of an ancient text, no critical edition is final. Unless the missing archetype is recovered, its reconstruction must always be a matter of greater or lesser probability. When the editor is fortunate enough to have an effective consensus of extant MSS, he may choose to constitute a composite text, distilling similarities and filtering out discrepancies. If the text data are more disparate, he may propose an eclectic text, guided first by one witness, then by another, then by his own conjecture. Either of these approaches permits editorial emendation. Having detected a corrupt passage, the editor corrects it according to available criteria: the types of error to which the particular scribe is prone; the evidence of other witnesses; compatibility with the author's thought and expression. A successful emendation may be truer to the archetype than the copy it corrects. On the other hand, an unwarranted emendation corrupts the text still further. In the view of some text critics, emendation involves an unacceptable level of subjectivity on the part of the editor. The term "diagnostic conjecture" describes a more cautious approach by which the editor indicates the kind of correction required without substituting an emended text.

The most cautious approach to assembling a critical edition is to choose one extant text which best represents an authentic recension and to follow it with the least possible alteration. Rather than fabricating a composite, eclectic, or emended text, the editor presents a diplomatic text, or *codex optimus*, and lets the critical apparatus carry all the data necessary for the reconstruction of other possible versions. The *codex optimus* is chosen according to the criteria of external relationship and internal integrity discussed above. That MS whose transmission and transcription are judged most reliable may be considered the best extant witness. Since this MS gives the greatest number of correct readings where there are objective grounds for decision, it is assumed to give the correct reading where no such grounds exist. This argument from probability is the basis for the primacy of the *codex optimus* in a critical edition. It is presented as the base text against which variant readings are compared. Should the base text be defective in places, the critical apparatus furnishes the attested alternatives for correction.

Of course this method, too, has its limitations. While composite, eclectic, or emended editions may leave too much in the hands of the editor, a *codex optimus* may leave too little. Editors preferring a diplomatic text have been accused of being deliberately uncritical, i.e., too loyal to the base MS and too reluctant to improve it.[2] Since no MS is impeccable, excessive reliance on one can be criticized as a retreat from the editor's task. Rather he should exercise his own judgment in choosing the correct reading or emending by conjecture. A diplomatic text, concludes A. Dain, is "une solution de paresse."[3]

Nonetheless, the virtue of a critical edition based on a *codex optimus* is that it does not claim more than the evidence can bear. Rather than producing a theoretical text, it reproduces an extant one modified by the aggregate of other witnesses. If a diplomatic text stops short of reconstructing the archetype, it also stops short of reifying it. For ancient works of established authorship and ancestry, subjective reconstruction may be feasible. But for those texts whose history and composition are less certain, the first step must be the thorough presentation of the MSS and their readings. Such is the case with ancient rabbinic literature.

Unlike those classical texts that have been the subject of philological activity for hundreds of years, rabbinic literature has yet to receive extensive critical study. Only a few rabbinic works have been published in critical editions, and many of these are either incomplete or methodologically tentative. For most ancient and medieval rabbinic compositions, even the preliminary presentation of MSS and secondary quotations has yet to be accomplished. As a science, rabbinic text criticism is still in its infancy.

Part of the reason for such slow progress is the traditional Jewish reverence for received rabbinic texts and the resistance to regarding them as mere literature. But as the critical program has been undertaken in the last century, obstacles have emerged that are intrinsic to the literature itself. Most ancient rabbinic works are compilations of discrete traditions held in a loose external framework. Consequently, additions or deletions are not always felt by the reader, and transpositions are the rule rather than the exception. Inheriting many interchangeable components, copyists were free to edit the text in accord with parallel traditions or by their own lights. Moreover, ancient rabbinic compositions are corporate documents. The earliest stages of textual development are so fluid that the existence of a single corpus of readings cannot be assumed. A work of rabbinic literature routinely draws upon multiple sources, sometimes preserving a borrowed formulation, sometimes recasting its language or its substance. Attributions may change from one source to the next. Internal inconsistencies, contradictory interpretations, and successive recensions generate multitudes of alternate readings. In such a textual situation, it is difficult to justify the search for an archetype, let alone its reconstruction.

Further complications attend the determination of origins in rabbinic literature. We have little idea of whether a given text originated in oral form, or when it was first written down, or whether it was edited from written sources. Antecedent materials are masked by the tendency of redactors to treat all traditions as part of a dialectical whole rather than a historical sequence. For this reason it is difficult to distinguish between original and secondary versions: the latter may be as original as the former. As Jacob Neusner has demonstrated in his analysis of the Mishnah, the literary forms as we now have them were imposed primarily within the process of editing. Redaction, not authorship, is the governing act of formulation.[4] Attributions, too, often adhere to the formal traits and requirements of the redacted document, regardless of independent origin. In rabbinic literature it is not always possible to distinguish editorial decisions from antecedent texts. From his study of certain talmudic pericopae, E. S. Rosenthal doubts the prospect of accomplishing even the first goal of text criticism: deciding where redaction ends and text tradition begins.[5]

Despite the obstacles to producing critical editions of rabbinic texts, several have been attempted. Pioneering efforts include the editions of various midrashim published a century ago by Solomon Buber, Meir Friedmann (Ish-Shalom), Solomon Schechter, and David Hoffmann. Lacking a systematic methodology (by present standards), these works rely on editorial preferences that are not always explained or even identified. In the next generation of rabbinic scholarship, a more formal critical approach was introduced by Jacob Z. Lauterbach (Mekhilta de-R. Ishmael) and Henry Malter (Babylonian Talmud tractate Ta'anit).[6] Although both of these editions include detailed discussions of MSS and secondary witnesses, they are little different from their predecessors in following whatever reading the editor prefers. Malter claims that he tried but failed to organize the MSS into affinitive groups.[7] Lauterbach does not even go this far; in his introduction to the Mekhilta, there is no mention of any effort to assess the relationship among the various witnesses. Lauterbach bases his text on five "complete and independent sources," viz., two MSS and three printed editions. He describes his methodology as follows:[8]

> In the majority of cases...when the two manuscripts agree in a reading as against the reading of the editions, the former has been embodied in the accepted text. In case of disagreement between the two manuscripts, the reading of the one supported by the editions has been accepted. In many cases, however, the reading of the editions has been retained, because in the opinion of the editor it seemed to be more correct than the one found in the manuscripts....In some cases the accepted text is based upon only one of the five main sources, as against the reading or readings found in the other four, because the reading of the one source appeared to the editor to be more correct....

In some instances the accepted text is based upon a correct reading found only in one or more of the secondary sources, and not in any of the principal sources or fragmentary manuscripts.

For those who object to the subjective reconstruction of a missing text, Lauterbach's editorial procedure is a case in point. MSS and printed editions are accorded equal status regardless of descent relationships. Readings are usually chosen according to the majority of witnesses, as if the majority could not agree on a corrupt text. On the other hand, the editor also reserves the right to prefer an uncorroborated reading, even if it is from a secondary source and even if it is unattested in any of the witnesses on which he has based the text in the first place. In effect Lauterbach reduces the textual data to an undifferentiated sea of readings from which he fishes out the ones that, for reasons that he never specifies, are most pleasing to him. The final text, whatever its aesthetic merits, is a completely new recension composed by the editor. A fundamental premise of text criticism is the need to untangle lines of descent and conflation. Lauterbach's method accomplishes the opposite.

A less flagrant example of the eclectic method is Louis Finkelstein's edition of Sifre on Deuteronomy.[9] Finkelstein, like Lauterbach, is prone to rely on his own judgment even against the preponderance of textual evidence.[10] While basing his text of Sifre on a *codex optimus*, Finkelstein frequently interpolates passages from other MSS or secondary citations. Conjectural emendations abound, often without notification or explanation. On the other hand, Finkelstein opens new territory in rabbinic text criticism by presenting a *stemma codicum*.[11] He shows that the citations of Sifre in Midrash ha-Gadol are drawn from a different ancestor than the extant MSS and published editions. This means that, despite the disproportion of witnesses, a citation from Midrash ha-Gadol may be equal in value to the aggregate of MSS. Finkelstein's attempt at stemmatic analysis, however, is only probative; the connection between his stemma and his text is never made explicit. Owing to the profusion of editorial alterations, the extent to which Finkelstein is guided by stemmatic criteria is not clear.

In his review of Finkelstein's edition of Sifre, J. N. Epstein criticizes the incorporation of variants into the *codex optimus* unless the text is obviously defective. Epstein objects not only to the practice but to the principle of combining variants of tannaitic documents.

Alternate readings may represent ancient traditions distinct from
each other and from the recension at hand. In his own work on the
Mishnah, Epstein distinguishes between *Varianten* and *Versionen*.
The former are the consequence of the vagaries of oral or scribal
transmission; the latter are discrete recensions of the text. While certain *Varianten* are palpably corrupt, *Versionen* have equal textual
validity.[12] Epstein argues that an eclectic text such as Finkelstein's
does not distinguish between *Varianten* and *Versionen*. By mixing
unitary text traditions, it distorts the evidence. Epstein also criticizes
many of Finkelstein's emendations as unwarranted and
unsupportable.[13]

Saul Lieberman, the most eminent modern rabbinic philologist,
also takes exception to textual eclecticism and emendation. Review-
ing Lauterbach's Mekhilta and Finkelstein's Sifre,[14] Lieberman
faults both editions for failing to distinguish scribal errors from discrepant traditions. While appreciating Finkelstein's stemmatic analysis, Lieberman maintains that even if there once was a single original text, it comes to us in multiple versions, and each witness must
be evaluated on its own terms. The Mishnah, for instance, while
ostensibly an autonomous work, is not the same in the Palestinian
Talmud as it is in the Babylonian. Neither version is "wrong"; each
represents a tributary of text tradition. Lieberman points out that
scribal transmission is not merely the mechanical accumulation of
errors. Corrections also enter the received text from the copyist's
inherited usage. Consequently an editor should not mix readings
from different MSS. Each MS may represent a legitimate tradition
that editing only serves to mangle.

Introducing his own (incomplete) edition of the Tosefta,[15]
Lieberman argues that in its current state, rabbinic literature does
not readily admit to the same methodology as classical literature, the
texts of which have already been published in generations of critical
editions. Given the extant textual data, it is difficult to establish the
relationship, let alone the superiority, of one rabbinic witness to
another. Lieberman does not change the text of his *codex optimus*;
he copies the MS as it is, correcting only obvious errors and noting
these in the apparatus. His approach suggests that at this stage of
the critical endeavor, the editor of a rabbinic text should present the
evidence, not the verdict.[16]

In contemporary rabbinic scholarship, the caution of Lieberman
and Epstein has prevailed over the latitude of Finkelstein and

Lauterbach. Modern critical editions of rabbinic works rely on diplomatic texts revised from variants only in cases of obvious corruption.[17] Sustained stemmatic analysis has rarely been attempted. Lieberman, for instance, makes no effort to determine descent relationships among the three major MSS of the Tosefta utilized in his critical edition.[18] In other editions, e.g. Gen. R. (ed. Theodor-Albeck), Mekhilta de-R. Simeon b. Yoḥai (ed. Epstein-Melamed), Lev. R. (ed. Margulies), Pesiqta de-Rav Kahana (ed. Mandelbaum), She'eltot (ed. Mirsky) and Halakhot Gedolot (ed. Hildesheimer),[19] MS characteristics and affinities are mentioned, often with reference to their influence on printed editions. But there is little evaluation of witnesses in terms of genealogical relationships. Albeck concludes his introduction to Gen. R. with a few stemmatic speculations but concedes the likelihood of contamination.[20] He presents a stemmatic diagram that divides the witnesses into major groups, but no analytical criteria are set forth, nor do the editors furnish examples of convergent or divergent variation. Margulies and Mandelbaum divide their respective witnesses into classes or families but do not present formal stemmata.[21] Hildesheimer, while noting conjunctive MS errors suggesting a common exemplar, does not go beyond this observation.[22]

Among more recent critical editions of rabbinic texts, most of which are, to date, in a tentative or partial state,[23] the following methodological conventions are prevalent: 1) the division of witnesses into "families" based on frequent similarities in their readings; 2) the detection of affinities between primary witnesses and later *testimonia*; 3) the selection of the MS most likely to preserve original readings as the base text for the edition. Stemmatic analysis still tends to be avoided. For example, in his edition of the beginning portions of Ex. R., a medieval compilation, Avigdor Shinan provides an introduction describing the extant witnesses to the text.[24] He divides his six MSS into three groups but does not discuss stemmatic considerations.[25] He notes parallels from the Talmuds and amoraic midrashim but does not specify them. He mentions collateral sources (e.g. Yalqut Makhiri; the commentary of Ramban) used to corroborate the text but fails to define the extent of reliance or his criteria for accepting them. To establish a diplomatic text, Shinan follows one MS except for a missing section substituted from another source. However, he writes, "While I have not created an eclectic text, neither have I hesitated to elasticize it." No doubt a useful contribution to rabbinic scholarship, Shinan's work does not appear to constitute a methodological advance in text criticism.

In contrast, the critical edition of Seder Olam by Chaim Milikowsky exemplifies the application of sophisticated and thorough stemmatic analysis to a rabbinic text.[26] Assembling his base text from assorted fragmentary witnesses supplemented by the *editio princeps*, Milikowsky corrects obvious errors from variants but refrains from conjectural emendation. In this respect, his edition conforms to the Lieberman-Epstein model. However, Milikowsky's introduction includes an analysis of witnesses according to the stemmatic method of text criticism. Where possible, he seeks to apply the criteria of conjunctive and separative errors to determine the interrelationship of MSS and editions. He concedes that contamination defeats genealogical analysis but detects in the witnesses to Seder Olam a sufficient degree of vertical transmission to justify a stemmatic hypothesis.[27] While Milikowsky presents a *stemma codicum*, he does not extrapolate a reconstructed text from it. Stemmatic analysis, he argues, can help the editor to evaluate the witnesses even when it cannot produce an ultimate text. Where the *codex optimus* is defective, stemmatic criteria may indicate from which witness the text may be most plausibly corrected. Discovering MS ancestry is also crucial to choosing the *codex optimus* in the first place: it reduces both the number of eligible candidates and the number of legitimate variants.

Milikowsky's decision to base his text on a *codex optimus* recognizes the current state of rabbinic text criticism. But his stemmatic analysis of witnesses demonstrates the potential of the genealogical method to recover ancient texts, even in the vexing case of rabbinic literature.

This is not to say that classical stemmatics can be applied, *mutatis mutandis*, to rabbinic texts. As proposed by Karl Lachmann and elaborated by Paul Maas,[28] the stemmatic method of textual criticism traces the descent of MSS by noting what errors they have in common. The theory is that if two or more MSS agree on a textual anomaly, they must descend from a common ancestor. This assumes that textual anomalies can be distinguished from scribal corruptions, that conjunctive errors can be distinguished from coincidental ones, and that none of the descendants suffered emendation. Stemmatic theory also assumes that the identification of common ancestors, whether they survive or their existence is merely inferred, leads to a single archetype from which all witnesses descend. Finally, stemmatic analysis assumes that each scribe in the line of descent copied from only one exemplar, and that no variants entered the text from any other source.

If there are rabbinic texts that meet all of these criteria, BMM is not one of them. The MS tradition is thoroughly contaminated: textual transmission is both horizontal and vertical. Virtually every existing witness shares distinctive errors or variants with virtually every other witness. For example, MS A shares conjunctive errors or unique readings against other witnesses with: MS B (e.g. מן הפרכת, BMM 4:24); MS G¹ (e.g., omission of ומה ת"ל... , 5:28); MS G² (e.g. דברי ר' יהודה, 8:6); MS M (רחבו, 8:10); MS P (e.g. omission of scriptural citation, 2:14); and ed. V (e.g. omission of ורחבו חמש אמות, 11:4-5). Each of these witnesses in turn shares conjunctive errors or variants with at least one MS other than A against all witnesses including A, e.g.: MS B and ed. H (addition, 8:9-10); MS G² and MS P (addition, 7:9; cf. Appendix B, 7:9); MS M and ed. V (מבית, 5:30), ed. V and ed. H (omission, 8:4), etc. Contamination is also evidenced by separative errors or variants. For instance, MS A usually agrees with MS G¹, but not always (e.g. 14:2); MSS E and L are closely related but occasionally differ (e.g. 3:2); ed. D tends to follow MS M, but sometimes contradicts it (e.g. 3:9); MS V² almost matches ed. V but includes other readings (e.g. 2:7).

Clearly our witnesses to the text of BMM comprise an open recension. Each witness shares errors or unique variants with other witnesses in a bewildering variety of combinations. The more open the textual tradition, the less susceptible it is to stemmatic analysis. This is not to say that we despair of any genealogical conclusions. Even where stemmatic position cannot be determined with certainty, it is still possible to classify witnesses by conjunctive and separative characteristics. Once affinitive relationships within MS groups have been established, then the relationship (if any) among the groups can be explored.

Our method in the present edition is to measure the degree of textual affinity between witnesses by a distributional comparison of variants, and to interpret the results in terms of genealogical affiliation. From this data we propose a theoretical *stemma codicum*.

Our analysis does not confine variants to errors, as stemmatic theory requires. There are two reasons for this. First of all, Lachmann's original emphasis on errors was to restrict the pool of evidential var-

iants to a manageable number.[29] This does not mean that errors are
the only kind of textual evidence bearing upon genealogical relationship. All forms of textual variation—lexical, morphological, grammatical, orthographic—must be evaluated. More fundamentally, the
identification and even the definition of "errors" in ancient works
are problematic. In the strict sense, one cannot speak of "errors"
unless one knows exactly what the original text said and exactly
where the copy under examination differs from it. Given the contamination of our MS tradition and the impossibility of pure
stemmatic analysis, we do not wish to rule out any evidential variant
that might clarify the interrelationship of witnesses to the text.

Not all variants bear notice, however. Consistent distinctions
between *plene* and defective spelling, masculine and feminine numbers, and shortened words or abbreviations do not exist in any MS
of BMM. As we have seen in the preceding chapter, copyists of rabbinic texts mix these elements indiscriminately. The classification of
MSS by variants must consider whether a given variant is a genealogical indicator or merely a scribal idiosyncrasy. For our analysis
we have relied upon Henri Quentin's distinction between scribal and
codicological variants,[30] similar to J. N. Epstein's differentiation of
Varianten from *Versionen*.[31] This categorization seeks to separate
superficial affinities from fundamental ones by distinguishing horizontal from vertical transmission. Thus the scribal category includes
variants that can be explained by scribal phenomena: dittography,
haplography, metathesis, homoeoteleuton, associations by context,
etc. The codicological category includes variants attributable to
independent sources. Scribal variants originate with the copy;
codicological variants with the exemplar. Obviously the latter category is the only one with true genealogical significance. But as in
regard to errors, the distinction between scribal and codicological is
not always certain, e.g. in the event of an omission, transposition,
or other alteration of the text that may be attributed as plausibly to
the copy as to the exemplar. In effect the difference between scribal
and codicological variants is a matter of scale. Those variants least
likely to originate as scribal corruptions deserve the greatest weight
as genealogical indicators. But owing to ambiguities in the middle
of the scale, the entire spectrum of variants is needed.

For our comparative classification of MSS, we have adapted a
model of hierarchical cluster analysis that measures degrees of
resemblance and allows the formation of affinitive groups. In this

method, pairs of witnesses are compared by textual variants, and in succeeding stages the pairs are compared to the group as a whole.[32] To establish measurable criteria of similarity and distance, the number of variants shared in common is tabulated. A second tabulation is confined to codicological variants only. For those witnesses that are fragmentary or incomplete (MSS G^1, G^2, E, R, V^2; eds. H, V), we have factored in the proportion of BMM attested.[33] By this sorting procedure, we have sought to establish a reasonably objective basis for the classification of our MSS and the determination of their ancestry.[34]

The following table reports the tabulation of common variants between each pair of witnesses to the text of BMM. Each witness is summarized in three horizontal columns. The top column lists witnesses by siglum (see pp. 149-50 above). The middle column lists the sum of common scribal and codicological variants combined. The bottom column includes common codicological variants only. Those totals enclosed in parentheses are projected rather than actual numbers owing to partial attestations of our text.[35] Comparisons between two fragmentary witnesses are not included, since the combination of projections is too speculative to be meaningful.

MS A

B	G^1	G^2	L	M	E	P	D	H	V
90	(380)	(110)	81	84	(160)	59	73	(75)	(85)
36	(172)	(32)	30	29	(50)	30	23	(45)	(30)

MS B

A	G^1	G^2	L	M	E	P	D	H	V
90	(80)	(105)	83	62	(100)	73	70	(85)	(93)
36	(36)	(29)	22	24	(48)	26	26	(40)	(31)

MS G^1

A	B	G^2	L	M	E	P	D	H	V
(380)	(80)		(70)	(140)		(60)	(140)		
(172)	(36)		(24)	(56)		(32)	(56)		

MS G^2

A	B	G^1	L	M	E	P	D	H	V
(110)	(105)		(60)	(110)		(65)	(85)		
(32)	(29)		(26)	(46)		(20)	(40)		

MS L

A	B	G¹	G²	M	E	P	D	H	V
81	83	(70)	(60)	93	(290)	61	67	(80)	(62)
30	22	(24)	(26)	37	(140)	22	23	(35)	(21)

MS M

A	B	G¹	G²	L	E	P	D	H	V
84	62	(140)	(110)	93	(115)	48	158	(60)	(75)
29	24	(56)	(46)	37	(54)	26	77	(30)	(20)

MS E

A	B	G¹	G²	L	M	P	D	H	V
(160)	(100)			(290)	(115)	(70)	(120)		
(50)	(48)			(140)	(54)	(41)	(64)		

MS P

A	B	G¹	G²	L	M	E	D	H	V
59	73	(60)	(65)	61	48	(70)	43	(75)	(56)
30	26	(32)	(20)	22	26	(41)	16	(50)	(27)

Ed. D

A	B	G¹	G²	L	M	E	P	H	V
73	70	(140)	(85)	67	158	(120)	43	(30)	(49)
23	26	(56)	(40)	23	77	(64)	16	(5)	(14)

Ed. H

A	B	G¹	G²	L	M	E	P	D	V
(75)	(85)			(80)	(60)		(75)	(30)	
(45)	(40)			(35)	(30)		(50)	(5)	

Ed. V

A	B	G¹	G²	L	M	E	P	D	H
(85)	(93)			(62)	(75)		(56)	(49)	
(30)	(31)			(21)	(20)		(27)	(14)	

Although we have emphasized the importance of distinguishing between scribal and codicological variants, the data indicate that both measures of similarity tend to correspond, especially when there is a high degree of affinity between witnesses. For example, the following pairs demonstrate the closest resemblance by both scribal and codicological criteria: A-G[1]; L-E; M-D; P-H; and B-V. Two other pairs, B-E and M-G[2], are very nearly compatible on both scales. Only H evinces a marked disparity between scribal and codicological affiliations, and this may be explained by the unique editorial characteristics of Midrash ha-Gadol (discussed above, pp. 59-61) and by the fact that it is the most fragmentary of the eleven witnesses under comparison.

The congruity of scribal and codicological measures begins to break down at the lower levels of affinity. For instance, MS P stands at the greatest distance from the other witnesses when all variants are compared, but closer when the comparison is confined to codicological criteria. This corroborates our judgment rendered above (pp. 105-7) that MS P represents a separate recension of BMM yet preserves readings from the oldest and most reliable witnesses to the text. MS E and ed. H also register a greater degree of codicological than scribal similarity to the other witnesses. This is especially true of ed. H: for example, H is only eighth closest to MS A when all variants are considered, but third closest codicologically.

Emerging from the comparison of variants are three pronounced MS affinities: A-G[1]; L-E; and to a somewhat lesser degree, M-D. Our next step toward genealogical classification is to take these three pairs and compare each of their common variants to those of the remaining witnesses. In other words, each of the three affinitive pairs is compared as a unit to the nine other witnesses taken singly. Since our scribal and codicological measures have proven to be nearly congruent, the following table does not distinguish between the two. Of the three pairs, two include fragmentary witnesses; consequently their totals of correspondence with other witnesses are enclosed in parentheses to denote projected numbers based on the percentage of attestation.[36] Where fragmentary witnesses are compared to each other, the projections must be regarded as hypothetical.

MS A – MS G[1]

B	G[2]	L	M	E	P	D	H	V
(60)	(48)	(52)	(100)	(48)	(40)	(80)	(0)	(52)

MS L – MS E

A	B	G[1]	G[2]	M	P	D	H	V
(57)	(54)	(24)	(42)	(42)	(33)	(36)	(45)	(39)

MS M – Ed. D

A	B	G[1]	G[2]	L	E	P	H	V
32	27	(60)	(50)	30	(52)	14	(15)	(24)

Here the difficulty of tracing MS descent through a contaminated tradition becomes apparent. While each pair displays greater affinity to some MSS than to others, the differences are often slight and, given the use of projected totals, well within the margin of error. In the case of the pair L-E, for instance, we can assume that there is a closer relationship to A and B than to G[1] and P, but beyond that the discriminations are too narrow to warrant conclusions. Likewise M-D shows a closer affinity to G[1], G[2], and E than to P and H, but those witnesses in the middle of the scale stand at a similar distance from the affinitive pair. The widest range of correspondence is found in the comparison to A-G[1] common variants, where M and to a lesser extent D correspond to the pair while H shares not one variant. In this last case we must again point out that H is a fragmentary and somewhat anomalous witness to the text of BMM; accordingly we are reluctant to place too much store in the comparison of its variants.

In light of the degree of contamination reflected by the distribution of common variants among the witnesses, our attempt to classify the MSS of BMM and to construct a *stemma codicum* is necessarily heuristic. We begin with the most ancient surviving witness to the text, MS G[1]. As discussed in the previous chapter, this MS preserves not only the oldest but the most pristine and meticulous text of BMM. Unfortunately, only fragments of G[1] have survived. Therefore we required for our *codex optimus* the complete recension of BMM that best preserves the text of G[1]. As the comparison of variants shows decisively, this is MS A. G[1] and A display by far the greatest mutual affinity of any two witnesses. Moreover, they preserve in common numerous readings, most notably the lengthy citation of M. Sheq. 5:1-2 (BMM 12:20-27), attested in no other witness. A is not identical to the surviving text of G[1]; there are some divergences in scribal phenomena and usage (e.g. A's tendency to omit the accusative particle את). But A is unquestionably the most faithful surviving descendant of G[1], and its entire text is intact and well-preserved. Given the additional factor of its consistent internal characteristics and careful transcription (discussed in the previous chapter), MS A is an obvious choice to serve as the base text of the present edition.

Although MS B is the product of cross-contamination, we have already shown that one of its exemplars was almost certainly MS A (see above, p. 100). The distributional comparison of variants, while reflecting a considerable measure of similarity (A is second nearest to B in codicological agreement), confirms that A was not B's only source. Eds. H and V, together with MS P, are closer to B than to any other witness. V is most similar to B by both scribal and codicological criteria. H, which as we have seen tends to resist any pattern, shares more codicological variants with P than with any other source.

We turn next to the branch of MS descent generated by our second oldest witness, MS G². As described in the previous chapter, this fragmentary MS also preserves a valuable text. Comparison of G² to G¹ is hampered by the scarcity of joint attestations. Extant parallels show that the two are similar but not identical. Some of the differences are scribal, e.g. ולמקדש (G¹) vs. למקדש (G²), BMM 1:4; כולם היו כשרין vs. כולן היו כשרות, 8:16; others represent distinctive variants, e.g. כמין עשת או כמין קורה vs. כמין קורה, 1:6; עושין גופו vs. נעשה ממנו, 10:1. There are also a few discrepancies in scriptural citations, e.g. at 1:11 and 10:7-12. When the two MSS attest the same reading, G¹ preserves a superior text to that of G², which is marred by dittography (e.g. 9:14) and homoeoteleuton (e.g. 10:3-4).

To assess those portions of G² for which there is no surviving attestation in G¹, we turn to MS A. It does not include a number of passages found in G², e.g. at 1:14-15; 3:6; 4:14-16. However, each of these omissions appears to be a transcription error in A. Otherwise, with the exception of a few variants (e.g. המאור [A] vs. המשחה [G²], 1:6; בה vs. אותה, 4:2), A and G² corroborate the same recension. Further evidence for this conclusion is supplied by the numerical comparison of variants, in which A is the closest to G² of any witness in the total of all common variants and third closest by codicological measure.

The closest codicological partner to G² is MS M, which has already been paired with ed. D. There is little doubt that D, the *editio princeps*, relies upon the text tradition represented by M as its principal source. But the comparison of variants also reveals a strong correspondence between D and MS E, whose total of common codicological variants is second only to that of M. Other than MS L, with which it has already been paired, E's closest partner with respect to all common variants is MS A. Our hypothesis is that E, a sixteenth century copy, is descended from two genealogical branches represented by A (thirteenth century) and M (fourteenth century). D, the *editio princeps*, draws upon both lines of descent, thus explaining its affinity to M and the number of variants it preserves in common with G^1.

To summarize our comparative classification of witnesses and to advance a theory of interrelationship, we utilize the model of a *stemma codicum*. Owing to the contamination of our textual tradition, the stemma is only speculative. It cannot be regarded as historically exact: lines of descent do not indicate proof of direct dependence, nor have we attempted to infer hyparchetypes. Our purpose is to propose the routes, if not the precise itinerary, by which the surviving witnesses have come down to us.

Century C.E.

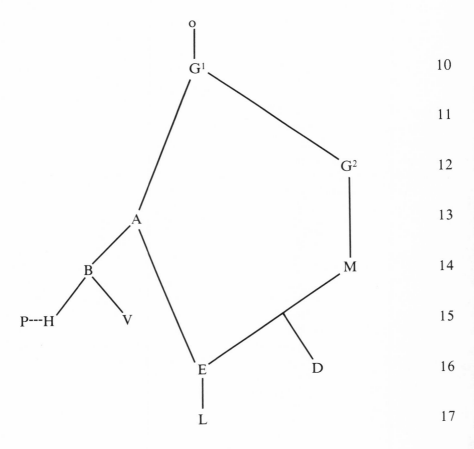

Notes to Chapter Six

TEXT CRITICISM AND STEMMATIC ANALYSIS

1. This principle of text criticism is discussed by Martin L. West, *Textual Criticism and Editorial Technique* (Stuttgart, 1973), 49-53.

2. See, e.g., L. Bieler, "The Grammarian's Craft," *Folia*, Studies in the Christian Perpetuation of the Classics, Holy Cross College 10 (1958): 1-42.

3. A. Dain, *Les manuscrits* (Paris, 1949), 157.

4. Jacob Neusner, "The Modern Study of the Mishnah," *The Study of Ancient Judaism* I, ed. J. Neusner (New York, 1981), 3-26.

5. See the summary of Rosenthal's research by David Goodblatt, "The Babylonian Talmud," *Aufstieg und Niedergang der Römischen Welt* II:19:2 (Berlin/New York, 1979), 268-73. Cf. Peter Schaefer, "Once Again the *Status Quaestionis* of Research in Rabbinic Literature," *JJS* 40 (1989), 89-94, who aptly characterizes this literature as "an open continuum in which the process of emergence is not to be separated or distinguished from that of transmission, (nor) the process of transmission from that of redaction." See also K. H. Rengstorf, "Grundsätzliches und Methodisches," introd. to *Die Tosefta* I, Seder Zera'im (Stuttgart, 1983), ix-xxiii, concerning Gerhard Kittel's term Zuwachs-Traditions-Literatur ("literature of expanding tradition") and its application to rabbinic texts: "Er bedinge eben, dass alle verfügbaren Handschriften wie auch alle Drucke, auch die ältesten Handschriften eingeschlossen, immer nur im Zug der Weitergabe zustandegekommene Textrezensionen böten, aber nicht mehr. Ziehe man aus diesem Sachverhalt Konsequenzen, so komme man notwendig dahin, auf grosse textliche Aspirationen zu verzichten...." (xviii).

6. *Mekilta de-Rabbi Ishmael*, ed. and tr. J. Z. Lauterbach (Philadelphia, 1933-35); *The Treatise Ta'anit of the Babylonian Talmud*, ed. and tr. H. Malter (New York, 1930).

7. Malter, ibid. Hebrew pagination 14.

8. Lauterbach, op.cit. 1:xxxvi-xxxvii.

9. *Sifre on Deuteronomy*, ed. L. Finkelstein (New York, 1969).

10. A graphic example of Finkelstein's propensity for uncorroborated emendation may be found in his "Prolegomena to the Edition of the Sifre on Deuteronomy," *PAAJR* 3 (1932): 3-42, where he produces (at 21-24) a table of proposed emendations divided into columns labeled "Erroneous Reading," "Correct Reading," and "Authority for Emendation," viz., a variant or parallel. For four of the ten emendations, the "Authority" column is blank.

11. Ibid. 38.

12. J. N. Epstein, *Mavo le-Nusah ha-Mishnah* (Tel Aviv, [2]1964), 1-7.

13. Epstein's review of Finkelstein's edition is published in *Tarbiz* 8 (1936/37): 375-92.

14. *Kiryat Sefer* 12 (1935/36): 54-65; *Kiryat Sefer* 14 (1937/38): 323-36 respectively.

15. *The Tosefta according to Codex Vienna with Variants from Codex Erfurt, Geniza MSS and Editio Princeps* v. 1, ed. S. Lieberman (New York, 1955), Hebrew pagination 12.

16. Lieberman, *Tosefeth Rishonim* v. 4 (Jerusalem, 1939), 12-13, 15, describes the problem with respect to the Tosefta: "In the MSS of the Tosefta there is a mixture of different traditions. Of two MSS known to have originated in the same place, one attests a Palestinian tradition and the other another. Thus what appear to be errors in MSS or medieval citations may actually be remnants of different traditions that once circulated.... Consequently, we must regard these MSS and citation variants with respect. It cannot be decided if one version only is correct, although historically there was one (original)." Lieberman assumes that rabbinic text versions must have expanded from a single archetype. Shamma Friedman, however, has suggested that the reverse may be true: rabbinic texts begin with multiplicity and advance toward unity or consensus once they are published; see his article "Le-Ilan ha-Yohasin shel Nushe Bava Mezia," *Mehqarim ba-Sifrut ha-Talmudit*, Israel Academy of Sciences and Humanities (Jerusalem, 1983), 93-147 at 139. If the history of rabbinic text transmission is in fact a centripetal rather than a centrifugal phenomenon, the search for a single archetype is not only hopeless but groundless.

17. An eclectic approach is still defended in certain respects by Shamma Friedman, "A Critical Study of Yevamot X with a Methodological Introduction" (Hebrew), *Mehqarim u-Mesorot* I, ed. H. Z. Dimitrovsky (New York, 1977), 275-441 at 319-20. Friedman argues that any MS based on more than one exemplar is already an "eclectic" text; eclecticism is inevitable. In our view, however, one does not solve the problem of contamination by compounding it.

18. The closest Lieberman comes to evaluating his witnesses is to suggest tendencies; e.g., regarding a fragmentary MS of Tosefta, he writes (*Tosefta*

ki-Feshutah [New York, 1955], 3:13): "It is nearest to MS Erfurt, but often its readings correspond to the printed editions and MS Vienna. It belongs to its own unique family." Chaim Milikowsky, who cites this example "Seder Olam: A Rabbinic Chronography," [Ph.D. diss., Yale Univ., 1981], 170-71 n. 44), points out that from a genealogical perspective Lieberman's statement is unintelligible.

19. *Midrash Bereshit Rabba*, ed. J. Theodor/H. Albeck, 3 vols. (Jerusalem, ²1965); *Mekhilta D'Rabbi Simon b. Jochai*, ed. J. N. Epstein/E. Z. Melamed (Jerusalem, 1955); *Midrash Wayyiqra Rabba*, ed. M. Margulies, 5 vols. (Jerusalem, 1953-60); *Pesikta de Rav Kahana*, ed. B. Mandelbaum, 2 vols. (New York, 1962); *She'eltot de Rab Ahai Gaon*, ed. S. K. Mirsky, 5 vols. (Jerusalem, 1982); *Sefer Halakhot Gedolot*, ed. E. Hildesheimer, 3 vols. (Jerusalem, 1971-88), not to be confused with the earlier edition (Berlin, 1888-92) edited by A. Hildesheimer.

20. *Bereshit Rabba*, ed. Theodor/Albeck, v. 3, introd. pt. 1, p. 137.

21. *Wayyiqra Rabba*, ed. Margulies, v. 5, introd. 34-37; *Pesikta de Rav Kahana*, ed. Mandelbaum, Hebrew introd. 17-19.

22. *Halakhot Gedolot*, ed. E. Hildesheimer, v. 1, introd. 15-21. V. 3 includes an extensive introduction by N. Z. Hildesheimer; however, there is no discussion of MS filiation.

23. To cite several examples: "Seder Olam: A Rabbinic Chronography," ed. Ch. Milikowsky; *Midrash Mishle: A Critical Edition* (Hebrew), ed. B. Visotzky (New York, 1990); *Midrash Shemot Rabbah, Ch. 1-14: A Critical Edition based on a Jerusalem MS with Variants, Commentary and Introduction* (Hebrew), ed. A. Shinan (Tel Aviv, 1984); "Mishna Aboda Zara: A Critical Edition with Introduction" (Hebrew), ed. D. Rosenthal (Ph.D. diss., Hebrew University, 1980); Eliezer Segal, "The Textual Traditions of Tractate Megillah in the Babylonian Talmud" (Hebrew), (Ph.D. diss., Hebrew University, 1981).

24. *Midrash Shemot Rabbah* ed. Shinan, ibid. 24-29.

25. Shinan is content with vague filiation claims: "Generally it agrees with....For the most part it is similar to...." etc. No examples or explanations accompany these conclusions.

26. "Seder Olam: A Rabbinic Chronography," op.cit. Stemmatic analysis has also been applied (in more limited fashion) to MSS of Gen. R. by Lewis Barth, *An Analysis of Vatican 30* (Cincinnati, 1973), esp. 81-89; Michael Sokoloff, *The Geniza Fragments of Bereshit Rabba* (Hebrew; Jerusalem, 1982), esp. 51-55.

27. Milikowsky, "Seder Olam," 123-27, 137-38, 141-62.

28. Paul Maas, *Textual Criticism*, tr. B. Flower (Oxford, 1958).

29. See S. Timpanaro, *La Genesi del Metodo del Lachmann* (Florence, 1963).

30. Henri Quentin, *Essais de critique textuelle* (Paris, 1926), ch. 9.

31. J. N. Epstein, *Mavo le-Nusaḥ ha-Mishnah* (Tel Aviv, [2]1964), 1-7.

32. See, e.g., Patricia Galloway, "Clustering Variants in the *Lai de l'Ombre* Manuscripts: Techniques and Principles," *Association for Literary and Linguistic Computing Journal* 3 (1982): 1-7. I am grateful to Dr. John Dawson of the Literary and Linguistic Computing Center at Cambridge University for calling my attention to this article.

33. The rough percentages of attestation: MSS A, B, L, M, P, ed. D = 100%; ed. V = 85%; MS G^2 = 35%; MSS E, V^2 = 30%; MS G^1 = 25%; ed. H = 20%. We omit MS R (5%) as too small to be significant. For the present purpose of determining MS filiation, the attestations of V/V^2 and H/H^2 are combined.

34. Our approach is similar but not identical to that proposed by J. G. Griffith, "Numerical Taxonomy and Some Primary Manuscripts of the Gospels," *Journal of Theological Studies* n.s. 20 (1969): 389-406. Griffith's method compares MSS by creating a numerical series of each one's agreements with the others, expressed as a graduated scale. No distinction is made between scribal and codicological variants as we have defined them, although agreements that seem to be coincidental are excluded. Those MSS with the most discrepant patterns appear at opposite ends of the scale; those most in agreement appear side by side and are grouped as distinct taxa. As M. L. West, *Textual Criticism and Editorial Technique* (Stuttgart, 1973) points out (p. 47), the problem with this procedure is that it may affiliate a group of MSS only because they do not agree with others, rather than because of any mutual affinity. This may prove only that the MSS are "equally promiscuous"; it does not prove that they are mutually dependent. Our procedure is, more simply, to examine the pattern of agreement and disagreement among the witnesses through the distributional comparison of scribal and codicological variants. Our conclusions will necessarily be more cautious than Griffith's.

35. See n. 33.

36. See n. 33.

Explanation of Transcription and Apparatus

Transcription

The present text of BMM is a diplomatic transcription of MS A (Oxford Bodleian 370.11). The transcription preserves the original text in all respects, including scriptural citations (even when at odds with the Masoretic text), abbreviations, shortened words, and chapter numeration. We also attempt, insofar as possible, to reproduce the line spaces of MS A which separate various pericopae.

Our policy is to correct or modify the text only where errors or defects appear to be certain. In such cases we do not rely on our own conjecture but on the attestation of other witnesses to the text, with priority assigned to the readings of MSS G^1 and G^2. The source of each correction is easily identified by consulting the apparatus.

Corrupt letters or words are enclosed in {braces}. When a substitute text is required, it appears immediately afterward in ⟨angle brackets⟩. Similarly, where there is an obvious omission, we enclose the restored passage in ⟨angle brackets⟩. Where MS A is illegible, doubtful transcriptions are marked by a small circle above each letter (˚). When the text quotes the Hebrew Bible, we add the location of the citation in (parentheses).

Text lineation is numbered at the right margin in increments of five. Numeration is sequential within each chapter. A chapter and line number summary appears at the top margin of each page. Pagination continuous with the Introduction is found at the upper corner of each page but is not used for reference.

Apparatus

Correlation of text and apparatus is accomplished by line number (introduced by a hyphen, —) and lemmata (marked by a left square bracket, [ ). A lemma may consist of one word or several. Extended lemmata are marked by an ellipsis (...) between the first and the last word; the intervening text will be found at the text line location indicated. When a word appears more than once on a text line, the lemma includes a supralinear Arabic numeral to distinguish the proper referent, e.g. מכאן² 13— referring to the second occurrence of מכאן on line 13.

Variants are recorded after each lemma. The reading is given first, followed by the siglum. When other witnesses concur, their sigla are added, but the first siglum is the actual source of the cited variant. When the text represented by a lemma is wanting from a given witness, the abbreviation ח' (for חסר) appears before the siglum.

The order of siglum citation places direct MS tradition before secondary attestations, as follows:

גֹ¹ גֹ² ב (בֹ¹ בֹ²) מ ע ל ד ו וֹ¹ ה הֹ² פ ר

Four of the sigla are cited selectively: בֹ¹ and בֹ² (only when they differ); וֹ¹ (only when it differs from ו); and הֹ² (only when it differs from ה). On the rare occasions when MS A (א) is quoted in the apparatus, it is listed before the other witnesses. When abbreviation or illegibility necessitates, we depart from the order of citation, reporting first the most fully preserved version of the variant, then reverting to the regular sequence. Each siglum citation is separated from the next variant by a period (.). When all variants for a given lemma have been presented, a vertical line (|) introduces the next lemma.

{Braces} and ⟨angle brackets⟩ appearing in the text are transferred intact to the lemmata in the apparatus. [Square brackets] denote lacunae or supplemented text owing to physical damage. Circles above letters (˚) indicate doubtful transcriptions owing to illegibility. (Parentheses) in the apparatus serve two functions. First, they are reserved for editorial comments, e.g. identifying erasures, marginal interpolations or corrections, etc. Second, parentheses serve to epitomize incongruities between similar variants, especially in lengthy passages when repetition would swell the apparatus beyond reason. This form of citation also contributes to a clearer picture of MS affiliation. Parenthetical insertions are always marked with sigla to identify their source. The insertions function in two ways: either to substitute another reading for the immediately preceding word(s), or to add on, in which case the insertion is preceded by an ellipsis (...).

We shall cite several examples. At BMM 6:22, the apparatus includes:

ומשה לא משה] ומשה לא משו מקרב (מתוך עו.) המחנה בעלוף.

This means that witnesses בעלוף agree except for one difference: ע and ו have מתוך instead of מקרב.

At 1:34 the apparatus reports:

ארכו] ארכה של כל אחת (...ואחת ד.) במד.

This indicates that במד agree except that ד adds on ואחת.

A third example may be found at 6:25:

שילה וגו'] שילה ויקחו (ויצאו פ.) משם את ארון ברית יי (...יושב הכרובים ג².) ג²בדפ.

This means that ג²בדפ preserve a similar reading but with two differences among them: פ has ויצאו instead of ויקחו, and ג² adds on יושב הכרובים.

A final example reports a more involved citation at 12:11:

על המשכן ועל המזבח] ואת קלעי (וקלעי ה.) החצר (...סביב ופ.) אשר על המשכן ועל המזבח (...סביב בוהפ.) בלוהפ.

In this example בלוהפ attest a similar reading but with three differences among them: ה has וקלעי instead of ואת קלעי; ו and פ add on סביב to החצר; and בוהפ add on סביב to המזבח. This last is an atypical instance; few of the epitomized citations contain multiple substitutions.

The apparatus is organized as a negative entry system, i.e., the variants cited are readings that disagree with the base text (MS A). The advantage of this system is that it makes for an apparatus of reasonable size and utility. The disadvantage is that in the case of fragmentary witnesses, one cannot distinguish between concurrence and lacunae. We have sought to remedy this problem in two ways. First, we have already listed (pp. 96-97) the precise attestations of each witness by chapter and line number of the text of BMM. Should it appear uncertain whether the absence of a given witness from the apparatus indicates an agreement or a lacuna, the answer may be found by consulting this table. Second, previously unpublished fragments of the two most important partial witnesses (G¹ and G²) are found not only in the collation of variants but in full transcription in Appendix A. This has spared us the necessity of including broken or otherwise unintelligible readings in the apparatus. Since the Genizah fragments (particularly G¹) represent the most ancient and accurate evidence of the text of BMM, we deemed their complete presentation a *desideratum*.

Unique difficulties are posed by variant citations from MS P, a divergent recension of BMM. Interpolations from MS P that would unduly burden the apparatus have been removed to Appendix B, where they are cited according to text line and lemma. Variants in parallel with other witnesses are incorporated in the apparatus. Lacunae present a particular citation problem, since MS P fails to attest extensive sections of BMM. Our practice is the same as with variant readings: lacunae are cited only in those portions of MS P that parallel other witnesses.

An utterly comprehensive apparatus is not practical. If the collation of variants is too minute, the history of the text tends to disappear in a mass of non-evidential data. We impose a number of limitations on the citation of variants. First, except when *matres lectionis* might affect the morphology of a word, *plene* or defective spelling distinctions are not considered significant. As we have seen, each of our witnesses freely mixes the two. The spelling in each variant is given according to the text of the first siglum cited. Second, abbreviations or shortened words are not entered as variants unless their expansions are not obvious. Third, the terms 'וג or 'וכו to conclude scriptural citations are often included in the apparatus but owing to their ubiquity are not treated as variants. Fourth, in regard to numbers, neither gender nor form of scribal notation is brought as a variant, since our witnesses are inconsistent in both respects. Finally, chapter separations and headings are not included in the apparatus; they are described by MS in chapter 5.

Register of Parallels

Located between the transcription and the apparatus is a register of parallels from tannaitic, amoraic, and geonic sources. Medieval citations are not included here; the major ones (e.g., Sefer ve-Hizhir, Midrash ha-Gadol) have been incorporated into the apparatus.

Correlation with the text is accomplished by line number and hyphen. Lemmata are separated from the citations by a period. Each lemma indicates where the parallel begins; lengthy parallels are indicated by subsequent references (e.g. הנ״ל, שם) to the initial citation.

The exact scope of each parallel, indexed by BMM line number and by source, may be found by consulting the tables in chapter 3 of the Introduction, where each passage is discussed in detail.

Critical Symbols and Sigla

Symbols

Text:

( )	biblical citation
⟨ ⟩	addition or correction from parallel source
{ }	deletion
°	doubtful transcription

Apparatus:

( )	editorial comment or alternate reading
⟨ ⟩	addition or correction from parallel source
{ }	deletion
°	doubtful transcription
[	lemma
[ ]	lacuna or supplemented text
...	ellipsis
•	conclusion of sigla citation
|	separation of lemmata
'ח	wanting

Sigla

Apparatus	Introduction	MSS and Editions
א	A	MS Oxford Bodleian 370.11 (base text)
ב	B	MS Oxford Bodleian 151.3
¹ב	B¹	F. 155a-b
²ב	B²	F. 157a-b
¹ג	G¹	MS Genizah Taylor-Schechter A45.24, K21.20, F11.32

149

ג²	G²	MS Genizah Dropsie 83, Adler 2940, Taylor-Schechter K21.82
ד	D	Ed. Venice 1602 (*editio princeps*)
ה	H	Midrash ha-Gadol Genesis and Exodus (ed. Margulies), Leviticus (ed. Steinsaltz), Numbers (ed. Rabinowitz)
ה²	H²	Midrash ha-Gadol Leviticus (ed. Steinsaltz)
ו	V	Sefer ve-Hizhir (ed. Freimann)
ו²	V²	MS Sopron (Oedenburg) Hungary 2
ל	L	MS Jewish Theological Seminary L899a.24
מ	M	MS Munich Bayerische Staatsbibliothek Cod. Hebr. 95
ע	E	MS Epstein 31.11 (now lost)
פ	P	MS Paris Bibliothèque Nationale 353.5
ר	R	MS Parma Biblioteca Palatina 2198

ברייתא דמלאכת המשכן

פרק א 1-3

ר' אומ' עשר תרומות הן תרומה ותרומת מעשר וחלה ובכורים ותרומת

נזיר ותרומת תודה ותרומת הארץ ותרומת מדיין ותרומת שקלים ותרומת

משכן   תרומה ותרומת מעשר וחלה ובכורים ותרומת נזיר ותרומ'

—1 ר'] ח' **מפ.** | אומ'] תניא פ. | הן] הם ל. | תרומה] תרומה גדולה **מעל.** | ותרומת מעשר] תרומת מעשר ל. | וחלה] חלה ג[2]**בעלד.** ותרומת חלה **ה.** | ובכורים] ובכורים ב**עפו**[2]. וביכור [ ] ג[1]. ותרומת בכורים **ה.** —2-1 ותרומת נזיר] ח' **בופ.** ותרומת איל נזיר **מ.** תרומת איל נזיר ל. —2 ותרומת[1] תרומת ל. | תודה] לחמי תודה **מל.** התודה פ. | ותרומת הארץ] תרומת הארץ ל. | ותרומת מדין ל. ותרומת שקלים פ. | ותרומת מדיין] ותרומת מדין ג[2]**במעד.** תרומת מדיין ל. ותרומת הארץ ו. ח' פ. | ותרומת שקלים] תרומת שקלים ל. ותרומת השקלים ו. ותרומת הארץ פ. —2-3 ותרומת משכן] ותרומת משכן (המשכן **מד.**) ותרומת חוצה לארץ **במדו.** תרומת המשכן ל. ותרומת המשכן ותרומת מדין ותרומת הדשן פ. —3 תרומה] תרומת לכהנים פ. | ותרומת מעשר] ותרומת מעשר ללויים ומן הלוים לכהנים פ. | וחלה] חלה ג[2]**בפ.** וחלה ותרומת (ותרומה ו[2].) חוצה לארץ וו[2]. | ובכורים] ביכורים פ. | ותרומת נזיר] ח' **בופ.** ותרומת איל נזיר **מל.** —3-4 ותרומ' תודה] ותרומת לחמי תודה **מל.** ותרומת תודה ותרומת חוצה לארץ **ה.** |

151

תוֹדה לכהן תרומ' הארץ לכהנים וללוים ולנתנים ולמקדש ולירושלים

5   תרומ' מדין לאלעזר (הכהן) תרומ' שקלים לאדנים תרומ' משכן ממנה

נעשה משכן ושמן המאור וקטרת הסמים ובגדי כהנים ובגדי כהן גדול

משכן ארכו שלשים אמות ורחבו עשר אמות וגבהו עשר אמות

ר' יוסה אום' {ארכן} ⟨ארכו⟩ שלשים ואחד אמות כיצד היה מעמיד

הקרשים היה נותן עשרים קרשים בצפון ועשרים בדרום ושמנה במערב

—4 לכהן] לכהנים ג²במלדוהפ. | תרומ' הארץ] תרומת שלמים ותרומת הארץ ב. | ותרומת
הארץ מו. תרומת הארץ למלך המשיח ה. | לכהנים] ולכהנים ה. | וללוים] ללוים ד. |
ולמקדש] למקדש ג²ה. ח' פ. | ולירושלים] ולירושלם ג²מו². | ולירושלם ולמקדש פ. —5 |
מדין] מידין ב. מדיין ל. | לאלעזר] לאליעזר ב. | (הכהן)] הכהן תרומת הדשן אצל המזבח
פ. | תרומ' משכן] תרומ' המשכן משכן ג²מ. | ממנה] שממנה ג²מ. שממנו בדרף. —6 |
נעשה] היו עושין ג²בדוה. עשו פ. | משכן] ממנו משכן ג¹. גופו של משכן ג²בדוהפ. גוף
המשכן על. | ושמן...גדול] ח' מ. | המאור] המשחה ג²עלה. | כהנים] כהונה עלפ. | ובגדי
כהן גדול] ח' ל. ובגדי כהן גדול שמונה פ. —7 משכן] ח' מ. המשכן ד. | ארכו] אורכן
פ. | אמות¹] אמה ג¹ג²במלדוהפ. | אמות²] אמה בלף. | עשר אמות³] עשר אמה בפ. כרחבו
מל. | —8 יוסה] יוסי ג¹ג²במלדוהפ. | {ארכן} ⟨ארכו⟩] ח' ב. | אמות] אמה ג²במלדוהפ. ח' ע.
אמה במה נחלקו בעבין שלקרשים נחלקו ה. | כיצד] כאיצד ו. כאיזה צד ו². | היה מעמיד]
מעמיד מע. הקים משה ה. היה משה מעמיד פ. —9 הקרשים] את הקרשים ג²במעלדופ.
את המשכן ה. | היה נותן] נותן על. | קרשים] קרש במלדו². | בצפון] ח' פ. | בדרום] קרש
בדרום ג¹בלדו². קרשים בדרום ג²וף. |

פרק א 10-14

10 במזרח לא היה קרשים אלא ארבע עמודים שעליהן {המסך} ⟨הפרוכת⟩ שנ'

{ועשית מסך} ⟨ונתת את הפרוכת וג'⟩ (שמות כו לג) ⟨ונתתה אותה על

ארבעה עמודי שטים⟩ (שם כו לב)   היה עושה האדנים חלולין והקרש

חרוץ מלמטה רביע מכאן ורביע מכאן וההרוץ חציו באמצע ועושין לו

שתי יתידות כמין שני חמוקים ומכניסן לתוך שני אדנים שנ' שני

—10 במזרח] אבל במזרח ג^{2}במלדוה. ובמזרח פ. | היה] היה שם ג^{2}במלדדה. היה בו ופ. היה בה ו^2. | קרשים] קרש ג^{1}ג^{2}במלדוהפ. | ארבע] ה' פ. | עמודים] עמודי ⟨ע⟩]די ג^2.⟩ שטים ג^{2}במלדוה. עמודי שטים מצופים זהב פ. | שעליהן] שעליהם נותנין ג^{2}מל. שעליהם נותנים ע. שעליהן היו נותנין בהפ. שעליה' היו נותנים ד. שהיו נותנין עליהם ⟨עליהם ו^1.⟩ וו^2. | ⟨הפרוכת⟩] את הפרוכת ג^{2}במלדוה. מסך הפתח לפתח המשכן פ. | —11 ⟨ונתת את הפרוכת וג'⟩] ח' ג^{2}מה. ונתת אותה על. ונתת את הפרוכת תחת הקרשים דו^2. ונתת' את הפרכת תחת הקרש ו. | ונתתה אותה] ונתת מ. ח' לו. וכתוב ונתת אותם ד. | —11-12 על ארבעה] ח' ו. | —12 שטים] שטים מצפים זהב ג^2. | היה] והיה מדו^2. | האדנים] את האדנים במדוה. את האדנים אדני כסף פ. אדנים ל. | חלולין] חלולים לדוהפ. | —12-13 והקרש חרוץ] וחורץ את הקרש במדהו^{2}פ. וחורץ הקרש על. וחורץ את הקרשים ו. | —13 מלמטה] למטה על. מלמטן ה. | מכאן'] מכאן בו. מיכן בו. מיכאן ג^{2}פ. | מכאן^2] מכן בו. מיכן בו. מיכאן פ. | והחרוץ] וחורץ ג^{2}מעלה. והחריץ בפ. והחרץ ד. והחורץ ו. | באמצע] באמצעת ב. | ועושין לו] ועושה לו במדוה. ועושה ל. ועושה לקרש פ. | —14 יתידות] ידות בלפ. יתדות מד. | כמין] כמו פ. | שני'] ח' פ. | שניין] ח' פ. | חמוקים] חמוקין ⟨]וקין ג^2.⟩ ג^{2}מלדו. חוקין ע. חמוקי יריכים פ. | ומכניסן לתוך שני אדנים] ומכניס שתיהן לשני אדנים פ. | —14-15 שני שני אדנים] שנ' שני אדנים תחת הקרש (תחת הקרש האחד ו. תחת הקרש האחד לשתי ידותיו ה.)

פרק א 15-17

15 אדנים (שם כו יט)   היה חורץ את הקרש מלמעלה אצבע מכאן ואצבע

מכאן ונותנן לתוך טבעת אחת של זהב כדי שלא יהו נפרדין זה מזה שנ'

ויהיו תאמים (שם כו כד) שאין ת"ל אל הטבעת האחת (שם) ומה ת"ל אל

בוה. תחת הקרש האחד ושני הׄסׄנׄין יוצאין מתוך הקרשים שנים לכל אחד ואחד שמשקיע
הזכר בתוך הנקבה שנ' משלבות אשה אל אחותה דברי ר' נחמיה שר' נחמיה אומ' אין ת"ל
משולבות מה ת"ל מלמד שעשה להם שלבין כסולם המצרי מ. תחת הקרש וב' הׄסׄנין יוצאין
מתוׄך הקרשים שנים לכל א' וא' שמׄכׄנׄיׄסׄין את הזכר לתוך הנקבה שנ' משלבות אשה אל
אחותה דברי ר' נחמיה שהיה ר' נחמיה אומר שאין ת"ל משולבות ומה ת"ל משולבות שעשה
להם שלׄיׄבׄון כסולם המצרי ל. (וכעין קטעי ע.) שנ' שני אדנים תחת הקרש האחד לשתי
ידותיו הניפין (והוסף בסוגריים: ס"א סניפין וס"א הסנין) יוצאים מן הקרשים שנים שנים לכל
אחד ואחד שמשקיע את הזכר בתוך הנקבה שנא' משלבות אשה אל אחותה דברי ר' נחמיה
שר' נחמיה אומר אין ת"ל משולבות מה ת"ל מלמד שנעשה להם שולפים כסולם המצרי ד.
(וכעין קטעי ג².) | —15 היה חורץ] וחורץ בפ. חרץ ו. | והיה חורץ ה. | את הקרש] את
הקרש ע. הקרשים ל. הקרש ו. | מלמעלה] מלמעלן מו. למעלה על. | מכאן] מיכאן ג²פ.
מיכן בו. | —16 מכאן] מיכאן ג²פ. מיכן בו. | ונותנן] ונותן בוהפ. | לתוך] בתוך (בת]
ג².) ג²בדוהפ. | טבעת אחת] טבעות מעלד. | כדי] ח' ל. | יהו] יהיו לדה. יהיה ו. | נפרדין]
נפרדים ד. | —17 ויהיו] והיו בלופ. | תאמים] תואמים מלמטה ב. תואמים מלמטה ויחדו
יהיו תמים על (אל ה.) ראשו את הטבעת האחת (אל הטבעת האחת לו²ה.) מלו²ה. תאמים
מלמטה ויחדיו יהיו תמים וגו' ד. תואמים מלמטה וגו' וטבעות זהב לבדים פ. | שאין ת"ל
אל הטבעת האחת] ח' ב. | —18-17 ומה ת"ל אל הטבעת האחת] | לומר אל הטבעת
ג¹. ח' מ. ומה ת"ל הטבעת האחת ה. |

פרק א 21-18

הטבעת האחת מקום שנותנין בו את הבריח   אר" נחמיה הקרשים מלמטן

עוביין אמה ומלמעלן כלין והולכין עד כאצבע שנ' ויחדיו יהיו תמים

20 (שם) ולהלן הוא אומ' תמו ונכרתו (יהושע ג טז) ר' יהוד' או'

מלמטן ומ̇למעלן עוביין עובייין אמה שנ' ויחדיו יהיו תמים (שמות כו כד)

—18 אר" נחמיה. שבת צח, ב.

—18 מקום שנותנין] אלא הוא מקום שנותנים ע. | בו] בו] ח' במעלדוה. | את] ח' ע. | הבריח]
הבדים ב. הקרשים ו. הטבעת ה. | —18-21 אר' נחמיה... תמים] ח' ד. ר' נחמיה אומר
([מיה או' ג'.) ג'מעלה.| הקרשים] ח' מ. עובין של קרשים] —19-18 מלמטן עובייין
עובייין מלמ̇] | ג'. עביין מלמטה ב. עובין של קרשים מלמט' מ. עובייין מלמטן ע. עובייין
מ̇למ̇טה ל. מלמטן ו. היו רחבין מלמטה ה. היה עובייין מלמטה פ. | —19 אמה] אמה אחת
במוהף. ח' ל. | ומלמעלן] ומלמעלה בופ. ומלמעלן מ. ולמעלה ל. | כלין] היו כלין בופ.
היו כולין ה. ח' מ. | והולכין הולכי' מ. | כאצבע] בעצבע ג'. | באמצע ו'2. | ויחדיו] והיו
תואמ' מלמטה ויחדיו ב. ח' ו'2ה. | יהיו] היו ב. והיו ו. ויהיו ה. | תמים] תמים] תמים על ראשו
בעף. תאמים מלמטה ו. תאומים מלמטה ויחדו יהיו תמים אל ראשו ה. | —20 תמו ונכרתו]
תמו נכרתו ג'על. היורדים עד (על ה.) ים הערבה ים המלח תמו נכרתו מה להלן כלין
והולכין אף כאן כלין והולכין בהף (וכעין ו.). תמו נכרתו מה להלן כלין והולכין אף כאן
כלין והולכין מ. | יהוד'] יודה ו. | —21 מלמטן ומ̇למעלן] ח' במוף. מלמטה ומלמעלן ל.
הקרשים היו רחבין אמה מלמטה ואמה מלמעלה ה. | עובייין] הקרשים עובין מו. קרשים היו
עובייין פ. ח' ה. | אמה] אמה אחת למטה ואמה אחת למעלה ב. אמה אחת מלמטה ואמה
אחת מלמעלה מפ. אמה אחת מלמטן ואמה אחת מלמעלן ו. ח' ה. | ויחדיו] יחדו מ. והיו
תואמים ויחדיו ה. ויהיו תואמים מלמטה ויחדיו פ. | תמים] תמים תמים על ראשו עלף. תמים
מלמד שכולן כאחד שוין ה. |

פרק א 22-25

כיצד היה מעמיד הקרשים היה נותן ארבעים אדני כסף בצפון וארבעים

בדרום וששה עשר במערב וארבעה במזרח הרי מאה אדנים שנ' מאת אדנים

(שם לח כז)   כל קרש וקרש היו בו שתי טבעות זהב אחת מלמעלה

25 ואחת מלמטה שבהן היו נותנין הבריחים והבריחים ארכו של כל אחד

—22 כיצד] כאיצד ו²‎. כאיצן² ‎. | ג'‎¹. ת״ר כאיזה צד ה.‎ | היהן] היו מל. ח‎' ד.‎ | מעמיד] מקיימין מ. מקימין ע.‎ מקרין (והוסף בסוגריים: פי' מעמיד) ד.‎ | הקרשים] את המשכן בעלדוהפ.‎ את המסוכן מ.‎ | ים ג'‎. | נותן] נותן בו מל. מעמיד ה.‎ | אדני כסף] אדנים של כסף ה.‎ | בצפון] בדרום מלפ.‎ —23-22 וארבעים בדרום] וארבע' אדני כסף בדרום בו.‎ וארבעים אדני כסף בצפון מ.‎ וארבעים אדני כסף בדרום וכן בצפון ע.‎ וכן בצפון ל.‎ ומ' בצפון פ.‎ —23 וששה עשר] י״ח ג'‎. | במזרח] במערב ו. ח' פ.‎ | הרי] ח' ל.‎ | מאה] מאת במדרו²הפ. ח' ל.‎ | אדנים] אדני' ב. ח' עלפ.‎ | שנ'] ח' פ.‎ | אדנים²‎ אדנים למאת (למאה ב. למא' מ.‎) הכבר וג' במלו²ה. אדנים למאת הכבר ככר לאדן דפ.‎ —24 כל] וכל ג'‎ במלדוף.‎ ונותן הקרשים בתוך האדנים וכל ה.‎ | קרש וקרש] קרש בל. ככר וככר מ.‎ היו] היה פ.‎ | בון לו על.‎ | זהב] של זהב דה.‎ | אחת] ח' לפ.‎ מלמעלה] למעלה בעל.‎ למעלן ו. מלמעלן הפ.‎ —25 ואחת] ושתי טבעות זהב פ.‎ | מלמטה] למטה בעל.‎ למטן ו. מלמטן ה.‎ | שבהן] בהם מל.‎ ובהם ע.‎ שבהם וה.‎ ח' ה.‎ | היו] היה מל.‎ | נותנין] נותן מלפ.‎ נותנים עד.‎ | הבריחים] את הבריחים במעלדוף.‎ את הבריחים ואמצען חלול לבריח התיכון ה.‎ והבריחים] ח' בודהפ.‎ והבריחים שתים העליונים ושתים התחתונים של רוח דרום דמ.‎ —26-25 ארכו של כל אחד ואחד] אורכן של כל אחת ואחת ב.‎ ארכן שכל (של כל ו².‎) אחד ואחד מו²‎. ח' על.‎ אורכן‎ | אחד ג'‎. | ארכן של בריחים ה.‎ אורכן של כל אחד ואחד

פרק א 26-30

ואחד שלשים אמות כנגד עשרים קרשים והאמצעי ארכו שתים עשרה אמה

כנגד שמנה קרשים שמשוקע בקרשים באמצען למזרח ולמערב שנ' והבריח

התיכון מבריח וגו' (שם כו כח)   כשם שהיה עושה לקרשים שבצפון

כך היה עושה לֹקרשים שבדרום אבל מערב אינו כן אלא ארכו של כל אחד

30 שמנה אמות כנגד ששה קרשים והקרשים והבריחים והאדנים והעמודים

מן הבריחים פ. | —26 שלשים] חמש עשרה אמה נמצא השתים ארכן שלשים דמפ. ארכן
שלשים ל. ח' ע. | אמות] ח' ע. | במעדו. אמה לפ. | כנגד... והאמצעי] ח' ע. | כנגד] כשיעור
פ. | קרשים] קרש שנ' ואמה וחצי האמה רוחב הקרש האחד פ. | והאמצעי] והאמצע ב.
והאמצעי שלמערב ה. | ארכו] אורכן ב. ארכן ע. | שתים עשרה] שלשים מעד. שמֹנים ל. |
אמה] ח' ע. | —27 שמנה] עשרים מעד. עֹ ל. | קרשים] קרשים וכריח אחת בצפון ב.
קרשים והאמצעי ארכו י"ב כנגד שמנה ע. אמה ל. | שמשוקע... ולמערב] ח' ה. | שמשוקע]
שמשקע ב. שמשקיע מעלדו. | בקרשים באמצען] באמֹצען ג[1]. באמצע הקרשים בלד.
באמצע קרשים מעו. | למזרח ולמערב] למערב ולמזרח ב. מן המזרח למערב דמ. לצפון
ולדרום ולמערב מן הקצה אל הקצה ל. | שנ'] ח' פ. | —28 מבריח] ח' ג[1]ה. בתוך הקרשים
במלד. בתוך ו. בתוך הקרשים מבריח מן הקצה אל הקצה פ. | כשם... שבדרום] ח' ה. |
כשם] וכשם ב. | לקרשים] בקרשים ו[2]. | —29 היה] היוה ב. | לקרשים] בקרש [ ] ו[2]. |
מערב] במערב במעלדו. השאר במערב ה. | של] ח' ו[2]. | כל] ח' מלד. | אחד] אחד ואחד
בעוה. אחד מן העליונים והתחתונים מד. | —30 שמנה] תשעה ב. שש מד. ח' ע. | אמות]
אמות ארבעה קרשים והאמצעי שתים עשרה מד. י"ב ע. | ששה] שמנה מעד. | והקרשים]
ח' מלוה. | והאדנים והעמודים] והעמודים והאדנים בד. |] מודים והאדנים ו[2]. והעמודים
מלו. מצופין זהב והטבעות של זהב עבין שלקרשים ה. |

פרק א 35-31

ומקום עוביין של קרשים מצופה זהב שנ' ואת הקרשים תצפה זהב

(שם כו כט) שאין ת״ל בתים לבריחים (שם) ומה ת״ל בתים לבריחים

מקום שהבריח התיכון נ[כנס]   ויצף את הבריחים זהב (שם לו לד)

כיצד היה עושה היה מביא שפופרֹת זהב ארכו אמה וחצי וגובהו חצי

35 אמה ונותן בחללו של קרש מקום שנותנין הבריח

31— ומקום] מקום ב ד וה. | עוביין] רחבן ל. הבריחים ה. | של קרשים] שבקרשים ו. ח' ה. | מצופה] מלצפה ב. מצופן ל. היו מצופין ה. | זהב[1]] זהב וצדדי הקרשים פ. | תצפה] צפה ו. זהב[2]] זהב בתים לבריחים **מעלד**. זהב ואת טבעתיהם תעשה זהב בתים לבריחים הפ. —32 ומה ת״ל בתים לבריחים] זהב (ונמחק: כיצד היה עושה) לבריחים ב. ומה תל' לו' ו'[2]. | —33 שהבריח התיכון נ[כנס]] שהבריחים נכנסין מבלו. שהבריח נכנס ד. שהבריח יהיה מצופה זהב ה. שהבריח נכנס תצפה זהב פ. | ויצף את הבריחים זהב] ח' ה. ואת הבריחים תצפה זהב פ. | —34 כיצד] כאיצד ו. כאיזה צד ה. | היה עושה] היה עושה ע. עושים ל. | היה מביא] מביא ל. היה נוטל ה. | שפופרֹת] שני פיפיות ב. שתי שפיפיות מ. שתי שפפרות ע. ב' שפופרת ל. שתי שפיפיות ד. אותו שפיפיות ו. שתי שפיפות ה. שפיפות פ. | זהב] של זהב **במלדוהפ**. | ארכו] ארכה של כל אחת (... ואחת ד.) במד. לאורכן של כל א' וא' ל. וארכה של כל אחד ואחד ו. וארכה של כל אחת ה. ואורכה של כל אחת ואחת פ. | וחצי] ומחצה **מלדוה**. וחצי האמה כנגד רחבו של קרש פ. | —35-34 וגובהו חצי אמה] ח' במלדוהפ. | —35 ונותן] ונותנו בד ו[2]. | ונותנין מו. ונותנן ה. | בחללו] היה מביא שני בחללו ב. בתוך הללו פ. | מקום] במקום כניסתו ע. במקום כ[ני]סתן ל. | שנותנין הבריח] שנותנין את הבריח בה. שהבריחים נותנין מ. ונתינתו של בריח ע. ונתינתם של בריחים ל. שנותנין את הבריחים ד. שהברים נותנין ו. שהבריחים] ו[2]. הכנסה הבריחים פ. |

פרק ב 1-7

פרק ב"   כיצד היו מקרין המשכן היו מביאין עשר יריעות של

תכלת ושל ארגמן ושל תולעת שני ושל שש שנ' ואת המשכן תעשה עשר

יריעות של וגו' (שם כו א) וחוטן כפול שלשים ושנים על שלשים ושנים

דברי ר' נחמיה שהיה אומ' חוט אחד כפול לשנים שזור לארבעה משזר

5   לשמנה נמצא חוטן כפול שלשי' ושנים על שלשים ושנים וחכמי' אומ'

חוט אחד כפול לשנים שזור לשלשה משזר לששה נמצא חוטן כפול לעשרים

וארבעה   היה מחברן לשתי אחת של חמש ואחת של חמש שנאמ'

4 חוט אחד. ירוש' שקלים פ"ח ה"ד נא ע"ב.—

1—כיצד] כאיצד ו. | היו] ח' ב. היה לדפ. | מקרין] מקרה פ. | המשכן] את המשכן
במלדופ. | היו מביאין] היה מביא במדופ. מביא ל. —2 ושל ארגמן] וארגמן בלפ. |
2-3 ושל תולעת... וגו'] ח' ב. | ושל תולעת שני] ותולעת שני לפ. | ושל שש] ושל משזר
מ. ושש משזר לפ. ושל שש משזר ד. —3 יריעות] ח' ו². | של] ח' מלדופ. | וחוטן] חוטן
אחד מד. חוטן ל. וחוטין ו². | תנו רבנן היריעות חוטן ה. | שלשים ושנים¹] ח' ה. —4
דברי] דב ב. | שהיה אומ'] שהיה ר' נחמיה אומ' במלדהפ. שהיה רנ"א ו. —5 חוטן חוטם
ל. חוטין ו. חוט ה. חוטו פ. | —5-6 שלשי'... כפול²] ח' ל. | שלשי' ושנים¹] לשלשים ושנים
במדפ. על שלשים ושנים ה. | על שלשים ושנים²] ח' מדה. —6 שזור] מדה. | משזר]
משזור ב. | חוטן] חוטין ו. חוטו פ. —7 היה מחברן] והיה מביא לשתים ומחברן ב. והיה
מחברן מו². | והיו מחברן ו. | והיה תופרן פ. | לשתי] לשתים ל. | וילאות] חבילאות ב. לולאות
מעו². ח' ל. ויאלות ד. | יריעות ו. | אחת של חמש] אחת אחת של חמש ע. וכל אחת ל. |
ואחת] ואחד ואחד ב. |

פרק ב 8-12

{שנא'} חמש היריעות (שם כו ג) והיה מחברן בלולאות של תכלת שנ'

ועשית ללאות תכלת (שם כו ד) והיה מחברן לחמשים קרסי זהב שנ'

10 ועשית חמשים קרסי זהב (שם כו ו) ונראין קרסים בלולאות ככוכבים

ברקיע   אורך היריעה עשרים ושמנה אמה (שנ' אורך היריעה האחת

שמנה ועשרים באמה) (שם כו ב) צא מהן עשר לגגו של משכן נשתיירו

—10 ונראין. ירוש' מגילה פ"א ה"יד עב ע"ג-ע"ד; שבת צח, ב-צט, א; פסיקתא דרב כהנא פ"א ס"ג, מהר' מנדלבוים 8.

—8 היריעות] היריעות תהיינה (תהיין לו.) חוברות וגו' בלדו. יריעו' תהיין חוברות אשה אל אחותה מ. | בלולאות] ללולאות בו. | לחמשים קרסי זהב מ. ללאות ד. ללואות ו[2]. | של תכלת] תכלת בד. ח' מו. | —9 תכלת] תכלת על שפת היריעה מ. | והיה מחברן] והיה וחברן ב. ומחברן ל. | לחמשים] בחמשים ל. | —9-10 שנ'... זהב] ח' בו. | —10 ונראין קרסים] והקרסים היו נראין במד. הקרסים נראים ל. והיו הקרסים נראין ו. והקרסים [ו[2]. ונראים קרסי זהב פ. | בלולאות] במלדו. | ככוכבים] ככבים ב. | —11 ברקיע] ברקיע (והוסף בסוגריים: עיין בשב' פ' הזורק דף צ"א ע"ב) ד. | אורך] אורכן בו[2]. ארכן מדלו. ואורכן פ. | היריעה'] של יריעות במלדופ. | עשרים ושמנה] שמנה ועשרי' בפ. | אמה] באמה ב. אמות מדו. | —12 באמה לרוחבו של משכן פ. | שמנה ועשרים באמה)] ח' מו. | —12-13 צא... מכאן[2]] ח' ב. | צא] תן פ. | מהן] מהם מל. | מהם עשר אמות מן המזרח למערב ו. | עשר] עשר אמות מלדפ. ועשר אמות ו. | לגגו] לרחבו מלד. לגבהו ו[2]. לרוחב גגו פ. | נשתיירו] ח' פ. | —12-14 נשתיירו... נשתיירו] ח' ו. |

פרק ב 15-13

מהן שמנה עשרה אמה תשע אמה מכאן ותשע מכאן רחב היריעות ארבעים אמה

‏(שנ׳ ורחב ארבע באמה) (שם) צא מהן שלשים לגגו של משכן נשתיירו

15 עשר אמות למערב לפי אורך הקרשים

13— מהן שמנה עשרה אמה] שם מד. ח׳ לפ. | תשע מכאן ותשע מכאן] תשע אמות מצד
זה ותשע אמות מצד זה שהם (שהן ד.) יורדות ומכסות את הקרשים עד שמגיעות לאדנים
הא למדת שהאדנים גבהן אמה מד. תשע מכאן ותשע מכאן שהם יורדות ומכסות הקרשים
עד שמגיעות לאדנים הא למדת שהאדנים גבהם אמה ל. ותשע מהן לציידי המשכן בדרום
וט׳ מהן לציידי המשכן בצפון פ. | רחב היריעות] רחבן של יריעות מל. ורחבן של יריעות
ד. ארבעים] ארבע ב. | אמה[2] אמות ב. | —14 באמה) | אמה ב. באמה היריעה האחת מל.
באמה היריעה וגומ׳ ד. | צא מהן שלשים] שלשים אמות מן המזרח למערב ב. צן   [מן
המזרח למערב שלשים אמות מ. צא מהן ל׳ אמה ממזרח למערב על. צא מהן שלשים אמות
מן המזרח למערב ד. | לגגו של משכן] ועשר אמות שנותנן לגגו של משכן ב. שנתן לגגו
של משכן מד. ח׳ על. | מ. | —14-15 נשתיירו עשר אמות] ועשר ב. ע   ] ‏ . ועשר אמות
לדפנו של משכן על. ועשר אמות דו. (נמחק: ועשר אמות למערבו ו.[2]) | —15 למערב לפי
אורך הקרשים] למערבו ומותר (והמותר מו.) שביריעות פורפן (פורפון ו.) לאחוריו במו.
למערבו לפי קומת הקרשים על. למערבו לאחורי המשכן הרי ארבעים ד. |

פרק ג 1-6

פרק ג״   היה מביא אחת עשרה יריעות מנוצה של עזים ארכן של כל

אחת ואחת שלשים אמה שנ׳ ועשית יריעות עזים (שם כו ז) והיה מחברן

לשתי וילאות אחת של חמשה ואחת של ששה שנ׳ ויחבר את חמש היריעות

לבד וג׳ (שם כו ט; לו טז)   והיה עושה חמשים לולאות בכל אחת

5   {ומחברן בקרסי נחשת} והיה מחבר לולאות חמישים בקרסי ‹נחשת› חמשים

שנ׳ ועשית לולאות חמישים (שם כו י) ואו׳ ועשית קרסי נחשת חמשים

1— היה] והיה ב. | אחת] אחת ב. | אחת] עשתי בופ. | מנוצה] מן הנוצה **מעלד**. | מן נוצה] של נוצה פ. |
1-2 ארכן... אמה] ח׳ **על**. | ארכן] וארכה **מד**. | ארכה] וא֗ר֗כֹה ב.). | וארכו ו. | 2— אחת ואחת]
אחד ואחד ו. אחת ד. אחת אחת פ. | אמה] באמה ו. אמה ורוחב ד׳ אמה פ. | ועשית] ועשרים
ועשית ב. | עזים] עזים לאהל על המשכן **מעפ**. עזים ועשית לולאות תכלת וג׳ **ל**. 2-5—
והיה... נחשת] ח׳ **ל**. | והיה מחברן] והוה מחברם **ע**. והיה מחברו פ. | 3— וילאות] חבילות
ב. לולאות **מופ**. ללאות ו[2]. | הוילאות ד. | 4— לבד וג׳] לבד ואת שש היריעות לבד **בד**. |
4-5 והיה... נחשת] ח׳ **מו**. | והיה עושה] והיה מחברן **בד**. והוא מחברן **ע**. | חמשים לולאות]
ללולאות חמשים ב. בחמשים לולאות **ע**. בלולאות של חמשים ד. 4-5— בכל אחת {ומחברן
בקרסי נחשת} שנ׳ ועשית חמישים לולאות ב. שנ׳ ועשית לולאות חמשים וג׳ **ע**. שנאמר
ויעש לולאות חמשים וג׳ ד. שנ׳ ויעש לולאות תכלת חמשים על שפת היריעה פ. 5—
והיה מחבר] והיה מחברתן ב. והיה מחברן **על**. | לולאות] לולאות הלולאות **מדו**.
ח׳ **בעלפ**. | חמשים] לחמישים **במדו**. בחמשים **על**. | בקרסי ‹נחשת› חמשים] קרסי נחשת
בעלדופ. קרסים נחשת **מ**. 6— ועשית לולאות חמישים ואו׳] ח׳ **במעלדו**. | ועשית קרסי
נחשת חמשים] ועשית חמשים קרסי נחשת (קרסי נחשת חמשים ד.) ארכן של יריעות שלשים
אמות צא מהם (מהן ד.) עשר אמות לרחבו נשתיירו עשר אמות מצד זה ועשר

פרק ג 7-11

(שם כו יא) רוחב היריעות ארבעים וארבע שנ' ורחב ארבע באמה

היריעה האחת (שם כו ח) צא מהן שלשים (אמה) לגג המשכן ועשר

לאחוריו נשתיירה שם יריעה אחת שכופלה על פני האהל שנ' וכפלת את

10 היריעה הששית אל מול פני האהל (שם כו ט) ר' יוסי אומ' כופל

חצייה אל פני האהל וחצייה היה סורח אחורי המשכן שנ' וסרח העודף

(... אמות ד.) מצד זה שהם יורדות ומכסות לעמודים והאדנים מד. (וכעין קטעי ג².). וע] [
קרסי נחשת ו². | —11-7 רוחב... העודף] ח' ג². | —7 רוחב היריעות] רוחבן של יריעות
במעלד. | ארבעים וארבע] ארבעים וארבע אמות מעלד. | —8-7 ורחב ארבע באמה
היריעה האחת] אורך היריעה (... האחת ו.) בו. וארבע אמות רוחב (... היריעה וגו' ד.) מד.
וארבע באמה רוחב היריעה האחת ל. | —8 צא מהן] צא מהם מלו². | הוצא מהן ע.] (אמה)
אמות מד. | לגג המשכן] ואורכו של משכן ב. לארכו של משכן מעלד. של משכן ו. לאורך
גגו של משכן פ. | (ועשר] ועשר אמות במע. ועשר אמה ד. עשר אמות ו. י' מהן פ. | —9
לאחוריו] שנותן לרוחבו של משכן ב. שנותן למערבי' של משכן מ. לרחבו שנותן ע. שנותן
לרחבו ל. לאחורי המשכן הרי ארבעים ד. לרחבו (לגבהו ו².) של משכן ו. לאחוריו המשכן
כנגד קומתו של קרשים פ. | נשתיירה] נשתייר ו. | שם] ח' ב. | שכופלה] שכופל ב. שכפולה
מעלד. | (על] אל מול מל. אל ו. | —9-10 וכפלת את היריעה] וכפל' את היריע מ. | —10
אל מול פני האהל] ח' במלו. | יוסי] יהוד' מעלד. | —10-11 כופל חצייה] חציה היה כופל
בלד. חציה מ. חצייה היה כפול ע. חצה כפול ו. וחצי היריעה היה כופל פ. | —11 אל
פני האהל] על פני האהל ב. אל מול פני האהל מלדפ. ח' ו. | וחצייה היה סורח] וחצי
היריעה היה כופל ב. וחציה היה סרוח מלדו. | אחורי] של אחורי ל. לאחורי ו. אחורי (וכתוב
תחת השורה) מ. | העודף] עד ש] [גיעות לארץ אמה מיכאן ואמה מיכאן | [

פרק ג 12-16

(שם כו יב) היה מביא כלי אחד של עור ארכו שלשים אמה ורחבו עשר

אמות ומלבישו לאהל שנ' ועשית מכסה לאהל (שם כו יד) וכמין פספיסין

היו למעלה דברי ר' נחמיה ר' יהוד' אומ' שני כלים היו התחתון של

15 עורות אלים מאדמים והעליון של עורות תחשים שנ' מכסהו ומכסה התחש

אשר עליו מלמעלה (במדבר ד כה)

והאמה מזה והאמה מזה בעודף ג². העודף ביריעות האהל וגו' ד. | 12— היה מביא] דתניא
היה מביא ה. | אחד] אחד גדול ג²מלדוה. | עור] עורות אלים מאדמים מלפ. | עור אילים
מאדמים ד. | ארכו] ארכן ל. | אמה] ח' במו. אמה כנגד אורכו של משכן פ. | 13— אמות]
אמה כנגד רחבו של משכן פ. | ומלבישו] שמלבישו ג²במלד. שמלבשין וה. שמלבישן ו².
ופורש פ. | לאהל¹] לאהל מן המזרח (ן) | מזרח ג²) למערב ג²בלוה. לאהל על המשכן מן
המזרח למערב מד. על היריעות פ. | מכסה] וכסה ב. | לאהל²] לאהל עורות וגו' ד. לאהל
עורות אלים מאדמים פ. | וכמין] כמין ה. | פספיסין] פסיפסין ג²ו²ה. פספסין במלד. פסופסין
ו. | 14— היו למעלה] עשוי מלמעלה ג²במד. עשוי למעלה לו²ה. | ר' נחמיה] ח' ב. ר'
יוסי וה. | יהוד'] יהודה ו². | שני] כמין שנא' ו. כמין שני ה. | כלים] מכסאות ג². | התחתון]
תחתון ג². התחתון היה ד. | 15— עורות] עורותי ח' ב. | אלים] אילים בו²ה. | מאדמים] מאדמים
שנאמ' מכסה עורות אלים מאדמים ג². מאודמים ב. ח' ו. | והעליון] ועליון ג². והעליון היה
ד. | מכסהו] ומכסהו מדוה. | 16— מלמעלה] ח' בו. |

פרק ד 1-5

פרק ד"   היה אורג הפרכ{ו}ת עשר אמות על עשר אמות ועושה בה

ארבע {תסברין} ⟨תוברין⟩ ותולה בה בֹאונקלאת שעל גבי העמודים שנ'

ונתתה הפרכת (שמות כו לג) שם היה נתון צנצנת המן וצלוחית של שמן

המשחה ומקלו של אהרן שקדיה ופרחיה ובגדי כהנים ובגדי כהן גדול שם

5   היה אהרן הכהן נכנס ארבע פעמים ביום הכיפורים   מחוץ לפרכת

—1 ועושה בה. פירוש הגאונים לסדר טהרות, כלים כה, א, מהד' אפשטיין ע' 67. —3
צנצנת המן. תוספתא יום הכיפורים ג, ז; תוספתא סוטה יג, א; ירוש' שקלים פ"א ה"א מט
ע"ג = ירוש' סוטה פ"ח ה"ג כב ע"ג; יומא נב, א; כריתות ה, ב; הוריות יב, א. —5 אהרן
הכהן נכנס. תוספתא כלים ב"ק א, ז.

—1 הפרכ{ו}ת] את הפרכות ג²במלדופ. | אמות¹] ח' ו. | אמות²] אומת ב. ח' ו. | ועושה
בה] ועושה בו ב. ותולה בה פ. | —2 ארבע] ח' ל. | ⟨תוברין⟩ תוביריז ג². | תובדין מ. תיברין
ד. | בה בֹאונקלאת] אותה באנקלאות ג². אורכה בֹאונקלאת ב. אורכה באונקלאו' מ. ארכה
באונקלא' לו². | אותה באונקלאות ד. | | באנקלאות ו. בה אורכה באנקלאות פ. | שעל
גבי] על גבי מד. שע"ג ל. | העמודים] העמו{ו}דים מכוונת היתה תחת הקרסים ג². | —3
הפרכת] את הפרכת תחת הקרסים וג' ג²מדו. את הכרוכת (הפרוכה פ.) תחת הקרסים בפ.
את הפרכת וג' ל. | שם היה] ושם היה מד. | ולפנים הימנה פ. | נתון] ארון נתון ג²מד.
הארון עם הלוחות וספר תורה וכפורת עם שני כרובים פ. | צנצנת] וצנצנת ג²מדפ. | —3-4
המן... ופרחיה] ח' (והוגה בגליון ביד אחרת: המן וצלוחית שמן המשחה ומקלו של אהרן
ושקידיה ופרחיה ב.). | —3-4 המן] שלמן ג². | —4 שקדיה] וצלוחית של שמן המשחה] ח' פ. | —4 שקדיה]
ושקדיה ג²עד. בשקדיה מו. | ובגדי כהנים] ח' מד. (והוגה בגליון ביד אחרת: | כהני'
ובגדי ב.). ובגדי כהונה ל. | וצלוחית של שמן המשחה פ. | ובגדי כהן גדול] ח' מדפ. | שם]
ושם ג²בלדפ. ולשם מו. | —5 היה] ח' פ. | אהרן] ח' בו. | הכהן] ח' ג²במלדופ. | נכנס]
נכנס כהן גדול בו. | ארבע פעמים] ארבעה פרקי' ד. שנים פעמי' פ. | ביום] בֹיום פעם אחת
בשנה ביום ג². | פעם אחת ביום ב. | מחוץ] ומחוץ ופ. |

פרק ד 6-12

היה שולחן ומנורה מונחים אלא ששולחן בצפון ומנורה כנגדו בדרום

שנ' ושמת השולחן {באהל מועד} וגו' (שם כו לה) ואומ' ואת המנורה

נכח השולחן (שם)   {ששולחן בצפון ומנורה כנגדו בדרום וגו'}

כשם שהיו מונחים באהל מועד כך היו מונחים בבית עולמים אלא שאהל

10 מועד ארכו שלשים אמה ורחבו עשר אמות ובית עולמים ארכו ששים ורחבו

עשרים הא למדת שאהל מועד רביע של בית עולמים   כשם שהיה אורג

הפרכת כך היה אורג את האפוד ואת החשן אלא שבאילו היה נותן חוט

—6 היה] היו **מד.** | ומנורה[1] | והמנורה **ל.** | מונחים] מונחין ג[2]**במופ.** | אלא] ח' **פ.** | ששולחן] שהשולחן **במלד.** שהשלֹחָן ג[2]. שהמנורה **ו.** שולחן **פ.** | בצפון] בדרום **ו.** | ומנורה[2] | והמנורה **ע.** והשלחן **ו.** | כנגדו בדרום] כנגדו ב. בדרום כנגדו **לדפ.** בצפון **ו.** —9-7 שנ'... אלא] ח' **ע.** —8-7 שנ'... השולחן] ח' **פ.** —7 השולחן] את השולחן וג' **בלו.** את השלחן מחוץ לפרכת **מד.** | ואומ'] וכת ב. ח' **מלדו.** —8-7 ואת המנורה נכח השולחן] ח' **לו.** —9 כשם] וכשם ב**מלדופ.** | מונחים[1] | מונחין ב**פ.** ח' **ו.** | מונחים[2] מונחין **מופ.** —10-9 שאהל מועד] ח' **ל.** —10 ארכו] אורכן **בל.** | אמה... עולמים] ח' **ל.** | ורחבו] ורחבן ב. | אמות] אמה ב**מפ.** | עולמים] העולמים ב. | ארכו[2] ארכן **ל.** | ששים] ששים אמה ב**מלדופ.** | ורחבו[2] ח' **מ.** —11 עשרים] עשרים אמה ב**לופ.** ח' **מ.** עשרים אמות **ד.** | למדת] למדנו **פ.** מועד] ח' **מ.** | רביע] רְבִֽֿיעַ (נמחק) ב. רביעי **מ.** רביעו **עו**[2]**.** רביעי **ו.** כחציו **פ.** | עולמים] העולמים ב. | כשם] וכ | **מ.** וכשם **ו.** | אורג] אורג **פ.** —12 הפרכת] את הפרוכת ב**מלדופ.** | אורג] אורך **פ.** | את האפוד ואת החשן] חושן ואפוד **פ.** | אלא] א'ל **מ.** | שבאילו היה נותן] שבאלו היה **בו.** שבאלו היה **לד.** שב |] היה בהם **מ.** שבאפוד ובחושן היה **פ.** | —13-12 חוט אחד יתר של זהב] חוט אחד של זהב יותר **בל.** חוט זהב יתר **מ.** חוט בהן

פרק ד 13-18

אחד יתר של זהב שנ' וירקעו את פחי הזהב (שם לט ג)   כשם שהיה

אורג הפרכת כך היה אורג את המסך אלא שהפרכת מעשה חשב (שנ' ועשית

15 פרכת תכלת וארגמן) (שם כו לא) והמסך מעשה רקם (שנ' ועשית מסך

לפתח האהל) (שם כו לו) דברי ר' נחמיה שהיה או' כל מקום שנ'

(מעשה) חשב שתי פרצופות (מעשה) רקם פרצוף אחד   וקני המנורה

היו מכוונים כנגד רחבו של שלחן הזהב   מזבח הזהב היה נתון בתוך

<hr>

15— מעשה רקם. ירוש' שקלים פ"ח ה"ד נא ע"ד; יומא עב, ב. —16— ר' נחמיה. תוספתא
שקלים ג, יד. —18— מזבח הזהב. ירוש' שקלים פ"ו ה"ד נ ע"ב.

יתר של זהב ע. חוט של זהב יתר ו. | —13— הזהב] הזהב וקצץ פתילים מד. הזהב וקיצץ
פתילין לעשות בתכלת ובארגמן וגו' פ. | כשם] וכשם ו. | —14— הפרכת] את פרפת המסך
ב. פרכת המסך מו. את הפרוכת המסך ל. את פרכ' המסך דו[2]. | את הפרוכת פ. | המסך]
מסך הפתח במלדו. מסך הפתח לפתח האוהל פ. | שהפרכת] שפרוכת ב. | —14-15— (שנ'...
וארגמן)] ח' לופ. | —15— והמסך] ומסך הפתח במלו[2]. | ומעשה הפתח ו. | —16— האהל] ח'
ו. | שהיה או'] שהיה ר' נחמיה או' ג[2]מלדופ. | —17— פרצופות] פרצופות יש בו. פרצופין
מד. פרצופין הם ל. | (מעשה)] ומעשה בל. | פרצוף] אין בו אלא פרצוף ג[2]. אינו אלא פרצוף
במ. אינו | פרצוף ל. | אחד] אחד בלבד ג[2]בלדופ. | המנורה] מנרה ג[2]. מנורה מלדו. |
—18— היו מכוונים] היו מכוונין מונחין ג[2]. מכווניו ב. היו מכווניו מו[2]. מכווניו היו ו. היו
מכווניו | | פ. | הזהב'] ח' ג[2]מלדופ. | מזבח] ושולחן ב. ומזבח מלדופ. | הזהב[2]] ח'
פ. | נתון] נותן ל. | —18-19— בתוך הבית] באמצע הבית ג[2]. כנגד הפתח ב. |

פרק ד 24-19

הבית וחולק הבית מחציו ולפנים והיה מכוון כנגד {הכפרת} {הפרכת}

20 שנ' {ונתת את מזבח הזהב לקטרת לפני ארון העדות} (שם מ ה) {ונתת

אותו לפני הפרכת אשר על ארון העדות} (שם ל ו) מן הקרשים שבדרום

עד קני המנורה שתי אמות ומחצה ומן המנורה עד השלחן חמש {חמש}

אמות מן השלחן ועד הקרשים שבצפון שתי אמות ומחצה הא למדת שרחבו

עשר אמות מן הקרשים שבמערב עד הפרכת עשר אמות מן הפרכת עד

19— וחולק] וחילק ג². | והיה חולק ל. | הבית²] את הבית ג²ב¹מלדוף. | מחציו] ומחציו
ג³מעלדוף. | ולפנים] לפנים מ. | והיה מכוון] היה מכוון עג². | מכוון] היה בדו. מכוון מלו²
מכוון והיה פ. | (הפרכת)] אמצע הפרכת ע. | 21— אותו] את ב¹. לפני ו. ח' ו²ל. | לפני]
פני ב¹. לפני (ונמחק: עדות) ב². | אשר על ארון העדות] ח' במעדוף. | מן] כמן ג². ומן
בפ. | שבדרום] שמדרום ע. | 22— קני] קנה מ. ח' ע. | המנורה¹] מנורה ג²לד. | ומן] ומקני
בד. מקנה מ. ומן קני לפ. | מן קני ו. מקני ו². | המנורה²] מנורה לד. מנורה שבדרום פ.
עד²] ועד ל. | השלחן] השולחן שבצפון פ. | 23— מן] ומן בלדפ. | ומן] מן ב²מוף. |
24-23— שבצפון... הקרשים] ח' (והוגה בגליון: נ"ל חסר כאן) מ. | שרחבו] שברוחב ב².
24— מן¹] ומן בל. | הקרשים] הקרשים (ולהלן: ארכן של יריעות שלשים אמה שנ' ארך
היריעה האח' שלש' באמ' צא מהן עשר לרחבו שלמשכן נשתיירו שם עשר אמות מצד זה
ועשר אמות מצד זה שהן יורדות ומכסות את הקרשים ואדנים עד שמגיעות לארץ אמה מיכן
ואמה מיכן שנ' והאמה מזה והאמ' מזה בעודף) ו². | עד הפרכת] עד קני מנורה ג². עד קני
המנורה דו. עד קנה המנורה מ. עד המנורה ע. ועד קני המנורה ל. עד קני המנורה שנגד
הפרוכת פ. | מן הפרכת] מקני מנורה ג². ומן הפרוכת ב. | מקנה המנורה מ. מן קני המנורה
עו. ומקני המנורה ל. מקני המנורה דפ. | 25-24— עד השלחן] ועד השלחן ג²מל. עד קני
המנורה ב. |

פרק ד 25-26

25 השלחן חמש אמות מן השולחן עד מזבח הזהב חמש אמות מ‏מזבח הזהב עד

הפתח עשר אמות הא למדת שארכו שלשים אמה

25—חמש‏[1]] עשר ו. | מן השולחן] מקני המנורה ב. | ומן השולחן ל. | עד מזבח

ב‏[1]. ועד מזבח על. | ממזבח] מזבח ב‏[1]. | וממזבח על. | 25-26—עד הפתח] עד פתחו של

אהל ג‏[2]. עד הקרשי׳ שבמזרח (והוגה בגליון: איני מבין כי לא היו קרשי׳ במזרח מ.) מד.

עד (ועד ל.) העמודים שבמזרח על. עד שבמזרח ו. עד פתח המשכן פ. | 26—עשר] חמש

מ. ט״ו ע. | אמות] אמה ע. | שארכו] שארכן ג‏[2]ל. שאורכו של משכן פ. |

פרק ה 6-1

פרק ה" החצר ארכה מאה אמה ורחבה חמשים אמה שנ' ועשית חצר

המשכן וגו' (שם כז ט) אבל אין אתה יודע כמה רחבה של קלע כשהוא

או' וקומה ברחב חמש אמות (שם לח יח) הוי או מ' מה קומה חמש אמות

אף רחב חמש אמות כיצד היה מעמיד החצר היה נותן עשרים אדנים של

5 נחשת בצפון ועשרים בדרום ועמוד בתוך כל אחד ואחד וטבעת קבועה

באמצע היה נותן הקונטסין במיתרים ובעמודים והקונטיסין ארכו של

---

1 —החצר] חצר ג[2]במעוף. חצר היה ד. | ארכה] אורכו ב[2]. | ורחבה] ורוחבו ב[2]. | אמה[2]
ח' ב'. | חצר] את חצר ג[2]במדוף. את החצר ל. | —2 המשכן] המשכן לפאת נגב תימנה
ג'. ח' לו. | אין] אי ג[2]בעל. | אתה... של] ח' ע. | רחבה] רחבו ג[2]לו. ח' ב'. | —2-3 כשהוא
או'] שנ' ג[1]ג[2]ע. | ממה שנ' ב. שתדרע בה גובהה של חצר כיון שכתוב מ. כמה היה דכתי'
ל. שתדרע בה גבה של חצר כשהוא אומר ד. אלא ממש"כתי' ו. | —3 ברחב] ח' מד. | הוי
או מ'] ח' ג[2]במעלדו. הוי ב[1]. | מה קומה חמש אמות] כמה קומה חמש [| ג[2]. מה
קומה הוי חמש אמות ב[2]. מה קומת קלע חמש מ. ח' ע. | —4 אמות] ח' מ. | כיצד] כאיצן [
ג[1]. | החצר] את החצר במלדו. | אדנים] אדונים ב[1]. | —5 ואחד] ואחד ב[1]. ואחד וקונטיסין
היו שם מד. | וטבעת] וטבעת קבועה בתוכו (בתוכה ב[2].) של כל אחד ואחד וטבעת ב. |
—6 באמצע] במציעתן ב[1]. באמצעית' ב[2]. באמצעיהם מל. באמצעיתן ד. באמצעתן ו.
היה] והיה במלדו. | הקונטסין] את הקונטסין ג[2]ד. את הקונטיסין במל. את הקונטסין ו. |
במיתרים] במיתריהן ל. במתרים ו. | ובעמודים] ועמודי' ב. ובעמודיהן ל. | והקונטסין]
| קונטסין ג[2]. והקונטיס מ. | ארכו] ח' ל. |

פרק ה 7-12

כל אחד {עשרה} ⟨ששה⟩ טפחים ורחבו שלשה ותולה את הטבעת בתוך

האונקלי וכורך בה את הקלע כמין קלע זו של ספינה נמצא הקלע יוצא

מן העמוד שתי אמות ומחצה {ו}מצד זה ושתי אמות ומחצה מצד זה וכן

10 לעמוד השיני הא למדת שבין עמוד לעמוד חמש אמות   היה מחבר את

הקונטיסין במיתרים ובעמודים ומחברן לתוך יתידות של נחשת כשם שהיו

יתידות למשכן כך היו יתידות לחצר שנ' לכל כלי המשכן וגו'

7— אחד] אחד ואחד ג¹במלדו. שלשה] שלשה טפחים ל. | הטבעת] הטבעות ב². | 8—
האונקלי] האונקלי שבעמוד מ. האונקלי שבעמוד ד. | וכורך] ותולה מ. | זו] ח' מ. | זה לדו.
נמצא] נמצאת ג¹מ. | יוצא] יתר ב. יוצאת מ. | 9— זה] זה¹ ו. | 10-9— ושתי... השיני] ח'
ו. | ושתי אמות ומחצה מצד זה²] ושתי אמות ומחצה ב¹. (הוגה בגליון: ושתי אמות ומחצ'
מצד זה ב²). | וכן מצד זה מ. | 10— השיני] השני מלד. | הא למדת]] למדתה ג¹.
הא למדת וכן לעמוד השני ו. הרי פ. | שבין עמוד לעמוד חמש אמות] ה' אמות בין עמוד
לעמוד פ. | את] ח' ו. | 11— הקונטיסין] הקנטיסין ו. | במיתרים] במיתרין ג¹. | במיתריהן
ל. במתרים ו. | ובעמודים] ובעמודין ג¹ב². | ובמודין ב¹. | לתוך] בתוך ג¹במלדו. | יתידות
של נחשת מ. יתידות האהל מ. יתדות של נחשת לד. | כשם] וכשם במלדו. | 12— יתידות¹]
יתידות ג¹מד. | למשכן] לאהל כך היו יתידות לאהל ב¹. לאוהל ב². | יתידות²] יתדו[ן]
ג¹. יתדות מד. | 12-13— שנ'... של חצר] ח' ו. | המשכן] המשכן בכל עבודתו ב. |

פרק ה 13-19

(שם כז יט) אבל אין אתה יודע כמה מן הקֿלעים עד פתחו של חצר כשנא'

את קלעי החצר וגו' (במדבר ד כו) מה מן המשכן ולמזבח עשר אמות כך

15 מן הקלעים ועד פתחו של חצר עשר אמות אבל אין אתה יודע כמה פתחה

של חצר שנ' ומסך שער החצר מעשה רקם וקומה ברחב (שמות לח יח) שאין

ת"ל חמש אמות (שם) ומה ת"ל חמש אמות אלא ללמד שארכו עשרי' אמות

ורחבו חמש אמות　　　　　　וכן לצפון מאה אמות שנ' וכן לפאת צפון

(שם כז יא) למערב חמשי' אמה שנ' ולפאת ים קלעים חמשים אמה

13— אין] אי בד. ח' ל. | הקֿלעים] הקלע ב. | עד פתחו] לפתח ב¹. | לפתחה ב²מלד. |
כשנא'] שנ' ג¹בלו. משכתו' מ. כשהוא אומר ד. | —14 את] ואת במלדו. החצר וגו'] החצר
ואת מסך וג' ל. החצר ואת מסך שער החצר ד. | מה מן המשכן] כשם שמן המשכן ל. | מה
בין המשכן ד. מה מן משכן ו. | ולמזבח] למזבח בלדו. | —15 ועד פתחו] עד פתחה בל. ועד
פתחה מ. לפתחה דו. | אין] אי בלד. | אתה] את ב. | פתחה] גובה פתחה מד. רחבו של פתח
ל. | —16 של חצר] החצר ל. | שנ'] כיון שנ' מע. כשהוא אומר ד. | ומסך] מיסך ב¹. מיסך
פתח ב². ומסך פתח] פתֿח ל. | מעשה רקם] ח' מלדו. | וקומה ברחב] וקומה ברוחב חמש אמות
במל. ח' ד. קומה ברחב ו. | —17 אלא] ח' במלדו. | ללמד] ללמֿד במלדו. שארכו] ארכו
ב. | אמות³] אמה במדו. ח' ל. | —18 אמות¹] ח' בו. אמה מ. | לצפון] לצפון צפֿון במד.
לפאת צפון בארוך קלעים פ. | אמות²] אמה במלדו. ח' פ. | וכן¹] ח' ב². | צפֿון] צפון בארוך
וג' ב. צפון מאה בארוך ד. | —19 למערב] למערב... אמה²] ח' ב. | למערב] ולמערב מלדו. | ולפאת]
וכן לפאת מ. ורוחב החצר לפאת פ. | —19-20 חמשים... ולפאת] ח' ל. | חמשים²] חמש
עשרה פ. |

פרק ה 20-27

20 (שם כז יב) ולמזרח חמשים אמות שנ' ולפאת קדמה מזרחה חמשי' אמה

(שם כז יג) צא מהן חמש עשרה אמות שנ' חמש עשרה אמה קלעים לכתף

(שם כז יד) ואו' ולכתף השנית מזה ומזה לשער החצר וגו' (שם לח טו)

ומן הקלעים שבדרום ועד האהל עשרים אמות והאהל עשר אמות

ומן האהל ועד הקלעים שבצפון עשרים אמות הא למדת שרחבה חמשים אמה

25 מן הקלעים שבמזרח עד האהל חמשים והאהל שלשים {ואחת} (אמה) ומן

האהל ועד הקלעים שבמערב עשרים אמה הא למדת שארכה מאה אמה שנ'

אורך החצר מאה באמה (שם כז יח)   ר' יוסה או' שאין ת"ל חמשים

20—ולמזרח חמשים אמות] ולמזרח חמשים (חמשים ב¹.) אמה בדו. ח' מפ. | שנ' ולפאת] ורוחב החצר לפאת פ. | חמשי' אמה] ח' לו. | —21 צא מהן] צא מהם מלד. הוצא מהם ע. אמות] אמה בדו. ח' מל. | חמש²] וחמש מו. קלעים חמש ד. | אמה] ח' במ. | קלעים ח' בד. | —22 ואו'] ח' במלדופ. | ולכתף... החצר וגו'] ח' מ. | השנית] השני ד. השיניה פ. | מזה ומזה] מזה ב¹. ט"ו ל. ח' ו. | לשער החצר וגו'] ח' במלדו. | —23 ומן] מן במלדו. | ועד] עד במלדו. | אמות¹] אמה ב¹. | אמות² אמה ב¹. | —24 ומן מן בו. | ועד] עד ו. | שבצפון] שבצפון ב¹. | אמות] אמה במלדו. | שרחבה] שרחבו ב²ל. | חמשים] עשרים ד. | —25 מן] ומן במעלד. | שבמזרח] שבמערב מד. ח' לו. | עד ועד מלד. חמשים] חמשים אמה בו. שלשי' אמה מד. | והאהל שלשים (אמה)] ח' מד. והאהל ל' אמות ו. | —25-26 ומן האהל ועד הקלעים] ומן (ונמחק: קלעים ב².) האהל עד הקלעים ב. מן האהל עד הקרשים ו. | —26 שבמערב] שבמזרח ג¹מד. שׁבׁמׁעׁרׁב ל. | עשרים אמה] נ' אמה ג¹מד. ח' ל. | שארכה] שאורכו ל. | —27 ר' יוסה] ר' יוסי ג¹במעלד. ר"י ו. | שאין] אין מד. |

פרק ה 28-31

בחמשים (שם) אלא ללמד שארכה מאה אמה ורחבה חמשים   כפתחו של

{היכל} (אהל) כך פתחו של אולם כפתח החצר כך פתחו של היכל מכאן

30 היה ר׳ יוסה ב״ר יהודה או׳ קרפף שהוא (כ)בית סאתים כחצר המשכן

מטלטלין בתוכה בשבת

—30 קרפף. עירובין כג, ב.

—28 אלא] ומה ת״ל חמשים בחמשים זה לפני האהל במדו. ומה ת״ל ולפאת ים קלעים חמשים אמה ולמזרח חמשים בחמשים זה לפני האהל ל. | ללמד] הא למדת במלדו. הכי ללמדך ע. | אמה] ח׳ במ. | ורחבה] ורחבו ב. | חמשים] חמשים אמה בל. חמשים ברחב מ. חמשים אמה ברחב ד. | —28-29 כפתחו... אולם] ח׳ מ. (ובסוגריים: כפתחו... אולם בפתחה של חצר כך פתחה של היכל ד.) | כפתחו] כפתחן ב. ופתחו פ. | —29 כך פתחו של אולם] כך פתחו של היכל ב. כפתחו של היכל י׳ אמה פ. | כפתח החצר] כפתה החצר ב׳. פתח של חצר ב׳. פתחה של חצר מ. כפתחו של חצר ל. פתחו של חצר ד. כפתחה של חצר ו. | פתחו של היכל] פתחן פתחן של אולם ב. פתחו של היכל בגובה פתחו של היכל כך רוחב פתחו של אולם מד. | —29-30 מכאן היה] מיכן היה ג׳ב. מכאן אמר מלד. מיכן אמר ו. | —30 יוסי ג׳במלדו. או׳] ח׳ במלדו. מיכאן אמרו חכמים פ. | קרפף] קרפין (עם סימן שאלה) ב. קרקף ל. | שהוא (כ)בית] שהוא (כ)בית בלפ. בבית בלפ. | יותר מבית מ. שהוא עד בית ד. יתר מבית ו. | כחצר המשכן] כחצר משכן ג׳. בחצר המשכן ד. שהוא כחצר המשכן פ. | —31 מטלטלין] ויטלטלין ב. אין מטלטלין מו. | בתוכה] לתוכה ב. בתוכו מלדופ. |

פרק ו 1-6

פרק ו" ארון שעשה משה במדבר ארכו שתי אמות ומחצה (ו)רחבו אמה

ומחצה וגובהו אמה ומחצה שנ' ועשו ארון עצי שטים וגו' (שם כה י)

ר' (מאיר) אומ' באמה בת ששה טפחים הרי חמשה עשר טפחים צא מהן

שתים עשר טפחים לרחבן של לוחות וטפח מכאן וטפח מכאן מקום הנחת

5 הלוחות וחצי טפח מכאן לעובי(ו)] של ארון {שארבעה לוחות היו בו

שנים שלימין ושנים שבורין והלוחות ארכן של כל אחד ואחד ששה טפחים

—1 ארון. בבא בתרא יד, א. —3 באמה בת ששה. ירוש' שקלים פ"ו ה"א מט ע"ד = ירוש'
סוטה פ"ח ה"ג כב ע"ג – ד.

—1 ארכו שתי אמות ומחצה] אמתים וחצי ארכו פ. | —2-1 (ו)רחבו... ומחצה] ח' ל. | ואמה
וחצי רחבו פ. | —2 וגובהו אמה ומחצה] ואמה וחצי קומתו פ. | שנ'... וגו'] ח' פ. | ועשו]
ועשית ג¹. | עצי שטים] ח' ג¹.ו. | —3 באמה] ח' פ. | בת] של בה. | הרי] הרי כאן ד. הרי
ארכו שלארון ה. | טפחים²] טפחים ר. | טפחים והלוחות ארכן ששׁ' ורחבן ששה ועובין שלשה טפחים מ.
טפיח ו. טפח ה. | טפחים אורכו של ארון ורוחבו ט' טפחים פ. | צא מהן] הוצא מהן ע. | צא
מהם ל. | —4 שתים עשר] ה"י ג¹. | חמשה ו. ששה פ. | טפחים] טפח ה. ח' פ. | לרחבן ח'
ב. רחבן ל. רחבו ו. | וטפח מכאן וטפח מכאן] וטפח (טפח ו.) מיכן וטפח מיכן ג¹בו. | וטפחיים
מד. וחצי טפח מכאן ע. טפח מכאן וטפח מכאן ל. ח' ה. | חצי טפח מיכאן וחצי טפח מיכאן
פ. | —5-4 מקום הנחת הלוחות] מקום שספר תורה מונה במדו. ח' לה. מקום הנחת שברי
לוחות פ. | וחצי טפח מכאן] [   ] מיכן וחצי טפח מיכן ג¹. | וחצי טפח (... מיכן ו.) וחצי
טפח מיכן בו. | וחצי טפח מכאן וחצי טפח מכאן מדה. ואצבע מיכאן ואצבע מיכאן פ. |
לעובי(ו)] לעבין ב¹. | —8-5 ארון... הנחת] ח' מ. | —5 של ארון] שלארון [   ] ים שלימין
ושנים שבורים והלוחות [   ] ששה טפחים ורחבו ששה ועביו [   ] ג¹. | של ארון נשתיירו
שם שני טפחים ששם ס"ת מונח ע. של ארון נשתיירו שם שני טפחים מקום ספר תורה ה.
של ארון הרי ט"ו טפחים פ. |

פרק ו 7-12

ורחבן שלשה ועוביין שלשה} ורחבן של ארון תשעה טפחים צא מהן ששה

טפחים לארכן של לוחות ומקום הנחת ספר תורה שני טפחים חצי טפח

מכאן וחצי טפח מכאן לעוביין של ארון ר' יהודה אומ' באמת בת חמשה

10 טפחים הרי שנים עשר טפחים ומחצה וארבעה לוחות היו בו שנים שלימין

ושנים שבורין והלוחות ארכן של כל אחת ששה טפחי' ורחבן שלשה צא

מהן שנים עשר טפחים לרחבן של לוחות ואצבע מכאן ואצבע מכאן

—9 באמת בת חמשה. ירוש' שקלים שם = ירוש' סוטה שם. —10 וארבעה לוחות. ירוש'
שקלים שם = ירוש' סוטה שם. —11 והלוחות. בבא בתרא יד, א.

—7-9 ורחבן[2]... מכאן[2]. ח' ל. | —7 ורחבן[2]] ורחבו בעדוה. | צא מהן] צא מהם ג[1]. הוצא
מהן ע. | —8 טפחים[1]] טפחין ג[1]. ח' בו. | ומקום] מקום בו. | ספר] לספר מ. | תורה] תרוה
ב[1]. | שני טפחים] טפחים בעוה. טפחים (טפחים ד.) כדי שלא יהא נכנס ויוצא בדוחק
מד. | —8-9 חצי טפח מכאן וחצי טפח מכאן] וחצי טפח מיכן וחצי טפח מיכן ב. וחצי טפח
מכאן וחצי טפח מכאן מדה. וחצי טפח מכאן על. וטפח וחצי מיכן וטפח וחצי מיכן ו. |
—9 באמת] באמה במוה. | בת] של במה. | —10 טפחים[1]] טפטחים ב[1]. | הרי] הרי כאן
מדו. | טפחים ומחצה] ח' (והוגה בגליון: וחצי) ב. טפח ומחצה ארכו שלארון ה. | היו בו] היו
שם מ. נתונות בו על. | היו מונחים בו ד. היו ד. | שלימין] שלמים ב[1]מדוף. שלמות ל.
שלמין ה. | —11 שבורין] שבורים בדו. שבורות ל. | והלוחות] הלוחות ב. | ארכן ארכו
ג[1]במלוה. | של כל אחת] ח' ל. | אחת] אחד ואח' ב[2]מו. | אחת ואחת ד. אחד ה. אחד ואחד
אורכו פ. | טפחי'] ח' ל. | ורחבן] ורחבו בהפ. | שלשה] ששה בעלה. | ששה ועובין שלשה
מ. ששה (ובסוגריים: ס"א שלשה) ועבין שלשה ד. ששה טפחים וף. | —11-12 צא מהן]
הוצא מהן ע. צא מהם לה. | —12 טפחים] טפח ג[1]וה. | לרחבן] לרוחב ב[2]. | לארכן פ. |
לוחות] (ונמחק: ארון א.) לוחות וטפחים מקום ספר תורה מונה מ. לוחות ואצבע ומחצה
מכאן ע. | —12-15 ואצבע[1]... הלוחות. ח' ל. | ואצבע מכאן ואצבע מכאן] ואצבע מוכן ואצבע

פרק ו 13-16

לעוביו של ארון ורחבו של ארון שבעה טפחים ומחצה צא מהן ששה

טפחי׳ לארכן של לוחות וחצי טפח מכאן וחצי טפח מכאן מקום הנחת

15 הלוחות ואצבע מכאן ‹ואצבע מכאן› לעׄוביו של ארון אבל ספר תורה

לא היה נתון אלא מן הצד שנ׳ לקוח את ספר התורה הזה וגו׳

מוכן ב[1]. ואצבע מיכן ואצבע מיכן ב[2]ו. וחצי טפח מכאן וחצי טפח מכאן מ. ואצבע מיכאן
ואצבע פ. —13 ארון[1] ארון וב׳ אצבעות הן חצי טפח פ. | ורחבו] ורוחב פ. | שבעה] תשע׳
מ. ו׳ פ. | צא מהן] הוצא מהם ע. | —14 טפחי׳] ח׳ במ. | לארכן] לרחבו פ. | לוחות] לוחות
‹ולהלן: צא מהם לספר תורה טפחים כדי שלא יהא נכנס ויוצא בדוחק וחצי טפח מכאן וחצי
טפח מכאן לעביו של ארון ר׳ יהוד׳ אומ׳ באמה של חמשה טפח׳ הרי כאן שנים עשר טפח
ומחצה וארבעה לוחות היו שם שנים שלמים ושנים שבורין וארכו של הלוחות ארכו של כל אחד ואחד
ששה טפחי׳ ורחבן ששה ועבין שלשה צא מהן שנים עשר טפח לרחבן של לוחו׳ ואצבע מכאן
ואצבע מכאן לעביו של ארון ורחבו של ארון שבע׳ טפחים ומחצה צא מהן ששה טפחים
לארכן של לוחות מ. וראה לעיל שורות 7-14). | וחצי טפח מכאן וחצי טפח מכאן] וחצי טפח
מיכן וחצי טפח מיכן ב[1]ו. וטפח אחד (אחר ד.) מד. וחצי טפח מיכאן וחצי טפח מיכאן פ. |
—15 הלוחות] שברי הלוחות ב. העמודים (העמו⟨   ⟩) מ. ועליו מפורש בקבלה אפריון עשה
לו המלך שלמה מעצי הלבנון דמ. הלוחות הראשונות ה. הלוחות פ. שברי לוחות פ. | ואצבע מכאן
‹ואצבע מכאן›] ואצבע מיכן ואצבע ואצבע מיכן ב[1]ו. ואצבע ומחצה מכאן ע. אצבע מכאן ואצבע
מכאן ל. ואצבע מיכן ואצבע ואצבע מיכאן פ. | ארון] ארון וב׳ אצבעות הן חצי טפח פ. | תורה]
תרוה ב[1]. | —16 נתון] נתון בו ע. מונה בו ל. | בארון פ. | מן] בארגז ומן פ. | הצד] הצד
היה נתון פ. | שנ׳] וכן הוא אומ׳ פ. | לקוח את ספר התורה הזה וגו׳] לקוח את ספר התורה
וגו׳ ג[2]. ושמתם אותו מצד (מן הצד ב[2].) ארון ברית יי לבד. לקוח את ס״ת הזה (הזאת פ.)
ושמתם (... אותו מצד ארון ברית יי מהפ.) עמהפ. ושמת אתו מצד ו. |

פרק ו 20-17

(דברים לא כו) ועליו מפורש בקבלה אפריון עשה לו שלמה וגו'

(שיר השירים ג ט) ר' יהוד' בן לקיש אומ' שני ארונות היו שם

אחד שהיה עמהם במחנה ואחד שהיה יוצא עמהם למלחמה והיו בו שברי

20 לוחות שנ' וארון ברית יי נוסע לפניהם (במדבר י לג) וזה שהיה

18— ר' יהוד' בן לקיש אומ'. תוספתא סוטה ז, יח; ירוש' שקלים פ"ו ה"א, מט ע"ג. —20
וארון ברית יי. ספרי במדבר בהעלתך פב, מהד' האראוויטץ 78.

17— ועליו מפורש בקבלה אפריון עשה לו שלמה וגו'] ועליו מפורש בקבלה אפריון עשה
לו המלך שלמה וכן הוא אומר בפלשתים ואת טהורי הזהב (כלי זהב ל.) אשר השבותם (...לו
אשם תשאו בארגז מצדו ל.) ג²ל. ועליו מפורש בקבלה אפריון עשה לו המלך שלמה (שלמה
המלך ב².) וכן הוא אומ' בפלשתים ואת כלי הזהב תשימו בארגז (...מצדן ב¹. מצידן ב².)
ב. וכן הוא או' בפלשתים (וכן בפלשתים הוא אומר ד.) ואת כלי הזהב אשר השיבתם לו
אשם תשימו (תשאו ד.) בארגז מצדו מד. ועליו מפורש בקבלה אפריון עמודיו עשה כסף
וכן הוא אומר בפלשתים ע. ועליו מפורש בקבלה אפריון עשה לו המלך שלמה וכ"ה אומר
בפלשתים תשימו בארגז מצדו ו. ועליו מפורש על פי שלמה ברוח הקדש אפריון עשה לו
המלך שלמה מעצי הלבנון וכהֹא בפלשתים וכהֹא ואת כלי הזהב אשר השבותם לו תשימו בארגז
בצידו פ. | 18— יהוד'] שמעון ע. | 19-18— ארונות... למלחמה] ח' ב¹. | שם] ח'
ג²ב²מלדופ. | 19— אחד] אחת היו בו לוחות האחרונים שלימים פ. | שהיה¹... שהיה פ. | ואחד] ח'
ל. | שהיה¹] היה ב²מו. | והיה פ. | עמהם¹] יושב ב²דופ. ח' מ. | במחנה] במחנה ואינו זז
ממקומו פ. | שהיה²] היה ב²מו. | מהן היה פ. | עמהם²] עמהן ב²מדפ. | למלחמה] במלחמה
ג²ב²דפ. | והיו בו] זה שהיה יוצא עמהם במלחמה (למלחמה ע.) היה ז (היו ע.) בו ג²ע. וזה
שהיה בו מ. ובו היו ל. שהיו בו פ. | 19-20— שברי לוחות] ספר תורה ג². | 21-20— שנ'...
במחנה] ח' מ. | 20— שנ'... נוסע] ח' פ. | 22-20— נוסע... יי] ח' ו. | לפניהם] לפניהם דרך
שלשת ימים וגו' ע. | וזה] וא' ל. אין שם ספר תורה מונח אלא זה פ. |

פרק ו 21-25

{יוצא} עמהם {למלחמה} (במחנה) היה בו ספר תורה שנ' וארון ברית

יי ומשה לא משו (שם יד מד) וכן הוא או' בשאול ויאמר שאול לאחיה

הגישה את ארון האלהים (שמואל א יד יח) וכן הוא או' באוריה הארון

ויש' יושבים בסוכֿה (שמואל ב יא יא) אבל ארון הברית לא יצא עמהם

25 למלחמה אלא פעם אחת בלבד שנ' וישלח העם שילה וגו' (שמואל א ד ד)

—23 הגישה את ארון. ירוש' שקלים הנ"ל.

—21 עמהם] המנ ב'. | עומד ב². | יושב ל. | (במחנה)] במחנה הוא היה זה ממקומו פ. | היה
בו] וכן הוא היה בו ב'. | היו בו ב². | והיה ל. | ושם היה פ. | ספר תורה] שברי לוחות ג². | ספר
תורה ולוחות אחרונות (האחרונות ע.) מע. ספר תורה מונח (... בו ל.) לפ. | שנ'] ח' מד.
וזהו שכתו' פ. | —21-24 וארון... אבל] ח' מ. | —21-22 ברית יי] ברית ברית ה' נוסע
לפניהם דרך שלשת ימים וגו' וזה ע. | —22 ומשה לא משו] ח' ג². | ומשה לא משו מקרב
(מתוך ער.) המחנה בעלוף. | וכן הוא או'] ואמ' פ. | ויאמר] ויאו ב. | לאחיה] אל אחיה
גדלדפ. | —23 הגישה את ארון האלהים] הגישה ארון האלהים וגו' ג². | הגישה את האפוד
ב. הגישה האפוד לדו. הגישה האפוד ארון אלהים וגו' פ. | וכן הוא או'] | | הוא אמ' ב.
וכן ד. ואומ' פ. | באוריה] באוריה החתי בו. | הארון] ח' ל. ויאמר אוריה אל דוד הארון פ.
—24 ויש'] וישראל ויהודה ג²בלדופ. | יושבים בסוכה] ח' ג². | יושבים בסוכות בלדפ.
ישבים בסכת ו. | ארון] זה שהיה עמהן במחנ' שהוא ארון מ. הארון ו. | הברית] ברית ל.
הברית ששם לוחות האחרונים פ. | עמהם] ח' ג²מלדופ. עמהן ב. | —25 למלחמה] ח' מ.
במלחמה ד. | אלא] ולא ו. | בלבד] במלחמה מ. ח' ד. ולמ] | אז לא היה יוצא אלא במלחמה
פלשתים פ. | וישלח] ושלח ו. | שילה וגו'] שילה ויקחו (ויצאו פ.) משם את ארון ברית יי
(... יושב הכרובים ג².) ג²בדפ. שילה ויקחו משם ארון ברית ה' ל. |

פרק ו 26-27

ר' יהוד' או' לא היה בארון אלא שני לוחות בלבד שנ' אין בארון רק

שני לוחות וגו' (מלכים א ח ט)

<hr/>

26—לא היה בארון. בבא בתרא יד, א.

<hr/>

26 יהוד'] יודה ו. | היה] היו ב²מע. | בארון] בארון'] בארון הברית פ. | אלא... בארון²] ח' ע. | אלא] זולתי פ. | שני] ח' מד. | לוחות] הלוחות ג². לוחות הברית במלדו. לוחות הברית הם שני לוחות האחרונים שלמים פ. | בלבד] ח' פ. | 26-27 רק שני לוחות וגו'] רק שני לוחות האבנים (אבנים ע.) אשר הניח שם משה בע. רק שני לוחות הברית (... אשר הניח שם משה בחורב פ.) מדפ. רק ב' לוחות האבנים ל. |

פרק ז 1-7

פרק ז"   כיצד עשה בצלאל הארון עשה שלש תיבות שתים של זהב

ואחת של עץ נתן של עץ בתוך של עץ ונתן של זהב בתוך של עץ וחיפה

שפתיו העליונות בזהב שנ' וצפית אותו זהב טהור (שמות כה יא) שאין

ת"ל תצפנו (שם) ומה ת"ל תצפנו מלמד שחיפה שפתיו העליונות בזהב

5 כפרת של זהב נתונה עליו מלמעלה שנ' ונתת את הכפרת על הארון

מלמעלה (שם כה כא) וארבע טבעות זהב היו {מוקבעות} ⟨מקובעות⟩ בו שתים

בצפון ושתים בדרום שבהן היו נותנין את הבדים שלא יהו זזים משם לעולם

—1 כיצד עשה בצלאל. ירוש׳ שקלים פ״ו ה״א מט ע״ד = ירוש׳ סוטה פ״ח ה״ג כב ע״ד.

—1 כיצד] כאיזה צד מ. | כאיצד ו. | הארון] את הארון ג²במלדופ. | עשה²] עשאו²] עשאו ג²במופ.
עשה אותו] עשאן ל. עשאן ד. | שלש] ח' ע. | —2 עץ²] עצי שטים ל. | שלי²] ח' מ. | ונתן של
זהב] ושל זהב ג²במלדופ. | וחיפה] וחפה ג²מד. | —3 בזהב] של זהב פ. | אותו] אותם
מ. | טהור] טהור וגו' ויצף אותו זהב טהור מבית ומחוץ ג². | טהור מבית ומחוץ תצפנו בל.
ח' ו. | —3-4 שאין ת״ל תצפנו] ח' ד. | —4 מלמד] ח' ע. | שחיפה] שציפה בופ. שחופה
מד. שיחפה ע. | בזהב] זהב ד. של זהב פ. | —5 נתונה] היתה נתונה ג²ב'מלו. נתונה
היתה ב². | היה נתון פ. | —6 מלמעלה] ח' מדו. | וארבע] ארבע ג²במופ. | זהב] זהב של זהב
ג²במו. | היו] ח' ל. | {מקובעות} קבועין ב. קבועות לדו. קובעין פ. | בו] בו בארון ב. |
—7 בצפון] בצפונו מלדופ. | בדרום] בדרומו מלדופ. | שבהן] שבהם ג²לד. | היו נותנין]
היו נותנים לדו. היה נותן פ. | את] ח' מלדו. | שלא] ולא בד. | יהון היו במד. | יהיו ל.
הי' ו. | זזים] זזין ב. | משם] ח' ל. |

שנ' בטבעות הארון יהיו הבדים (שם כה טו) וֹאֹעֹ֗פֹ֗י שעשה שלמה תבנית

כל הכלים תבנית הארון לא עשה שנ' ויבואו כל זקני ישר' וגו'

10 (מלכים א ח ג) אמרת היה ארון נתון בתוך הבית וחולק את הבית עשר

אמות על עשר אמות ושנים כרובים של זהב היו עומדים על רגליהם בארץ

מכותל לכרוב חמש אמות מכרוב לארון חמש אמות מניין אתה או'

{מ} כיון שהכניסו הארון האֹ֗ריכו הבדים והגיעו לפרוכת והגיעו לפתח

13— האריכו הבדים. תוספתא יום הכיפורים ג, ז; ירוש' שקלים פ"ו ה"א מט ע"ג; יומא נד,
א; מנחות צח, א – ב.

---

9 — .8— יהיו הבדים] יהיו הבדים לא יסורו ממנו בל. ח' ו. | ואֹ֗עֹ֗פֹ֗י] אע"פ ג²במדפ. |
הכלים] הכלים כולן ב. | הארון] ארון ו. | כל²] ח' פ. | ישר'] ישראל וישאו הכהנים את הארון
במדלפ. ישראל וישאו הכהנים את הארון ויביאו הכהנים את ארון יי אל דביר [| הקדשים
כול' כי הכרובים פורשי כנפים וגו' | ג². | 10 — אמרת] הארון בל. אמנת (והוגה בגליון:
נ"ל [| כת] מ. ח' ופ. | היה] היה ארון נתון] היה [| תון] ג². | היה נתון בלדופ. היה נותן מ.
ארון היה נתון ע. | בתוך הבית] בדביר פ. | וחולק] וחלק ב. חולק מ. | את] ח' ב². | הבית²]
הדביר בתוך פ. —11 — של זהב] עצי שמן פ. | היו] ח' ב². | עומדים] עומדין ג²מופ. |
רגליהם] רגליהן ג²ו. | בארץ] ח' ל. — 12 — מכרוב] ומכרוב ג²במלדו. | לארון] לארץ ב². |
מניין] ומנין בל. — 13 — מכיון] שכיון ג²מלד. כיון ב. ח' ו. וכיון פ. | שהכניסו הארון]
שהכניסו (שכשהכניסו ו.) הכהנים את הארון ג²במלדופ. שבשעה שהכניסו ו. | ע. |
האריכו] שהאריכו ע. | הבדים] את הבדים מ. | והגיעו לפרוכת] הגיעו לפרכת ג²מ. והגיעו
לפרוכת ב¹. ח' ל. והגיעו בפרוכת פ. | והגיעו לפתח] והגיעו לפתח ונגעו בפתח ג²במלדו. עד

פרק ז 14-19

‹לפיכך› לא ננעלו דלתות בית קדשי הקדשים שנ' ויאריכו הבדים

15 (שם ח ח, דברי הימים ב ה ט) אי איפשר לומ' ולא יראו (שם) שכבר

נא' ויראו (שם) אי איפשר ‹לומר› ויראו שכבר נאמ' ולא יראו הא

כיצד בולטים בפרכת ונראין כשני דדי אשה ומניין שהאריכו בפנים שנ'

ולא יראו החוצה (שם) הא למדת שהאריכו בפנים ומניין שהאריכו מבחוץ

שנ' ויאריכו ראשי הבדים מן הבית וגו' (שם)   ומניין שכשם

—17 ונראין כשני דדי אשה. ירוש' שקלים שם; יומא שם; מנחות שם.

שהגיעו בפתחה קדש קדשים פ. | —14 דלתות] דלתי ב². ח'ו. | בית קדשי הקדשים] בית
קדש הקדשים מעולם ג²ד. בית קדשי הקדשים מעולם (לעולם ב.) במ. של בית קדשי קדש
הקדשים מעולם ל. בית קה״ק מעולם ו. קדש הקדשים מעולם פ. שנ'] ח'ו. | הבדים]
הבדים ויראו (... ולא יראו החוצה ו.) בו. ראשי הבדים מל. | —15 ולא יראו] לא יראו
ג²מו. ויראו ב. שלא יראו ד. | —16 ויראו] לא יראו ב. | אי] ואי ג²במעלד. | ויראו²]
לא יראו ב². | ולא יראן] ויראו ב². לא יראו מד. | —16-17 הא כיצד] ח' מ. הא כאיצד ו.
אלא פ. | —17 בולטים] היו בולטין ג²מעוף. בולטות היו ב¹. היו בולטים ד. | בפרכת]
לפרכת מ. | ונראין] ונראין בהיכל ג²במו. ונראים בהיכל ד. ונראין בפרוכת פ. | כשני] כעין
שני על. | אשה] אשה שכן כתו' בין שדי ילין פ. | —17-18 שהאריכו... ומניין] ח' ל. |
בפנים] מבפנים ג²במד. בארק ו. | —18 ולא יראו החוצה] ויאריכו שני הבדים ו. | הא למדת
שהאריכו בפנים] ח' ב. | —18-19 הא למדת... הבית וגו'] ח' ו. | הא למדת] למדנו ג²מד. |
בפנים] מבפנים ג²מד. | —19 ויאריכו] ויראו ג²במל. וירו ד. | מן הבית
וגו'] ח' ג²מלד. מן הקודש על פני הדביר ב. | ומניין] ומנין אתה אומ' ג²במלד. | שכשם]
כשם בל. |

פרק ז 20-25

20 שנמתחו הבדים כך נמתחו כנפיהם וכיסו הארון וחיפו את בדיו מלמעלה

שנ' ויסכו את הארון ועל בדיו מלמעלה (מלכים א ח ז)   היכן ארון

נתון ⟨ר' יהודה בן לקיש אומר⟩ במקומו בבית קדשי הקדשים הוא שנ'

ויהי שם עד היום הזה (דהי"ב ה ט, מ"א ח ח) וחכמי' או' בלשכת

דיר העצים ר' אל(י)עז ⟨אומר⟩ לבבל ירד שנ' ולא יוותר דבר אמר יי

25 (מ"ב כ יז, ישעיה לט ו) ואין דבר אלא דברות הארון ר' או' יאשיהו

—21-22 היכן ארון נתון. תוספתא שקלים ב, יח; ירוש' שקלים פ"ו ה"א מט ע"ג.

—20 הבדים] ראשי הבדים לבו. | נמתחו] נמתחו (ובסוגריים: ס"א נפתחו) ד. | כנפיהם] כנפי
הכרובים ג²במלד. ראשי כנפי הכרובים ו. | וכיסו הארון] וכסו את הארון ג²מלד. | וכיסו
את הארון ב. | וסיבו את הארון ו. | וחיפו את בדיו] וחפוי את הבית מ. וחפו את הבית עד.
וחפו ל. וחיפו את הבית ו. | מלמעלה] ח' ב. | —21 ויסוכו את הארון ועל בדיו מלמעלה]
ויסכו הכרובים על הארון ועל בדיו מלמעלה ג²בד. ויסכו הכרובי' מ. ויסוכו הכרובים על
הארון ל. ויסבו הכרובים וגו' ו. | היכן] והיכן בלדוף. | —21-22 ארון נתון] היה ארון נתון
ג². היה הארון נגנז ב. היה נתון מ. גנזו הארון לפ. היה ארון (הארון ו.) גנוז דו. | —22
יהודה] שמעון ע. | במקומו] במקומו גנזו ל. | קדשי] קדש ג²לדפ. | הוא] ח' ג²במלדופ. |
—23 ויהי] ויהיו מלדו. ח' פ. | עד] ח' ד. | —24 דיר העצים] דור העצים מ. דיר העצים
גנזו ל. | לבבל] לבבל בל ו. בבבל ב. בבבל ל. | ולא] לא ג²מלו. אל ד. | יוותר] (נמחק: אותי) פ. | אמר
יי] ח' בל. | —25 ואין] אין ג²מדו. | אלא דברות] אלא עשרת דברות (הדברות ופ.) לופ. |
הארון] שבו ג²במלדו. ח' פ. | יאשיהו] ישעיהו ו. ירמיהו ויאשיהו פ. |

פרק ז 26-31

גנזו שנ' ויאמר ללוים המבינים את העם וגו' (דהי"ב לה ג) אמ'

לא ירד עמכם לבבל שתעלו אותו בכתף 　בית קדש הקדשים שעשה

שלמה היה לו כותל פתח ודלתות שנ' ויעש דלתות להיכל ולקדש

(מעין דהי"ב ד כב) אבל בבניין האחרון לא היה שם כותל אלא שני

30 פסין ארכו של כל אחד ואחד אמה ומחצה ושתי פרכות של זהב היו

פרוסות עליהן מלמעלה והיה נקרא מקום הטרקסין

—26 ויאמר ללוים המבינים. ירוש' שקלים שם.

—26 גנזו] גנזו אותו פ. | ללוים] אל הלוים ב**מלד**. | המבינים את העם וגו'] המבינים לכל
העם הקדשים ליי ג[2]. | המבינים לכל ישר' הקדושים תנו את הארון הקודש בבית אשר בנה
שלמה בן דוד וילך ישר' אין לכם משא בכתף עתה עבדו את יי אלהיכם ואת עמו ישר'
הדלתות לא ננעלו מפני הבדים היוצאים בפתח והפרכות היתה פרוסה (ונמחק: עלי) בפני
הפתח לצניעות ב. ח' מו. | המבינים תנו את הארון אל הבית כי אין להם משא בכתף ועתה
עבדו וגו' ע. המבינים ו**נֿאֿ**' כי אין לכם משא בכתף ל. | אמ'] או' להן ב. אמר להם ל**ד**. ח'
ו. | —27 לא ירד] לא יעלה **ד**. יעלה ו. | עמכם] עמהם **מ**. | לבבל] בבבל ל. | בכתף] בכסף
ד. | בית] בבית ופ. | קדש] קדשי **מד**. | שעשה] שעשה לו מ**דו**. | —28 היה] היו ב. | פתח]
ופתח לו. | שנ'... ולקדש] ח' ל. | ולקדש] ולדביר ב**ו**. ח' פ. | —29 אבל] ח' פ. | בבניין]
בינ[י]ין ב. בבנה ל**ד**. | ובבית קדש הקדשים פ. | האחרון] בית שני ע. | היה] עשה **מ**. | שם]
בו ב. ח' ע. | כותל] ח' **ד**. | —30 פסין] פסין היו שם ג[2]**מפ**. פסין היו לו ב. פסים היו שם
ל**דו**. | ארכו] וארכו ג[2]ב**מלד**. | ואחד] ח' **מ**. | פרכות] פרוכות **ד**. | היו] היו שם **מד**. ח' ו.
| —31 עליהן] עליהם **על**. | והיה נקרא] והיה נקרא שמו ג[2]. | ונקרא ע. | מקום הטרקסין]
מקום טרקסין **מ**. אמה טרקסין ע. מהן הטרקסין ו. |

פרק ח 6-1

פרק ח״   שולחן שעשה משה במדבר ארכו שתי אמות ורחבו אמה

וגבהו אמה ומחצה שנ׳ ועשית שלחן וגו׳ (שמות כה כג)   ר׳ יהוד׳

אומ׳ באמה של חמשה טפחים מכאן אמרו השלחן ארכו עשרה ורחבו חמשה

ולחם הפנים ארכו עשרה ורחבו חמשה נותן ארכו כנגד רחבו של שלחן

5   וקופל שני טפחי׳ ומחצה מכאן ושני טפחים ומחצה מכאן נמצא ארכו

של לחם ממלא רחבו של שולחן דברי ר׳ יהודה ר׳ מאיר או׳ השלחן

3— השלחן ארכו עשרה. משנה מנחות יא, ה.

1— ארכו שתי אמות] אמתים ארכו פ. | ורחבו אמה] ורחבו אמה ומחצה ו. ואמה רוחבו פ. |
2— וגבהו אמה ומחצה] וקמתו אמה ומחצה בד. ח׳ לו. ואמה וחצי קומתו פ. | שנ׳... וגו׳]
ח׳ פ. | שלחן] שלחן עצי שטים ג²בדו. | יהוד׳] יהוד׳ יודה ו. —3— של] ח׳ מ. בת לפ. | טפחים]
טפחים הרי עשרה טפחים ג²ד. טפחים הוי עשרה ב. טפחים הרי עשרה מו. | מכאן] מיכאן
ג²פ. מיכן ב. ח׳ ו. | אמרו] אמרו של לחם הפנים לרוחבו של שולחן פ. | השלחן]
שולחן במדו. נִמְצָא שולחן ל. | עשרה] עשרה טפחים לפ. | חמשה²] ה׳ טפחים לפ. —4—
ולחם... חמשה] ח׳ וה. | ולחם] לחם פ. | עשרה] י׳ טפחים לפ. | ורחבו חמשה] ח׳ ל. | נותן]
ונותן ע. נתן ד. | ארכו²] ארכו של לחם הפנים דפ. —5-8— וקופל... שלחן] ח׳ ל. |
וקופל] כופל ג²ב. קפל מ. וכופל עה. קופל ה. | שני טפחי׳] טפחים ג²מדה. טפחיים בעפ. |
מכאן¹] מיכאן ג²פ. מיכן בו. | ושני טפחים] וטפחים ג²מדה. וטפחיים בוף. | מכאן²] מיכאן
ג²פ. מיכן בו. | נמצא] נמצאו פ. —6— של לחם] ח׳ במדוה. של לחם הפנים פ. | ממלא]
כנגד פ. | דברי ר׳ יהודה] (ונמחק: אומ׳) א. ח׳ במדופ. | ר׳ מאיר או׳ במדוף. | תנו רבנן כיצד סדר
המערכה ר׳ מאיר או׳ ה. —6-7— השלחן ארכו] ארכו ג²ב. | ארכו של שלחן מד. באמה בת
ששה טפחים ארכו ע. | שולחן ארכו ו. | אמה של שולחן באמה בת ששה טפחים נמצא

פרק ח 7-12

ארכו שנים עשר ורחבו ששה לחם הפנים ארכו עשרה ורחבו חמשה נותן

ארכו כנגד רחבו של שלחן וקופל טפחיים מכאן וטפחיים מכאן וטפחיים

ריוח באמצע כדי שתהא הרוח מנשבת בהן אבא שאול אומ' נותן ארכה

10 כנגד ארכו של שלחן ורחבה כנגד רחבו של שלחן שנ' ונתת על המערכת

לבונה זכה (ויקרא כד ז) אמרו לו והלא כבר נאמ' ועליו מטה מנשה

(במדבר ב כ) וארבע טבעות של זהב היו קבועות בו שנים בצפונו

9— אבא שאול אומ'. משנה מנחות שם.

שולחן אורכו פ. | —7 עשר] עשר טפחים מ**דפ**. עשר טפח ה. | ורחבו ששה] ורחבו ששה
טפחים מ**ד**. רחבו ששה ה². ח' פ. | לחם] ולחם ג²ב**מעדוה**²פ. | עשרה] י' טפחים פ. | ורחבו
חמשה] ח' ופ. | נותן] ונותן טפחיים ע. | ונתן ד. ח' ו. ונותן פ. | —8 ארכו] ח' ו. אורכו של
לחם הפנים פ. | כנגד] ח' פ. | וקופל] כופל ג²בל. קפל מ**ד**. וכופל ה. (והוגה בגליון ע.)
טפחיים] טפחים ג²מ**ה**². טפח ד. | מכאן¹] מיכאן ג²ה. מיכן בו. | וטפחיים¹] וטפחים ג²ה².
וטפחים ריוח מ. וטפח ד. ח' ו. | מכאן²] מיכן ג²ה**פ**. מיכן ב. ח' ו. | וטפחיים²] וטפחים
ג²מ**דה**². ח' ו. | —9 ריוח] רוח ג². | וריוח ו. | באמצע] ח' פ. | בהן] בהם ל**ד**. ביניהן ה. |
—9-10 אבא... שלחן²] ח' פ. | אומ'] או' שם היו נותני' שני (... בזיכי לבונה שללחם הפנים
ה.) בה. | —9-10 נותן... שלחן²] נותן ח' ב. | נותן] ח' ל. | ארכה] ארכו ל**ד**. | —10 ארכו] רחבו
ל**ד**. רחבה ו. | ורחבה כנגד רחבו של שלחן] ג²ל. ורחבו כנגד רחבו של שלחן מ**ד**. ורחבה
כנגד ארכה של שלחן ו. | המערכת] השולחן המערכת ב. | —11 זכה] זכה על בסמוך פ.
אמרו... מנשה] ח' פ. | אמרו לו] אמרו לו והלא נאמ' ונתת על המערכ' לבונה זכה או' להן
ב. | כבר ח' במדו. | נאמ'] נאמ'... מנשה] ח' ו. | —15-12 וארבע... וגו']

ושנים בדרומו שנ' ועשית ארבע טבעות זהב (שמות כה כו) ר' יהוד'

אומ' שתי ידות למטה מרגל לרגל ומסגרת של זהב הייתה לה שנ' ועשית

15 לו מסגרת וגו' (שם כה כה) אע׳פ׳ שעשה שלמה עשרה שולחנות כולן

היו כשירין ולא היו משתמשין בהן אלא בשל משה שנ' ויעש שולחנות

עשרה וינח בהיכל חמשה מימין וחמשה משמאל (דהי״ב ד ח) ואם תאמר

חמשה מן הדרום וחמשה מן הצפון והלא (שלחן מן) הדרום פסול ומה

ת״ל חמשה מימין וחמשה משמאל (שם) אלא חמשה מימין השלחן

15— עשרה שולחנות. תוספתא מנחות יא, ט; ירוש' שקלים פ״ו ה״ד נ ע״א; מנחות צט, א.

ארבע טבעות שלזהב היו קבועות בו ושתים בצפונו ושתים בדרומו שנ' ועשית לו ארבע
טַבָּעֹ֫ת זָהָב ונתת את הטבעות על ארבע הפיאות וגו' רבי יהודה אומ' שתי ידות למטה מרגל
לרגל ומסגרת שלזהב היתה סובבת את לחם הפנים שנ' ועשית לו מסגרת ג׳². (וכעין קטע
ג׳.) ח׳ במלדוהפ. | 15— אע׳פ׳ו ואע׳פ׳ ב. אעפ״ו ד. | כולן] כולם ג׳. | כולן] וכולם בלדוף. וכולם
ד. | 16— כשירין] כשרין ג׳מ. כשרות לעבודה ג׳². | כשירין לעבודה בפ. כשירים לעבודה
ל. כשרין לעבודה דו. | ולא] לא בלדוף. | משתמשין בהן] משמשין בהן ג׳². | משתמשין
במדפ. משתמשין ל. משמשין ו. | בשל] בזה שעשה ג׳²בפ. בזה של מו. | ויעש] ויעש
שלמה בלוף. | 16-17— שולחנות עשרה] עשרה שולחנות ב. ח׳ ו. עשרה שלמה פ. | 17—
חמשה] מאי ו. | וחמשה] ומאי ו. | ואם] אם מדוף. | 18— מן הדרום'] מן הצפון ג׳²מפ.
| צפון ג׳. | בדרום ב. בצפון ל. | מן הצפון] מן הדרום ג׳¹ג׳²מפ. בצפון ב. בדרום ל.
| והלא] הלא עד. | מן] הדרום²] בדרום ג׳²מעלו. | פסול] לעולם פסול ו. והשולחן
תתן על צלע צפון פ. | 18-19— ומה... משמאל] ח׳ עלו. | ומה] אלא מה בדף. מה מ. |
19— ת״ל] ויעש עשרה שולחנות וינח בהיכל פ. | אלא] ח׳ ב. | השלחן] שולחן של משה

פרק ח 20-21

20 וחמשה משמאל שולחן של משה שנ' ואת השולחנות ועליהם לחם הפנים

(שם ד יט)

ג²**מעד.** שולחן שעש' משה ב**פ.** שולחן משה ל. שולחנו של משה ו. | —20 וחמשה... משה]
ח' ב**מ.** | וחמשה] וחמשה שולחנות פ. | משמאל] משמאלו ו. | שולחן של משה] שלחן משה
ג¹ל. שלחן של משה ר' אלעזר בן שמוע אומר בכולן היו מסר ה' ע. ח' ו. שולחן שעשה
משה פ. | ואת] ויעש את ב. את מ. ח' פ. | השולחנות] השולחן פ. | ועליהם] ועליהן ג².
ועליו ב. | לחם הפנים] ח' ל. |

פרק ט 1-6

פרק ט"   מנורה שעשה משה במדבר הייתה באה משל זהב מקשה

וטעונה גביעים כפתורים ופרחים שנ' ועשית מנורת זהב טהור וגו'

(שמות כה לא) שומע אני שיעשה איברים ויחברם לה ⟨ת"ל ממנה יהיו⟩

(שם) ⟨מניין לרבות נרותיה⟩ ת"ל תעשה (שם) יכול לרבות נרותיה

5 ולהוציא גביעים כפתורים ופרחים אחר שריבה הכתוב מיעט מרבה אני

נירותיה שנעשין עמה ומוציא אני גביעיה כפתוריה ופרחיה שאין נעשין

—3 שיעשה איברים. ספרי במדבר בהעלתך סא, מהד' האראוויטץ 59. —4 ⟨מניין לרבות
נרותיה⟩. מנחות פח, ב.

—1 הייתה באה] ח' ו. | משל] של ל. | מקשה פ. | מכבר פ. | מקשה] וטעונה מקשה ג²מלד. —2
וטעונה] ח' ו. | כפתורים וכפתורים לו. | טהור] ח' מ. | —3 שומע אני] שומעני ו. | שיעשה]
יעשה ג²בלדר. יעשם מ. | איברים] אברים מ. אברים אברים מ. איברים איברים לדו. | ויחברם לה]
וידבקם לה ג²ו. | וידבקם בה ב. | וידביקם לה מד. ח' ל. | יהיו] ח' מ. | —4 ⟨מניין לרבות
לרבות מ. | יכול שאני מרבה על. ממנה לרבות ד. אי ממנה יכול לרבות ו. | נרותיה⟩ נירותיה
שיהיו ממנה ו. | תעשה] יעשה (והוגה בגליון: נ"ל חסר] מ. אותה ע. | יעשה אותה וכו' | [
ל. | יכול] יכול שאני מרבה (מוציא על.) גביעים כפתורים ופרחים ת"ל אותם (אותה ג².
תעשה ע. ואת כל כליה ל.) ומה ראית (מה ריאתה ג².) ג²מעלד. | לרבות²] להוציא² על. |
נרותיה] נרותיה שהיו עשויין ממנה ו. | —5 ולהוציא] ולרבות על. ונוציא ו. | גביעים
כפתורים ופרחים] גביעיה כפתורי' ופרוחיה (ופרחיה שאין עשויין עמה ו.) בו. | שריבה] שרבה
ד. | הכתוב] הכתו' (ונמחק: הקתוב) ג². | מיעט] מיעות ב. | ומיעט ו. | מרבה אני] מרבה מ.
מוציא אני על. | —6 נירותיה] את נרותיה ג²מלדו. | שנעשין] שנעשין שאין נעשין על. שנעשים
ד. שהן נעשין ו. | ומוציא] ומרבה על. | גביעיה] את הגביעים (הגבי' מ.) ג²מ. את גביעה
ד. | כפתוריה] כפתורים ג²מ. | ופרחיה] ופרחים ג²מ. ופרוחיה ב. | שאין נעשין] שאינן נעשין
ג²מ. שנעשין ע. שאין נעשים ד. |

פרק ט 7-10

עמה ומניין לרבות מלקחיה ומחתותיה ולהוציא הצבתים ואת המלקטאות

אחר שריבה הכת' מיעט מרבה אני מלקחיה ומחתותיה שמשמשין עמה

ומוציא אני את הצבתים והמלקטאות שאין משמשין עמה   כשהיא באה

10 של זהב טעונה גביעים כפתורים ופרחים כשאינה באה משל זהב אינה

—8 מרבה אני מלקחיה ומחתותיה. מנחות שם.

—7 ומניין] מנין ג²**מד**. | לרבות] לרבות מלקחיה ומחתותיה ת"ל תעשה יכול שאני מרבה את הצבתים (הצביתים **מ**.) ואת המלקטאות (...ת"ל אותם ומה ראית לרבות **ד**.) ג²**מד**. לרבות מלקוחיה (מלקחיה **ו**.) ומחתותיה ת"ל תעשה (... המנרה **ו**.) יכול שאני מרבה את הצבתים והמלטואות (ואת המלקטאות **ו**.) ת"ל אותה ומה ראית לרבות ב**ו**. לרבות מלקחיה ומחתותיה ת"ל תעשה ל. | —7-9 מלקחיה... עמה] ח' **ל**. | מלקחיה ומחתותיה] ח' ג²**מ**. את מלקחיה ומחתותיה ב. | ולהוציא הצבתים ואת המלקטאות] ח' ג²**מ**. ולהוצי' הצבתי' והמלקטאות (הוגה בגליון) ב. | ולהוציא את הצבתים **ד**. | —8 שריבה] שרבה **מד**. | מיעט] מיעות (הוגה בגליון) ב. מעט **מ**. | מלקחיה ומחתותיה] את מלקחיה ואת מחתותיה ג². את מלקחיה ומחתותיה **מ**. | שמשמשין] שהן משמשין ג²**ו**. | —9 הצבתים] הצביתין **מ**. הצבתין **ד**. | והמלקטאות] ואת המלקטאות ג²במדו. | שאין] שאינן **מד**. | משמשין] משתמשין **ו**. | כשהיא] וכשהיא **ל**. | —10-9 באה של זהב] באה משלזהב ג²**ו** (ונמחק: משמשין ב.). באה זהב **ל**. | —10 טעונה] טעונה מקשה כשאינה באה משלזהב (של זהב **מד**.) אינה טעונה מקשה כשהיא באה משלזהב (של זהב **מד**.) טעונה ג²**מד**. באה מקשה **ל**. | באה מקשה] | אינה באה מקשה] באה **ע**. | —10-11 גביעים... טעונה] ח' (והוגה בגליון: באה משל זהב אינה טעונ' גביעי' כפתורי' ופרחי' וכשהי') ב. | גביעים כפתורים ופרחים] כפתורי' גביעי' ופרחים **מ**. גביעיה כפתורים ופרחיה **ל**. | כשאינה] וכשאינה ג²**ו**. אינה **ל**. | משל זהב] של זהב **מד**. זהב **ל**. | מן הזהב **ו**. | —10-11 אינה טעונה] אינה באה **ע**. אינה באה מקשה **ל**. באה ככר **ו**. |

פרק ט 11-15

טעונה גביעים כפתורים ופרחים   כשהיא באה משל זהב באה ככר

וכשאינה באה זהב אינה באה ככר ר' יהושוע בן קרחה או' אותה מככר

ואין נירותיה מככר שנ' ככר זהב טהור (שם כה לט) ומה אני מקיים

⟨כל⟩ כליה (שם לז כד) זהב טהור אבל חצוצרות שעשה במדבר לא היו באות אלא

15 משל כסף שנ' עשה לך שתי חצוצרות כסף (במדבר י ב)

—11 כשהיא באה משל זהב באה ככר. מנחות כח, א; מנחות פח, ב.

—11 גביעים כפתורים ופרחים] גביעיה כפתוריה ופרחיה לו. | כשהיא] וכשהיא ג‏². | וכשאי‏
(נמחק) ב. כשהיה ע. וכשהיה ל. | משל זהב] של זהב מד. זהב על. מן הזהב ו. | באה‏²] ח'‏
מ. היא טעונה דו. | ככר] ככר של זהב ד. | —12 וכשאינה] וכשאין ב. כשאינה מד. אינה‏
ע. | זהב] משלזהב ג‏²ב. של זהב מד. מן הזהב ו. | באה‏²] טעונה דו. | ככר] ח' ב. ככר זהב‏
ד. | —12-13 ר' יהושוע... נירותיה] (הוגה בגליון: ר' יהושוע בן קרחה או' אותה מככר ואין‏
נרותיה מככר שנ') ב. | קרחה] קרחא לד. | מככר] היה מככר ל. | —13 נירותיה] היה‏
ונרותיה ל. כליה ו. | מככר] ככר מ. באים מככר ל. | שנ'...] שנ'] ככר זהב טהור תעשה‏
אותה ג‏². שנ' ככר זהב מ. ח' ל. | —14 (כל)] ואת כל ג‏²במעלד. | זהב] כל כליה זהב‏
ג‏²ב. שיהיו מזהב ע. שיהיו של זהב ל. | טהור] טהור ולא ככר ב. ח' מ. | שעשה] שעשה‏
משה ג‏²במעלדוף. | במדבר... אלא] במדבר היו ע. ח' ל. במדבר אינן באות אלא פ. |‏
—15 משל כסף] של כסף על. משל כסף וכן כל כינופיא בשל כסף פ. | שתי חצוצרות‏
כסף] ח' ו. שתי חצוצרות כסף מקשה תעשה אותם והיו לך למקרא ולמסע את המחנות פ. |

פרק י 1-6

פרק י"א   כיצד עשה בצלאל את המנורה עשאה כמין קורה ועשאה

{מרובה} ⟨מיריכה⟩ למטה גביעיה כפתוריה ופרחיה ומשך ממנה שני

קנים אחד אילך ואחד אילך ומשך הימינה שני קנים אחרים אחד אילך

ואחד אילך ומשך ממנה שני קנים אחד אילך ואחד אילך שנ' ששה קנים

5   יוצאים מצידיה (שמות כה לב) אבל לא למדנו לגביעים המשוקדים שנ'

ובמנורה ארבעה גביעים (שם כה לד) איסי בן יהוד' או' חמשה דברים

—6 איסי בן יהוד' או'. יומא נב, א – ב.

—1 כיצד] כאיצד ו. | בצלאל] משה ב. | עשאה] עשתה ב. עשאן מ. עשאו עד. | כמין
קורה] כמין עשת או כמין קורה (קרח ע.) ג²מעד. כמין עשת או קורה ל. | ועשתה
ב. ועשה מעד. | —2 ⟨מיריכה⟩] מרובה בו. ח' ל. מריבה ד. | למטה] ולמטה ד. | ולמשה
(והוגה בגליון: נ"ל ולמטה) מ. | גביעיה כפתוריה ופרחיה] גביעים כפתורים (וכפתורים מ.)
ופרחים ג²מלד. | ומשך] ומושך ג². | ממנה] הימנה ג¹ג²במדו. ממנה ועוד עשה ע. | —3
אחד אילך ואחד אילך] ע. א' מכאן וא' מכאן ל. אילך ואילך ו. | ומשך... אילך]
ח' ג²בל. ומשך הימנה שני קנים (... אחרים אילך ואילך ד.) מד. ממנה מצד אחד ושני
קנים ע. ומשך הימנה עוד שני קנים אילך ואילך ו. | —4 ומשך... אילך]
קנים אחרים אילך ואילך ג'. ח' ג²בל. אחד אילך ואחד אילך מ. ממנה מצד אחד ע. ומשך
הימנה שני קנים אילך ואילך דו. | שנ'] וכן עשה למטה וקנים היוצאים ממנה שני' ל. | ששה]
ושנה ג²במלדו. | —5 יוצאים מצידיה] ח' מ. יוצאים ל. יוצאים מצדים ד. | לגביעים] אם
גביעים ל. | המשוקדים] המשוקדים בה ג². משוקדי' ב. אם הם משוקדים או כפתריה ע.
משוקדים או כפתורים ופרחים ל. | —7-6 דברים בתורה] מקראות לה. |

פרק י 7-12

בתורה אין להם הכרעה ואילו הן שאת ארור מחר משוקדים וקם הלא אם

תטיב שאת (בראשית ד ז) או שאת אם לא תיטיב (שם) ארור אפם כי עז

(שם מט ז) או (כי) באפם הרגו איש וברצונם עקרו שור ארור

10 (שם מט ו-ז) מחר אנכי נצב (שמות יז ט) או והלחם בעמלק מחר (שם)

משוקדים כפתוריה ופרחיה (שם כה לד) או ארבעה גביעים משוקדים

(שם) וקם העם וזנה (דברים לא טז) או הנך שוכב אם אבותיך וקם (שם)

—7 ואילו הן. ירוש' עבודה זרה פ"ב ה"ז מא ע"ג-ד; יומא שם.

—7 להם] להן בה. | הכרעה] הכרע (הכרעה ע.) מן התורה מ. הכרע בע. הכרע מ. הכרע בתורה
ה. | ואילו הן] אלו הן מד. ואלו הם ל. | —7-12 שאת... וקם²] שאת ארור ומחר משוקדים
וקם הלא אם תטיב שאת וג' ארור אפם כי עז מחר אנכי נצב על ראש הגבעה וקם העם הזה
וזנה וג' או הנך שוכב עם אבותיך וקם ג². ארור מחר משוקדי' שאת ארור אפם כי עז או
וברצונם עקרו שור ארור מחר צא הלחם בעמלק מחר או מחר אנכי נצב ארבעה גביעי'
משוקדי' או משוקדי' כפתריה ופרחי' הנך שוכב עם אבותי' וקם או וקם העם הזה הלא אם
תטיב שאת ב. שאת ארור מחר משוקדים וקם (...שאת מ.) הלא אם תטיב שאת (...או שאת
ד.) ואם (אם ו.) לא תטיב ארור אפם כי עז (...או כי באפם הרגו איש מד.) וברצונם עקרו
שור ארור מחר אנכי נצב (...על ראש הגבעה ו.) או צא הלחם בעמלק מחר משוקדים כפתוריה
ופרחיה או ארבעה גביעים משוקדים וק העם וזנה (הזה ד.) או הנך שוכב עם אבותיך וקם
מדו. (וכעין קטע ג.¹). שאת ארור מחר משוקדים וקם שׁאֹת וג' משוקדים וַאֹרְבָעָה גְבִיעִים
משוקדים או משוקדים כפתוריה ל. הלא אם תיטיב שאת או שאת ואם לא תיטיב וברצונם
עקרו שור ארור או ארור אפם כי עז וצא הלחם בעמלק מחר או מחר אנכי נצב ובמנורה
ארבעה גביעים משוקדים או משוקדים כפתוריה ופרחיה הנך שוכב אם אבותיך וקם או

פרק י 13-18

אילו חמשה דברים בתורה אין להם הכרעה   איסי בן {עקשיא} (עקביא)

אומ' מעשה והייתה יתירה דינר זהב והכניסוה לכור שמנים פעמים

15 גופה של מנורה שמנה עשרה טפחים הרגלים והפרח שלשה טפחים

וטפחיים חלק וטפח וטפח גביע שבו כפתור ופרח וטפחיים חלק וטפח וטפח כפתור

ושני קנים יוצאים ממנו אילך ואילך וטפחיים חלק וטפח וטפח כפתור ושני

קנים יוצאים ממנו אילך ואילך וטפחיים חלק וטפח וטפח כפתור ושני קנים

---

14 מעשה והייתה יתירה דינר. ירוש' שקלים פ"ו ה"ד נ ע"ב; מנחות כט, א. —15 גופה
של מנורה שמנה עשרה טפחים. מנחות כח, ב.

וקם העם הזה וזנה ה. (וכעין קטעי ע.). —13 אילו... הכרעה] ח' ל. | אילו] הרי אילו ב. |
דברים בתורה] דברים ב. ח' מ. | אין] שאין במד. | להם] להן ב. | הכרעה] הכרע ג.[2]מ. הכרע
בתורה ב. | —13-14 איסי... פעמים] ח' מל. | (עקביא)] עקביא)] יהודה ג.[2] יהוד' עקבי' ב. עקיבא
דו. | —14 דינר] דינור ב. | זהב] של זהב ד. | והכניסוה] והכניסו] (ונמחק: הוציאו) ב.
והוציאוה והכניסוה ו. | פעמים] פעמים עד שעמדה על ככר ע. | —15 גופה] גובהה בל. |
שמנה עשרה] שמנה מ. היה י"ח ל. | טפחים[1]] טפח הפרח ו. | הרגלים] הרגלים והרגלים ו. | טפחים[2]
ח' ל. | —16 וטפחיים חלק[1]] ח' מ. וטפחים חלק ד. | שבו] שבן ב. | גביע] גביעי ו. | כפתור[1]
וכפתור ל. | וטפחיים[2]] וטפחים מד. | —17 ממנו] ממנה במ. ממנה ו. | אילך ואילך] אחד
היל ואחד אילך ואחד אילך מדו. אחד אילך ואחד אילך ב. | —17-19 וטפח... ואילך] ח' מ. | —18 יוצאים]
יוצאין ב. | ממנו] הימנו ב. הימנה ד. ממנה ו. | אילך ואילך] אחד היל ואחד היל ב. אחד
אילך ואחד אילך ו. | וטפחיים] וטפח ב. וטפחים ד. | —18-19 וטפח... ואילך] ח' ל. |

פרק י 19-23

יוצאים ממנו אילך ואילך נשתיירו שם שלשה טפחים שבהן גביעין

20 כפתורין ופרחין שנ' שלשה גביעים משוקדים (שמות כה לג) נמצאו

גביעיה ⟨עשרים ושנים⟩ וכפתוריה אחד עשר ופרחים תשעה גביעים למה

הן דומין לכוסות אלכסנדריים כפתורים למה הן דומין לתפוחים

הבירותיים פרחים למה הן דומין לפרחי העמודין נמצאת או' שיש

—21-22 למה הן דומין. מנחות שם.

—19 יוצאים] יוצאין ב. | ממנו] ממנה ב. | אילך ואילך] אחד הילך ואחד הילך
וטפחיי' חלק ב. אחד אילך ואחד אילך ו. | שם] ח' מ. | שבהן] שבהם מלדו. | —19-20
גביעין כפתורין ופרחין] גביעי' כפתור ופרח ב. גביעים כפתורים ופרחים מו. גביעים וכפתור
ופרח ל. גביעיה כפתוריה ופרחיה ד. | —20 שנ'... משוקדים] ח' ל. | משוקדים] ח' מו. |
נמצאו] נמצאו שם ב. | —21 גביעיה ⟨עשרים ושנים⟩ עשרים ושני' גביעים במלו. גביעים
עשרים ושנים ד. | וכפתוריה אחד עשר] | כפתרים י"א ג[1]. ואחד עשר כפתורי' במלו.
וכפתורים אחד עשר ד. | ופרחים תשעה] ותשעה פרחי' במלו. | גביעים] גביעין ד. | —22
הן] הם לו. | דומין] דומים מו. רומזים ל. | לכוסות] כמין כוסות ב. | אלכסנדריים]
אלכסנדרים ג[1]. אליכסנדריא ד. | כפתורים] כפתוריה ד. | הן[2]] הם לו. | דומין[2]] דומים
מלו. | לתפוחים] לתפוחי במד. | לטפוחים ל. | —23 הבירותיים] הברותים ג[1]. חברתי' ב.
הכותיים מ. הברתיים ע. הברותיים ל. הברתום (ובסוגריים: עיין סוף פרק הקומץ ובערוך
בערך תפוח) ד. הכדוניים ו. | פרחים] פרחין ג[1]. | הן] הם לו. | דומין] דומים מלו. | לפרחי]
לפרחי ל. לווי ו. | העמודין] העמודים דו. | של עמודים ל. | —23-24 נמצאת... הכלים] ח'
ו. | או'] אתה אומ' במל. את למד ד. |

פרק י 24-28

במנורה קושי ושבח כנגד כל הכלים מגיד שהראה הקב'ה כלים עשויים

25 ומנורה עשוייה שנ' וראה ועשה כתבניתם (שם כה מ) א'עפ'י שעשה

שלמה עשר מנורות כולן היו כשירות לעבודה ולא היו משתמשין אלא

בשל משה שנ' ויעש המנורו' עשר וגו' (דהי"ב ד ז) ואם תאמר חמש

מן הצפון וחמש מן הדרום והלא מנורה מן הצפון פסולה ומה ת"ל חמש

26— עשר מנורות. תוספתא מנחות יא, י; ירוש' שקלים פ'ו ה"ד נ ע"ב; מנחות צט, א.
27— ואם תאמר חמש. ירוש' שקלים שם.

24— קושי ושבח] שבח וקושי גדול ב. קישוי ושבח מ. קשוי ושבח ד. | כנגד ל. | ח' ל. |
הכלים] הכלים כולם מ. הכלים כלן מ. | מגיד] ומגיד הכתוב ב. הכתו' מ. ח' על. מגיד
הכתוב דו. | שהראה] שהראהו מ. הראהו ע. הראה ל. | הקב'ה] הקב'ה למשה בל. המקום
למשה מד. הֹבֹהֹ] ע. הק' למשה ו. | כלים] ח' ל. | עשויים] עשויין ג'ב. | 25— ומנורה]
למנורה ב. | עשוייה] עשויה ונעשת מ. עשויה ונעשית מאליה ע. עשויה ונעשית ל. | וראה]
תעשה המנורה ואומר וראה ע. | כתבניתם] ח' מ. כתבנית אשר אתה מראה בהר ע. | 26—
עשר] ח' פ. | מנורות] מנורות מנורת זהב ע. | כולן... לעבודה] ח' ו. | כולן] כולם ג'. וכולן בעלפ. |
היו כשירות] כשרות היו מ. היו כשרות עד. כשירות ל. | ולא] לא עלוף. | היו משתמשין]
שמשו בו. | 27— בשל משה] בזה שעשה משה ב. בזה מ. בשל משה בלבד ל. בזו של
משה ד. במנורה של משה ו. באותה שעשה משה פ. | המנורו' עשר] את המנורת עשר ג'.
מנורו' זהב טהור ב. מנורת זהב מד. מנורות זהב ה' מימין וה' משמאל ל. מנורות ו. מנורת
זהב עשר וינח בהיכל יי חמש מימין וחמש משמאל פ. | ואם תאמר] את במו. | 28— מן
הצפון'] בצפון ב. בדרום ע. מדרום ל. מן הדרום דפ. | מן הדרום] בדרום ב. בצפון ע.
מצפון ל. מן הצפון דפ. | מנורה] המנורה ל. | מן הצפון²] בצפון במלד. | אינו כשירה אלא
מן הדרום שנ' על ירך המשכן הימנה פ. | פסולה] לעולם פסולה ו. ח' פ. | 28-29— ומה...
מימין'] ח' עלוף. | ומה] מה מ. | 28-29— חמש משמאל וחמש מימין] ה' מן השמאל וה'
מימין ג'. | חמשה מימין וחמשה משמאל בד. חמש מימין וחמש משמאל מ. |

פרק י 32-29

משמאל וחמש מימין (שם) חמש מימין מנורת משה וחמש משמאל מנורת

30 משה שנ' מנורת זהב ונרותיהם וגו' (שם יג יא)   והם מכלות זהב

(דהי"ב ד כא) הם כולם זהב של שלמה כיצד מדשנן מעבירם מעל גבי המנורה

ומניחם באהל ומקנח בספוג נמצאו כל הכהנים עסוקין בנר אחד דברי

—30 והם מכלות דהב. ירוש' שקלים שם.

—29 חמש מימין] ח' מ. אלא חמש מימין עפ. אלא ה' המנורות מימין ל. אלא חמש מן
ו. | מנורת משה] מנורה (מן   [רה מ.) של משה במעלפ. מנורת של משה ד. —30-29
וחמש²... משה] ח' מ. | וחמש²] וה' מנורות ל. —29-30 מנורת משה] מנורה של משה בעל.
מנורה שעשה משה פ. | —31-30 שנ'... זהב] ח' ע. | —30 מנורת זהב] מנורות זהב ג'לו.
ח' ב. | ונרותיהם] ונרותיהם בערם כמשפט לפני הדביר זהב סגור ב. ונרותיה (ונרותיה
דו.) לבערם כמשפט לפני הדביר זהב סגור הפרח (והפרח' ו.) והנרות והמלקחי' זהב מדו.
כמשפט לפני הדביר ל. | —31-30 והם... שלמה] ח' ל. | והם] והם ג'ד. והיא ג'ד. הוא ב. והוא מו. |
מכלות] מוכלות מ. | —31 הם כולם זהב של שלמה]   זהבו שלמשה ג'. | שכילו לכל
של זה שלמה ב. וגם כלו זהבו של משה מ. ר' אלעזר בן שמוע אומר בכולם היו מדליקין
שנ'   ] הם כלם זהבו של שלמה ע. הם כלה זהבו של משה (ובסוגריים: ס"א שלמה) ד.
והן זהב כלים של שלמה ו. | כיצד] כיצד (ונמחק: עשה) עשר מנורות עשה שלמה וכל אחת
ואחת הביא' לה אלף ככר זהב והכניסוהו אלף פעמי' לכור והעמידוהו על ככר ומה שכתב
אין כסף נחשב בימי שלמה לא אומה זהו כשאר מיני זהב אבל זהב סגור כילה כיצד ב.
באיזה צד פ. | מדשנן] היו מדשנן ל. היו מדשנין את הנרות פ. | מעבירם] מעבירן במלדוה.
מעבירו פ. | מעל גבי] מגבי מד. מנגב ו. | המנורה] מנורה מוה. | —32 ומניחם] ומניחן
ג'במלדוה. ומניחו פ. | ומקנח] ומקניח ג'. | ומקנחן] ומקנחן במדוה. ומקנחן באהל ומקנחן ל.
ומקנחו פ. | בספוג] בספוג מיכאן אתה אומ' שלא היו קבועות נרות במנורה פ. | הכהנים]
כהנים פ. | עסוקין] עסוקים לופ. עסיקין ה. | בנר] בדבר ע. |

פרק י 37-33

ר' {מאיר} וחכמי' אומ' לא היו מזיזן ממקומן אלא על גבי מנורה

מדשנן שנ' על המנורה הטהורה (ויקרא כד ד) ומזרחיים היו דולקין

35 כנגד נר האמצעי מכאן היה ר' נתן או' האמצעי משובח שנ' אל מול

פני המנורה וגו' (במדבר ח ב) שהיה דליקתן שוה ונרותיהן שוות

והם דומות זה לזה

—35 היה ר' נתן או'. ספרי במדבר בהעלתך נט, מהד' האראוויטץ 57; מנחות צח, ב.

—33 ר'] רבי ג'. ר' יוסי מד. ר' יוסי הגלילי ל. | היו] היה לדוה. | מזיזן בו. מזיזין
אותן פ. | ממקומן] ממקומו ב. ממקומם ל. | אלא] ח' פ. | מנורה] המנורה ג'ל. | —34
מדשנן] היה מדשנן בל. מדתנן ד. ח' ה. | הטהורה] הטהורה יערך (...את הנרות דהפ.)
לבדהפ. | ומזרחיים] וכולן ל. | היו] ח' מל. | דולקין] דולקים מדפ. | —35 האמצעי]
האמצעי שפניו כלפי מערב פ. | מכאן] מיכן בו. מיכאן פ. | או'] ח' ד. | האמצעי[2] אמצעי
ע. | משובח] מכובד במפ. היה מכובד ד. | —35-37 שנ'... לזה] ח' פ. | שנ'] ח' ב. | —36
המנורה] המנורה יאירו (...ז' הנרות ל.) בלדו. | שהיה] שתהא ב. שיהא מלדו. | דליקתן]
דליקן מד. דולקין על. דליקין ו. | שוה] בשוה על. ח' ו. | ונרותיהן] ונרותיהם ג'מלו. |
שוות] דומות ושוות ל. | —37 והם... לזה] ח' ל. | והם] ח' ג'. והן בדו. והיו מ. | דומות]
למין ב. דומין מדו. | זה לזה] זו לזו ע. |

פרק י"א"　　מזבח הקטרת ארכו אמה ורחבו אמה וגובהו שתי אמות

שנ' (ועשית) מזבח וגו' (שמות ל א)　　וכולו היה מצופה זהב שנ'

וצפית אותו זהב טהור וגו' (שם ל ג) שלשה שמות נקרא (לו) מזבח הקטרת

מזבח הזהב מזבח הפנימי　　מזבח העלה ארכו חמש אמות (ורחבו

5　חמש אמות) שנ' ועשית מזבח העלה וגו' (שם לח א) דברי ר' מאיר

אמ' לו ר' יוסה ממשמע שנ' חמש על חמש איני יודע שהוא רבוע ומה

—1 ארכו אמה] ארכו אמה ומחצה מ. אמה אורכו פ. | ורחבו אמה] ורחבו אמה פ. | ואמה רוחבו פ. | וגובהו
שתי אמות] גבהו שתי אמות מ. וגבוה שתי אמות ו. | ואמתים קומתו גובהו כפליים כארכו
וכן ברוחבו פ. —2 שנ'... וגו'] ח' פ. | מזבח] מזבח מקטר קטורת (...אמה ארכו מ.
במלדו. | וכולו] וכולן בפ. | היה] היתה ד. ח' פ. | מצופה] מצפה ב. | זהב] בזהב מדפ. |
3-2 שנ'... וגו'] ח' פ. —3 טהור] ח' לד. | שלשה] ושלשה פ. | נקרא (לו)] נקראו לו
למזבח בו. | נקראו לו מל. יש לו למזבח ד. | הקטרת] הזהב לו. —4 מזבח¹] ומזבח
מלפ. | הזהב] הקטורת ל. הפנימי ו. | מזבח²] ומזבח מופ. | הפנימי] הפנימין ו. | מזבח³
ומזבח ל. דתניא מזבח ה. | ארכו חמש אמות] חמש אמות אורך פ. —5-4 (ורחבו חמש
אמות)] ורח' חמש אמות וגבהו שלש אמות למדה. ח' ו. וחמש אמות רוחב רבוע היה המזבח
ושלש אמות קומתו פ. —5 שנ'... וגו'] ח' פ. | מזבח] את מזבח במעלדוה. | העלה] העולה
עצי שטים ה' אמות אורך ל. —6 יוסה] יוסי במלדוהפ. | חמש על חמש] ה' אמות אורך
וה' אמות רוחב לוה. חמש אמות רוחב פ. | איני] אינו ב. | שהוא רבוע] שרבוע היה המזבח
פ. | ומה] מה מלדה. |

פרק י"א 7-12

ת"ל רבוע (שם) מופנה להקיש לדון ממנו גזירה שוה נאמ' כאן רבוע

ונאמ' להלן רבוע (שם ל ב) מה ⟨רבוע האמור⟩ להלן גובֿהו כשנים

כרחבו אף רבוע האמור כאן גובהו כשנים כרחבו אמ' לו ר' מאיר ⟨אם⟩

10 כדבריך נמצא גבוה מן הקלעים אמ' לו ר' יוסי הרי הוא אומ' על

המשכן ועל המזבח (במדבר ד כו) מה משכן עשר אמות אף מזבח עשר

אמות   חוט של סיקרא חוגרו באמצע להבדיל בין דמים העליונים

—7 ת"ל רבוע. זבחים נט, ב – ס, א. —11 מה משכן עשר אמות. זבחים שם. —12 חוט
של סיקרא. משנה מידות ג, א; זבחים י, ב; נג, א.

—7 רבוע¹] רבוע אלא ב**מדפ.** רבוע יהיה המזבח ל. רבוע יהיה אלא ו**ה.** | להקיש] להקש
ה. | לדון... שוה] ח' **פ.** | לדדון] ולדון ב**מל.** | ממנו] ח' **ב.** הימנו מל**ד.** | כאן] כאן ו. במזבח
העולה **פ.** | רבוע²] ח' **מ.** —8 להלן¹] במזבח הזהב **פ.** | ⟨רבוע האמור⟩ להלן] להלן ל.
רבוע שנאמר ו. רבוע האמור כאן במזבח הזהב **פ.** | גובהו] גובֿהו (הוגה בגליון **א.** גובהן ב.
כשנים] שנים מב**דוה.** פי שנים ל. כפליים **פ.** —9 כרחבו¹] ברחבו מ**ה.** כארכו **פ.** | רבוע
האמור] ח' ל**וה.** | כאן] להלן ו. במזבח העולה **פ.** | גובהו] גובהן ב. כשנים] גובהן ב**מדוה.**
פי שנים ל. כפלים **פ.** | כרחבו²] כרוחבן ב. ברחבו מ**עה.** כארכו **פ.** —10 נמצא] נמצא
מזבח במ**לדוה.** נמצא מזבח העולה **פ.** | גבוה] גובה ב. | מן הקלעים] מן הקלעים חמש אמות
ב**הפ.** מהקלעים ⟨מן הקלעים ו.⟩ עשר אמות **מו.** | יוסי] יוסין יוסף **ה.** | הרי] והלא ב**לדוה.** עז
מ. | הוא אומ'] כבר נאמ' ב**לדוהפ.** נאמר מ. —10-11 על המשכן ועל המזבח] ואת קלעי
⟨וקלעי **ה.**⟩ החצר ⟨...סביב ו**פ.**⟩ אשר על המשכן ועל המזבח ⟨...סביב בו**הפ.**⟩ ב**לוהפ.** את
קלעי החצר את עמודיה ואת אדניה ואת מסך מ. ואת קלעי החצר וגו' ל**ה.** | —12 חוט של
סיקרא] חוט של סיקרין ב. חוט הסיקרא ל. חוט ⟨וחוט **פ.**⟩ של סיקרא היה ד**פ.** | חוגרו]
חוגרן ג'. חוגר **פ.** | באמצע] ובאמצע **פ.** | —12-13 להבדיל... התחתונים] ח' **פ.** |

פרק י"א 13-17

לדמים התחתונים מחוט הסיקרא ולמטה חמש אמות אמה יסוד ושלש

אמות ברקים ואמה סובב ושם היו נותנין דמים הניתנים למטה ומחוט

15 הסיקרא ולמעלה חמש אמות אמה קרנות ושלש אמות ברקים ואמה כולי

עורב ושם היו נותנין דמים הניתנין למעלה   דמים הניתנין מחוט

הסיקרא ולמטן שנתנם מחוט {מחוט} הסיקרא ולמעלן פסולין והניתנין

—13 הסיקרא] סיקרא מ. סקרא ד. | אמות] אמות ומחוט (מחוט ל.) הסיקרא ולמטה (ולמעלה
ל.) חמש אמות על. אמה] ח' מד. | יסוד] ביסוד בד. | —14 ברקים] כרכב מלדו. גופו
פ. | סובב] סובבו פ. | —14-16 ושם... עורב] ח' פ. | נותנין] נותנים ד. | הניתנין] הניתנים
ב. הנמצאים ו. | למטה] למטה אלו חמש אמות התחתונות ע. למטה אלו ה' התחתונות חמש
העליונות ל. | —14-15 ומחוט הסיקרא ולמעלה] מחוט הסיקרא (סקרא ד.) ולמעלה מלד.
ח' ע. | —15 חמש אמות] וחמש אמות ע. ח' ל. | אמה] ח' ע. | אמות²] אמות ושלש או מ.
ח' ע. אמה ד. | ברקים] כרכב מעלדו. | כולי] כולה ב. ח' ל. כלה ד. כילו ו. | —16
נותנין] נותנים דמים העליונים ל. | דמים¹] דמין ד. | הניתנין¹] התנין ג¹. | למעלה] ח'
בלד. | —16-17 דמים²... הסיקרא] ח' ל. | דמים²] ודמים במעדוף. | הניתנין²] הנתנין מו.
הנתנין ד. | —17 הסיקרא¹] הסקרא ג¹ד. | ולמטן] ולמטה בדו. ח' מ. למטה ל. ולמעלה
פ. | שנתנם] שנתן ג¹. | אם נתן במ. אם נתנם עד. אם נתנן ל. אם נותן ו. אם ניתנם פ. |
מחוט הסיקרא] מחוט הסקרא | נין מחוט הסקרא ג¹. מחוט הסקרא ד. ח' ע. | ולמעלן]
ולמעלה מדלו. מלמעלה ע. ולמטה פ. | פסולין] ח' מעל. פסולים דו. | והניתנין] ודמים
הניתנין בלו. או דמים הנתנים מ. או הניתנין ע. ודמים הנתנים ד. ח' פ. |

פרק י"א 18-22

מחוט הסיקרא ולמעלן שנתנן מחוט הסיקרא ולמטן פסולין   מזבח שעשה

משה במדבר גובהו עשר אמות ושעשה שלמה גובהו עשר אמות ושעשו בני

20 הגולה גבהו עשר אמות ולעתיד לבא ⟨גבהו⟩ עשר אמות   מזבח

החיצון היה נתון באמצע עזרה כבש לדרומו כיור למערבו בית

המטבחיים לצפונו וכל ישר' במזרחו שנ' ויקרבו כל העדה וגו'

—18 מחוט הסיקרא¹] ח' ל. מחוט הסקרא ד. והני תני מחוט הסיקרא פ. | ולמעלן ו̇למעלן פ. | ולמעלן
פסולין ג¹. ולמעלה עד ו. | שנתנן פ. | והנתנים ג¹. | אם נתנן בל. אם
נתן מ. אם נתמן עד. אם נותן ו. אם ניתנין פ. | מחוט הסיקרא²] מחוט הסקרא ג¹ד. ח'
ע. | ולמטן] ולמטה במלדו. מלמטה ע. ולמעלה פ. | פסולין] פסולים ד. | —19 משה]
שלמה ל. | במדבר] ח' במעוף. | גובהו¹] גבוה מע. | ושעשה... אמות] ח' על. | גובהו²] גבוה
מ. | —19-20 ושעשו... אמות¹] ח' ע. | —20 גבהו¹] ח' בו. גבוה מ. | ולעתיד... אמות²] ח'
ב. | ולעתיד] לעתיד מעלדו. | ⟨גבהו⟩] גבוה מעד. אף כן פ. | אמות²] אמות שנא' וההראל
ו. | —20-21 מזבח החיצון] ח' בפ. מזבח הזהב מד. מזבח הנחשת על. מזבח ו. | —21
היה] ח' מעלד. | באמצע] בצפון פ. | עזרה] העזרה בלו. | כבש] והכבש ל. | כיור] והכיור
ל. וכיור ו. | בית] ח' מ. ובית ל. | —22 המטבחיים] המטבחים בד. | לצפונו] לציפונו ב. |
במזרחו] למזרחו ג¹במלדוף. | שנ'... העדה] ח' שנ'. | ויקרבו כל העדה ויעמדו מד. ויקרבו כל העדה ויעמדו כל העדה ל. ויקרבו כל
העדה ⟨ויקרב מ.⟩ כל העדה ויעמדו לפני ה' ו. ויקרבו כל העידה ויעמדו פתח האוהל פ. |

פרק י"א 23-24

(ויקרא ט ה)   שלשה שמות נקרא המזבח מזבח העלה מזבח הנחשת

מזבח הח(י)צון

23 שלשה] ושלשה פ. | נקרא המזבח] נקראו לו במעלוף. יש למזבח ד. | העלה] הנחשת‎—
ע. החיצון ל. | מזבח²] מזבח² עוף. | הנחשת] הקטרת מ. העולה ע. | 24 — מזבח ומזבח
עוף. | הח(י)צון] העולה ל. |

פרק י"ב 1-7

פרק י"ב   משה עשה כיור אחד (שנ' ועשית כיור נחשת)

(שמות ל יח) ושלמה עשה עשרה כיורות שנ' ויעש כיורות עשרה

(דהי"ב ד ו) שאין ת"ל חמשה מימין וחמשה משמאל (שם) ומה ת"ל

אלא חמשה מימין כיורו של משה וחמשה משמאל כיורו של משה   שלמה

5 הוסיף שעשה את הים שנ' ויעש את הים מוצק (מלכים א ז כג) ואו'

אלפים בת יכיל (שם ז כו) אי איפשר לומ' אלפים שכבר נאמ' שלשת

אלפים (דהי"ב ד ה) ואי איפשר לומ' שלשת אלפים שכבר נאמ' אלפים

—6 א' איפשר לומ' אלפים. תוספתא כלים ב"מ ה, ב; ירוש' עירובין פ"א ה"ה יט ע"א.

1—(שנ'... נחשת)] ח' פ. | נחשת] נחשת) ח' ל. | 2—ושלמה] שלמה **במעלפ.** | כיורות עשרה]
כיורות עשרה ויתנם בהיכל (...חמש מימין וחמש משמאל **על.) מעלד.** עשר כיורות נחשת
ו. כיורות עשרה נחושת פ. —3 שאין ת"ל] ויתן פ. | ומה ת"ל] ומה ת"ל חמש מימין וחמש
משמאל **בו.** מה ת"ל חמשה מן הימין וחמשה מן השמאל מ. ח' **לפ.** ומה ת"ל חמש ביומין
וה' בשמאל ד. —4 אלא] ח' **במו.** | כיורו] כיורו] כיור **במדו.** הכיור ל. | משמאל] משמאלו פ. |
כיורו²] כיור **במדו.** הכיור ל. ח' פ. | של משה²] ח' פ. | שלמה] שלמה] ח' פ. ועוד ו. —5 הוסיף שעשה
את הים] הוסיף עליהם שעשה את הים ב. הוסיף מדעתו הים ע. הוסיף הים מדעתו ל. הוסיף
מעשה שעשה את הים פ. | מוצק] מוצק מוצק עשר באמה משפתו וגו' ועוביו טפח ושפתו וגו' ב.
מוצק עשר באמה משפתו אל שפתו (... ועביו טפח מ.) **מד.** מוצק עשר (עשרים פ.) באמה
לפ. | ואו'] ח' **במדוף.** וכ' ל. —6 אלפים בת יכיל] ח' **בו.** אלפים בה יכיל ד. | אי איפשר]
אי איפשר מ. ח' ל. | לומ' אלפים] ח' פ. | שכבר נאמ'] וכתו' אחר אומ' פ. —7-6 שלשת
אלפים] שלש אלפים פ. (ובסוגריים: עיין פ"ק דעירובין דף י"ד ע"א וע"ב) ד. שלשת אלפיים
בת יכיל פ. —7 ואי איפשר] ואי איפשר מ. | לומ'] ח' ב. | שלשת] ח' פ. |

פרק י"ב 8-11

הא כיצד אלפים בלח שהן שלשת אלפים ביבש   וכמה היא הבת הרי

הוא אומ' עשרת הבתים חומר (יחזקאל מה יד) תנם עשרה בתים לכל כור

10 מאתים כור צא מהן חמשים כור תנם חמשים על חמשים הרי מאה וחמשי'

מקואות ⟨שכל מקוה ומקוה מחזיק ארבעים סאה ומניין שמחזיק מאה

—8 הא כיצד] ח' ל. | ומה ת"ל אלפים ומה ת"ל שלשת אלפים ו. | בלח] אמה בלח ו. | שהן]
שהם מד. ח' ופ. | שלשת] ושלש ו. ושלשת פ. | וכמה] אבל אי את (אתה ד.) יודע כמה
בדו. אבל אינו יודע כמה מ. אבל אי אתה יודע מכמה על. ח' פ. | היא הבת] הוא הבת
לד. והכת היא מידה איפה פ. | —8-9 הרי הוא אום' ת"ל ב. שנ' מעדו. ח' פ. | —9
עשרת הבתים חומר] האיפ' והבת תוכן אחד להם וג' ואו' עשר הבתי חומר ב. האפה והבת
תוכן אחד (...הוא ד.) ואומר עשרת הבתים (בתים מ.) חומר מלד. והאיפה והבת אחד להן
ע. האיפה והבת תוכן אחד יהיה ואי עשרת הבתים חומר ו. והאיפה והבת תוכן אחד לשנ̇יה
הוא ואומ' כי עשרת הבתים חומר פ. | תנם] תן על. הים ו. | עשרה] עשרת בעלדופ.
כור] כור וכור בדו. חֹומֶר וֹכֹוֹר ל. חומר וחומר פ. | —10 מאתים כור] מאתי כור ב. הרי
מאתים כור מלד. אלפים בת מאתים אום' פ. | מהן] מהם דו. | כור²] ח' פ. | תנם] תנה ד.
ח' ו. | חמשים על חמשים] חמשים על חמשי' על חמשים ב. חמשים על חמשים חמשים על
חמשים ע. | —11 מקואות] מקוות ג'¹. מקוה טהרה בלדו. | | טהרה וטהרה מ. מקוה
של טהרה ע. מקוה הטהרה פ. | —11-12 ⟨שכל... מקואות⟩ (הוגה בגליון באותיות
קורסיביות: לכל מקוה ומקו' מחזיק ארבעי' סאה ומניין שמחזי' מאה וחמשי' מקו' טהרה) ב.
מחזיק ארבעי' סאה ומניין שמחזיק מאה וחמשים טהרה מ. שכל טהרה וטהרה מחזיקת מ'
סאה] | ע. מחזקת מ' סאה ומניין שמחזקת מן] | וחמשים מקוה טהרה ל. שכל מקוה
ומקוה מחזיק (שבו ו.) מ' סאה ומניין שמחזיק ק"נ מקוה טהרה דופ. |

פרק י"ב 12-14

וחמשים מקואות) אם תאמר כולו עגול אינו מחזיק אם תאמר כולו

מרובע מחזיק יותר ומניין שעגול למעלה שנ' ועוביו טפח (מ"א ז כו,

דהי"ב ד ה) למדנו שעגול למעלה ומניין שהוא מרובע מלמטה שנ' עומד

—12 אם תאמר כולו עגול. ירוש' עירובין שם.

—12 אם תאמר¹... מחזיק] וא"ת (הוגה בגליון באותיות קורסיביות) ב. ואֹ"ת כולו עגול ל.
ח' ופ. | אם תאמר²] וא"ת בל. | —12-13 כולו מרובע] מרובע כולו פ. | —13 מחזיק] מחזיק
הוא במד. הוא מחזיק ל. | יותר] יותר על כן כרובים ותימורים (ותימורות ו.) ופטורי ציצים
בו. יותר על כן אלא שתי אמות העליונות היו עגולו' תנם (... על מ.) עשר באמ'
על עשר באמ' הרי מאה אמ' תנם מאה (... אמה מ.) על מאה הרי מאה טהרה מכאן שערו
(שיערו ל.) חכמי (...מי מ.) מקוה ארבעים סאה שלש אמו' התחתונות היו מרובעו' תנם שבעים
וחמש (...על ע"ה ל.) הרי מאה וחמש' תנם חמשי' על חמשי' הרי חמשי' טהרה הא למדת
שהמרובע יתר על העגול רביע מד. יותר אלא ב' אמות העליונות היו עגולות וב' אמות
התחתונות היו מרובעות [   ] מקוה טהורה שיערו חכמים מקוה מ' סאה שלש אמות
התחתונות היו מרובעות וב' אמות העליונות עגולות תנם שבעים וחמש על שבעים וחמש
הרי [   ] חמשים מקוה טהורה הא למדת שהמרובע יותר על העגול רביע ל. [
מי מקוה ארבעים סאה ובהם אמה על אמה ברום שלש אמות הא למדת שהמרובע יותר על
העיגול רביע ע. | ומניין שעגול] ומניין שעגול טפח ב. | ומניין שהעגול ל. אלא עגול פ.
למעלה] מלמעלה במלדו. מלמעלה ומרובע מלמטה פ. | ועוביו טפח] ועוביו טפח ושפתו
כמעשה שפת כוס (כיס ה.) בד. ועביו טפח שפתו כמעשה שפת כוס פר' שושן אלפים בת
יכיל מ. כמעשה שפת כוס וגו' ל. ושפתו כמעשה שפת כוס ו. ועוביו טפח ושפתו כמעלה
פרח שושן פ. | —14 למדנו שעגול למעלה] הא למדת שעגול מלמעלה ב. למדנו שעגול
מלמעל' (מן [   ] ג¹.) ג¹מדו. ח' לפ. | ומניין שהוא מרובע] ומניין (ונמחק: שעגו ב.) שמרובע
מבו. ומניין שהיה מרובע לד. לארכו עגול מלמעלה ומרובע פ. | שנ'] ח' מ. מניין שנ' פ. |

פרק י"ב 15-19

15 עַל שְׁנֵי עָשָׂר בָּקָר וגו' (מ"א ז כה, דהי"ב ד ד) ומה ת"ל פונים פונים

(שם) ארבע פעמים אלא נכנס להיכל פונה לימין לעזרה פונה לימין

להר הבית פונה לימין עולה לראש המזבח פונה לימין שנ' ודמות בקר

תחת לו וג' (דהי"ב ד ג) נמצאו ראשי שורות של ראשי שוורים

{במצבתם} ארבעה ארבעה (במצבתם) וכולו היה מוצק מרגל ועד ראש

15— בקר] בקר שלשה פונים צפונה פ. | ומה] מה מדפ. | פונים²] ח' מל. | 16 —נכנס]
מלמד שכשהיה נכנס ב. | לעזרה] נכנס לעזרה לו. | 17 —להר] נכנס להר ל. | לימין] ח'
מ. | עולה] ח' ב. | לראש המזבח] למזבח פ. | לימין²] ח' מ. | 17-18— ודמות בקר תחת לו]
ודמות בקרים תחת לו ג'.¹ ודמות בקרים תחת לו סביב סביבי' אותו עשר באמה מקיפים
את הים סביב ב. | ודמות בקר מתחת לבקרי' סביב סובבים אותו עשר באמה מקיפי' את הים
סביב דמ. | ודמות בקרים ל. | ודמות בבקר מתחת לבקרים ו. | ודמות בקר מתח' לבקרים סביב
סוכו אותו עשר באמה מקיפות אותו הים סביב פ. | 18 —נמצאו] נמצא פ. | ראשי שורות]
שורים ל. | של] על ע. | 19— ארבעה ארבעה] של ד' ד' ג'.¹ופ. של ארבע ב. ארבע ארבע
שמשתמשים לכל הצדדין ואת הבקר ושני (ושנוי ד.) טורי הבקרי' מוצקים (ומוצקים ד.) מד.
ד' ד' שמשתמשין לכל הצדדין שנ' ואת הים האחד (אחד ל.) ואת הבקר שנים עשר תחת
הים ושני טורי הבקרים (הב' ל.) על. | (במצבתם)... ראש] ח' ל. | (במצבתם)
במצבתיו מ. במצבתו ע. במצבתן ופ. | וכולו] וכולן ב. | היה] היה מ. | והיה מ. | מרגל ועד ראש
מרגליו של שור ג'.¹ופ. מרגלו של שור מ. מראשו של שור ע. |

פרק י"ב 20-27

20 אילו הן הממונים שהיו במקדש יוחנן בן פנחס על החותמות

ואחיהו על הסלתות מתתיהו בן שמואל על הפייסות פתחיה על הקינין

ולמה נקרא שמו פתחיה שפותח דברים ודורשן ויודע בשבעים לשון בן

אחיה על חולי מעים נחמיה חופר שיחין גביני בן גבר על נעילת

שערים הוגרס בן לוי על השיר בית גרמו על מעשה לחם הפנים בית

25 אבטינס על מעשה הקטרת אלעזר על הפרכות פנחס על המלבוש אין

פוחתין משבעה אמרכלין ומשלשה גזברין ואין עושין סררה על הצבור

בממון פחות משנים

—20 אילו הן הממונים. משנה שקלים ה, א. —25-26 אין פוחתין. משנה שקלים ה, ב.

—20-27 אילו... משנים] ח' במעלדוף. | —20 אילו] תנו רבנן אילו ג'. | פנחס] פינחס ג'. | —21 מתתיהו] מתייה ג'. | —22 דברים] בדן | ג'. | —24 גרמו] גורמו ג'. | —25 פנחס] פינחס ג'. | —27 פחות] בפחות ג'. |

פרק י״ג 7-1

פרק י״ג   כיצד היו הלוים משמרין במקדש בני קהת היו משמרין

בדרום שנ' משפחת בני קהת יחנו על וגו' (במדבר ג כט) והם היו

ממונין על כלי הארון שנ' ומשמרתם הארון והשלחן וגו' (שם ג לא)

חוצה להם שלשה שבטים ראובן גד שמעון   בני גרשון היו {היו}

5   משמרין במערב שנ' משפחות הגרשוני אחורי המשכן וגו' (שם ג כג)

והם היו ממונים על המשכן (שנ' ומשמרת בני גרשון באהל מועד וג')

(שם ג כה) וחוצה להם שלשה שבטים אפרים מנשה ובנימן   בני

---

1 משמרין] משמרים ד. | משמרין[2] משמרים ד. —2 יחנו על] יחנו על ירך המשכן
(...יחנו פ.) תימנה בלדפ. ח' מ. | והם] והן ב. —2-3 היו ממונין] היו משמרין כל כלי
האור ממונין ע. היו משמרים ל. היו ממונים ד. —3 כלי הארון] כל כלי הקדש ע. כל
כלי האורג ל. הארון ועל כל תשמישיו פ. | שנ'... וגו'] ח' פ. | ומשמרתם... והשלחן]
ומשמרתם הארון מד. ונשאו את יריעות המשכן ל. —4 חוצה] וחוצה פ. | להם] להן בפ.
ח' ד. | שלשה שבטים] ח' פ. | ראובן גד שמעון] ראובן ושמעו' וגד ב. ראובן שמעון וגד
מל. אפרים ומנשה ובנימין ע. ראובן שמעון לוי ד. דגל מחנה ראובן פ. —4-5 היו משמרין]
משמרת ב. היו משמרים לד. משמרין פ. —5 משפחות הגרשוני] ומשפחו' גרשו' ב. בני
הגרשו' פ. | אחורי] אחרי במדפ. על ירכתי ע. על ירך ל. | המשכן] המשכן יחנו ימה בעל.
המשכן ימה פ. —6 והם... וג'] ח' פ. | והם] והן ב. | היו] ח' ל. | ממונים] ממונין מ.
משמרין ע. | על המשכן] על האהל ב. כל כלי האהל ע. על כלי הקדש ל. | ומשמרת...
וג'] ונשאו את יריעו' המשכן מד. (ונשאו [   ] ע.) ומשמרתם הארון והשלחן וגו' ל.
—7 וחוצה] חוצה מלדפ. | להם] להן ב. | אפרים] ב. | אפרים] דגל מחנה בני אפרים פ. |

פרק י"ג 8-12

מררי היו משמרין בצפון שנ' ונשיא בית אב למשפחותם מררי וגו'

(שם ג לה) והם היו ממונים על הקרשים והקרסים והבריחים שנ' ופקדת

10 משמרת בני מררי וגו' (שם ג לו) וחוצה להם שלשה שבטים דן ואשר

ונפתלי   למזרח משה ואהרן ובניו שנ' והחונים לפני המשכן קדמה

וגו' (שם ג לח) וחוצה להן שלשה שבטים יהודה ויששכר וזבולון

8—היו משמרין] משמרת ב. משמרים ל. היו משמרים ד. על ירך המשכן יחנו פ. | בצפון]
לצפון מ. צפונה פ. | שנ'... וגו'] ח' פ. | למשפחותם מררי] למשפחות מררי מבד. וג' על
ירך המשכן [   ] יחנו צפונה ל. | —9 והם] והן ב. | ממונים] ממונין במפ. | הקרשים
והקרסים] הקרשים ב. הקרסים ועל הקרשים מד. הקרשים ועל הקרסים ל. קרשי המשכן
פ. | והבריחים] ועל הבריחים ב. ועל הברי' (והבריחים ד.) והעמודי' ועל אדני המשכן מד.
ועל הבריחים ועל אדני המשכן ל. ח' פ. | ופקדת] ופקודת בפ. | —10 משמרת] (נמחק:
משפחת) א. | בני מררי] ח' מ. בני מררי קרשי המשכן וגו' ועמודי החצר פ. | וחוצה] חוצה
מלפ. | להם] להן בפ. | דן ואשר] דן אשר בג'מלד. דגל מחנה בני דן אשר פ. | —11
למזרח] (נמחק: מש) ב. ח' ל. במזרח היו משמרין פ. | ובניו] ובניו משמרים במזרח ל. | לפני
המשכן] (הוגה בגליון ב.) ח' פ. | קדמה] קדמה לפני ב. ח' ל. קדמה לפני אהל מועד מזרחה
משה ואהרן ובניו ד. קדמה מזרחה לפני אהל מועד משה ואהרן ובניו עד והזר הקרב יומת
פ. | —12 וחוצה] חוצה מלפ. | להן] להם מלדפ. | שלשה שבטים] ח' מל. | יהודה] דגל
מחנה בני יהודה פ. | ויששכר] יששכר ג'במדפ. | וזבולון] וזבולן ג'. | וזבולון מ. זבולון ד. |

פרק י"ג 13-17

מחנה ישר' ⟨היה⟩ שנים עשר מיל על שנים עשר מיל דגלו של

יהודה ארבעה מילין מחנה שכינה ומחנה לוייה ארבעה מילין דגלו של

15 ראובן ארבעת מילין   מן הצפון לדרום שנים עשר מילין דגלו של

אפרים ארבעת מילין מחנה שכינה ומחנה לוייה ארבעת מילין דגלו של

דן ארבעת מיל נמצא בארבעת זוויות המשכן ארבע מחנות שמשמשין לכל

13— מחנה] ומחנה ב. כל מחנה מד. | ⟨היה⟩ היתה מ. | ⟨היה⟩ על שנים עשר מיל] על י"ב מילים
ג'. על י"ב מיל מן המזרח (ממזרח ל.) למערב י"ב מיל (...מחנה פ.) בלפ. ח' מד. | 13-14—
דגלו של יהודה] דגל יהודה ל. | 14— מילין] מיליון] מילין על שנים עשר מיל מן המזרח למערב
שנים עשר מיל דגלו של יהוד' ארבעה מילין מ. מיל על ד' מיל פ. | מחנה שכינה ומחנה
לוייה] מחנה לוייה ומחנ' שכינה במלד. | ⟨ ⟩ | מחנה שכינה ג'.). דגלו מחנה לוי ומחנה
שכינה פ. | מילין] מילים ג'. | 14-15— דגלו... מיליון] ח' ב. | 14-15—
דגלו של ראובן] דגל אפרים ל. דגלו של ראובן שבתימן פ. | 15— מיליון] ח' מ. מיל על
ד' מיל פ. | מן הצפון לדרום] ח' בד. ומצפון לדרום ל. מתימן לצפון פ. | שנים עשר מילין]
ח' בד. ארבע' מילין מל. | 15-16— דגלו של אפרים] דגל אפרים ב. דגל דן ל. דגלו של
אפרים שבמערב פ. | 16— מיליון] מילים ג'. | מילין ומן הצפון לדרום י"ב מילין דגלו של
ראובן ד' מילי' ב. מיל על ד' מיל פ. | מחנה... לוייה] ומחנה לוייה ושכינ' ב. מחנה לוייה
ומחנה שכינה מלד ⟨ ⟩ | שכינה ג'.). ח' פ. | ארבעת מילין] ד' מילים ג'. ודגלו ארבעה
מילין מ. ח' פ. | 16-17— דגלו של דן] ודגלו של דן מ. דגל ראובן ל. דגלו של דן שבצפון
פ. | 17— מיל] מילין מלד. | נמצא] נמצאו בעלדפ. | ונמצאו מ. | בארבעת] ד' בעלדפ. |
המשכן] שלמשכן ג'מד. של בעל. של מחנה ישראל פ. | ארבע מחנות] ארבע מחנות (ונמחק זוויות
ב.) מילין בע. ד' ד' מילין ל. ארבע מילין על ארבע מילין לכל דגל ודגל פ. | שמשמשין]
משמשין על. המשמשין פ. | 17-18— לכל הצדדין] בכל הצדדין ב. בהן

פרק י"ג 18-24

כיון שהיו ישר'   הצדדין שנ' איש על דגלו וגו' (שם ב ב)

נוסעין היה עמוד הענן מקופל וממושך על גבי (בני) יהודה כקורה

20 תקעו והריעו ותקעו נסע דגל יהודה תחילה שנ' ונסע דגל מחנה

יהודה וגו' (שם י יד) מיד נכנסו אהרן ובניו ופירקו הפרכות וכיסו

בה את הארון שנ' ובא אהרן ובניו (שם ד ה) תקעו הריעו ותקעו ונסע

דגל מחנה ראובן שנ' ונסע דגל מחנה ראובן וגו' (שם י יח) מיד

נכנסו בני גרשון ובני מררי ופירקו המשכן וטענו אותו בעגלות

— 19 כקורה. ירוש' עירובין פ"ה ה"א כב ע"ג.

18— רווח מיכאן ורווח מיכאן פ. | דגלו] ידו ג[1]. | ידו לדגליהם מלד פ. דגלו באותות ב. |
19— נוסעין] נוסעים ל. | עמוד] ח' ע. העמוד עומד ד. | הענן עומד עליהם פ. | הענן] ענן
ב. ח' דפ. | מקופל] מקפל ב. מקופר ועומד מ. מקופל ועומד על. | וממושך] וממשיך ב.
ונמשך מעלד. וממשך פ. | גבי] מחנה ב. דגל פ. | (בני)] ח' לפ. | כקורה] כמין קורה בלד.
כמו קורה פ. | 20-26 תקעו... וגו'] ח' מ. | 20— ותקעו] ותקעו בחצוצרות פ. | נסע]
ונסע בלדפ. | דגלי... שנ'] ח' ב. | דגלי] שנ' ב. | יהודה] מחנה בני יהודה פ. | ונסע ויסע
פ. | דגלי[2] ח' ב. | 21— יהודה] בני יהודה ב. יהודה וגו' ב. ראשונה יסעו ל. בני יהודה
לצבאותם ועל צבאו נחשון בן עמינדב פ. | 21-22 מיד... שנ'] ח' פ. | נכנסו] נכנסי' ב.
נכנס ד. | אהרן ובניו] בני אהרן ובניו ב. בני אהרן על. | ופירקו] ופירקו בעלד. | הפרכות]
את הפרכת ג[1]. את הפרוכת לב. את הפרכת ד. | וכיסו] וכסו בלד. | 22— הארון] ארון
העדות ב. | ובא] ומיד בא פ. | ובניו] ובניו בנסוע המחנ' בד. ובניו בנסוע המחנה וגו' וכלה
אהרן ובניו לכסות את הקדש פ. | 22-23 תקעו... וגו'] ח' ד. | הריעו] והריעו בלפ.
23— דגל מחנה ראובן] דגלו של ראובן פ. דגלו של ראובן החונים תימנה ב. | שנ'... וגו']
ח' ל. | ראובן[2] בני ראובן ב. בני ראובן לצבאותם פ. | מיד] ומיד ב. | 24— נכנסו] נכנסו
ב. | ופירקו] ופרקו בלד. | המשכן] את המשכן ג[1]בלדפ. | בעגלות] בעגלים ב. בעגלה ד. |

פרק י"ג 25-31

25 והעמידוהו עד בוא בני קהת שנ' {ונשאו} ⟨ונסעו⟩ הקהתים נושאי

וגו' (שם י כא) תקעו והריעו ותקעו ונסע דגל אפרים שנ' ונסע

דגל מחנה בני אפרים (שם י כב) מיד נכנסו בני קהת ופירקו את

הקודש וטענו אותו בכתף שנ' וכלה אהרן ובניו וגו' (שם ד טו)

תקעו והריעו ותקעו ונסע דגל דן שנ' ונסע דגל מחנה בני דן וגו'

30 (שם י כה) נמצאו שני דגלים מלפניהם ושנים מאחריהם ומחנה שכינה

ולוייה באמצע שנ' ונסע אהל מועד (שם ב יז)   כשם שהיו חונין

31-32 כשם שהיו חונין כך היו נוסעין. ירוש' עירובין פ"ה ה"א כב ע"ג.

---

25 והעמידוהו] והעמידו אותו **בדפ.** | שנ'] ח' **פ.** | נושאי] ח' **פ.** | נושאי] ח' ב. נושאי המקדש **לד.** נושא
המשכן **פ.** | —26 תקעו] ותקעו **ד.** | ונסעו'] ונסעו ונסע **פ.** | דגל אפרים] דגל מחנה אפרים
ל. דגלו של אפרים **ד.** דגל מחנה בני אפרים לצבותם **פ.** | 26-28 שנ'... וגו'] ח' **פ.** |
26-27 שנ'... אפרים] שנ' ונסע דגל בני אפרים ב. ח' **לד.** | 27 מיד] ח' **מד.** | נכנסו
בני קהת] נכנסי' בני קהת ב. ח' ל. | ופירקו] ופרקו **במד.** פרקו ל. | —28 אותו] ח' **בל.** |
וכלה] וכלו ב. | ובניו] ובניו לכסות ב. | —29 תקעו] ותקעו ל. | ונסע'... שנ'] ח' **פ.** | דגל
דן] דגלו של דן **בד.** דגל מחנה דן ל. | בני דן] דן] | ל. בני דן מאסף לכל המחנות **פ.** |
—30 נמצאו] ונמצאו **פ.** | מלפניהם] לפניהם **בל.** לפני המשכן **פ.** | ושנים] ושני דגלים
דבלפ. ח' **מ.** | מאחריהם] לאחוריהן ב. ומאחריהם **מ.** מאחרי המשכן **פ.** | —30-31 ומחנה
שכינה ולוייה] ומחנה לויה ומחנה שכינה לבדה **בדפ.** ומחנה שכינה **מ.** | —31-32 באמצע... היוי]
ח' **מ.** | 31 באמצע] בתוך **פ.** | שנ'] ח' **פ.** | מועד] שנ'... מועד] ח' **פ.** | מועד] מועד מחנ' הלוי' בתוך המחנ'
ב. | כשם] וכשם **בלד.** וכמו **פ.** | —31-32 שהיו חונין כך היו נוסעין]

פרק י"ג 32-37

כך היו נוסעין שנ' כאשר יחנו כן יסעו (שם)   על פי שלשה היו

ישר' נוסעים על פי הקודש על פי משה על פי חצוצרות על פי הקודש

מניין שנ' על פי יי יסעו (שם ט יח) על פי משה שהיה או' להם

35 מבערב בהשכמה אתם נוסעים התחילו ישר' לתקן בהמותם ואת כליהם

לצאת על פי חצוצרות שנ' ותקעתם תרועה ונסעו המחנות (שם י ה)

תקיעה תרועה תקיעה על כל דגל ודגל ר' יהודה אומ' על כל מטה ומטה

שהיו חונים כך היו נוסעים לד. שהיו נוסעים כן היו חונים פ. | 32— יסעו] יסעו דגל מחנה
בני דן לצבעותם פ. | שלשה] ג' דֹּבְֹֹרֹי ֹל. | 32-33— היו ישר' נוסעים] נוסעי' ישר' ב. היו
ישראל נוסעים וחונים ע. | 33— הקודש] רוח הקדש על. ה'ב'ה' פ. | על[1] ועל בד. | על[2]
ועל בדפ. | הקודש] רוח הקדש לע. ה'ב'ה' פ. | 34— מניין] ח' בל. | שנ'] ח' מ. דכתו'
פ. | יין יי יחנו ועל פי יי פ. | יסעו] יסעו בני ישר' בד. | משה] משה כיצד מד. משה מניין
שנ' דבר אל בנ"י ויסעו ע. | משה שנ'] על פי ה' ביד משה ל. | משה מניין שכשהיה ה'ב'ה'
חפץ לנסוע פ. | שהיה או' להם] שהיה או' להן ב. | משה היה אומר להם מלד. והיה (היה
פ.) אומר להם משה עפ. | 35— נוסעים] יוצאין מ. יוצאים ד. | התחילו ישר' לתקן] מיד
היו ישר' מציעין ב. מיד מוצאין יש' ל. מיד התחילו ישראל להיות מוצאין ד. מיד התחילו
ישראל לתקן פ. | בהמותם ואת כליהם] את בהמתם ואת | ג[1]. בהמתן ומתקני' כליהם
ב. את בהמתם מ. את בהמותיהם ומתקנין כליהם ל. בהמתם ומתקנים את כליהם ד. בהמתן
וכלי המשכן כדי לנסוע בבקר פ. | 36— לצאת] ח' פ. | על פי חצוצרות וחצוצרות ל.
שנ'... המחנות] שנ' ותקעת תרועה ונסעו ב. ח' מד. שנאמר ובני אהרן | ע. מניין
דפ. | 37— תקיעה תרועה תקיעה] תקיעה ותרועה ותקיעה ג[1]. תקעו והריעו ותקעו (...שלש
תקיעות לב.) במלד. תקעו הריעו שלש תקיעות היו ע. | ר' יהודה' אומ'] ח' ע. | על כל
מטה ומטה] שלש תקיעו' על כל מטה ומטה בד. | שלש על כל מטה ומטה על. תקעו והריעו
ותקעו על כל שבט ושבט פ. |

פרק י"ד   כיון שהיו ישר' חונים היה {עומד} עמוד הענן מתמר

ועולה ונמשך על גבי בני יהודה כמין סוכה ומחפה את האהל מבפנים

וממלא המשכן מבחוץ שנ' ויכס הענן וגו' (שמות מ לד) וזה {אחד}

משבעה ענני כבוד ששימשו לישר' (במדבר) ארבעים שנה אחד מימין

5 ואחד משמאל אחד מלפניהם ואחד מאחריהם ואחד למעלה מהם וענן שכינה

ביניהם ואחד נוסע לפניהם משפיל לפניהם הגבוה ומגביה לפניהם את

—4 משבעה ענני כבוד. ספרי במדבר בהעלתך פג, מהד' האראוויטץ 79.

| חונים] חונין ג'ב. | —2 ונמשך] וממשך פ. | בני יהודה] יהודה מ. דגל בני יהודה פ. | כמין] ומסכך כמין פ. | —3] ג'. | ונקפל ונוקמן ומחפה ב. ומסכך פ. | את האהל] אותם ל. | מבפנים] מבפנים פ. | —3 המשכן] את המשכן ג'במלדר. | מבחוץ] מבחוץ פ. | הענן] הענן את אהל מועד בדר. הענן את האהל לפ. | וזה] וזהו פ. | —3-4 {אחד} משבעה ענני כבוד] אחד מענני כבוד (הכבוד ר.) ג'במלדפר. | —4 ששימשו] ששמשו דר. שהיו משמשין פ. | לישר'] את ישר' במלדפר. | (במדבר)] במדבר משבעה מ. ח' פ. | ארבעים שנה] ח' במ. ארבעים שנה ארבעה מד' רוחותיהן פ. | —5-4 אחד מימין... מהם] ח' פ. | —5-4 אחד מימין ואחד משמאל] אחד מימינם ואחד משמאלם בלדר. | —5 אחד מלפניהם] ואחד מלפניהם מלד (ואחד |] ג'.). ואחד לפניהם ר. | מאחריהם] מלאחריהם בל. מלאחוריהם ד. | למעלה] מלמעלה ב. | מהם] מהן ג'ב. | וענן שכינה ל. | וא' על גביהן וא' ביניהם הוא ענן השכינה פ. | וענן (והוגה בגליון: שכינה) ר. | —6 ביניהם] מביניהם ב. שביניהם ד. ח' פ. | ואחד] ואחד ח' פ. | ועמוד ענן ב. וענן ל. | ועמוד הענן ד. נוסע] שנוסע ד. שהולך פ. | לפניהם] מלפניהם ב. | —7-6 משפיל... השפל] ח' פ. | לפניהם²] ח' בל. להם ע. | הגבוה] את הגבוה במלד. | לפניהם³] להן ב. להם ע. ח' ל. |

פרק י"ד 7-11

השפל והורג את הנחשים ואת העקרבים ושורף קוצים {כבירים} {וסירים}

{ומרחיבים} ‹ומדריכם› בדרך ישר' וענן שכינה שהיה באהל ר' שמעון בן יוחי אומ'

כל ארבעים שנה שהיו ישר' במדבר לא נצרך אחד מהם לא לאור החמה ביום

10 ולא לאור הלבנה בלילה אלא האדים היו יודעים ששקעה החמה הלבין

היו יודעים שזרחה החמה מסתכל בחבית ויודע מה שבתוכה בטפיח ויודע

—7 והורג... העקרבים] והורג נחשי' ועקרבים **במלדר** ‹והורג נחשים ועק| ג¹.). | והורג
לפניהם | ע. | והורג לפניהם נחשים ועקרבים ומשפיל לפניהם הגבוה ומגביה לפניהם
את השפל פ. | ושורף קוצים ‹וסירים› ושורף קוצים וברקנים ב. | ושורף לפניהם שיחים וקוצים
ע. | ושורף סירים וקוצים ל. ח' פ. | —8 ‹ומדריכם› ומדריכן בלר. | ומדריכן במסילה ע. |
—8-9 וענן... מהם] ח' פ. | שהיה] היה מ. | באהל] באהל מה משמש ע. | באהל מועד מה היה
השמש ל. | ר' שמעון בן יוחי אומ'] ר' שמעון בן יוחאי או' מ. אר"ש בן יוחי ל. רבי שמעון
בן יוסי אומר ד. | —9 כל ארבעים] כל אותן ארבעי' ב. כל אותם מ' ל. | ישר'ן ח' ל. |
נצרך] צרך ר. | החמה] חמה ל. | ביום] ח' ב. | —10 הלבנה] לבנה ל. | אלא] אלא אלא מאין היו
יודעים בין היום ובין הלילה ע. ח' ל. אלא לאור השכינה שנ' באורך נראה אור פ. | האדים
הלבין ענן ע. האדים הענן פ. | יודעים] יודעין בפ. | ששקעה החמה] ששקעה מ. שזרחה
החמה ע. שהחמה זורחת ל. | הלבין] האדים הענן ע. הלבין הענן פ. | —11 יודעים] יודעין
ג¹במפ. | שזרחה] ששקעה על. | שזרח פ. | החמה] חמה מ. | מסתכל] מסתכל היה אדם מסתכל ע.
ומסתכל לדר. | ומסתכלין פ. | בחבית] בחבית בלילה ע. | ויודע מה שבתוכה] רואה כל מה
שבתוכה ע. | ויודע מה שבתוכו ד. ח' פ. | בטפיח] בטפיח ובטפיח לפ. בטפיס ד. | ויודע] רואה כל
ע. ויודעין פ. |

פרק י"ד 12-15

מה שבתוכו מפני ענן השכינה (שביניהם) שנ' לעיני כל בית ישר'

(שם מ לח) ואו' קומי אורי וגו' (ישעיה ס א) ואו' לא יהיה לך

עוד השמש לאור יומם וגו' (שם ס יט) ואו' לא יבא עוד שמשך וגו'

15 (שם ס כ) ואו' והיה לך יי לאור עולם (שם ס יט) מהיכן היתה

12—שבתוכו] שבתוכה **במד**. בתוכה **ר**. | מפני ענן] מפני נוגה ענן **ע**. כשׁנוגה ענן **ל**. | השכינה] שכינה **במע**. | (שביניהם)] שהיה באהל **ע**. ואף לעתיד לבא יהיה להם כן **ל**. שביניהן **ד**. | שנ'] **מ**. ח' | לעיני כל בית ישר'] לעיני כל בית ישראל בכל מסעיהם **בדר**. לכל עיני כל בית ישר' **מ**. |] ולעתיד לבא גאולת ישראל עתיד הקב"ה להחזירה להם **ע**. והיה ה' לך לאור עולם וגו' **ל**. לעיני כל בית ישראל בכל מסעיהם וכן יהיה לעתיד לבא **פ**. | 13—ואו' קומי אורי וגו'] ח' **פ**. ואו'[1] ואו' ולעתיד כן שנ' ב. שנ' **ע**. | אורי] אורי כי בא אורך ג'[1]**במלדר**. | 13-15—ואו'[2]... עולם] ח' **ל**. | ואו'[2] שנ' **פ**. | לא] לא] **ר**. | לך] ח' **דר**. | 14—עוד השמש] עוד שמש (וה"א הידיעה הוסף ביד אחרת: השמש) **ב**. השמש **מ**. השמש עוד **פ**. | יומם] יומם ולנוגה הירח לא יאיר לך והיה יי לאור עולם **פ**. | ואו'] ח' **ד**. וכתו' **פ**. יותׁר **ר**. | לא] ולא **ר**. | עוד] ח' **ר**. | שמשך] שמשך וירחך ג'[1]. שימשך (שמשך **פ**.) וירחך לא יאסף **בפר**. | 15—ואו'] ח' **בדפ**. יותׁר **ר**. | והיה לך יי לאור עולם] כי יי יהיה לך לאור עולם **ב**. והיה לך יי לעולם **מ**. והיה ה' (...לך **ד**.) לאור יומם ושלמו ימי אבלך **דר**. ח' **פ**. | מהיכן] אוׁר שכינׁה]] מׁדבֹרת מהיכן **ל**. | היתה] היה **פר**. |

פרק י"ד 16-20

שכינה מדברת עם משה ר' נתן אומ' מן האהל שנ' ונתת אותו לפני

הפרכת אשר אֿועד (שמות ל ו) ר' שמעון בן עזאי או' ממזבח הקטרת

שנ' ושחקת ממנו הדק וגו' (שם ל לו) תלמידיו של ר' ישמעא' או'

מאצל מזבח העולה שנ' עולת {ה}תמיד לדורותיכם וגו' (שם כט מב)

סליקא ברייתא דמלאכת המשכן

20

—16 שכינה מדברת] ח' ל. מדבר ה'ב'ה' פ. שכינה מדבר ר. | —19-16 ר'] נתן... וגו'] ח'
פ. | מן] מעם בלדר. מעל ע. | האהל] מזבח הקטורת בלר. (ובסוגריים: ס"א מעם האהל
ד.). מזבח קטרת ע. | —17-16 ונתת... אֿועד] ונתת אותו לפני הפרוכת (הכפרת ר.) אשר
על (...ארון בר.) העדות (...ולפני הכפורת אשר על העדות אשר אועד לך שמה ב.) בדר.
ונתת אותו לפני הפרכת מ. ונתת ממנה לפני העדות באהל מועד אשר אועד לך שמה ל. |
—17 ר' שמעון בן עזאי] בן עזאי ל. רבי שמעון בן יוחאי ה. שמעון בן עזאי ר. | ממזבח
הקטרת] מאצל מזבח הקטורת בדר. מעם הפרכת על. | —18 ושחקת... הדק] ושחקת ממנה
הדק (...ונתת ממנה לפני העדות באוהל מועד אשר אועד לך שמה ב.) במדר. ונתת אותו
לפני הפרוכת וֿגֿ' אֿשֿר אועד לך שמה ל. | תלמידיו של] תלמידיו של במלדר. תלמידי ע. |
—19 מאצל] מעם ל. | לדורותיכם וגו'] לדורותיכם פתח אהל מועד לפני יי אשר אועד לכם
שמה (שם גֿ.) (...לדבר אליך שמה בגֿ.) גֿ2בל. | —20 סליקא... המשכן] וסליק מעשה
המשכן פירקי] | ברוך העֿ] | גֿ. סליק פירקין ב. ת"ם ונשל"ם תהלה לאל עולם ית' מֿ.
תושלב"ע ל. ותהי השלמת המלאכה מלאכת הקדש ד. סליקא לה ברייתא דמשכנא ופרקהא
כ"ז חזק ונתחזק נשלם פירקא דמשכנא דמנחות הצור ינהלינו על מי מנוחות פ. תם סליק
הפרקים] | בריית' דמלאכת המשכן] | ר. |

Note on Translation and Transliteration

Two previous translations of BMM have been published: an English translation by Joseph Barclay, in *The Talmud* (London, 1878); and a German translation by Heinrich Flesch, *Die Barajtha von der Herstellung der Stiftshütte* (Konitz, 1899). The latter is based on an inferior transcription of MS Munich Cod. Hebr. 95, as discussed above in chapter 5 of the Introduction. The evident deficit of Hebrew comprehension that nullifies the transcription also damages the translation, rendering it of little use for our purposes. The Barclay translation of BMM is included in a selection of talmudic tractates that, according to the translator's Preface (p. v), "contain the particular mode of thought against which the deepest woes of the New Testament are denounced; while, at the same time, they afford much information concerning the inner life of the Jews at the period of our Saviour's sojourn upon earth." Despite the tendentious aspect of the translation, it is on the whole quite faithful to the Hebrew, if occasionally mystified by dense passages. The Hebrew source of the translation is not identified; it is apparently one of the printed editions based on the *editio princeps* (Venice, 1602; see ch. 5 above). Neither of these translations makes use of the Hebrew text presented in this edition, necessitating the new translation that follows.

Any translation is an approximation. The distance between mishnaic Hebrew and modern English is vast, chronologically and conceptually. In the case of BMM, added difficulty is posed by the uniquely technical language of architectonic description. Moreover, BMM is predicated upon biblical accounts (e.g. Ex. 25-27, 35-40, 1 Ki. 7-8, 2 Chr. 4) that are obscure to begin with. We note these obstacles in order to stress the conjectural aspect of our translation.

Every translator tries to strike a balance between fidelity and felicity. Since BMM is more technical than literary in character, we have translated it with more emphasis on precision than style. A freer rendering is offered only where literal translation is unintelligible.

221

Words, phrases, explanations and references set off in [brackets] are added by the translator for the sake of clarity and continuity. We have sought, whenever possible, to base bracketed additions on alternate MS readings. For Hebrew pronouns with ambiguous antecedents, the noun is substituted in brackets.

The Hebrew Bible is cited by chapter and verse set off in (parentheses). We rely primarily on the Jewish Publication Society (JPS) translation (1962/1978/1982) with ancillary reference to JPS (1917) and the Revised Standard Version (RSV). Occasionally BMM diverges from the Masoretic text; at other times the nature of the citation has required departures from the given translations. The biblical verses as now numbered are rarely supplied by BMM in their entirety, and often only a few words from a verse are cited. When fuller citation is necessary for comprehension or context, the expansions are added in [brackets] within the quotation marks. The frequent Hebrew abbreviations WGW or WKW (lit. "etc.") are rendered as an ellipsis (...).

On the few occasions when comprehension depends upon an untranslatable Hebrew association (e.g. BMM 1:19-21, 7:24-25, 8:10-11, 12:22) the Hebrew consonants are transliterated in upper case English letters. The same transliteration system is used in the supplementary notes.

M	=	מ	ʼ	=	א
N	=	נ	B	=	ב
S	=	ס	G	=	ג
ʻ	=	ע	D	=	ד
P	=	פ	H	=	ה
Ẓ	=	צ	W	=	ו
Q	=	ק	Z	=	ז
R	=	ר	Ḥ	=	ח
Š	=	שׁ	Ṭ	=	ט
Ś	=	שׂ	Y	=	י
T	=	ת	K	=	כ
			L	=	ל

Transitive verbs or participles are sometimes rendered in the passive voice in order to convey in English the collective force of the Hebrew, e.g. BMM 1:12, "The sockets were hollowed out" (lit. "He hollowed out the sockets"). This is especially necessary because the substantive is not always identified by BMM, referring most often to Moses but also to Bezalel, Oholiab, all "the skilled" among the Israelites (e.g. Ex. 36:8), etc. When the substantive is identified by BMM, e.g. Bezalel (BMM 7:1, 10:1), Moses (8:1, 9:1), Solomon (10:25-26, 12:4-5), the translation assumes the active singular voice.

Regarding the frequent term of measure 'MMH ("cubit"), the singular form may also signify the plural and is translated accordingly.

The notes to the translation are confined primarily to philological and lexical matters. We have also sought to clarify various discrepancies and obscurities in the text in light of variant readings, rabbinic commentaries, realia and mathematical notation. Cross-references are intended to supplement the parallels discussed in chapter 3 of the Introduction and cited in the register of the Hebrew text. For an extended commentary on BMM, focusing on the conciliation of conflicting rabbinic data, the indispensable work is still that of M. Friedmann (Meir Ish-Shalom), whose edition is described above in chapter 5.

Baraita on the Construction of the Tabernacle

CHAPTER 1

Rabbi [Judah ha-Nasi] says: [There were] ten heave-offerings:[1] [regular] heave-offering,[2] tithe heave-offering,[3] dough-offering,[4] firstfruits,[5] Nazirite heave-offering,[6] thanksgiving heave-offering,[7] heave-offering of the Land,[8] heave-offering of [the tribute of] Midian,[9] heave-offering of shekels,[10] and heave-offering for the tabernacle.[11] [Regular] heave-offering, tithe heave-offering, dough-offering, firstfruits, Nazirite heave-offering, and thanksgiving heave-offering were for the priest[s]. Heave-offering of the Land was for the priests, for the Levites, for the Nethinim,[12] for the Temple and for Jerusalem. Heave-offering of [the tribute of] Midian was for Eleazar the priest. Heave- offering of shekels was for the sockets [of the tabernacle]. Heave-offering for the tabernacle provided for the tabernacle, oil for the light, the aromatic incense, the priests' vestments, and the high priest's vestments.

The tabernacle was thirty cubits in length, ten cubits in width, and ten cubits in height. R. Jose says: Its length was thirty-one cubits. How were the planks set up? Twenty planks were placed on the north, twenty on the south, and eight on the west. On the east there were no planks but four posts upon which was [hung] the veil, as it is said, "Hang the veil..." (Ex. 26:33); "Hang it upon four posts of acacia wood" (Ex. 26:32). The sockets were hollowed out, and each plank was cut out at the bottom, a fourth [of a cubit] from each [edge] and half [of a cubit] cut out of the middle. For each [plank] two tenons[13] were made in the shape of two rungs[14] and inserted into two sockets, as it is said, "[And you shall make forty silver sockets under the twenty planks,] two sockets [under the one plank for its two tenons]" (Ex. 26:19).

225

Each plank was cut out at the top, a fingerbreadth from each [edge], and placed inside one ring of gold[15] so that they would not separate one from the other, as it is said, "They shall match [at the bottom and terminate alike at the top inside one ring]" (Ex. 26:24). Now Scripture does not [need to] say "inside one ring" (Ex. 26:24); why then does Scripture say "inside one ring"? [To designate] the space where they insert the bar.

R. Nehemiah said: The planks were one cubit thick at the bottom, but at the top they tapered to a fingerbreadth, as it is said, "And they shall terminate (TMMYM) alike" (Ex. 26:24), and elsewhere it says, "The waters... ran out (TMMW) completely" (Josh. 3:16). R. Judah says: At the bottom and at the top they were one cubit thick, as it is said, "And they shall terminate alike" (Ex. 26:24).

How were the planks set up? Forty sockets of silver were placed on the north, forty on the south, sixteen on the west and four on the east, a total of one hundred sockets, as it is said, "[The one hundred talents of silver were for casting the sockets of the sanctuary and the sockets for the curtain,] one hundred sockets [to the one hundred talents]" (Ex. 38:27).

Each plank had two rings of gold on it, one at the top and one at the bottom, into which the bars were inserted. The length of each bar was thirty cubits corresponding to twenty planks.[16] The length of the center [bar] was twelve cubits corresponding to eight planks, for it was sunk through the center of the planks to the east and to the west, as it is said, "The center bar [halfway up the planks] shall run [from end to end]" (Ex. 26:28).

As the planks were made on the north, so also were the planks made on the south, but on the west it was not so; rather the length of each [bar] was eight cubits corresponding to six planks. The planks, the bars, the sockets, the posts and the thickness of the planks were overlaid with gold, as it is said, "Overlay the planks with gold [and make their rings of gold, as holders for the bars]" (Ex. 26:29). Now Scripture does not [need to] say "holders for the bars" (Ex. 26:29); why then does Scripture say "holders for the bars"? [To designate] the space where the center bar entered.

"And they overlaid the bars with gold" (Ex. 36:34). How was [this] done? A tube of gold was produced, one and a half cubits in length and half a cubit in height, and it was placed in the hollow space of the plank where they insert the bar.

CHAPTER 2

How did they cover the tabernacle? They brought ten strips of cloth of blue, purple and crimson yarns and fine linen, as it is said, "As for the tabernacle, make it of ten strips of cloth; [make these of fine twisted linen, of blue, purple and crimson yarns]" (Ex. 26:1). Their thread was folded thirty-two [times]: [these are] the words of R. Nehemiah. For R. Nehemiah said: "Thread" [by itself indicates] one [strand]; "folded" indicates two; "twisted" indicates four; "fine-twisted" indicates eight; thus their thread was folded thirty-two [times].[17] But the sages say: "Thread" [by itself indicates] one [strand]; "folded" indicates two; "twisted" indicates three; "fine-twisted" (Ex. 26:31) indicates six; thus their thread was folded twenty-four [times].[18]

[The cloths] were fastened into two [sets of] curtains, one of five and the other of five, as it is said, "Five of the cloths [shall be joined to one another]" (Ex. 26:3). To these were fastened loops of blue wool, as it is said, "Make loops of blue wool [on the edge of the out-ermost cloth]" (Ex. 26:4). To these were fastened fifty clasps of gold, as it is said, "And make fifty gold clasps [and couple the cloths to one another with the clasps]" (Ex. 26:6). The clasps in the loops looked like stars in the sky.

The length of each cloth was twenty-eight cubits, as it is said, "The length of each cloth shall be twenty-eight cubits" (Ex. 26:2). Subtract ten [cubits] for the roof of the tabernacle; this leaves eighteen cubits, nine on each [side]. The width of the [fastened] cloths was forty cubits, as it is said, "The width of each cloth shall be four cubits" (Ex. 26:2).[19] Subtract thirty [cubits] for the roof of the tabernacle; this leaves ten cubits to the west, coinciding with the length of the planks.

CHAPTER 3

Eleven cloths of goat's hair were produced. The length of each one was thirty cubits, as it is said, "You shall then make cloths of goat's hair [for a tent over the tabernacle; make the cloths eleven in num-ber. The length of each cloth shall be thirty cubits]" (Ex. 26:7-8). They were fastened into two [sets of] curtains, one of five and the other of six, as it is said, "Join five of the cloths by themselves [and the other six cloths by themselves]" (Ex. 26:9, 36:16). On each one fifty loops were made, and the fifty loops were fastened to fifty clasps of bronze, as it is said, "Make fifty loops [on the edge of the outermost cloth]" (Ex. 26:10); and it says, "Make fifty clasps of bronze [and fit the clasps into the loops]" (Ex. 26:11).

The [fastened] cloths were forty-four [cubits] in width, as it is said, "And the width of each cloth shall be four cubits" (Ex. 26:8).[20] Subtract thirty cubits for the roof of the tabernacle and ten [cubits] for the back of it;[21] this leaves one cloth folded over the front of the tent, as it is said, "And fold over the sixth cloth at the front of the tent" (Ex. 26:9).

R. Jose says: Half of it was folded over the front of the tent, and half of it overlapped the back of the tabernacle, as it is said, "As for the overlapping excess [of the cloths of the tent, the extra half-cloth shall overlap the back of the tabernacle]" (Ex. 26:12).

A covering[22] of skin was produced, thirty cubits in length and ten cubits in width, and it was draped over the tent, as it is said, "And make for the tent a covering [of tanned ram skins]" (Ex. 26:14). It resembled a checkered pattern[23] on top: [these are] the words of R. Nehemiah. R. Judah says: There were two coverings, the lower one of tanned ram skins and the upper one of dolphin skins, as it is said, "Its covering, the covering of dolphin skin that is on top of it" (Num. 4:25).

CHAPTER 4

The veil was woven ten cubits by ten cubits. Four loops[24] were made in it, and it was hung from hooks that were on the posts, as it is said, "Hang the veil [under the clasps]" (Ex. 26:33). Stored there were the jar of manna,[25] the flask of anointing oil,[26] the staff of Aaron [with] its almonds and blossoms,[27] the priests' vestments, and the high priest's vestments. There Aaron the priest entered four times on the Day of Atonement.

Outside the veil were placed the table and the lampstand, the table on the north and the lampstand opposite to it on the south, as it is said, "Place the table [outside the curtain]" (Ex. 26:35); and it says, "And the lampstand opposite the table [by the south wall of the tabernacle]" (Ex. 26:35). As they were placed in the tent of meeting, so also were they placed in the Temple,[28] except that the length of the tent of meeting was thirty cubits and its width was ten cubits, while the length of the Temple was sixty [cubits] and its width was twenty [cubits]. Thus you learn that [the area of] the tent of meeting was one fourth of [the area of] the Temple.

As the veil was woven, so also were the ephod and the breastpiece woven, except that in these an extra thread of gold was placed, as it is said, "They hammered out sheets of gold [and cut threads to be worked into designs]" (Ex. 39:3).

As the veil was woven, so also was the screen woven, except that the veil was worked into designs, as it is said, "You shall make a curtain of blue, purple [and crimson yarns, and fine-twisted linen; it shall have a design of cherubim worked into it]" (Ex. 26:31); while the screen was done in embroidery, as it is said, "You shall make a screen for the entrance of the tent [of blue, purple and crimson yarns, and fine-twisted linen, done in embroidery]" (Ex. 26:36): [these are] the words of R. Nehemiah. For he said: Wherever it is said [in Scripture] "worked into designs," [this signifies] two faces;[29] "done in embroidery" [signifies] one face.[30]

The branches of the lampstand were aligned opposite the width of the golden table. The golden altar was placed inside the house,[31] and it divided the house[32] from its midpoint inward. It was aligned opposite the veil, as it is said, "Place it in front of the veil that is over the ark of the testimony" (Ex. 30:6).

From the planks on the south to the branches of the lampstand was [a distance of] two and a half cubits. From the lampstand to the table was [a distance of] five cubits. From the table to the planks on the north was [a distance of] two and a half cubits. Thus you learn that the width [of the tabernacle] was ten cubits.

From the planks on the west to the veil was [a distance of] ten cubits. From the veil to the table was [a distance of] five cubits. From the table to the golden altar was [a distance of] five cubits. From the golden altar to the entrance was [a distance of] ten cubits. Thus you learn that the length [of the tabernacle] was thirty cubits.

CHAPTER 5

The enclosure was one hundred cubits in length and fifty cubits in width, as it is said, "You shall make the enclosure of the tabernacle:

[on the south side, a hundred cubits... For the width of the enclosure, on the west side, fifty cubits]" (Ex. 27:9-12). But you do not know the width of a hanging. Yet Scripture [also] says, "Its height—or width—was five cubits, [like that of the hangings of the enclosure]" (Ex. 38:18). You must infer that as the height was five cubits, so also the width was five cubits.

How was the enclosure set up? Twenty sockets of bronze were placed on the north and twenty on the south, a post [was placed] inside each one, and a ring was attached in the middle. The stakes were held in place by cords and the posts. The length of each of the stakes was six handbreadths, and its width was three [handbreadths]. The ring hung from the hook, and the hanging wrapped around it like the sail of a ship. Consequently the hanging extended two and a half cubits from the post on one side and two and a half cubits on the other side; so also with the second post. Thus you learn that between the posts there was [a distance of] five cubits.

The stakes were fastened by cords and the posts. These were held fast by pegs[33] of bronze. As there were pegs for the tabernacle, so also were there pegs for the enclosure, as it is said, "All the utensils of the tabernacle [for all its service, as well as all its pegs and all the pegs of the enclosure, shall be of bronze]" (Ex. 27:19). But you do not know the distance[34] from the hangings to the entrance of the enclosure. Yet it is also said, "The hangings of the enclosure, [the screen at the entrance of the gate of the enclosure that surrounds the tabernacle, the cords thereof, and the altar]" (Num. 4:26). [You must infer that] as [the distance] from the tabernacle to the altar[35] was ten cubits, so also [the distance] from the hangings to the entrance of the enclosure was ten cubits. But you do not know the measure[36] of the entrance of the enclosure. Yet it is said, "The screen of the gate of the enclosure, done in embroidery, [...was twenty cubits long...]; its height—or width [—was five cubits]" (Ex. 38:18). Now Scripture does not [need to] say "five cubits" (Ex. 38:18). Why then does Scripture say "five cubits"? To teach that the length [of the entrance of the enclosure] was twenty cubits, and its width was five cubits.

So also on the north, [the length of the enclosure] was one hundred cubits, as it is said, "Again [a hundred cubits of hangings for its length] along the north side" (Ex. 27:11). On the west [the width of the enclosure] was fifty cubits, as it is said, "[For the width of the enclosure] on the west side, fifty cubits of hangings" (Ex. 27:12). On the east [the width of the enclosure] was fifty cubits, as it is said, "[For the width of the enclosure] on the front, or east side, fifty cubits" (Ex. 27:13). Subtract fifteen cubits, as it is said, "Fifteen cubits of hangings on the one flank" (Ex. 27:14); and it says, "And fifteen cubits of hangings on the other flank—on each side of the gate of the enclosure" (Ex. 38:15).

[The distance] from the hangings on the south to the tent was twenty cubits. The tent was ten cubits.[37] [The distance] from the tent to the hangings on the north was twenty cubits. Thus you learn that the width [of the enclosure] was fifty cubits. [The distance] from the hangings on the east to the tent was fifty [cubits]. The tent was thirty cubits.[38] [The distance] from the tent to the hangings on the west was twenty cubits. Thus you learn that the length [of the enclosure] was one hundred cubits, as it is said, "The length of the enclosure shall be a hundred cubits [and the width fifty by fifty[39]]" (Ex. 27:18). R. Jose says: Now Scripture does not [need to] say "fifty by fifty" (Ex. 27:18), except to teach that the length [of the enclosure] was one hundred cubits and its width was fifty [cubits].

As was the entrance of the tent, so was the entrance of the porch [of the Temple]; as was the entrance of the enclosure, so was the entrance of the great hall [of the Temple]. On this [basis] R. Jose b. R. Judah said: An enclosed area [outside of a settlement][40] of two seahs' space[41] is equivalent [in area] to the enclosure of the tabernacle; [therefore it is permitted to] carry [objects] within it on the Sabbath.

CHAPTER 6

The ark that Moses made in the wilderness was two and a half cubits in length, one and a half cubits in width, and one and a half cubits in height, as it is said, "They shall make an ark of acacia wood [two and a half cubits long, a cubit and a half wide, and a cubit and a half high]" (Ex. 25:10). R. Meir says: The [ark] cubit measured six handbreadths; thus [the length of the ark] was fifteen handbreadths. Subtract twelve handbreadths for the width of the tablets, a handbreadth on either side for space to rest the tablets, and half a handbreadth on [either] side for the thickness of the ark. The width of the ark was nine handbreadths. Subtract six handbreadths for the length of the tablets, two handbreadths for space to rest the scroll of the Law, and half a handbreadth on either side for the thickness of the ark.

R. Judah says: The [ark] cubit measured five handbreadths; thus [the length of the ark] was twelve and a half handbreadths. There were four tablets in [the ark], two whole ones and two broken ones. The length of each of the tablets was six handbreadths, and its width was three [handbreadths]. Subtract twelve handbreadths for the width of the tablets and a fingerbreadth on either side for the thickness of the ark. The width of the ark was seven and a half handbreadths. Subtract six handbreadths for the length of the tablets, half a handbreadth on either side for space to rest the tablets, and a fingerbreadth on [either] side for the thickness of the ark. But the scroll of the Law was placed at the side [of the ark], as it is said, "Take this book of Teaching [and place it beside the ark of the covenant of the Lord your God]" (Deut. 31:26).

Concerning [the ark] it is explained in the later Scriptures,[42] "King Solomon made him a palanquin [of wood from Lebanon; he made its posts of silver, its back of gold, its seat of purple wool]" (Cant. 3:9).[43] R. Judah b. Laqish says: There were two arks there, one that was with them in the camp and one that went forth with them to battle. In [the latter] were the broken tablets, as it is said, "The ark of the covenant of the Lord traveled in front of them" (Num. 10:33). In the one that was with them in the camp was the scroll of the Law, as it is said, "Neither the Lord's ark of the covenant nor Moses stirred [from the camp]" (Num. 14:44).[44] Likewise it says of Saul, "Thereupon Saul said to Ahijah, 'Bring the ark of God here'" (1 Sam. 14:18); likewise it says of Uriah, "[Uriah answered David,] 'The ark and Israel and Judah abide in booths'" (2 Sam. 11:11). But the ark of the covenant went forth with them to battle only once, as it is said, "So the troops sent men to Shiloh; [there Eli's two sons, Hophni and Phinehas, were in charge of the ark of the covenant of God, and they brought down from there the ark of the covenant of the Lord of Hosts enthroned on the cherubim]" (1 Sam. 4:4). R. Judah says: There were only two tablets in the ark, as it is said, "There was nothing inside the ark but the two tablets [of stone which Moses placed there at Horeb]" (1 Ki. 8:9).

CHAPTER 7

How did Bezalel make the ark? He made three boxes, two of gold and one of wood. He placed the one of wood inside one of gold and placed [the other] one of gold inside the one of wood. He overlaid its upper edges with gold, as it is said, "Overlay it with pure gold; [overlay it inside and out]" (Ex. 25:11). Now Scripture does not [need to] say "overlay it" [the second time] (Ex. 25:11); why then does Scripture say "overlay it" [the second time]? It teaches that he overlaid [the ark's] upper edges with gold.

The cover of gold was placed on top of [the ark], as it is said, "Place the cover on top of the ark" (Ex. 25:21). Four rings of gold were attached to it, two on the north and two on the south. Into these were inserted the poles, which were never moved from there, as it is said, "The poles shall remain in the rings of the ark; [they shall not be removed from it]" (Ex. 25:15). Although Solomon made a pattern of all the vessels, he did not make a pattern of the ark, as it is said, "When all the elders of Israel had come, [the priests lifted the ark and carried up the ark of the Lord]" (1 Ki. 8:3-4). You must deduce: the ark was placed inside the house[45] and divided the house ten cubits by ten cubits.[46] Two cherubim of gold stood with their feet on the ground.

From the wall to [each] cherub [the distance] was five cubits; from [each] cherub to the ark [the distance] was five cubits. How do you derive [this from Scripture]? When they brought in the ark, the poles extended as far as the veil and the entrance; consequently the doors of the holy of holies were not closed, as it is said, "The poles projected [so that the ends of the poles were visible in the sanctuary in front of the shrine, but they could not be seen outside]" (1 Ki. 8:8; 2 Chr. 5:9). Now it is not possible [for Scripture] to say, "But [the ends of the poles] could not be seen" (1 Ki. 8:8; 2 Chr. 5:9), since it is also said, "[The ends of the poles] were visible" (1 Ki. 8:8; 2 Chr. 5:9); nor is it possible [for Scripture] to say, "[The ends of the poles] were visible," since it is also said, "But [the ends of the poles] could not be seen." How can this be [resolved]? [The poles] protruded through the veil and were visible like the two breasts of a woman. How is it derived [from Scripture] that [the poles] extended inside? As it is said, "[The ends of the poles] could not be seen outside" (1 Ki. 8:8; 2 Chr. 5:9). Thus you learn that they extended inside. And how is it derived [from Scripture] that [the poles] extended outside? As it is said, "[The poles] projected [so that] the ends of the poles [were visible] in the sanctuary" (1 Ki. 8:8; 2 Chr. 5:9).

How is it derived [from Scripture] that as the poles were extended, so also were the wings [of the cherubim] extended, concealing the ark and coverings its poles from above? As it is said, "[And the cherubim] shielded the ark and its poles from above" (1 Ki. 8:7).

Where was the ark deposited? R. Judah b. Laqish says: In its place in the holy of holies, as it is said, "And there it remains to this day" (2 Chr. 5:9; 1 Ki. 8:8). But the sages say: In the chamber of the woodshed.[47] R. Eliezer says: It went down to Babylon, as it is said, "[A time is coming when everything in your palace which your ancestors have stored up to this day will be carried off to Babylon;] not one thing (DBR) will remain behind, saith the Lord" (2 Ki. 20:17; Is. 39:6). "Thing" (DBR) refers here to the Decalogue (DBBRWT) [in] the ark. Rabbi [Judah ha-Nasi] says: Josiah hid it, as it is said, "He said to the Levites [consecrated to the Lord] who taught the people,[48] ['Put the holy ark in the house that Solomon son of David, King of Israel, built; as you no longer carry it on your shoulders, see now to the service of the Lord your God and His people Israel]'" (2 Chr. 35:3). [Josiah] said: [The ark] will not go down to Babylon with you, for you [must] carry it on [your] shoulders.

The holy of holies that Solomon made had a wall, an entrance, and doors, as it is said, "And he made doors for the great hall and for the holy of holies" (cf. 2 Chr. 4:22). But in the Second[49] Temple there was no wall but rather two partitions,[50] each of them one and a half cubits in length. Two veils of gold were spread over the top of them. It was called the partition space.[51]

CHAPTER 8

The table that Moses made in the wilderness was two cubits in length, a cubit in width, and a cubit and a half in height, as it is said, "You shall make a table [of acacia wood, two cubits long, one cubit wide, and a cubit and a half high]" (Ex. 25:23). R. Judah says: The [table] cubit measured five handbreadths. On this [basis] they said: The length of the table was ten [handbreadths] and its width was five [handbreadths]. The length of the bread of display was ten [handbreadths] and its width was five [handbreadths]. It was placed lengthwise across the width of the table, and two and a half handbreadths on each side were folded over; thus the length of the bread filled the width of the table: [these are] the words of R. Judah.

R. Meir says: The length of the table was twelve [handbreadths] and its width was six [handbreadths]. The length of the bread of display was ten [handbreadths] and its width was five [handbreadths]. It was placed lengthwise across the width of the table, and two handbreadths on each side were folded over. A space of two handbreadths was [left] in the middle so that the wind could blow between [the loaves].

Abba Saul says: [The bread of display] was placed lengthwise across the length of the table and breadthwise across the width of the table, as it is said, "With ('L) each row you shall place pure frankincense [which is to be a token offering for the bread]" (Lev. 24:7). They said to him: But is it not said, "Next to it ('LYW) the tribe of Manasseh"? (Num. 2:20).[52]

Four rings of gold were attached to [the table], two on the north and two on the south, as it is said, "Make four gold rings [for it, and attach the rings to the four corners at its four legs]" (Ex. 25:26). R. Judah says: [There were] two arms[53] below from leg to leg. [The table] had a rim of gold, as it is said, "Make a rim [of a hand's breadth] around it" (Ex. 25:25).

Although Solomon made ten tables, all of them valid [for divine service], they were not used; rather that of Moses was used, as it is said, "He made ten tables and placed them in the great hall, five on the right and five on the left" (2 Chr. 4:8). Now if you say five [tables] were on the south and five on the north, would not a table on the south be invalid?[54] Why then does Scripture say "five on the right and five on the left" (2 Chr. 4:8)? Rather [it means] five on the right of the table [of Moses] and five on the left of the table of Moses, as it is said, "[And Solomon made all the furnishings that were in the house of God: the altar of gold] and the tables for the bread of display" (2 Chr. 4:19).[55]

CHAPTER 9

The lampstand that Moses made in the wilderness was wrought from hammered gold and required cups, calyxes, and petals, as it is said, "You shall make a lampstand of pure gold; [the lampstand shall be made of hammered work; its base and its shaft, its cups, calyxes, and petals shall be of one piece]" (Ex. 25:31). I might infer that its members were made [separately] and fastened to it; [therefore] Scripture says "of one piece" (Ex. 25:31). How is it derived [from Scripture] to include its lamps? Scripture says "shall be made"[56] (Ex. 25:31). I might think [that Scripture means] to include its lamps but to exclude cups, calyxes, and petals. After it amplifies, Scripture limits:

[therefore] I include its lamps that were made with it, and I exclude its cups, calyxes, and petals that were not made with it. How is it derived [from Scripture] to include its tongs and fire pans[57] and to exclude the pincers and the forceps?[58] After it amplifies, Scripture limits: [therefore] I include its tongs and fire pans that were used with it, and I exclude the pincers and the forceps that were not used with it.

If it was wrought of gold, it was wrought of the talent;[59] if it was not wrought of gold, it was not wrought of the talent. R. Joshua b. Qorḥa says: It was wrought of the talent, but its lamps were not [wrought] of the talent, as it is said, "[And it shall be made with all these furnishings] out of a talent of pure gold" (Ex. 25:39).[60] But how do I explain [the verse], "[He made it and] all its furnishings [out of a talent of pure gold]"? (Ex. 37:24).[61] [All of its furnishings were of] pure gold. But the trumpets that [Moses] made in the wilderness were wrought of silver, as it is said, "Have two silver trumpets made" (Num. 10:2).

CHAPTER 10

How did Bezalel make the lampstand? He made it like a beam, and from its base[62] below he made its cups, calyxes, and petals. From it he extended two branches, one on either side, and from it he extended two other branches, one on either side, and from it he extended two [more] branches, one on either side, as it is said, "Six branches shall issue from its sides, [three branches from one side of the lampstand and three branches from the other side of the lamp-stand]" (Ex. 25:32). But we would not have learned that the cups were shaped like almond-blossoms unless it was said, "And on the lampstand itself there shall be four cups [shaped like almond-blossoms]" (Ex. 25:34).

Isi b. Judah says: There are five verses in the Torah that are uncertain [in syntax], and they are as follows: "shall it not be lifted up" (Gen. 4:7); "cursed" (Gen. 49:7); "tomorrow" (Ex. 17:9); "shaped like almond-blossoms" (Ex. 25:34); "rise up" (Deut. 31:16). [The meaning could be either] "If you do right, shall it not be lifted up" or "Shall it not be lifted up if you do no right" (Gen. 4:7). [The meaning could be either] "Cursed be their anger so fierce" (Gen. 49:7) or "For when angry they slay men, and when pleased they maim oxen that are cursed" (Gen. 49:6-7). [The meaning could be either] "Tomorrow I will stand" or "Do battle with Amalek tomorrow" (Ex. 17:9). [The meaning could be either] "shaped like almond-blossoms, the calyxes thereof and the petals thereof" or "four cups shaped like almond-blossoms" (Ex. 25:34). [The meaning could be either] "And the people will rise up and go astray" or "You are soon to sleep with your fathers and rise up" (Dt. 31:16). These are the five verses in the Torah that are uncertain [in syntax].

Isi b. Aqavya says: Once it happened that there was an extra golden denar [in the talent], and they placed it in the furnace eighty times.[63]

The lampstand itself was eighteen handbreadths [in height]: three handbreadths for the legs and the petal;[64] two handbreadths [left] plain; a handbreadth for a cup, calyx, and petal; two handbreadths [left] plain; a handbreadth for a calyx and two branches issuing from it on either side; two handbreadths [left] plain; a handbreadth for a calyx and two branches issuing from it on either side; two handbreadths [left] plain; a handbreadth for a calyx and two branches issuing from it on either side; leaving three handbreadths for cups, calyxes, and petals, as it is said, "[On one branch there shall be] three cups shaped like almond-blossoms [each with calyx and petals; and on the next branch there shall be three cups shaped like almond-blossoms, each with calyx and petals; so for all six branches issuing from the lampstand]" (Ex. 25:33). [The lampstand had] a total of twenty-two cups, eleven calyxes, and nine petals.

What did the cups resemble? Alexandrian goblets.[65] What did the calyxes resemble? Cypress cones.[66] What did the petals resemble? Blossom ornaments of columns.[67] Thus you conclude that the lampstand entailed as much difficulty and [earned] as much praise[68] as all of the [other] vessels. This shows that the Holy One, blessed be He, revealed the finished vessels and the finished lampstand, as it is said, "Note well, and follow the patterns for them [that are being shown you on the mountain]" (Ex. 25:40).

Although Solomon made ten lampstands, all of them valid for the [divine] service, they used only that of Moses, as it is said, "He made ten lampstands [of gold as prescribed, and placed them in the great hall, five on the right and five on the left]" (2 Chr. 4:7). Now if you say five were on the north and five were on the south, would not a lampstand on the north be invalid?[69] Why then does Scripture say "five on the left and five on the right"? (cf. 2 Chr. 4:7). [It means]

five on the right of the lampstand of Moses and five on the left of
the lampstand of Moses, as it is said, "They kindle the golden lampstand and the lamps thereof" (2 Chr. 13:11).[70] "[The petals, lamps,
and tongs] of purest gold" (2 Chr. 4:21): [this means that] they were
all [wrought from] the gold of Solomon.[71]

How were [the lamps] trimmed? They were removed from the
lampstand, set down in the tent, and wiped off with a sponge. Thus
all the priests were occupied with one lamp: [these are] the words of
Rabbi [Judah ha-Nasi]. But the sages say: [The lamps] were not
moved from their places; rather they were trimmed upon the lampstand, as it is said, "[He shall set up the lamps] upon the pure lampstand" (Lev. 24:4). The eastern [lamps] burned facing the center
lamp.[72] On this [basis] R. Nathan said: The center [lamp] is specially
cherished, as it is said, "[Let the seven lamps give light] at the front
of the lampstand" (Num. 8:2), for the flames were equal, the lamps
were equal, and they were alike one to the other.

CHAPTER 11

The incense altar was a cubit in length, a cubit in width, and two
cubits in height, as it is said, "You shall make an altar [for burning
incense; it shall be a cubit long and a cubit wide—it shall be
square—and two cubits high]" (Ex. 30:1-2). It was overlaid completely with gold, as it is said, "Overlay it with pure gold, [its top,
its sides round about, and its horns; and make a gold molding for it
round about]" (Ex. 30:3). It was called by three names: incense altar,
golden altar, inner altar.

The altar of burnt-offering was five cubits in length and five cubits
in width, as it is said, "[He made] the altar for burnt-offering [of
acacia wood, five cubits long and five cubits wide—square—and
three cubits high]" (Ex. 38:1): [these are] the words of R. Meir. R.
Jose said to him: By deduction from what is said, "five [cubits] by
five [cubits]" (cf. Ex. 38:1), do I not know that [the altar of burnt-
offering] was square? Why then does Scripture say "square"? (Ex.
38:1). It is eligible to be considered a comparison for the purpose of
analogy. "Square" is mentioned here [Ex. 38:1, concerning the altar
of burnt-offering] and "square" is mentioned there [Ex. 30:2, concerning the incense altar]. Just as there [where] "square" is mentioned, its height was twice its width, so here [where] "square" is
mentioned, its height was twice its width. R. Meir said to him:

According to what you have said, [the altar of burnt-offering] was higher than the hangings. R. Jose said to him: [Scripture] says: "[The hangings of the enclosure, the screen at the entrance of the gate of the enclosure] that surrounds the tabernacle and the altar" (Num. 4:26). As [the height of] the tabernacle was ten cubits, so also [the height of] the altar was ten cubits.

A red line encircled [the altar of burnt-offering] in the middle to separate between the blood [sprinkled] above and the blood [sprinkled] below.[73] From the red line downward was [a distance of] five cubits: a cubit for the base; three cubits for the ledges;[74] and a cubit for the surround. There they sprinkled the blood assigned for sprinkling below [the red line]. From the red line upward was [a distance of] five cubits: a cubit for the horns; three cubits for the ledges;[75] and a cubit for the scarecrow.[76] There they sprinkled the blood assigned for sprinkling above [the red line].

Blood assigned for sprinkling below the red line was invalid if it was sprinkled above the red line. [Blood] assigned for sprinkling above the red line was invalid if it was sprinkled below the red line.[77]

The altar that Moses made in the wilderness was ten cubits in height; the one that Solomon made was ten cubits in height; the one that the exiles [returned from Babylon] made was ten cubits in height; and in the time to come its height will be ten cubits.

The outer altar was placed in the center of the [Temple] court. To the south of it was the ramp; to the west of it was the laver; to the north of it was the slaughterhouse;[78] and to the east of it was all Israel, as it is said, "And the whole community came forward [and stood before the Lord]" (Lev. 9:5). The altar was called by three names: altar of burnt-offering; bronze altar; outer altar.

CHAPTER 12

Moses made one laver, as it is said, "Make a laver of bronze [and a stand of bronze for it, for washing]" (Ex. 30:18). Solomon made ten lavers, as it is said, "He made ten lavers [for washing; he set five on the right and five on the left]" (2 Chr. 4:6). Now Scripture does not [need to] say "five on the right and five on the left" (2 Chr. 4:6). Why then does Scripture say [this]? Rather [it means] five on the right of the laver of Moses and five on the left of the laver of Moses.[79]

Solomon added [to these], for he made the [molten] sea, as it is said, "Then he made the molten sea"[80] (1 Ki. 7:23), and it says, "Its capacity was two thousand baths" (1 Ki. 7:26). Now it is not possible [for Scripture] to say [its capacity was] "two thousand [baths]" (1 Ki. 7:26), since it is also said [the molten sea held] "three thousand [baths]" (2 Chr. 4:5); nor is it possible [for Scripture] to say [the molten sea held] "three thousand [baths]," since it is also said [its capacity was] "two thousand [baths]." How can this be [resolved]? "Two thousand" (1 Ki. 7:26) refers to liquid measure, which is equivalent to "three thousand" (2 Chr. 4:5) in dry measure.[81]

What was the quantity of a bath? [Scripture] says: "Ten baths make a homer" (Ezek. 45:14). Allow ten baths per kor;[82] [the capacity of the molten sea was] two hundred kors.[83] Subtract fifty kors; allow fifty [kors] for fifty [mikvahs]: [this makes] a total of one hundred fifty mikvahs, for a mikvah holds forty seahs.[84] How is it derived [from Scripture] that [the molten sea] held one hundred fifty mikvahs? If you say it was completely round, it could not have held [one hundred fifty mikvahs];[85] if you say it was completely square, it would have held more [than one hundred fifty mikvahs].[86] How is it derived [from Scripture] that it was round on top? As it is said, "It was a handbreadth thick [and its brim was made like that of a cup]" (1 Ki. 7:26; 2 Chr. 4:5). Thus we learn that it was round at the top. And how is it derived [from Scripture] that it was square on the bottom? As it is said, "It stood upon twelve oxen, [three facing north, three facing west, three facing south, and three facing east, with the sea resting upon them]" (1 Ki. 7:25; 2 Chr. 4:4). Now why does Scripture [need to] say "facing" (1 Ki. 7:25; 2 Chr. 4:4) four times? Rather [it means] one who enters the great hall [of the Temple] must turn to the right; [one who enters] the [Temple] court must turn to the right; [one who enters] the Temple mount must turn to the right; one who ascends to the top of the altar must turn to the right.[87] As it is said,[88] "Beneath were figures of oxen [set all around it, of ten cubits, encircling the sea; the oxen were in two rows, cast in one piece with it]" (2 Chr. 4:3). They were standing so that there were four heads of oxen at the head of each row.[89] All of it was cast from the foot [of each ox] to the head.

These were the officers in the Temple: Johanan b. Phineas in charge of the seals;[90] Ahijah in charge of the drink offerings; Mattithiah b. Samuel in charge of the lots;[91] Petahiah in charge of the bird-offerings. Why was he called Petahiah (PTHYH)? Because he opened (PWTH) matters and explained them and knew seventy languages. Ben Ahijah was in charge of bowel sickness; Nehemiah[92] was the trench-digger; Gabini was the herald; Ben Geber was in charge of closing the gates; Hugros b. Levi was in charge of the singing; the house of Garmu was in charge of preparing the bread of display; the house of Abtinas was in charge of preparing the incense; Eleazar was in charge of the curtains; Phineas was in charge of the garments.

There were no fewer than seven supervisors and three bursars, and no fewer than two [people] were given jurisdiction over the public in [matters of] property.

CHAPTER 13

How did the Levites guard the sanctuary? The Kohathites guarded the south, as it is said, "The clans of the Kohathites were to camp along [the south side of the tabernacle]" (Num. 3:29). They were in charge of the ark vessels, as it is said, "Their duties comprised the ark, the table, [the lampstand, the altars, and the sacred utensils that were used with them]" (Num. 3:31). To their exterior were three tribes: Reuben, Gad, Simeon.

The Gershonites guarded the west, as it is said, "The clans of the Gershonites were to camp behind the tabernacle [to the west]" (Num. 3:23). They were in charge of the tabernacle, as it is said, "The duties of the Gershonites in the tent of meeting [comprised the tabernacle, the tent, its covering, and the screen for the entrance of the tent of meeting]" (Num. 3:25). To their exterior were three tribes: Ephraim, Manasseh, and Benjamin.

The Merarites guarded the north, as it is said, "The chieftain of the ancestral house of the clans of Merari [was Zuriel son of Abihail; they were to camp along the north side of the tabernacle]" (Num. 3:35). They were in charge of the planks, the clasps and the bars, as it is said, "The assigned duties of the Merarites [comprised the planks of the tabernacle, its bars, posts and sockets, and all its furnishings]" (Num. 3:36). To their exterior were three tribes: Dan, Asher, and Naphtali.

To the east were Moses, Aaron and his sons, as it is said, "Those who were to camp before the tabernacle, in front, [before the tent of meeting, on the east, were Moses and Aaron and his sons]" (Num.

3:38). To their exterior were three tribes: Judah, Issachar, and Zebulun.

The Israelite camp was twelve miles by twelve miles. The standard of Judah was four miles. The camp of the divine Presence[93] and the Levites was four miles. The standard of Reuben was four miles.

From north to south [the camp] was twelve miles. The standard of Ephraim was four miles. The camp of the divine Presence and the Levites was four miles. The standard of Dan was four miles. Thus at the four corners of the tabernacle there were four camps, so that they served on all of the sides, as it is said, "[The Israelites shall camp] each with his standard [under the banners of their ancestral house; they shall camp around the tent of meeting at a distance]" (Num. 2:2).

Whenever Israel set out, the pillar of cloud rolled up and stretched out over the children of Judah like a beam.

They sounded [on the trumpets[94]] a sustained blast, a quavering blast, and a sustained blast.[95] The standard of Judah set out first, as it is said, "[And in the first place] the standard of the camp of the children of Judah set forward" (Num. 10:14). Aaron and his sons immediately proceeded to take down the veil,[96] and they covered the ark with it, as it is said, "[At the breaking of camp] Aaron and his sons [shall go in and take down the veil of the screen and cover the ark of the testimony with it]" (Num. 4:5). [Next] they sounded [on the trumpets] a sustained blast, a quavering blast, and a sustained blast, and the standard of the division of Reuben set out, as it is said, "The next standard to set out [troop by troop] was the division of Reuben" (Num. 10:18). The Gershonites and the Merarites[97] immediately proceeded to take down the tabernacle and load it on to wagons, and [at their destination] they would set it up by the time the Kohathites arrived, as it is said, "Then the Kohathites who carried [the sacred objects] would set out; [and by the time they arrived, the tabernacle would be set up again]" (Num. 10:21).

[Next] they sounded [on the trumpets] a sustained blast, a quavering blast, and a sustained blast, and the standard of Ephraim set out, as it is said, "The next standard to set out [troop by troop] was the division of Ephraim" (Num. 10:22). The Kohathites[98] immediately proceeded to remove the sacred furniture, which they carried on their shoulders, as it is said, "When Aaron and his sons have finished [covering the sacred furniture, and all the sacred vessels at the breaking of camp, only then shall the Kohathites come to bear them]" (Num. 4:15). [Next] they sounded [on the trumpets] a sustained blast, a quavering blast, and a sustained blast, and the standard of Dan set out, as it is said, "The standard of the division of Dan would set out" (Num. 10:25). Thus there were two standards in front of [the Israelites] and two standards behind them, and the camp of the divine Presence and the Levites was at the center, as it is said, "Then the tent of meeting [with the camp of the Levites] shall set out [midway between the divisions]" (Num. 2:17).

As they camped, so they set out, as it is said, "As they camp, so shall they set out, [each in his place by their standards]" (Num. 2:17).

At three behests the Israelites set out: at the behest of the Holy One, at the behest of Moses, at the behest of the trumpets. How is it derived [from Scripture that they set out] at the behest of God? As it is said, "On a sign from the Lord the Israelites broke camp" (Num. 9:18). [They set out] at the behest of Moses, who said to them in the evening: You will set out early in the morning. The Israelites then began to prepare their cattle and their belongings for departure. [They set out] at the behest of the trumpets, as it is said, "But when you sound short blasts, the divisions [camped on the east] shall move forward" (Num. 10:5). They sounded [on the trumpets] a sustained blast, a quavering blast, and a sustained blast for each standard. R. Judah says: For each tribe.

CHAPTER 14

When the Israelites were camped, the pillar of cloud rose straight up and stretched out over the children of Judah like a sukkah. It covered the tent from inside and filled the tabernacle from outside,[99] as it is said, "The cloud covered [the tent of meeting, and the glory of the Lord filled the tabernacle]" (Ex. 40:34). This was one of the seven clouds of glory that ministered to Israel for forty years in the wilderness: one on the right, one on the left, one in front of them, one behind them, one above them, the cloud of the divine Presence in their midst, and one advancing before them, lowering the high places and raising the low places before them, killing serpents and scorpions, consuming thorns and briers,[100] and guiding them by a straight way.[101]

[Regarding] the cloud of the divine Presence that was in the tent, R. Simeon b. Yoḥai says: During all of the forty years that the Israelites were in the wilderness, not one of them had need of the light of the sun by day nor the light of the moon by night. For when [the cloud] reddened, they knew that the sun had set; when it whitened, they knew that the sun had risen. One who looked into a jug knew what was in it; [one who looked] into a pitcher knew what was in it, owing to the cloud of the divine Presence in their midst, as it is said, "[For over the tabernacle a cloud of the Lord rested by day, and fire would appear in it by night] in the view of all the house of Israel" (Ex. 40:38); and it says, "Arise, shine, [for your light has dawned; the glory of the Lord has shone upon you]" (Is. 60:1); and it says, "No longer shall you need the sun for light by day" (Is. 60:19); and it says, "Your sun shall set no more" (Is. 60:20); and it says, "For the Lord shall be your light everlasting" (Is. 60:19).

From where did the divine Presence speak with Moses? R. Nathan says: From the tent, as it is said, "Place it in front of the veil [that is over the ark of the testimony, in front of the cover that is over the testimony], where I will meet [with you]" (Ex. 30:6). R. Simeon b. Azzai says: From the incense altar, as it is said, "Beat some of it into powder [and put some before the testimony in the tent of meeting, where I will meet with you]" (Ex. 30:36). The students[102] of R. Ishmael say: From beside the altar of burnt-offering, as it is said, "It shall be a regular burnt-offering throughout the generations [at the entrance of the tent of meeting before the Lord; for there I will meet with you, and there I will speak with you]" (Ex. 29:42).

Notes to the Translation

BARAITA ON THE CONSTRUCTION OF THE TABERNACLE

1. Jacob Milgrom, *The JPS Torah Commentary: Numbers* (Philadelphia/New York, 1990), 426-27, suggests "dedication" or "contribution" as a more accurate translation, describing the transfer of object from owner to deity.

2. E.g., Num. 18:8.

3. E.g., Num. 18:24.

4. Num. 15:19-20.

5. Cf. Num. 5:9; Sifre Num. ad loc., ed. Horovitz (Jerusalem, 1966), p. 8.

6. Num. 6:19-20.

7. Cf. Lev. 7:14, Rashi ad loc.

8. Ezek. 48:12.

9. Num. 31:41.

10. Ex. 30:13.

11. Ex. 25:2.

12. See M. Qid. 4:1 ff.

13. YTYDWT, referring here to the biblical YDWT ("tenons," e.g. Ex. 26:17) rather than YTDWT ("pegs," e.g. Ex. 27:19).

14. ḤMWQYM; cf. Cant. 7:2, where the usage suggests a rounded shape. Other MSS have ḤWWQYM ("rungs"); cf. b. Er. 77b, Rashi ad loc. who translates into Old French *echelon*.

15. See JPS notes at Ex. 26:24, 36:29; the meaning of the Hebrew is uncertain.

16. The following data concerning the correspondence of the length of the bars to the number of planks appear to conflict with the scriptural description at Ex. 26:26-27, which evidently prescribes five bars per enclosed side, one center bar spanning the length of each wall and four bars of half the length, one pair above the center bar and one pair below. The MSS differ from each other in this regard.

17. I.e., each of the four threads (blue, purple, crimson, linen) was twined eight-fold. See following note.

18. I.e., each of the four threads was twined six-fold. The translation of the foregoing discussion of the thread relies upon the interpretation of *Pene Moshe* (R. Moses b. Simeon Margoliot, 18th c., Lithuania), y. Sheq. 8:2 ad loc. Cf. a similar discussion with respect to the priestly garments, b. Yoma 71b-72a.

19. 10 x 4.

20. 11 x 4.

21. Viz., the west wall.

22. KLY, in the sense of a garment, e.g., Num. 31:20. Cf. KLY PŠTN, b. Ket. 59b; KLY LBNYM, b. Shab. 114a.

23. PSPYSYN, checks, stripes; i.e., a variegated, patchwork appearance.

24. M. Kel. 25:1 = TWBRWT. See *Perush ha-Geonim le-Seder Tohorot*, ed. Epstein (repr. Jerusalem, 1982), p. 67 and notes thereto; *Arukh Completum*, ed. Kohut v. 5 (Vienna, ²1926), p. 201, s.v. TBR. The present translation follows the explanation of *Perush ha-Geonim*. Cf. M. Er. 10:15; M. Suk. 5:3.

25. Cf. Ex. 16:33.

26. E.g., Ex. 40:9.

27. Num. 17:23.

28. BYT 'WLMYM, a less common expression for the Temple, e.g., b. Suk. 5b; b. Sot. 16a.

29. I.e., images on both sides of the fabric; so *Pene Moshe* (R. Moses b. Simeon Margoliot, 18th c., Lithuania), y. Sheq. 8:2 ad loc.

30. I.e., an image on one side of the fabric only; so *Pene Moshe*, ibid.

31. BYT, lit. "house," referring here to the outer compartment of the tabernacle.

32. BYT ("house"), here meaning the tabernacle as a whole.

33. YTYDWT, "pegs" as in the biblical description, e.g. Ex. 27:19; but cf. n. 13 above, where YTYDWT denotes the biblical YDWT (e.g. Ex. 26:17, "tenons").

34. KMH, lit. "how much."

35. Referring to the altar of burnt-offering, e.g. Ex. 30:28, as distinguished from the golden altar within the tabernacle.

36. KMH, lit. "how much."

37. In width, from north to south.

38. In length, from east to west.

39. Rather than "fifty by fifty," JPS = "fifty throughout." The present translation is substituted to clarify the explanation of R. Jose that follows. Cf. Rashi, Ex. 27:18.

40. Cf. M. Beẓ. 4:2.

41. Cf. M. Er. 2:5; 5:2-3. Two seahs' space = 70 cubits and a fraction by seventy cubits and a fraction = the approximate square root of 5,000 sq. cubits.

42. QBBLH, often translated "tradition," referring here to the post-Pentateuchal books of the Hebrew Bible; cf. b. BQ 2b, b. RH 7a, b. Ḥag. 10b.

43. Some MSS also cite 1 Sam. 6:8, "Take the ark of the Lord and place it on the cart, and put next to it in a chest the gold objects you are paying Him as indemnity." Both verses are brought to support the view that the scroll of the Law was not stored inside the ark; see b. BB 14a-b. Cf. Cant. R. (ca. 6th c.) 3:9: "Palanquin": this refers to the ark. What is a "palanquin"? A litter. It is as if a king had an only daughter, fair, gracious, and renowned, and he said to his servants...."Make for her a litter, for her beauty should be seen...." So the Holy One, blessed be He, said, "My Torah is fair, gracious and renowned....It is better that the beauty of My Torah should be seen outside of the ark."

44. There is some confusion in the MSS and parallels here; see Sifre Num., ed. Horovitz (Jerusalem, 1966), p. 78 n. 6. Note that the scriptural citations refer to the possible existence of two arks but not to their respective contents.

45. Referring here not to the tabernacle but to the holy of holies in Solomon's Temple.

46. The holy of holies in the Temple was 20 x 20 cubits (2 Chr. 3:8). The ark was placed at the center. If the ark's own dimensions are factored in, the division of the holy of holies area would leave less than ten cubits on either side; but according to b. Meg. 10b, "The ark took up no room."

47. Cf. M. Mid. 2:5.

48. Instead of "the people," 2 Chr. 35:3 = "all Israel."

49. AḤRWN, lit. "last" = the Herodian Temple.

50. Possibly "boards"; cf. 1 Ki. 6:16, M. Er. 2:1. According to an anonymous statement at M. Yoma 5:1, there were two curtains between the sanctuary and the holy of holies, separated by one cubit.

51. MQWM HṬṬRQSYN, more frequently 'MMH ṬRQSYN (e.g. M. Mid. 4:7). The word ṬRQSYN is apparently of Greek origin; its meaning was debated by the sages (e.g. y. Kil. 8:4, 31c). At b. Yoma 51b and b. BB 3a, 'MMH ṬRQSYN is understood not as a space but as a solid partition, to be differentiated from the two curtains that separated the sanctuary from the holy of holies in the Second Temple. Both of these passages state, in contradiction to BMM, that there was no 'MMH ṬRQSYN in the Second Temple.

52. The text of Abba Saul's statement is in evident disorder; see Introduction, p. 42.

53. YDWT ("arms"); cf. the usage of 1 Ki. 10:19, 2 Chr. 9:18, although elsewhere the meaning varies, e.g. "tenons" (Ex. 26:17); "stays" (1 Ki. 7:35); "axletrees" (1 Ki. 7:32). YDWT could also mean "handles"; cf. M. Yoma 3:1, M. Uq. 1:5.

54. According to Ex. 26:35, the table in the tabernacle was placed on the north, opposite the lampstand. Cf. y. Sheq. 6:3, 50a.

55. The text would seem to require the citation of 1 Ki. 7:48 rather than 2 Chr. 4:19; see Introduction, pp. 44-45 and notes thereto.

56. Two explanations may be adduced for this citation: 1) TY'ŚH ("shall be made") is written with a seemingly superfluous letter (cf., e.g., Ex. 35:2, T'ŚH); 2) the verb 'ŚH occurs twice (W'ŚYT, TY'ŚH) without apparent necessity. According to either explanation, Scripture refers to the lamps by the principle of amplification; see below.

57. Cf. Ex. 25:38.

58. The translations are approximate; both were apparently types of tongs. Neither term is attested in the various biblical descriptions of the tabernacle or Temple utensils. The Targums use the two words interchangeably to render the Bible's MLQḤYH (its "tongs"): ZBTH (its "pincers," Targum Onqelos); MLQṬYYH (its "forceps," Targum Jonathan), Ex. 25:38, 37:23, Num. 4:9. The present translation renders the latter term "forceps" because in rabbinic usage it was apparently a smaller instrument, e.g., M. Kel. 13:8, T. Kel. BM 3:14.

59. Cf. Ex. 25:39.

60. R. Joshua b. Qorḥa apparently deduces the exclusion of the lamps from the singular verb Y'ŚH, "It shall be made," in the protasis of the verse. A contrary deduction is found at b. Men. 88b. See following note.

61. B. Men. 88b cites Ex. 25:39, which would seem to connect more readily with the preceding statement of R. Joshua b. Qorḥa. BMM ed. Friedmann (Vienna, 1908), e.g., emends accordingly. However, the MSS of BMM unanimously attest the *lectio difficilior* KL KLYH (Ex. 37:24) rather than KL HKKLYM (Ex. 25:39).

62. At Ex. 25:31, YRKH ("base") denotes the separate base below the center shaft; QNH ("shaft") denotes the center shaft and (at Ex. 25:32 ff.) the branches. In BMM, YRKH refers to the base and center shaft combined.

63. I.e., the weight must be exactly one talent; cf. y. Sheq. 6:3, 50b; b. Men. 29a.

64. Cf. b. Men. 29a, where Num. 8:4 is interpreted to require a petal at the foot of the center shaft in addition to the petals specified at Ex. 25:31-34.

65. According to Rashi, b. Men. 28b, these were long and narrow. He translates to Old French *madernes*; cf. his comment at b. Ket. 65a, s.v. ŠWPRZY. Maimonides has the opposite view (Mishneh Torah, *Bet ha-Beḥirah* 3:9), describing an Alexandrian goblet as a short vessel with a wide mouth.

66. Reading HBBYRWTYYM as "cypresses" (e.g. Cant. 1:17; Gen. R. 15, ed. Theodor/Albeck [repr. Jerusalem, 1965] p. 136) and TPPWḤY (usually "apples") as "cones," referring to the shape (e.g. M. Tamid 2:2). The

cone of the cypress is globe-shaped and ends in a curved point. But the translation is uncertain and the meaning obscure. B. Men. 28b has HKKRTYYM ("Cretan"?), but the majority of MSS of BMM corroborate HBBYRWTYYM, and elsewhere the same Bavli tractate has HBBRTYM (b. Men. 63a; see also *Diqduqe Soferim*, ed. Rabbinovicz [repr. New York, 1976], b. Men. 28b). *Arukh Completum*, ed. Kohut v. 5 (Vienna, ²1926), p. 256 s.v. TPPWH, explains that the shape was greater in breadth than thickness, or (on the basis of b. Men. 63a) almost completely round. Maimonides (Mishneh ‚Torah, *Bet ha-Behirah* 3:9) understands the term to describe an oval shape similar to an egg.

67. Referring to the decorative design of capitals common in Greek architecture.

68. QWŠY WŠBH, with slight variations among the MSS. The meaning is uncertain; the present translation is based on Sifre Num. *be-Ha'alotkha* 61, ed. Horovitz (Jerusalem, 1966), p. 59, where Num. 8:4 is interpreted to confer praise (ŠBHW) on Moses for his precise execution of the prescribed lampstand design. Cf. b. Men. 29a, where this task is described as one of three supreme difficulties (QŠYN) presented to Moses.

69. According to Ex. 26:35, the lampstand in the tabernacle was placed by the south wall, opposite the table; cf. y. Sheq. 6:3, 50a.

70. Here the priority of the Mosaic lampstand is proven by the use of the singular "lampstand," the ten Solomonic lampstands (2 Chr. 4:7) notwithstanding. Cf. BMM 8:15-20, and see our Introduction, pp. 44-45.

71. Several MSS have "Moses" instead of "Solomon."

72. See Rashi, b. Men. 98b, who understands this to refer to the angle of the wick.

73. Cf. M. Mid. 3:1, T. Zev. 6:2.

74. BRQYM; meaning uncertain. Several MSS have KRKB ("ledge," Ex. 27:5), a term that is also obscure. At b. Zev. 62a, one opinion defines KRKB as a synonym for KYWR, the laver; another equates it with SWBB, the "surround," mentioned here (BMM 11:14) as a separate feature and at M. Mid. 3:1 in connection with the Herodian Temple. In its biblical usage, KRKB apparently refers to a kind of projecting rim; cf. Jacob Milgrom, "Altar," *EJ* 2:762.

However, the MSS adjudged by the present edition to be superior (including the most valuable witness, MS G¹) attest the reading BRQYM rather than KRKB. Given the paleographic similarity of K and B and the occasional interchange of K and Q attested elsewhere in MSS of BMM (e.g. at 8:5), a scribal error may explain the discrepancy. But aside from the principle of *lectio difficilior*, this explanation must be doubted. Nowhere else in the meticulous transcription of MS G¹ is there so flagrant a scribal mistake (see Introduction, p. 101); moreover, the presence of KRKB in the Scriptural account of the altar (Ex. 27:5) could hardly have been missed or mistaken.

While BRQYM does not appear in biblical descriptions of the tabernacle or the Temple, the word BRQ' occurs in the Babylonian Talmud in the context of architectural description. Evidently its meaning was variable. At b. Er. 15a, it seems to describe a kind of enclosed porch; Rashi ad loc. gives the synonym YZY' which he translates into Old French *apendiz*. At b. BB 61a, printed editions have BDQ' rather than BRQ', but MSS support the latter reading (see *Diqduqe Soferim*, ed. Rabbinovicz [repr. New York, 1976] ad loc., p. 38). Here too the meaning is unclear: it is offered with modifiers as a synonym for YZY' ("extension"), 'PT' ("balcony"?; cf. b. Ḥul. 92a); ZL' ("side-chamber," Ezek. 41:6); and T' ("cell," e.g. M. Mid. 4:7). *Arukh Completum*, ed. Kohut v. 1 (Vienna, ²1926), p. 200 s.v. BRQ', reports other possibilities, including an upper story, a portico, a scaffold, etc.

The present translation of BRQYM, "ledges," is a conjecture based in part on the talmudic attestations of BRQ' and in part on the biblical and rabbinic altar descriptions; cf. b. Zev. 62a, which mentions the existence of two KRKB, one for function and one for ornament. However, these descriptions are poorly understood. Possibly the Aramaic BRQ' is attested in BMM in its original Hebrew form as either a substitute for, or a refinement of, the scriptural KRKB.

75. See preceding note.

76. According to M. Mid. 4:6, the scarecrow was located on the roof of the Temple; cf. b. Shab. 90a, b. MQ 9a, b. Men. 107a, b. Ar. 6a, none of which describe it except to assume that it was made of iron. Josephus (*War* V, 5, 6, 224) mentions protruding golden spikes whose purpose was to prevent birds from settling upon or fouling the Temple roof. In Eupolemus' account of Solomon's Temple, a more elaborate and almost certainly fanciful scarecrow is described: a latticed network of bronze bells that cast a shadow over the entire sanctuary; see the discussion of Ben Zion Wacholder, *Eupolemus: A Study of Judaeo-Greek Literature* (Cincinnati, 1974), 196-200. BMM is the only source that describes a scarecrow on the altar; cf. Saul Lieberman, *Hellenism in Jewish Palestine* (New York, 1950), 173-77, who suggests (at 176) that scarecrows "were probably planted not only on the roof of the Temple but also near the altar...."

77. Cf. M. Zev. 2:1.

78. See M. Tamid 3:5.

79. Cf. BMM 8:15-20, 10:25-30.

80. JPS = "tank of cast metal."

81. Cf. T. Kel. BM 5:2.

82. "Homer" and "kor" are synonyms; see JPS ad loc., translator's note.

83. Viz., 2,000 baths (1 Ki. 7:26) divided by 10 = 200 kors.

84. One kor = 30 seahs; one mikvah = 40 seahs; thus 200 kors = 150 mikvahs (200 x 30 = 150 x 40). By first deducting 50 kors, the remaining

150 may be considered equivalent to 150 mikvahs. For this interpretation we rely on a note in BMM ed. Kanivsky (Bene Berak, 1961), Hebrew pagination 70.

85. According to 1 Ki. 7:23, the molten sea had a circumference of 30 cubits, a diameter of 10 cubits, and a depth of 5 cubits. If it was round, viz., a cylinder of 10 cubits in diameter and 5 cubits in height, its capacity would be $3 \times (\frac{10}{2})^2 \times 5 = 375$ cubits^3; 1 cubit^3 = 1 mikvah (b. Er. 14b), therefore 375 cubits^3 = 125 mikvahs rather than 150.

86. See preceding note. Assuming a square tank 10 x 10 x 5 cubits = 500 cubits^3 = 167 mikvahs rather than 150.

87. Cf. b. Zev. 62b.

88. This phrase usually ties the citation to what precedes it, but it does not appear to do so here. However, it is unanimously attested in the MSS. Possibly the citation is meant to include the following verse, 2 Chr. 4:4, which repeats 1 Ki. 7:25.

89. The meaning is uncertain. BMM ed. Friedmann (Vienna, 1908), pp. 79-80, attempts to explain such a configuration.

90. See M. Sheq. 5:3.

91. See M. Yoma 2:1-4.

92. Printed eds. of Mishnah have "Nehuniah" rather than Nehemiah.

93. MḤNH ŠKYNH, i.e., the tabernacle.

94. See Jacob Milgrom, *The JPS Torah Commentary: Numbers* (Philadelphia/New York, 1990), 372-73. The functions of trumpet and shofar overlap in biblical literature. A baraita explains that the trumpets were used only until the death of Moses (Sifre Num. 75 end; b. Men. 28b). From other (later?) rabbinic sources (e.g. b. Shab. 36a, b. Sot. 43a), it appears that the distinction between shofar and trumpet was no longer known.

95. Cf. M. Suk. 4:5, 5:4 ; M. RH 4:9, all with respect to the shofar.

96. The Hebrew spelling is plural, but the pronominal suffix of the preposition that follows ("with it") is singular; cf. Num. 4:5.

97. According to the scriptural sequence (Num. 10:17-18), the Gershonites and Merarites preceded rather than followed the division of Reuben.

98. According to the scriptural sequence (Num. 10:21-22), the Kohathites preceded rather than followed the division of Ephraim.

99. As noted in BMM ed. Friedmann (Vienna, 1908), p. 84, one would expect the reverse: to cover from the outside and fill from the inside. However, the MSS are virtually unanimous against this logic.

100. Both words, QWZYM (e.g. Is. 33:12) and SYRYM (e.g. Is. 34:13), are usually translated as "thorns"; the synonyms here seek to convey the effect of the Hebrew.

101. Cf. Ps. 107:7.

102. Or "student"; see apparatus at BMM 14:18.

Appendix A

Genizah Transcriptions

Except for MS Dropsie 83, already published by Louis Ginzberg, *Ginze Schechter* (repr. New York, 1969), 1:374-83, all known fragments of Baraita de-Melekhet ha-Mishkan (BMM) from the Cairo Genizah are transcribed in full in Appendix A.

Transcriptions are ordered in the sequence of the Sigla Table, pp. 149-50: 1) MS G^1 = T-S A45.24, K21.20, F11.32; 2) MS G^2 (except Dropsie 83) = Adler 2940, T-S K21.82. The lineation of each fragment is numbered at the right margin. [Bracketed] spaces indicate lacunae owing to physical damage. Unbracketed line space seeks to replicate the scribe's original spacing.

MSS G^1 and G^2 are described in chapter 5 of the Introduction, pp. 100-102. The citation of MSS G^1 and G^2 variants within the critical apparatus is described on pp. 145-46. The two sets of fragments are compared on p. 137. The portions of BMM attested are listed by chapter and line on p. 96.

Critical Symbols

[ ] lacunae owing to physical damage
˙ doubtful transcription

T-S A45.24 6(1) recto

1	
2	
3	
4	
5	
6	[אומר עשר תרומות הן ת] [
7	[וביכור] [רומת נזיר] [
8	[ותרומת שֹ] [
9	[עֹשר וחֹל] [

T-S A45.24 6(2) recto

1	[וֹמֹת] [
2	[לֹוים וֹל] [ולמקדֹש] [
3	[לעזר הכהן תרומת שקלי] [
4	[נעשה ממנו משכן ושמֹן] [
5	[גדי כהנים ובגדי כהן גדול] [
6	שֹימֹוש המֹשכֹן] [
7	[שכן ארכו שלשים אמה ורחבו עשר] [
8	[אמות ר' יוסי אומ' אורכו ל"א אמות] [
9	[ה מעמיד הקרשים היה נותן עשרים קר] [
10	וֹעשרים קרש בדרום ושמֹ] [ה במערב במ] [
11	קרש אלא ד' עמֹ] [
12	[קרשים וג'] [

T-S A45.24 6(1) verso

[	[שאין תלמוד לֹ] [ ] אל]	1
[	ד֞ לומר אל הטבעת מֹקוֹם]	2
[	מיה או' הקרשים עובײן מלֹמֹ]	3
[	הולכין עד באצבע שנ' ויחדו יֹה]	4
[	תֹמו נכרתו ר' יהודה או' מלמטן]	5
[	שֹנ' ויחדו יהיו תמים כאיצֹ]	6
[	ים היה נותן] [ ] עֹים אד]	7
[	י"ח במערב]	8
[	[וכל]	9
[	מֹל]	10

T-S A45.24 6(2) verso

[	יֹן אורכן] [ ] אחד [ ]	1
[	קרשים והאמצֹעי ארכו ש]	2
[	שֹים שמשוקע באמֹצען למֹ [	3
[	תיכון כשם שהיה עושה לקרשֹים	4
[	עֹושה לקרשים שבדרום אבל מער]	5
[	שלכל אחד ח' אמות כנגד ששה קר]	6
[	יחים והאדנים והעמודים ומקום עובײן	7
[	צופה זהב שנ' ואת הקרשים צפ' זה' ש]	8
[	לבריחים ומה תל' לו' בתים לבריחים מקום	9
[	יֹצֹף את] [ ] יחים זהב כיצד היה	10
[	אמה וחצי] [ ]	11
[	שנותנין] [ ]	12

T-S A45.24 7 recto

1	רחבה שלקלע שנ' וק]
2	אף רווחב ה' אמות כאיצ]
3	היה נותן עשרים אדנים של]
4	בֹדֹרום ועמוד בתוך כל אחד ו]
5	] מֹצע היה נותן את הקונטסין]
6	] וקונטסין ארכו שלכל אחד ואחד]
7	ותולה את הטבעת בתוך האונקלי]
8	ספינה נמצאת הקלע יוצא מן העמוד]
9	מצד זה וב' אמות ומחצה מצד זֹה]
10	למדתה שבין עמוד לעמוד ה' אמֹו]
11	במיתרין ובעמודין ומחברן בתוך י]
12	שהיו יתדות למשכן כך היו יתדוֹ]
13	המשכן וג' אבל אין אתה יודעֹ]
14	פתחו שלחצר שנ' את קלעי הח]
15	] מֹזֹבח י' אמות כך מן הקלעים וֹעֹ]
16	] ות אבל אין אתֹה יודע כמה פ]
17	] החצר מעשֹה] קֹם וקֹומה]
18	] ת ומה תל' לו' ה]
19	] חבו ה' אמוֹת]
20	צפון וג' ו]
21	ולמזרח]

T-S A45.24 7 verso

1 [שבמזרח נ' אמה הא למדתָ]

2 [ך החצר מאה באמה ר' יוסי או']

3 [חמשים אלא ללמד שאורכה]

4 [תֹחו שלאהל כך פתחו שלאולֹם]

5 [ ] פתחו שלהיכל מיכן היה ר' יוסי [ ]

6 [שהוא כבית סאתים כחצר משכן]

7 [שָׁבָּת סליק פירקא]

8 [במדבר ארכו שנים אמות ומחצה ורחבו]

9 [אמה ומחצה שנ' ועשית ארון וג' ר' מאיר]

10 [טפחים הרי ה"י טפחים צא מהן ה"י]

11 [ת וטפח מיכן וטפח מיכן מקום הנחת]

12 [וחצי טפח מיכן לעביו שלארון]

13 [ים שלימין ושנים שבורים והלוחות]

14 [ששה טפחים ורחבו ששה ועביו]

15 [ט' טפחים צא מהם ו' טפחין לארכֹן]

16 [ ] ת ספר תורה שני טפחים וחצי [

17 [ ] לעביו שלארֹ [ ] יהודה או' באמֹ [ ]

18 [ ] פֹחים וֹמחצֹ [ ] וֹארבעה לוחות ה [ ]

19 [ ] תֹ ארכו שלכל אחֹ [ ]

20 [טפח לרחבן]

21 [לארון ורחבו]

22 [לארכֹן של]

T-S A45.24 8 recto

1	[	[ור צא מהן נֿ]
2	[	[מקוות שכל מקוה]
3	[	[חֿזיק ק"ג מקוות אם תאמר]
4	[	תאמר כלו מרובע מחזיק יותר וֿ]
5	[	שנ' ועביו טפח וג' למדנו שעגול מ]
6	[	מֿרובע מלמטה שנ' עומד על שני עש]
7	[	[ ] נים פונים ד' פעמים אלא נכנס להֿי]
8	[	פונה לימין להר הבית פונה לימין עו]
9	[	פונה לימין שנ' ודמות בקרים תחת לו]
10	[	שורות שלראשי שוורים של ד' ד' במֿ]
11	[	מרגליו שלשור תנו רבנן אי]
12	[	במקדש יוחנן בן פינחס על החותמו]
13	[	מתייה בן שמואל על הפייסות]
14	[	נקרא שמו פתחיה שפותח בד]
15	[	לשון בן אחייה על חולי מעיים]
16	[	[ ] וז בן גבר על נעילת [ ] עֿרים]
17	[	[ ] גורמו על מעשה לחם הפנים]
18	[	[ ] ת אלעזר על הפרכות פינחס]
19	[	[ ] זֿ משבעה אמרכולין ומשלשה]
20	[	[ ] רה על הציבור בממון בפחות מש]
21	[	סליק פרקא כי]
22	[	[ ] מקד [ ] קהֿת היו משמרין בדֿ]
23	[	הֿם הי [ ]]

T-S A45.24 8 verso

[ ] [נשיא] [שנ' ו	1
[ ] [י] [וה] [ם ועל הקרשים	2
[ ] וחוצה להם ג' שבטים דן אשר	3
[ ] משה ואהרן ובניו שנ' והחנים לפני המש'	4
[ ] יהודה יששכר וזבולן מחנה	5
[ ] ם על י"ב מילים דגלו שליהודה ד'	6
[ ] מחנה שכינה ד' מילים דגלו שלראובן	7
[ ] דרום י"ב מילים דגלו שלאפרים ד' מילים	8
[ ] ל שכינה ד' מילים דגלו שלדן ד'	9
[ ] ע זויות שלמשכן ד' מחנות שמשמשין	10
[ ] על ידו כיון שהיו ישראל נוסעין היה	11
[ ] ל וממושך על גבי בני יהודה כקורה	12
[ ] ע' דגל יהודה תחילה שנ' ונסע דגל	13
[ ] [הרן ובניו ופירקו את הפרכות וכ	14
[ ] [ותק] תקעו והריעו [ ] [ן ובני	15
[ ] [דגל מחנה ראובן מיד נ'כ] [ן ון] [נ'	16
[ ] ירקו את המשכן וטענו אותו	17
[ ] [ ] בני קהת שנ' ונסעו הקהתי	18
[ ] [ ] סע דגל אפרים שנ' ונסע דגל מחנ	19
[ ] [ ] ופירקו את הקודש וטענו אתו בכ	20
[ ] תקעו והריעו ותקעו ונ'סע דגל	21
[ ] [ ] ניהם [ ] בני דן נ'מצאו שנ'י דגל	22
[ ] שנ'	23

T-S A45.24 9 recto

1	[ ]	[להם]
2	[ ]	[קן את בהמתם ואת]
3	[ ]	[תקיעה ותרועה ותקיעה ע]
4	[ ]	על כל מטה ומטה סליק]
5	[ ]	כיון שהיו ישראל חונין היה עמוד הענן]
6	[ ]	על גבי בני יהודה כמין סוכה ונוקמן ו]
7	[ ]	מבפנים וממלא את המשכן מבחוץ ש]
8	[ ]	אחד מענני כבוד ששימשו לישראל ב]
9	[ ]	שנה אחד מימין ואחד משמאל ואחד]
10	[ ]	מאחריהם ואחד למעלה מהן וענן]
11	[ ]	אחד נוסע לפניהם משפיל לפניהם אֹ]
12	[ ]	לפניהם את השפל והורג נחשים ועק]
13	[ ]	וסירים ומדריכם בדרך ישרה וענֹ]
14	[ ]	באהל ר' שמעון בן יוחי או' כל אֹ]
15	[ ]	[דבר לא נצרך אחד מהם לא לאֹ]
16	[ ]	[ר הלבנה בלילה אלא האדים]
17	[ ]	[ה הלבין היו יודעין שזרחה ה]
18	[ ]	[מה שבתוכה בטפיֹח ויודיע מ]
19	[ ]	[שכינה שביניהם שנ' לעיני כלֹ]
20	[ ]	[אורי כי בא אורך ואו' לא יהיה לך]
21	[ ]	[אֹ עוד שמשך וירחך וג' ואו]
22	[ ]	[ולם וג' מהיכן היתה שכינהֹ]
23	[ ]	[ן אומ' מן האהל שנ' ו]

T-S K21.20 *recto*

[	[יו מ] [מנשה וארב]	] 1
[	] ב' בצפונו וב' בדרומו שנ' ו]	] 2
[	] תֿת את הטבעות על ארבע הֿפֿ]	] 3
[	] ת למטה מרגל לרגל ומסגרת שֿ]	] 4
[	] הֿפנים שנ' ועשית לוֹ מסגרת]	] 5
[	] ה י' שלחנות כולם היו כשרין]	] 6
[	] משתמשין בהן אלא בשל משה שנ']	] 7
[	] וֹינח בהיכל חמ' מימין וה' משמאל]	] 8
[	] צֿפון וה' הן הדרום והלא שלחן]	] 9
[	] תלמ' לומ' ה' מימין וה' משמאל אלא]	] 10
[	] וה' משמאל שלחן משה שנ' וא]	] 11
[	] לחם הפנים סליק פיֿרֿ]	] 12
[	] נורה שעשה משה במדבר הי]	] 13
[	] שה וטעונה גביעים כפתורים]	] 14
[	] רת זהב טהור וג' שומע אני]	] 15
[	] קֿם לה] [לֿ' לֿוֹ' מֿ]	] 16

T-S K21.20 verso

[	[שהיא באה מ] [בא]	1
[	[אינה באה ככר ר' יהושע]	2
[	[כֹר ואין נירותה מככר שנ' כך]	3
[	[נֹי מקיים כל כליה זהב טהור אב]	4
[	[שה במדבר לא היו באות אלא]	5
[	[שתי חצוצרות כסף	6
[	[הַמְּנוֹרֹה]	7
[	[את המנורה עשאה כמין קורה ועשאה]	8
[	[כפתוריה ופרח ומשך הימנה שני קנים]	9
[	[ילך ומשך הימנה שני קנים אחרים]	10
[	[מנה שני קנים אחרים אילך ואילך]	11
[	[ם מצדיה אבל לא למדנו לגביעים]	12
[	[רה ארבעה גביעים איסי בן יהודה]	13
[	[הכרעה ואילו הן שאת ארור מחֹר]	14
[	[לא אם תטיב שאת או שאת אֹם]	15
[	[כי עז או כי באפם הרגו אֹיש וברצֹוֹ]	16
[	[ ] [נצב] [הלחם]	17
[	[ ] [מש]	18

T-S F11.32 recto

1	[שנ' שלשה גבי] [ ]
2	[כפתרים י'א' ופרחים ט] [ ]
3	כוסות אלכסנדרים כפתורים]
4	הֹברותים פרחין למה הן דומין]
5	[שיש במנורה קושי ושבח כנג] [ ]
6	שהראה ה'ק'ב'ה' כלים עשוין ומנורה]
7	וֹעשה כתבניתם וג' אף על פי שעש]
8	כולם היו כשירות לעבודה ולא היו מ]
9	משה שנ' ויעש את המנורת עשר וג']
10	הצפון וה' מן הדרום והלא מנורה מן הֹ]
11	לוֹ' ה' מן השמאל וה' מימין ה' מימין]
12	שנ' מנורות זהב ונרותיהם וג' והיא]
13	זהבו שלמשה כיצד מדשנ]
14	ומניחן באהל ומקניח בספוג נ]
15	בנר אחד דברי רבי וחכמ' אומ' ל]
16	אלא על גבי המנורה מדשנן שנ' עֹל]
17	ומזרחיים היו דולקין כנגד נר האמצ]
18	האמצעי משובח שנ' אל מול פני המ]
19	שווה ונרותיהם] [וֹֹת והֹן]
20	]
21	[ח הקֹטרת ארכו] [ ]

T-S F11.32 *verso*

[ ] מׄור כאן גבהו כ [ ]	[ ]	1
[ ] אׄ גבוה מן הקלעים אמ [ ]	[ ]	2
[ ] משכן ועל המזבח מה משכן	[ ]	3
[ ] אמות חוט שלסיקרא חוגרן	[ ]	4
[ ] דמים העליונים לדמים התחתונים	[ ]	5
[ ] מות אמה יסוד ושלש אמות ברקים	[ ]	6
[ ]וׄ נותנין דמים הניתנין למטן ומחוט	[ ]	7
[ ] אמות אמה קרנות וג' אמות ברקים	[ ]	8
[ ] ושם היו נותנין דמים התנין למעלה	[ ]	9
[ ] הׄסקרא ולמטן שנתן מחוט הסקרא	[ ]	10
[ ]נין מחוט הסקרא ולמעלן פסולין	[ ]	11
[ ]אׄ וׄלמעלן פסולין והנתנין מחוט הסקרא	[ ]	12
[ ]לין מזבח שעשה משה	[ ]	13
[ ]ות ושעשה שלמה גבהו י' אמות	[ ]	14
[ ]י' אמות ולעתיד לבא גבהו י' אמׄוׄת	[ ]	15
[ ] אמצע עזרה כבש לדרומו כיור למעׄ [ ]	[ ]	16
[ ]וׄ וכל ישראל למזרחו שנ' ויקרבו כל	[ ]	17
[ ] קרא המזבח מזבח העולה מזבח הנחשת	[ ]	18
[ ] סׄלׄיׄק כׄיׄוׄרׄ [ ]	[ ]	19
[ ] [ ] כיורות שנ' [ ]	[ ][ ]	20
[ ] יׄן וׄחׄמש משמאל [ ]	[ ][ ]	21

Adler 2940.1

[חלה [ ] 1

ובכורים ותרומת [ ] זיר וֹתְרֹוֹ [ ] תודה ותרומת הארץ 2

ותרומת מדין ותרומת שקלים ותרומת משכן 3

תֹ [ ] מה ותרומת מעשר חלה ובכורים ותרומת נֹזיר 4

ותרומת תודה לכהנים תרומת הארץ לכהנים וללוים 5

ולנתנינים למקדש ולירושלם תרומת מדין לאלעזר הכהן 6

תרומת שקלים לאדנים תרומת המשכן שממנה היו עושין 7

גופו שלמשכן ושמן המשחה וקטורת הסמים ובגדי 8

כהניֹם ובגדי כהן גדול   משכן ארכו שלשים אמֹה 9

ורח [ ] עשר אמות וגבהו עשר אמות ר' יוסי אומ' ארכו 10

של [ ] ת אמה   כיצד הֹ [ ] מעמיד את הקרשים 11

[ ] תֹן עשרים קרשים בצפון ועשרים קרשים בדרום 12

[ ] במֹערב אבל במזרח לא היה שם קרש אלא 13

[ ] עֹהֹ עֹ [ ] דֹי שטים שעליהם נותנין את הפרוכת שנ' ונתתה 14

[ ] ל ארבֹ [ ] מצפים זהֹב   היה עושה 15

[ ] נים חלולין וחֹ [ ] קֹרֹשֹ [ ] למטה רביע מיכאן ורביע 16

[ ] כֹאן וחֹורץ חציו באמֹ [ ] לֹוֹ [ ] תי יתידות כמין שני 17

וֹקין ומכנֹיֹסֹן לתוך שני אדנֹים [ ] שני אדנים תחת הקרש 18

[ ] ד לשתי ידוותיו   הסנין [ ] צֹאין מֹן הקרשים 19

[ ] ֹם לכל אחד ואחד שמשקיע את [ ] כֹֹר [ ] וד הנקבה 20

[ ] אֹל אחותה דֹברי ר'נחמיה שר' נחמֹ [ ] 21

[ ] משולבות מה ת״ל משולבות מלמד [ ] 22

[ ] בֹין [ ] סולם המצרי   היה חורץ את [ ] 23

[ ] מעלה אצבע מיכאן ואצבע מיכאן ונותנן בת [ ] 24

[ ] ת שלזֹהֹב כדי שלא יהו נפרדין זה מזה שנאמֹ [ ] 25

Adler 2940.2

1   אומרים מאצל מזבח העולה שנ׳ עולת תמיד לדורותי]

2   פתח אהל מועד לפני יי׳ אשר אועד לכם שם לדבר אליך ש]

3   מזבח היה מכוון כנגד חצי פתח שלהיכל וכן]

4   אחת מן הדלתות משוך]   [לפי דרום ור׳ יהודה אומ׳ מזבח]

5   ממוצע באמצע עזרה שהיה ושלשים]   [

6   אמות כנגד פתח שלהיכל אחת עשרה]   [

7   עשרה אמה מן הדרום נמצא מזבח מכוון כנגד היכל וכתליו

8   איזה הוא צפון מקירו שלמזבח צפוני עד כותל עזרה

9   כנגד מזבח דברי ר׳ יוסי בר׳ יהודה ר׳ אלעזר בר׳ שמעון מוסיף

10   מכנגד בין האולם ולמזבח עזרה צפוני ור׳ מוסיף מכנגד מקום

11   דריסת רגלי ישראל ומקום דריסת רגלי כהנים עד כותל עזרה

12   צפוני אבל מכנגד]   [ת החלפות ולפנים הכל מודים שהוא פסול

13   היה ר׳ נחמיה אומ׳ אהל מועד שעשה משה במדבר

14   כנגד כל מעשה בראשית שבעולם שלחן כנגד כל התבו]

15   שבעולם מזבח העולה כנגד כל הבהמות שבעולם]

16   הקטורת כנגד כל הבשמים שבעולם ומנורה כנגד]

17   [לבנה שיש ברקיע ושבעה נרות כנגד שבעה שמש]

18   שמשמשין] [ה ש] [ת] [שׁבהן העולם מ] [

19   ואלו הן חמה ולבנה כוכב נוגה שׁבתי וצדק ומאדים

20   סליק פירקא

21   וסליק מעשה המשכן

22   פירקי] [

23   ברוך העוֹזֵר

T-S K21.82 recto

[ ] [	עשר אמוׄ] [ ] מ	1
[ ] [שהׄן יורדות ומכסות את העמודים ואת	2
[ ] אׄדנים עד שׄ [ ] גיעות לארץ אמה מיכאן ואׄמׄה מיכאן	3
[ ] והאמה מזה והאמה מזה בעודף היה מביא	4
[ ] אחד גדול שלעור ארכו שלשים אמה ורחבו עשר אמות	5
שמלבישו לאהל מן [ ] [ ] מזרח למערב שנ' ועשית מכסה לאהל וג'	6
וכמין פסיפסין עשוי מלמעלה דברי ר' נחמיה ר' יהודה אומ'	7
שני מכסאות היו תחתון שלעורות אלים מאדמים שנאמ'	8
מכסה עורות אלים מאדמים ועליון שלעורות תחשים שנ'	9
מכסהו ומכסה התחש אשר עליו מׄל [ ] עׄלה	10
סליק פרקא	11
היה אורג את הפרוכת עשר אמות על עשר אמות ועושה	12
בה ארבעה תובירין ותולה אותה באנקלאות שעל גבי העמ [ ] דים	13
מכוונת היתה תחת הקרסים שנ' ונתתה את הפרכת תחת	14
הקרסים וגו' שם היה ארון נתון וצנצנת שלמן	15
וצלוחית שלשמן המשחה ומקלו שלאהרן ושקדיה ופרחיה	16
ובגדי כהנים ובגדי כהן גדול ושם היה אהרן נכנס ארבׄעה	17
פעמים בׄיום פעם אחת בשנה ביום הכפורים	18
מחוץ לפרכת הי [ ] שלחן ומנורה מונחין אׄלא שהשׄלׄחׄן בצפון	19

T-S K21.82 *verso*

1   [סך כך היה אוֹ]   [   ]

2   שהפרוכת מֹעֹשֹהֹ חשב שנ' ועשית [   ] ר [   ] ת [   ]

3   מעשה רקֹם שֹנ' ועשית מסך לפתח האהל [   ]

4   שר' נחמיה אוֹ [   ] כֹל מקום שנאמ' מעשה חשב שנֹי פרצֹ

5   מעשה רקם אין בו אלא פרצוף אחד בלבד   ו [   ]

6   מנרה היו מכווֹנין מונחין כנגד רחבו של שלחן מזבח הזהב

7   היה נֹתון באמצֹע הבית וחילק את הבֹית ומחציו ולפֹנים היה

8   מכֹוֹוֹן כנגד הפרכת שנ' ונתת אתֹו לפני הפרכת אשר עֹל ארֹון

9   העֹדֹות כמן הקרשים שבדֹרום [   ] ד קני מנורה שתֹי אמות

10   [   ] עֹד הֹשלחן חמש אמות מן השלחן

11   ועד הקרשים שבצפון שתי אמות ומחצֹה הא למדֹת שֹרֹחבו

12   עשר אמות מן הקרשים שבמערב עד קני מנורה עשר

13   אֹמות מקני מנורה ועד השלחן חמש אמות מן השלחן

14   עד מזבח הזהב חמש אמות ממזבח הזהב עד פתחו שלאהל

15   עשר אמות הא למדת שארכן שלשים אמה

16   סליק פירקא

17   חצר ארכה מאה אמה ורחבה חמשים אמה שנ' ועשית את

18   חצר המשכן לפאת נגב תימנה אבל אי אתה יודע כֹמה רחבו

19   שלקלע שנֹ' וקומה ברוחב חמש אמות כמה קומה חמש

Appendix A

Plates

*Reproductions courtesy of the Cambridge University Library,
the Library of the Jewish Theological Seminary of America,
and the Annenberg Research Institute Library.*

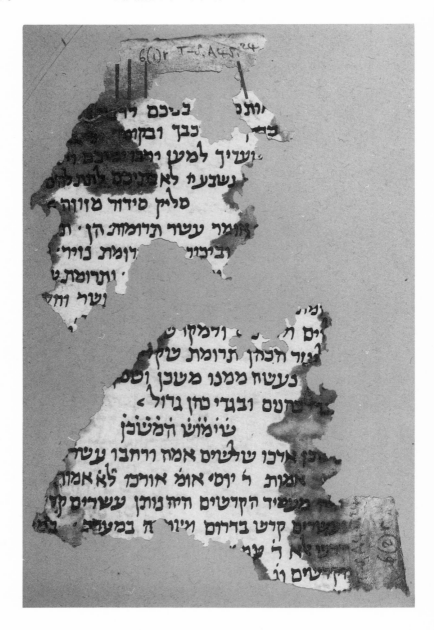

Cambridge University Library
T-S A45.24 6(1) recto
T-S A45.24 6(2) recto

רחבה ג' ל'קלע שנו...
אף רוחב ה' אמות ׳   כא'...
היה נותן עשרים אדנים ש...
...דרום ועמוד בתוך כל אחד...
...צע היה נותן את הקונטסין
...קונטוסין ארכו שלכל אחד ואח...
ותלה את הטבעת בתוך האונק...
ספינה נ'יאת הקלע יוצא מן השש...
...מ'נד זה וב אמות ומחצה מצד ...
...למ'דתה שבין עמוד לעמוד ה' אמ...
במ'תד'ן ובע'מוד'ן ומחבר'ן בתוך ...
...טוחין יתדות למשכן כך הין יתד...
...ה משכן ו...   אבל א'ן אתה יוד...
...פתחו שלחצר של את קלע' הח...
...מ'דח ג' אמות כך מן הקלע'ם ו...
...ות ׳   אבל א'ן צר'ד יודע כמה פ...
...החצר מעש... ׳   ...ם ור'מר...
...ג ומה תל לו ה...
...חבו ה' אמר...
...פ'ן וג' נ...
...נל מורה

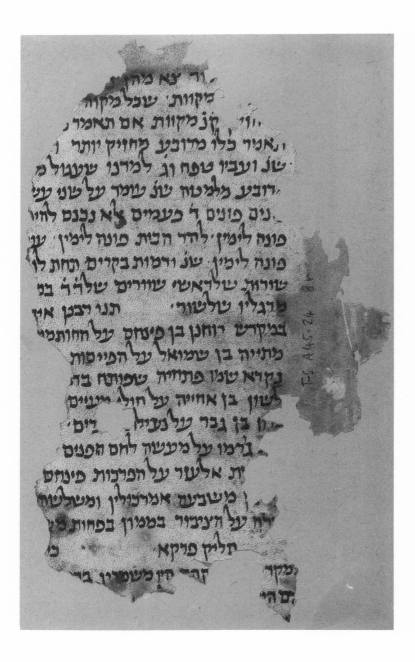

..ור צא מחן ..
מקוות שעל מקוה
יוסי.. קנ מקוות אם תאמר ..
ואמיר כלו מדובע קחזיק יותר ו..
שג ועבין טפח וג למדנו שעגול מ..
..דובע מלמטה שג עומד על טנו עי..
..נים פונים ד פעמים לא נכנס להיו
פונה לימין להד הבית פונה לימין עו..
פונה לימין שג ורמות בקרים תחת לו..
שורות שלדאש שוורים שלד'ד' בנ..
פדגלין שלשור תנו רבנן אין
במיקדש יוחנן בן פיצחק על מחותמ..
מתיה בן שמואל על הפייסות
נקרא שמו פתחיה שפותח בה
..שון בן אחייה על חולי מייניים
..ון בן גבר על נעיל ביים
בירמו על מעשה לחם הפנס
..ת אלעזר על הפרכות פינחם
..ן משבעה אמרכולין ומשלשה..
..יח על העצבור בממון בפחות מ..
תליק פורקא פ..
..מקר
זהר יין משורין בר..
..סהי

Cambridge University Library
T-S A45.24 8 recto

שנ ונטיא ו

ט וגבל הקרשים וה ...'

וחוצה להם ג שבטים דן אש

...טה ואהרן ובניו טנ והחנם לפנ המ'

יהורה ישטנבר וובולן , מחנה

ם עליב מיליס · רגלו טליחורה ד'

...חה שכינה ד' מילים · רגלו שלואובן

לריוק יצ מילים · רגלו שלאפרים ל' מילים

...אל שכינה ד' מיליס · רגלו שלדן ל'

...זויות טלמשכן ד' מיחנות טמטמטי

...עלידן· כיון שהיו ישראל נוסעין היד

...ומושך על גבי בנ יהורה בקורה

..ורגבל' יהורה תחילה טנ ונסע רג...

...הרן ובני ומירקו את הפרכות וכ...

...ובנ' תקעו והריעו ותק...

נ' ו נ ... ... נ' מחנה ראובן פיר

..יקו את המשכן וטעעו אות

..בנ קהת טנ ונסע הקהתי·

...רגל אפרים טנ ונסע רגל מחנ..

ומירדקו את הקורש וטעעו את ת..

תקעו והריעו ותקעו· ..מטרב

...ורבן ומצאו טיירו .. ..הם
שנ

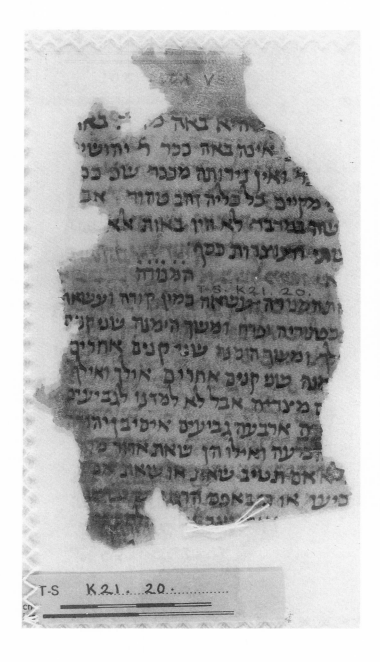

Cambridge University Library
T-S K21.20 verso

Cambridge University Library
T-S F11.32 recto

... כהן גבהן ...
... גבוה מן הקדשים א... ...
...שכן ועל המזבח מה משכן
...מות ... חוט שלסיקרא חוגרן
...מים העליונים לרמים התחתונים
...ות אמה יסור ושולטן אמות בריקים
... נותנין דמים העתונין למטן ומחוט
...מות אמה קרנות וגאמות בדקים
...שם היו נותנין דמים תתנן למעלה
...יסקרא ולמטן שטטן מחוט הסקרא
...גן מחוט הסקרא ולמעלן פסולין
...מעלן כמולין והנתנין מחוט הסקרא
... מזבח שעשה משה
...ת ושעשוק שולמה גבהן ... אמות
... אמות ולעעוד לבא גבהו אמ...
...מיצע עזרה כבש לדרומו כיור ל...
... וכל ישראל למזרחו שנ ויקרבו כל
...קרא המזבח מזבח ... ילה מזבח הנ...
... כו...
...ורות שנ...
... ... בסיור...

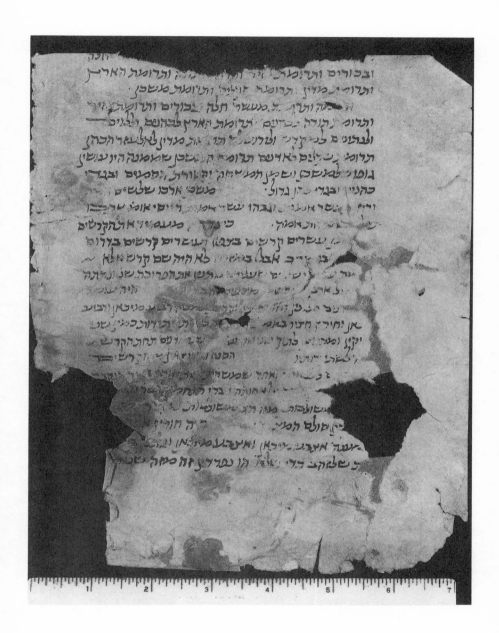

Jewish Theological Seminary Library
Adler 2940.1

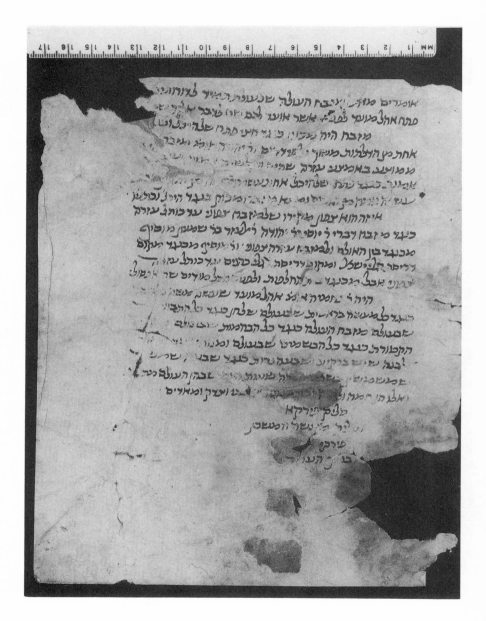

Cambridge University Library
T-S K21.82 recto

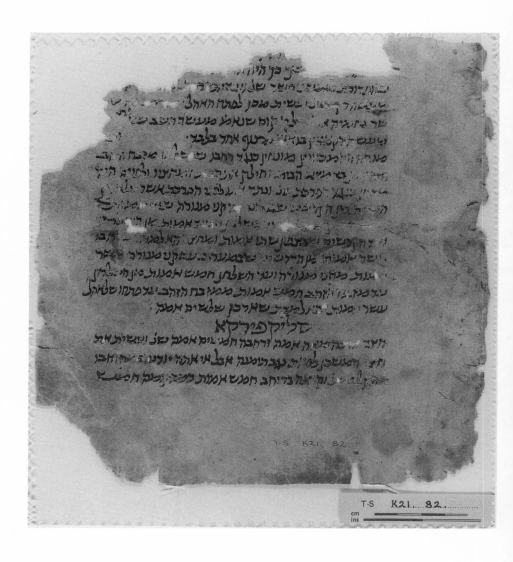

Cambridge University Library
T-S K21.82 verso

Annenberg Research Institute Library
MS Dropsie 83

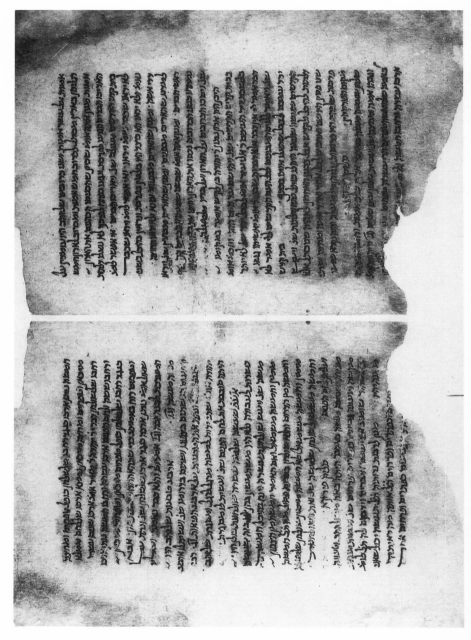

Annenberg Research Institute Library
MS Dropsie 83

Appendix B

MS Paris Addenda

MS Paris Bibliothèque Nationale 353.5 (MS P), a unique recension of Baraita de-Melekhet ha-Mishkan (BMM), contains additions and interpolations that could not be accommodated in the critical apparatus. They are presented in Appendix B.

Each passage is cited by BMM chapter and line (ch.:line) and by the word(s) after which the passage is found.

MS P is described in chapter 5 of the Introduction, pp. 105-7. The citation of MS P variants within the critical apparatus is described on p. 146.

Critical Symbols

[lemmata from BMM base text
( ) included in critical apparatus
[ ] lacunae
°   doubtful transcription

Appendix B

MS PARIS ADDENDA

תודה] ארבעים לחמי התודה ארבעה הן מיני לחם בתודה ועשרה מכל מן ומין וכתו' והקריב עליה אחד מכל קרבן

1:2

משכן] (ותרומת מדין ותרומת הדשן) ויש אומ' אף תרומת הקומץ שנ' והרים ממנו בקומצו וגו'

1:3

זהב] כדי שני חריצים של שני קרשים טבעת אחת לשני קרשים וטבעת אחת לשני קרשים מיכאן בחריצים והטבעות של זהב והקרשים מצופים זהב

1:16

וארבעה] אדנים בשליש המשכן למזרח תחת ד' עמודי שיטים שעליהן נתונה הפרוכת שנ' והבדילה הפרוכת לכם בין הקדש ובין קודש הקדשים שלפנים הימינה היה נתון הארון והכפורת והכרובים וצלוחית של שמן וצנצנת המן ומקלו של אהרן ושקדיה ופריחיה כשמצוע בבית עולמים שקדש הקדשים הדביר במקום הארון בשליש הבית שנ' והבית בהבנותו ששים אמה ארכו ועשרים אמה רחבו וגו' וכתו' לפני הדביר עשרים אמה אורך ועשרים אמה רוחב אף המשכן שעשה משה קדש הקדשים מקום הארון בשליש הבית

1:23

מבריח וגו'] (מבריח מן הקצה אל הקצה) ושנו חכמ' במקום אחר מן האשל אשר נטע אבינו אברהם בבאר שבע עשה אותו אורכו שבעים אמה כנגד היקיפו של משכן ובנס היה נכנס ובנס היה יוצא שהיה מקיף כעכנא שנ' מבריח מן הקצה אל הקצה ובברייתא זו שנינו שהבריחים שאחורי המשכן למערב לשמונה קרשים אורכו י"ב אמה בין צפון לדרום וכל בריחי מערב כן היא מידתן והבריח התיכון ממזרח למערב כן במלאכה וכמידה זו וכמידה זו לצפון ולדרום והקרשים וארבעה עמודי שטים שעליהם נתונה הפרוכת וחמשה עמודי שטים שעליהם נתון המסך לפתח האהל מצופים זהב וו' העמודים מצופים זהב

1:28

הבריח] סליק פרק א' פרק ב' קירוי המשכן היאך הוכן ביריעות הראשונות מתכלת וארגמן ותולעת שני ושש משזר שש זהו פשתן וכנגד ארבע יסודות של עולם דמות גוונים

1:35

והיה מחברן] חמש היריעות לבד וחמש היריעות לבד אורך היריעה האחת כ"ח באמה ורוחב ד' באמה מידה אחת לכולן חמשים לולאות תכלת בקצה החוברת האחת וכן במחברת השינית מקבילות הלולאות אשה אל אחותה ואחר כן עשה חמשים קרסי נחושת והיה מכניס ב' לולאות בקרס האחד

2:8

ברקיע] והיה פורש על המשכן רוחבוֹ של יריעות לאורכו של משכן רוחב עשר   2:11
יריעות [˚ ˚ ˚] באמה נותן להם ל' לאורך גגו של משכן וי' מאחורי המשכן
כצד קומת הקרשים הנהﬞ [˚] מדת רחבן של יריעות לאורך המשכן

תשע מכאן ותשע מכאן] נמצא המשכן לשֹׁוֹלֹיֹ צדדוֹ מ[ ] לה מלמטה אמה   2:13
אחת מיכאן ואמה אחת מיכאן כאדם שחלוקו ה[ ] ן שאר מבשרוֹ מבית כמעﬞ
קצור מחלוקו של מעל הנה שיעור ופיﬞרוש של עשר יריעות של מטה הראשונות
של תכלת וארגמן ותולעת שני ושש משזר

עזים] (לאהל על המשכן) היה תופרן ה' יריעות לבד כנגד ה' סיפרי תורה ושש   3:2
יריעות לבד כנגד ו' סידרי משנה

נחשת] לחבר את האהל להיות אחר [ ] ב' לולאות היה מכניס בקרס אחד והיה   3:6
פורשו על יריעות הראשונות רוחב כולו בכלל מﬞ' אמות פירש רחבו של יריעות
לאורכו של משכן

לאחוריו] (לאחורי המשכן כנגד קומתו של קרשים) חצי היריעה היה פורש   3:9
מאחור המשכן כאשה צנועה הפורפת שדיה לאחוריה

האהל] הרי יצאו מ"ד אמה של רוחבו של יריעות לאורכו של משכן ואורכן של   3:9
יריעות לרוחבו של משכן יצאו מהן י' אמות לרוחב גגו של משכן י' מהן לצידי
המשכן בצפון וי' מהן לצידי המשכן בדרום והאמה מזה והאמה מזה בעודף
שﬞאורך יריעות באהל יהיה סרוח על צדי המשכן מזה ומזה לכסֹותו בחלוק של
מעלה העורף על חלוק של מטה הרי יצאו שלשים

לאהל[2]] (אלים מאדמים) וכמידה זו עושה מכסה עורות תחשים מלמעלה וזה   3:13
תחש חיה טהורה היתה בﬞה כמה גוונים וקרן אחד היה לו ולפי שעה נזדמן לו
למשה ועשה ממנו מכסה למשכן ונגנז

המשכן] לפאת נֶגֶב הימנה קלעים לחצר שש משזר מאה באמה אורך ועמודיו   5:2
עשרים

אמות] ואדניהם עשרים נחושת ו' העמודים וחשוקיהם כסף   5:10

מאה אמות] אורך עמודיהם עשרים ואדניהם עשרים ו' העמודים   5:18
וחשוקיהם כסף

אמה[2]] עמודיו עשרה הרי חמש אמות בין עמוד לעמוד ואדניהם עשרה   5:19

לכתף] עמודיהם שלשה ואדניהם שלשה הרי ה' אמות בין עמוד לעמוד ואדניהם   5:21
שלשה

השנית] ט"ו קלעים עמודיו שלשה הר' ה' אמות בין עמוד לעמוד ואדניהם
שלשה ולשער החצר מסך עשרים אמה תכלת וארגמן ותולעת שני ושש משזר
מעשה רוקם הרי לך מפתחו של חצר רחבו כרוחב פתחו של אולם וכתו' קראו
אורך ועל ד' עמודי שיטים מחושקים כסף וויהם כסף וקומת שער החצר ה'
אמות

אולם] (י' אמה) נמצא החצר ק' אמה אורך ממזרח עד מערב מצד דרום וק' אמה
אורך ממזרח ועד מערב מצד צפון ורוחב בנ' בנ' היך מקלעי החצר שמצד מזרח
עד מכוון פתח האהל שהוא חצי מידה מכוונת של אורך החצר החצר רוח נ'
בנ' נ' ממזרח ועד מערב ונ' מצפון לדרום ומפתח האהל שבמזרח עד אחוריו
שבמערב אורך האוהל ל' אמה ורוחב י' אמה נמצא מן נ' אמות של חצר שהוא
רוחב נ' בנ' עד קלעי מערב של אחורי האהל נ' אמה בין צד דרום בין מצד
צפון לפי שאורך החצר ק' אמה ועד נ' אמה רוחב נ' בנ' ומן נ' מצד קלעי
דרום עד האהל אמה ומצד קלעי צפון עד האוהל עוד כ' אמה הרי מ' אמה
והאוהל רוחב מ' אמה ומצד קלעי מערב עד האהל עוד כ' אמה נמצא מחצי
החצי שהוא מכוון חצי מפתח האוהל בקו מתוח מצפון לדרום מאותו הקיו עד
קלעי צידי מערב נמצא רוחב אמה מצפון וכ' ממערב וכ' מדרום

לוחות] מקום הנחת שברי לוחות ו' טפחים הרי י"ב טפחים ספר תורה טפחיים
הרי י"ד טפחים

לוחות] צא מהם לספר תורה טפחים כדי שלא יהא נכנס ויוצא בדוחק וחצי טפח
מכאן וחצי טפח מכאן ומחצה וארבעה לוחות היו שם שנים שלמים ושנים
שבורין והלוחות ארכו של כל אחד ואחד ששה טפחי' ורחבן ששה טפחי' ובין שלשה
צא מהן שנים עשר טפח לרחבן של לוחו' ואצבע מכאן ואצבע מכאן לעביו של
ארון ורחבו של ארון שבע' טפחים ומחצה צא מהן ששה טפחים לארכן של
לוחות

יושר' וגו'] וכתו' ויביאו הכהנים את ארון ברית יי אל מקומו אל דביר הבית אל
קדש הקדשים אל תחת כנפי הכרובים

וחולק את הבית] (בתווך) ובנס היה עומד היך כי הדביר כ' אמה אורך וכ' אמה
רוחב והארון אמתים וחצי ארכו ואמה וחצי רחבו והוא היה נתון בתוך הדביר
והיה לו ריוח י' אמות לכל רוח

בארץ] ה' אמות כנף הכרוב האחד וה' אמות כנף הכרוב השני י' אמות מקצות
כנפיו אל קצות כנפיו ושני כרובים כנף זה נוגע לכנף זה ויסוכו הכרובים על
הארון

הבדים] ויראו ראשי הבדים בין הקדש וגו' דכתו' ויראו ראשי הבדים וכתו' ולא   7:14
יראו החוצה היאך ויראו והיאך לא יראו החוצה

אשה] (שכן כתו' בין שדי ילין) ומה הפרש בין קדש הקדשים שבבית ראשון   7:17
לקודש הקדשים שבבית שני בבית ראשון היה כותל מבדיל בין קדש ובין קדש
הקדשים וזהו ששנינו ואמה טרקסין שהיה בשלישו של בית ועוביו אמה ובבית
שיני היו שני פרכות מבדילות שתים היו החיצונה פרופה מן המזרח והפנימית
פרופה מן הדרום

גנזו] (אותו) בעת שמצא חלקיהו הכהן ספר תורה ומצא בו כתו' יוליך יי אותך   7:26
ואת מלכך אשר תקים עליך וגו'

חמשה] וקרנותיו ז' אצבעות ר' יהודה אום' שלא תטעה סימני לחם שתי הלחם   8:4
של לחם המוסרים אורכו ז' טפחים ורוחבו ד' טפחים וקרנותיו ד' אצבעות וסימ'
ז'ד'ד'

מכאן²] ורוחבו של לחם הפנים לאורכו של שולחן זה על גב זה וכן מצד זה   8:8
והשולחן אורכו י"ב טפחים נמצא בו מערכת למערכת

בהן] שלא יתעפש ובאותן טפחיים ריוח נותן בזך הלבונה וערך זה ובזך הלבונה   8:9
לערך זה

זכה] (על בסמוך) מיכאן ואילך סופה דברויית דלעיל עד סוף פרק ט...   8:11

זהב] עם גביעיה כפתריה ופרחיה ונירותיה ומלקחיה ומחתתיה ולדורות אם באה   9:1
משל כסף בדרך שעשו בית חשמונאים כשירה אבל אינה צריכה ככר ולא
גביעים כפתורים ופרחים ואם באה זהב לדורות צריכה ככר זהב וגביעים
וכפתורים ופרחים ומלקחיים ומחנות ולא צבתיים ולא מלקטאות באין ממנה

אמות] סליק פרק י"א פרק י"ז המזבח היה נבוב לוחות מלא אדמה שנ' מזבח   11:12
אדמה תעשה לי והיה מעצי שטים מצופה נחושת

יסוד] ושם שופכין את הדם שנ' ואת דמו ישפך אל יסוד המזבח   11:13

אחד] ומאיין עשאו כשהביאו אנשי ישראל מי כסף מי זהב והכסף לכסף פקודי   12:1
העדה והזהב לתנופה וכל אשר נמצא אתו תכלת וארגמן ותולעת שני היו
מביאין והנשיאים הביאו את אבני השוהם ואת אבני המילואים ולפי שהנשיאים
נשתהו בהבאה לפיכך כתו' והנשיאם חסר יוד נשאו הנשים ק"ו בעצמו ואמרו
ואנו לא נביא למלאכת המשכן כלים מיד נטלו מראיות שהיו להן מנחשת
מוצהב טוב ומהיכן היו להם אמ' ר' בנימן בר יפת כשהיו ישראל משועבדין

במצרים כל מי שהיה מארס אשה היה משגר לה מראית של נחושב טוב ומוצהב
כדי להסתכל בו וכשגזרו המצריים שיעבוד על ישראל בחומר ובלבנים ובכל
עבודה בשדה והיו חוזרין יגיעין מן העבודה היו הנשים יוצאות לשאוב מים
וה'ב'ה מזמן להם בכדים ומבשלות הדגים ומוכרות מהן ולוקחות בדמיהן
לחם ויין ומביאין הלחם והתבשיל והיין ומאכילות ומשקות בעליהן והיו שם
עמהן בשדה ולאחר שאוכלין ושותין היתה האשה נוטלת המראית של נחושת
שלה ומסתכלת בה היא ובעלה זאת אומרת אני נאה והלה אומ' אני נאה
מינֶיך והכל לשם שמים לדבר מצוה להרגילו לתשמיש כדי שלא יבטלו מפריה
ורביה עד שהיה נזקק לה לתשמיש וה'ב'ה פוקדה ומתעברת והיו עובריהן פרין
ורבין במעיהן רב יהודה ושמואל פליגי בה חד אמ' שנים בבטן כעניין שנ' ובני
ישראל פרו וישרצו וחד אמ' שנים עשר פרו שנים וישרצו שנים וירבו שנים
ויעצמו שנים במאד שנים מאד שנים הרי י"ב וחכמ' אומ' ששה כעניין שנ'
וישרצו גדול שבשבַרשْ שבשרצים עכבר ויולדת ששה בבטן ר' מאיר אומ' ששים
כעניין שנ' וישרצו והקטן שבשרצים עקרב ויולדת ששים בבטן רב הונא דרש
זה של ששים כנגד ששים ריבוא אמ' ריש לקיש עדיין לא דרש רב הונא כלום
מן הפסוק אין וישרצו אלא כעניין שנ' ישרצו המים שרץ נפש חיה כדג שהוא
משריץ כמה וכמה בלא מספר רב נחמן אמ' מהכא וידגו לרוב בקרב הארץ
ומאותן המראיות הביאו למלאכת המשכן וכשהביאום צף בהם משה ואמ' גדול
הוא זה שכל מי שיש לאשה בלא של בעלה הוא אמרו לו רבינו משה אילו
בימי אירוסינו שיֵּגّّרْו לנו בעלינו וליْטّבّعֿוْן נתנו לנו כעין קידושין מיד רמז
לו ה'ב'ה ואמ' על אילו אתה מבזה אילו הן המראות שגרמו להיוולד כל אילו
ציבאו צבאות שנ' יצאו כל ציבאות יי מארץ מצרים על צבאותם עכשיו טול
מידיהן ועשה בהן מלאכה נאה שיקדש בהן את הכלי הכיור הכהן ידיו ורגליו
בעת בואו לעבודה וזה הכלי יהיה מכשיר לעבודה שנ' ויעש את הכיור נחושת
ואת כנו נחושת במראות הצובאות אשר צבאו פתח אהל מועד וזהו שכתו'
ונחושת התנופה מאי תנופה תנّّוْפֿֿה והיא כלה שבו בלשון יוון קורין לכלה
נינפי כיוצא בדבר יפה נוף אמורפי נינפי ופירושו כלה נאה מיכאן אתה אומ'
כיור שעשה משה ממראיות של כלות עשאו

13:7   ובנימן] והם בני גרשום ממונים על המשכן והאהל מכסיהו ומסך פתח אהל
מועד וקלעי החצר ומסך פתח החצר

13:12   וזבולון] שנ' והחונים קדמה מזרחה דגל מחנה בני יהודה לצבאותם

13:21   יהודה] (לצבאותם ועל צבאו נחשון בן עמינדב) מדגליו יוצאות שלש מפאות
ודמות צבעם כמו דמות טור הראשון טור אבנים שעל חושן המשפט שעל לב
אהרן מפא אחת ירוקה אחת אדומה אחת ברקא בעניין גוון אותו של אותן
אבנים ג' טור אודם פטרֿה וברקת הטור האחד דמות המפות כדמות האבנים
ודמות האבנים כדמות המפות ושם ג' שבטים על ג' אבנים יהודה יששכר וזבולון
על הדגל על כל מפא ומפא שם השבט וכתו' בדגל קומה יי ויפוצו אויבך וינוסו
משנאיך מפניך וכן היה אומ' משה רבי' וביום העלות העֿנָן מעל המשכן ומֿת

ועולה ועומד כמין קורה עד שהיו ישראל מתקנין עצמן וטוענין כלי תשמישיו
בהמתן ומי שלא היה לו בהמה הענן סובל וטוען כלי תשמישיו ובאמצע הדגל
צורה גור אריה יהודה

ראובן וגו'] ועל צבאו אליצור בן שדיאור ושלש מפאות ברّגל כנגד שלשה   13:23
אבנים שבחושן המשפט שעל לב אהרן שבטור השני והם נופך ספיר ויהלום
ושם ג' שבטים חקוק על ג' אבנים ראובן שמעון גד ודמות ג' המפות כדמות
ג' האבנים ודמות ג' האבנים כדמות ג' המפות של דגל ושם של ג' שבטים
חקוק על ג' מפות ראובן שמעון גד וכתו' על הדגל שמע ישראל יי אלהינו יי
אחד ודמות איילה חקוק על הדגל

נושאי וגו'] והקימו את המשכן עד בואם ובני קהת ישאו על כתיפם שנ' ולבני   13:25-26
קהת לא נתן כי עבודת הקדש עליהם בכתף ישאו

דגל אפרים] ועל צבאו אלישמע בן עמיהוד והן מן המערב וג' מפות בדגל   13:26
ודמות ג' מפות כדמות ג' אבנים ודמות ג' אבנים כדמות ג' מפות והאבנים
שבחושן המשפט שעל לב אהרן שבטור השלישי לשם שבו ואחלמה ושם ג'
שבטים חקוק על ג' אבנים אפרים ומנשה ובנימן ושם ג' שבטים (ונמחק: חקוק)
אפרים ומנשה ובנימן חקוק על ג' מפות וחקוק בדגל וענן יי עליהם יומם בנסעם
מן המחנה ודמות זהב חקוק בדגל בנימן זאב יטרף

יסעו] (דגל מחנה בני דן לצבאותם) ועל צבאו אחיעזר בן עמישדי והדגל יש   13:32
בו ג' מפות דמות המפות כדמות האבנים ודמות האבנים שעל לב אהרן בחושן
המשפט כדמות ג' המפות והטור הרביעי תרשיש שוהם וישפה ושם ג' שבטים
חקוק על ג' אבנים דן נפתלי ואשר ושם ג' שבטים חקוק על ג' מפות דן נפתלי
אשר וחקוק בדגל דמות נחש יהי דן נחש עלי דרך וחקוק בדגל ובנוחה יאמר
שובה יי רבבות אלפי ישראל

חצוצרות] (מניין) דכתו' ותקעו מהן ונועדו אליך הנשיאים אל פתח אהל מועד   13:36
וכתו' תרועה יתקעו למסעיהם

שמשך] (ויירחך לא יאסף וגו') ועל כן נאמ' לא בלתה שמלתך מעליך ונעלך   14:14
לא בציקה וגו' לפי שאיירו של עולם מבלה תשמישו העולם והכלים וכשלא
היה שולט אותן ארבעים שנה האויר מפני עניני הכבוד והעננים היו מכבסין
ומנגבין ומגהצין שמלותיהן והילדים היו הן גדילין ושמלותיהן גדילין על גופן
ונעליהן על רגליהן כמו כן וסימן בעולם לדבר חלזון

משה] מעל הכפרת ולא מכפרת כולו אלא מצמצם שכינתו מאהבה ומדבר   14:16
מבין שני הכרובים שהן כמלא טפח שנ' ובא משה אל אהל מועד לדבר אתו
וישמע את הקול מדבר אליו מעל הכפרת מבין שני הכרובים אשר על ארון
העדות וידבר אליו

Appendix C

Biblical Citations
in Baraita de-Melekhet
ha-Mishkan

		BMM ch.:line			*BMM* ch.:line
Gen.	4:7	10:7-8	Ex.	26:9	3:3-4, 3:9-10
	49:6	10:9		26:10	3:6
	49:7	10:8, 10:9		26:11	3:6
Ex.	17:9	10:10		26:12	3:11
	25:10	6:2		26:14	3:13
	25:11	7:3		26:19	1:14-15
	25:15	7:8		26:24	1:17, 1:19, 1:21
	25:21	7:5-6		26:28	1:27-28
	25:23	8:2		26:29	1:31
	25:25	8:14-15		26:31	4:14-15
	25:26	8:13		26:32	1:11-12
	25:31	9:2		26:33	1:11, 4:3
	25:32	10:4-5		26:35	4:7-8
	25:33	10:20		26:36	4:15-16
	25:34	10:6, 10:11		27:9	5:1-2
	25:40	10:25		27:11	5:18
	26:1	2:2-3		27:12	5:19
	26:2	2:11-12, 2:14		27:13	5:20
	26:3	2:8		27:14	5:21
	26:4	2:9		27:18	5:2, 5:27
	26:6	2:10		27:19	5:12
	26:7	3:2		29:42	14:19
	26:8	3:7-8			

		BMM ch.:line
Ex.	30:1	11:2
	30:2	11:8
	30:3	11:3
	30:6	4:20-21, 14:16-17
	30:18	12:1
	30:36	14:18
	36:16	3:3-4
	36:34	1:33
	38:1	11:5
	38:15	5:22
	38:18	5:16
	38:27	1:23-24
	39:3	4:13
	40:5	4:20
	40:34	14:3
	40:38	14:12
Lev.	9:5	11:22
	24:4	10:34
	24:7	8:10-11
Num.	2:2	13:18
	2:14	13:31, 13:32
	2:20	8:11
	3:23	13:5
	3:25	13:6
	3:29	13:2
	3:31	13:3
	3:35	13:8
	3:36	13:9-10
	3:38	13:11-12
	4:5	13:22
	4:14	13:20-21
	4:15	13:28
	4:25	3:15-16
	4:26	5:14, 11:10-11
	8:2	10:35-36
	9:18	13:34
	10:2	9:15
	10:5	13:36

		BMM ch.:line
Num.	10:18	13:23
	10:21	13:25-26
	10:22	13:26-27
	10:25	13:29
	10:33	6:20
	14:44	6:21-22
Deut.	31:16	10:12
	31:26	6:16
Josh.	3:16	1:20
1 Sam.	4:4	6:25
	14:18	6:22-23
2 Sam.	11:11	6:23-24
1 Ki.	7:23	12:5
	7:25	12:14-15
	7:26	12:6, 12:13
	8:3	7:9
	8:7	7:21
	8:8	7:14, 7:18, 7:19, 7:23
	8:9	6:26-27
2 Ki.	20:17	7:24
Is.	39:6	7:24
	60:1	14:13
	60:2	14:14
	60:19	14:13-14, 14:15
Ezek.	45:14	12:9
Cant.	3:9	6:17
2 Chr.	4:3	12:17-18
	4:4	12:14-15
	4:5	12:6-7, 12:13
	4:6	12:2
	4:7	10:27
	4:8	8:16-17
	4:19	8:20
	4:21	10:30
	4:22	7:28
	5:9	7:14, 7:18, 7:19, 7:23
	13:11	10:30
	35:3	7:26

Selected Bibliography

EDITIONS OF RABBINIC TEXTS

MISHNAH

Faksimile-Ausgabe des Mischnacodex Kaufmann A 50. Ed. G. Beer. Jerusalem, 1969.
Shishah Sidre Mishnah. Ed. H. Albeck. 6 vols. Jerusalem, 1954-59.

TOSEFTA

The Tosefta according to Codex Vienna with Variants from Codex Erfurt, Geniza MSS and Editio Princeps. Ed. S. Lieberman. 4 vols. New York, 1955-73.
Tosephta. Ed. M. S. Zuckermandel. Jerusalem, 1965.

PALESTINIAN TALMUD

Talmud Yerushalmi Codex Leiden Scal. 3. 4 vols. Jerusalem, 1971.
Talmud Yerushalmi. Editio princeps. Venice, 1522/23. [Reprint, n.p., n.d.]
Talmud Yerushalmi. 7 vols. New York, 1959. [Reprint of ed. Vilna, 1922.]

BABYLONIAN TALMUD

Talmud Bavli Codex Munich 95. 3 vols. Jerusalem, 1971.
Talmud Bavli. 20 vols. New York, 1969. [Reprint of ed. Vilna, 1895.]
Diqduqe Soferim: Variae Lectionis in Mishnam et in Talmud Babylonicum. Ed. R. Rabbinovicz. 2 vols. New York, 1976.

BARAITA DE-MELEKHET HA-MISHKAN

Baraita de-Melekhet ha-Mishkan. Venice, 1602 [editio princeps].
Baraita de-Melekhet ha-Mishkan. Ed. I. Scheuer. Offenbach, 1802.
Baraita de-Melekhet ha-Mishkan. Ed. M. Friedmann (Ish-Shalom). Vienna, 1908.

Baraita de-Melekhet ha-Mishkan. Ed. Ch. Kanivsky. Bene Berak, 1961.
Baraita de-Melekhet ha-Mishkan [published with *Ma'aseh Ḥoshev*]. Ed. Sh. Shefer. Jerusalem, 1965.

TANNAITIC MIDRASHIM

Mechilta D'Rabbi Ismael. Ed. H.S. Horovitz/I.A. Rabin. Jerusalem, 1970.
Mekilta de-Rabbi Ishmael. Ed. J.Z. Lauterbach. 3 vols. Philadelphia, 1933-35.
Mekilta D'Rabbi Ismael. Ed. M. Friedmann (Ish-Shalom). Jerusalem, 1961.
Mekhilta D'Rabbi Sim'on b. Jochai. Ed. J.N. Epstein/E.Z. Melamed. Jerusalem, 1955.
Mekilta de-R. Simeon b. Yohai. Ed. D. Hoffmann. Frankfurt, 1905.
Midrash Tannaim. Ed. D. Hoffmann. 2 vols. Berlin, 1909.
Sifra de-ve Rav. Ed. I.H. Weiss. Vienna, 1862.
Sifra or Torat Kohanim according to Codex Assemani LXVI. New York, 1966.
Sifra on Leviticus. Ed. L. Finkelstein. 4 vols. New York, 1983-90.
Sifre de-ve Rav. Ed. M. Friedmann (Ish-Shalom). Vienna, 1864.
Siphre ad Numeros adjecto Siphre zutta. Ed. H.S. Horovitz. Jerusalem, 1966.
Sifre on Deuteronomy. Ed. L. Finkelstein. New York, 1969.

OTHER RABBINIC TEXTS

Aboth de Rabbi Nathan. Ed. S. Schechter. Vienna, 1887.
Aruch Completum. Ed. A. Kohut. 8 vols. Vienna, 1926.
Die Fastenrolle: Eine Untersuchung zur jüdisch-hellenistischen Geschichte. Ed. H. Lichtenstein. *HUCA* 8-9 (1931-32): 257-351.
Megillat Ta'anit. Ed. B.Z. Luria. Jerusalem, 1964.
Midrash Bereshit Rabba. Ed. J. Theodor/H. Albeck. 3 vols. Jerusalem, 1965.
Midrash ha-Gadol. Genesis: ed. M. Margulies. Exodus: ed. M. Margulies. Leviticus: ed. A. Steinsaltz. Numbers: ed. Z.M. Rabinowitz. Deuteronomy: ed. S. Fisch. Jerusalem, 1975-83.
Midrash Rabbah. 2 vols. Jerusalem, 1961. [Reprint of ed. Vilna, 1884-87.]
Midrash Shemot Rabbah 1-14. Ed. A. Shinan. Tel Aviv, 1984.
Midrash Tanḥuma. Jerusalem, 1971.
Midrash Tanḥuma ha-Qadum ve-ha-Yashan. Ed. S. Buber. 2 vols. Jerusalem, 1964.

Midrash Tehillim. Ed. S. Buber. Vilna, 1891.
Midrash Wayyiqra Rabba. Ed. M. Margulies. 5 vols. Jerusalem, 1953-60.
The Mishnah of Rabbi Eliezer or The Midrash of Thirty-Two Hermeneutic Rules. Ed. H.G. Enelow. 2 vols. New York, 1933.
Mishnat ha-Middot. Ed. S. Gandz. *PAAJR* 4 (1933): 54-112.
Perush ha-Geonim le-Seder Tohorot. Ed. J.N. Epstein. Jerusalem /Tel Aviv, 1982.
Perushe ha-Torah le-Rabbenu Moshe b. Naḥman (Ramban). Ed. C.D. Chavel. 2 vols. Jerusalem, 1959-60.
Perushe Rashi al ha-Torah. Ed. C.D. Chavel. Jerusalem, 1983.
Pesikta de Rav Kahana. Ed. B. Mandelbaum. 2 vols. New York, 1962.
Seder Olam. Ed. B. Ratner. New York, 1966.
"Seder Olam: A Rabbinic Chronography." Ed. Ch. Milikowsky. Ph.D. dissertation: Yale University, 1981.
Seder Tannaim ve-Amoraim. Ed. K. Kahana. Frankfurt, 1935.
Sefer Halakhot Gedolot. Ed. E. Hildesheimer. 3 vols. Jerusalem, 1971-88.
Sefer ve-Hizhir. Ed. I.M. Freimann. 2 vols. Leipzig, 1873 (v. 1); Warsaw, 1880 (v. 2).
Sheeltot de Rab Aḥai Gaon. Ed. S.K. Mirsky. 5 vols. Jerusalem, 1982.
Yalqut ha-Makhiri. Isaiah: ed. J.Z.K. Spira. Berlin, 1894.
Yalqut Shimoni. 2 vols. Jerusalem, 1973.
Yalqut Shimoni. Genesis: ed. A. Hyman/Y. Lehrer/Y. Shiloni. 2 vols. Jerusalem, 1973. Exodus: ed. A. Hyman/Y. Shiloni. 2 vols. Jerusalem, 1977-80. Leviticus: ed. A. Hyman/Y. Shiloni. 2 vols. Jerusalem, 1984.

SECONDARY LITERATURE

Albeck, Hanoch. *Mavo la-Mishnah.* Tel Aviv, 1979.
———. *Mavo la-Talmudim.* Tel Aviv, 1969.
———. *Meḥqarim be-Baraita ve-Tosefta.* Jerusalem, 1969.
———. *Untersuchungen über die halakischen Midraschim.* Berlin, 1927.
Aptowitzer, A. "The Heavenly Temple According to the Aggadah" (Hebrew). *Tarbiẓ* 2 (1931): 137-53, 257-87.
———. "Seder Elia." *Jewish Studies in Memory of George A. Kohut.* New York, 1935, 5-39.
Assaf, Simḥa. *Tequfat ha-Geonim ve-Sifrutah.* Jerusalem, 1976.
Avi-Yonah, Michael. *The Jews under Roman and Byzantine Rule.* Jerusalem, 1984.

Bacher, Wilhelm. *Die exegetische Terminologie der jüdischen Traditionsliteratur.* 2 vols. Darmstadt, 1965.
_____. *Tradition und Tradenten in den Schulen Palästinas und Babyloniens.* Berlin, 1966.
Bar-Asher, M., ed. *Mehqarim be-Lashon* I. Jerusalem, 1985.
Bar-Ilan, Meir. "The Character and Origin of Megillat Ta'anit" (Hebrew). *Sinai* 98 (1986): 114-37.
Barth, Lewis M. *An Analysis of Vatican 30.* Cincinnati, 1973.
Bédier, Joseph. *La tradition manuscrite du Lai de l'Ombre.* Paris, 1929.
Beit-Arie, Malachi. *Hebrew Codicology.* Jerusalem, 1981.
_____. "The Paleography of the Genizah Literary Fragments" (Hebrew). *Cairo Genizah Studies.* Ed. M.A. Friedman. Tel Aviv, 1980.
Bendavid, Abba. *Leshon Miqra u-Leshon Hakhamim.* 2 vols. Tel Aviv, 1967-71.
Benduhn-Mertz, Annette. "Methodological Aspects in Automatically Discovering Genealogical Dependencies Among Greek New Testament Manuscripts." *Association for Literary and Linguistic Computing Journal* 5 (1985): 31-35.
Ben-Hayyim, Z. "On the Chronology of an Article in the Historical Dictionary" (Hebrew). *Proceedings of the Fifth World Congress of Jewish Studies* 5 (1973): 3-11.
Bernheimer, Carlo. *Paleografia Ebraica.* Florence, 1924.
Bieler, L. "The Grammarian's Craft." *Folia,* Studies in the Christian Perpetuation of the Classics 10 (1958): 1-42.
Birnbaum, S.A. *The Hebrew Scripts.* 2 vols. London, 1954-57; Leiden, 1971.
Bloch, Renée. "Midrash." Tr. M.H. Callaway. *Approaches to Ancient Judaism: Theory and Practice.* Ed. W.S. Green. Brown Judaic Studies 1. Missoula, 1978, 29-50.
Bokser, Baruch M. "An Annotated Bibliographical Guide to the Study of the Palestinian Talmud." *Aufstieg und Niedergang der Römischen Welt* II:19:2. Berlin/New York, 1979, 139-256.
_____. *Post-Mishnaic Judaism in Transition.* Brown Judaic Studies 17. Chico, 1980.
_____. "Rabbinic Responses to Catastrophe: From Continuity to Discontinuity." *PAAJR* 50 (1983): 37-61.
Braude, W.G./Kapstein, I.J. *Pesikta de-Rab Kahana.* Philadelphia, 1975.
_____. *Tanna debe Eliyyahu.* Philadelphia, 1981.
Buber, Solomon. *Yeriot Shlomo.* Warsaw, 1896.

Chernick, Michael. *Le-Ḥeqer ha-Middot*. Hermeneutical Studies in Talmudic and Midrashic Literatures. Tel Aviv, 1984.

Cohen, Martin S. *The Shi'ur Qomah*. Lanham, 1983.

Collins, Marilyn. "The Hidden Vessels in Samaritan Traditions." *Journal for the Study of Judaism* 3 (1972): 97-116.

Dain, A. *Les manuscrits*. Paris, 1949.

Dearing, Vincent A. *Principles and Practice of Textual Analysis*. Berkeley, 1974.

DeVries, Benjamin. *Meḥqarim be-Sifrut ha-Talmud*. Jerusalem, 1968.

———. "The Problem of the Relationship of the Two Talmuds to the Tosefta" (Hebrew). *Tarbiẓ* 28 (1959): 158-70.

Dinur, B. "An Investigation of the Historiographic Fragments in Talmudic Literature" (Hebrew). *Proceedings of the Fifth World Congress of Jewish Studies*. Jerusalem, 1972: 137-46.

Elbaum, Jacob. "On the Character of the Late Midrashic Literature" (Hebrew). *Proceedings of the Ninth World Congress of Jewish Studies*. Jerusalem, 1986: 57-62.

Epstein, J.N. *Mavo le-Nusaḥ ha-Mishnah*. Second ed. 2 vols. Tel Aviv, 1964.

———. *Mevo'ot le-Sifrut ha-Amoraim*. Jerusalem, 1962.

———. *Mevo'ot le-Sifrut ha-Tannaim*. Tel Aviv, 1957.

Feldman, W.M. *Rabbinical Mathematics and Astronomy*. Third ed. New York, 1978.

Finkelstein, Louis. *Mavo le-Massekhtot Avot ve-Avot de-R. Nathan*. New York, 1950.

———. "Prolegomena to an Edition of the Sifre on Deuteronomy." *PAAJR* 3 (1932): 3-42.

Fishbane, Michael. *Biblical Interpretation in Ancient Israel*. Oxford, 1985.

Florsheim, Yoel. *Rashi la-Miqra be-Ferusho la-Talmud* I. Jerusalem, 1981.

Fraade, Steven D. "Sifre Deuteronomy 26 (ad Deut. 3:23): How Conscious the Composition?" *HUCA* 54 (1983): 245-301.

Fraenkel, Yonah. *Darko shel Rashi be-Ferusho la-Talmud ha-Bavli*. Jerusalem, 1975.

———. *Iyyunim be-Olamo ha-Ruḥani shel Sippur ha-Aggadah*. Tel Aviv, 1981.

Frankel, Zechariah. *Darkhe ha-Mishnah*. Tel Aviv, n.d.

Friedman, Shamma. "A Critical Study of Yevamot X with a Methodological Introduction" (Hebrew). *Meḥqarim u-Meqorot* I. Ed. H.Z. Dimitrovsky. New York, 1977, 275-441.

———. "Le-Ilan ha-Yoḥasin shel Nushei Bava Meẓia." *Meḥqarim ba-Sifrut ha-Talmudit.* A Study Conference in Honor of the Eightieth Birthday of Saul Lieberman. Israel Academy of Sciences and Humanities. Jerusalem, 1983, 93-147.

Friedmann, Meir (Ish Shalom). *Nispaḥim le-Seder Eliyyahu Zuta.* Vienna, 1904.

Gaehde, Joachim. "Carolingian Interpretations of an Early Christian Picture Cycle." *Frühmittelalterliche Studien* 8 (1974): 351-84.

Galloway, Patricia. "Manuscript Filiation and Cluster Analysis." *La pratique des ordinateurs dans la critique des textes.* Paris, 1979, 87-95.

_____. "Clustering Variants in the 'Lai de l'Ombre' Manuscripts: Techniques and Principles." *Association for Literary and Linguistic Computing Journal* 3 (1982): 1-7.

Gandz, Solomon. *Studies in Hebrew Astronomy and Mathematics.* New York, 1970.

Ginzberg, Louis. *Geonica.* 2 vols. New York, 1968.

_____. *Ginze Schechter.* 3 vols. New York, 1969.

_____. *Legends of the Jews.* 7 vols. Philadelphia, 1968.

Goldberg, Abraham. "The Duplicate Interpretations in Mekhilta de-Milluim" (Hebrew). *Sinai* 89 (1981): 115-18.

Goldin, Judah. *The Fathers According to Rabbi Nathan.* New Haven, 1955.

Goldstein, Naftali. "On Some Midrashic Conjunctive Terms" (Hebrew). *PAAJR* 49 (1982): 1-7.

Goodblatt, David. "The Babylonian Talmud." *Aufstieg und Niedergang der Römischen Welt* II: 19:2. Berlin/New York, 1979, 257-336.

_____. *Rabbinic Instruction in Sasanian Babylonia.* Leiden, 1975.

Goodenough, Erwin R. *Jewish Symbols in the Greco-Roman Period* XII. New York, 1965.

Goshen-Gottestein, Moshe. "Corpus, Genre and the Unity of Hebrew" (Hebrew). *Meḥqarim be-Lashon.* Ed. M. Bar-Asher. Jerusalem, 1985, 57-73.

Green, W.S. "What's in a Name? The Problematic of Rabbinic 'Biography.'" *Approaches to Ancient Judaism: Theory and Practice.* Ed. W.S. Green. Brown Judaic Studies 1. Missoula, 1978, 77-96.

Greenbaum, Aaron. "Baraita de-Melekhet ha-Mishkan within a Manuscript of Midrash ha-Gadol" (Hebrew). *Sura* 1 (1954): 490-513.

Greg, W.W. *The Calculus of Variants.* Oxford, 1927.

Gruenhut, L. *Sefer Ha-Liqqutim.* 2 vols. Jerusalem, 1898.

Gutmann, Joseph, ed. *The Temple of Solomon: Archaeological Fact and Medieval Tradition in Christian, Islamic and Jewish Art.* American Academy of Religion and Society of Biblical Literature: Religion and the Arts No. 3. Missoula, 1976.

Hachlili, Rachel. *Ancient Jewish Art and Archaeology in the Land of Israel.* Handbuch der Orientalistik VII. Leiden, 1988.

Hammer, Reuven. *Sifre: A Tannaitic Commentary on the Book of Deuteronomy.* New Haven/London, 1986.

Haran, Menaḥem. "The Law Code of Ezekiel XL-XLVIII and its Relation to the Priestly School." *HUCA* 50 (1979): 45-71.

————. *Temples and Temple-Service in Ancient Israel.* Winona Lake, 1985.

Hauptman, Judith. "Development of the Talmudic Sugya by Amoraic and Post-Amoraic Amplification of a Tannaitic Proto-Sugya." *HUCA* 58 (1987): 227-50.

Heinemann, Yiẓḥaq. *Darkhe ha-Aggadah.* Jerusalem, 1970.

Higger, Michael. *Oẓar ha-Baraitot.* 10 vols. New York, 1938-48.

Hoffmann, David. *Zur Einleitung in die halachischen Midraschim.* Berlin, 1887.

Hopkins, Simon. *A Miscellany of Literary Pieces from the Cambridge Genizah Collections.* Cambridge Univ. Library, 1978.

Horowitz, Chaim M. *Tosefata Attiqata* I. Frankfort am-Main, 1889.

Hyman, Arthur. *Meqorot Yalqut Shimoni.* 2 vols. Jerusalem, 1964.

Jacobs, Louis. "Are There Fictitious Baraitot in the Babylonian Talmud?" *HUCA* 42 (1971): 185-96.

————. "How Much of the Babylonian Talmud is Pseudepigraphic?" *JJS* 28 (1977): 46-59.

Jastrow, Marcus. *Dictionary of the Targumim, the Talmud Babli and Yerushalmi and the Midrashic Literature.* 2 vols. New York, 1886-1903.

Kaddari, M.Z., ed. *Erkhe ha-Milon he-Ḥadash le-Sifrut Ḥazal* II. Ramat Gan, 1974.

Kaplan, Julius. *The Redaction of the Babylonian Talmud.* New York, 1933.

Kirschner, Robert. "Apocalyptic and Rabbinic Responses to the Destruction of 70." *HTR* 78 (1985): 27-46.

————. "The Vocation of Holiness in Late Antiquity." *Vigiliae Christianae* 38 (1984): 105-124.

Kostof, Spiro. *A History of Architecture.* New York/Oxford, 1985.

Kraemer, David. "On the Reliability of Attributions in the Babylonian Talmud." *HUCA* 60 (1989): 175-90.

Krinsky, Carol. "Representations of the Temple of Jerusalem before 1500." *Journal of the Warburg and Courtald Institutes* 33 (1970): 1-19.

Kugel, James L. "Two Introductions to Midrash." *Prooftexts* 3 (1983): 131-55.

Kutscher, E.Y., ed. *Erkhe ha-Milon he-Ḥadash le-Sifrut Ḥazal* I. Ramat Gan, 1972.

————. *A History of the Hebrew Language.* Ed. R. Kutscher. Jerusalem/ Leiden, 1982.

————. "Mittelhebräisch und Jüdisch-Aramäisch im neuen Köhler Baumgartner Hebräische Worforschung." *Festschrift W. Baumgartner.* Leiden, 1967, 158-75.

————. et al, eds. *Sefer Zikkaron le-Ḥanokh Yalon.* Ramat Gan, 1974.

Lauterbach, Jacob Z. *Rabbinic Essays.* Cincinnati, 1951.

Lehmann, Manfred R. *Perush Rashi al ha-Torah.* New York, 1981.

Levine, Baruch. "The Descriptive Tabernacle Texts of the Pentateuch." *Journal of the American Oriental Society* 85 (1965): 307-18.

Lieberman, Saul. *Greek in Jewish Palestine.* New York, 1965.

————. *Hellenism in Jewish Palestine.* New York, 1950.

————. *Siphre Zutta.* New York, 1968.

————. *Tosefta Ki-Feshutah.* 8 vols. New York, 1955-73.

————. *Tosefeth Rishonim.* 4 vols. Jerusalem, 1937-39.

————. *Ha-Yerushalmi Ki-Feshuto.* Jerusalem, 1935.

Maas, Paul. *Textual Criticism.* Tr. B. Flower. Oxford, 1958.

Maier, Johann. *The Temple Scroll.* JSOT Suppl. 3. Tr. R.T. White. Sheffield, 1985.

Malter, Henry. *The Treatise Ta'anit of the Babylonian Talmud.* New York, 1930.

Mann, Jacob. *The Bible as Read and Preached in the Old Synagogue* I. New York, 1971.

McGann, Jerome J. *A Critique of Modern Textual Criticism.* Chicago/ London, 1983.

Meade, David G. *Pseudonymity and Canon.* Grand Rapids, 1987.

Melamed, E.Z. *Mavo le-Sifrut ha-Talmud.* Jerusalem, 1977.

————. *Midreshe Halakhah shel ha-Tannaim be-Talmud Bavli.* Second ed. Jerusalem, 1988.

Metzger, Mendel. "Quelques caractères iconographiques et ornementaux de deux manuscrits hébraïques du Xe siecle." *Cahiers de civilisation médiévale* 1 (1958): 205-13.

Metzger, Thérèse. "Les objets du culte, le sanctuaire du désert et le Temple de Jérusalem dans les bibles hebraïques médiévales enluminées." *Bulletin of the John Rylands Library* 52 (1970): 397-436.

Meyers, Carol L. *The Tabernacle Menorah.* AASOR Dissertation Series 2. Missoula, 1976, 4-11.

Milgrom, Jacob. *The JPS Torah Commentary: Numbers.* Philadelphia/ New York, 1990.

————. *Studies in Cultic Theology and Terminology.* Leiden, 1983.

Milikowsky, Chaim. "Seder Olam and Jewish Chronography in the Hellenistic and Roman Periods." *PAAJR* 52 (1985): 115-39.

Momigliano, Arnaldo. *On Pagans, Jews and Christians.* Middletown, 1987.

Morell, Samuel. "Sources of Halakhot Pesuqot: A Formal Analysis" (Hebrew). *PAAJR* 49 (1982): 41-95.

Moreshet, Menaḥem. "The Language of the Baraitot in the Babylonian Talmud is not MH" (Hebrew). *Sefer Zikkaron le-Ḥanokh Yalon.* Bar Ilan University Studies in Judaica and the Humanities. Ed. E.Y. Kutscher et al. Ramat Gan, 1974, 275-314.

_____. "Further Studies of the Language of the Hebrew Baraitot in the Babylonian and Palestinian Talmuds" (Hebrew). *Erkhe ha-Milon he-Ḥadash le-Sifrut Ḥazal* II. Ed. M.Z. Kaddari. Ramat Gan, 1974, 31-73.

_____. "The Language of Mishnat R. Eliezer" (Hebrew). *Annual of Bar Ilan University Studies in Judaica and the Humanities* 11. Ed. M.Z. Kaddari et al. Ramat Gan, 1973, 182-223.

_____. *Leqsiqon ha-Po'al she-Nitḥadesh be-Leshon ha-Tannaim.* (A Lexicon of the New Verbs in Tannaitic Hebrew). Ramat Gan, 1980.

_____. "New and Revived Verbs in the Baraitot of the Babylonian Talmud" (Hebrew). *Erkhe ha-Milon he-Ḥadash le-Sifrut Ḥazal* I. Ed. E.Y. Kutscher. Ramat Gan, 1972, 117-62.

Neubauer, Yekutiel. *Halakhah u-Midrash Halakhah.* Jerusalem, 1948.

Neugebauer, O. *The Exact Sciences in Antiquity.* Second ed. New York, 1969.

Neusner, Jacob. *A History of the Mishnaic Law of Purities.* 22 vols. Leiden, 1974-77.

_____. *Judaism: The Evidence of the Mishnah.* Chicago /London, 1981.

_____. *Judaism in Society: The Evidence of the Yerushalmi.* Chicago/ London, 1983.

_____. *The Memorized Torah: The Mnemonic System of the Mishnah.* Brown Judaic Studies 96. Chico, 1985.

_____. *Method and Meaning in Ancient Judaism.* Brown Judaic Studies 10. Missoula, 1979.

La paléographie hébraïque médiévale. Colloques Internationaux du Centre National de la Recherche Scientifique (C.N.R.S.). Paris, 1974.

Porton, Gary G. "Defining Midrash." *The Study of Ancient Judaism I: Mishnah, Midrash, Siddur.* Ed. J. Neusner. New York, 1981, 55-92.

Quentin, Henri. *Essais de critique textuelle.* Paris, 1926.

Qimron, Elisha. *The Hebrew of the Dead Sea Scrolls.* Harvard Semitic Studies 29. Atlanta, 1986.

Rabin, Chaim. "Hebrew and Aramaic in the First Century." *Compendia Rerum Iudaicarum ad Novum Testamentum* 1:2. Ed. S. Safrai/M. Stern et al. Assen/Philadelphia, 1976, 1007-39.

Ratner, B. *Ahawath Zion we-Jeruscholam.* 10 vols. Jerusalem, 1962.

Reynolds, L.D., and Wilson, N.G. *Scribes and Scholars: A Guide to the Transmission of Greek and Latin Literature.* Second ed. Oxford, 1974.

Rokeah, David. *Jews, Pagans and Christians in Conflict.* Jerusalem/Leiden, 1982.

Rosenthal, David. "Mishna Aboda Zara: A Critical Edition with Introduction" (Hebrew). 2 vols. Ph.D. dissertation: Hebrew University, 1980.

————. "Nusaḥ Ereẓ Yisrael ve-Nusaḥ Bavel be-Mishnat Avodah Zarah." *Meḥqarim ha-Sifrut ha-Talmudit.* A Study Conference in Honor of the Eightieth Birthday of Saul Lieberman. Israel Academy of Sciences and Humanities. Jerusalem, 1983, 79-92.

Roth, Abraham Naftali Ẓevi. "A Fragment from Midrash V'Hizhir" (Hebrew). *Talpiyyot* 7 (1958): 89-98.

Russell, D.S. *The Method and Message of Jewish Apocalyptic.* London, 1964.

Saldarini, Anthony J. "Reconstructions of Rabbinic Judaism." *Early Judaism and Its Modern Interpreters.* Ed. R.A. Kraft/G.W.E. Nickelsburg. Philadelphia/Atlanta, 1986, 437-77.

————. *Scholastic Rabbinism: A Literary Study of the Fathers According to Rabbi Nathan.* Brown Judaic Studies 14. Chico, 1982.

Sarason, Richard S. "The Significance of the Land of Israel in the Mishnah." *The Land of Israel: Jewish Perspectives.* Ed. L. Hoffman. Notre Dame, 1986, 109-36.

Sarfatti, Gad B. *Mathematical Terminology in Hebrew Scientific Literature of the Middle Ages* (Hebrew). Jerusalem, 1968.

————. "Some Remarks About the Prague Manuscript of *Mishnat ha-Middot.*" *HUCA* 45 (1974): 197-204.

Scheiber, Alexander. "The Prague Manuscript of *Mishnat ha-Middot.*" *HUCA* 45 (1974): 191-96.

Schiffman, Lawrence H. "The Temple Scroll in Literary and Philological Perspective." *Approaches to Ancient Judaism* II. Ed. W.S. Green. Brown Judaic Studies 9. Chico, 1980, 143-58.

Segal, Eliezer. "The Textual Traditions of Tractate Megillah in the Babylonian Talmud" (Hebrew). Ph.D. dissertation: Hebrew University, 1981.

Simon, Marcel. *Verus Israel.* Second ed. Paris, 1983.

Smith, Jonathan Z. *Map Is Not Territory: Studies in the History of Religions.* Leiden, 1978.

Sokoloff, Michael. *The Geniza Fragments of Bereshit Rabba.* Jerusalem, 1982.

_____. "The Hebrew of Genesis Rabbah According to MS Vatican 30" (Hebrew). *Leshonenu* 33 (1969): 25-42, 135-49, 270-79.

Strack, Herman L./Stemberger, Gunter. *Einleitung in Talmud und Midrasch.* Seventh ed. Munich, 1982.

Sussman, Jacob. "Mesoret Limmud u-Mesoret Nusah shel ha-Talmud ha-Yerushalmi." *Meḥqarim ba-Sifrut ha-Talmudit.* A Study Conference in Honor of the Eightieth Birthday of Saul Lieberman. Israel Academy of Sciences and Humanities. Jerusalem, 1983, 12-76.

Ta-Shema, Y.M. "The Library of the Sages of Ashkenaz of the Eleventh and Twelfth Centuries" (Hebrew). *Kiryat Sefer* 60 (1985): 298-309.

Towner, Wayne S. *The Rabbinic Enumeration of Scriptural Examples.* Leiden, 1973.

Vermes, Geza. "Bible and Midrash: Early Old Testament Exegesis." *Cambridge History of the Bible.* Ed. P. Ackroyd/C. Evans. Cambridge, 1970, 199-231.

_____. *Post-Biblical Jewish Studies.* Leiden, 1975.

Wacholder, Ben Zion. "The Date of the Mekilta de-Rabbi Ishmael." *HUCA* 39 (1968): 117-44.

_____. *The Dawn of Qumran.* Cincinnati, 1983.

_____. *Eupolemus: A Study of Judaeo-Greek Literature.* Cincinnati, 1974.

_____. *Messianism and Mishnah.* Cincinnati, 1979.

Weisenberg, E. "Problems Connected with the Ark of the Covenant" (Hebrew). *Essays Presented to Chief Rabbi Israel Brodie.* Ed. H.J. Zimmels et al (Hebrew vol.). London, 1967, 107-28.

Weiss, Abraham. *Al ha-Yezirah ha-Sifrutit shel ha-Amoraim.* New York, 1962.

Weiss, I. H. *Dor Dor ve-Dorshav.* 3 vols. Wilno, 1911.

Weiss Halivni, David. *Midrash, Mishnah, and Gemara.* Cambridge/London, 1986.

West, Martin L. *Textual Criticism and Editorial Technique.* Stuttgart, 1973.

Wilken, Robert L. *John Chrysostom and the Jews.* Berkeley/Los Angeles/London, 1983.

Winston, David. *The Wisdom of Solomon.* New York, 1979.

Yadin, Yigael. *Megillat ha-Miqdash.* 3 vols. Jerusalem, 1979.

_____. *The Temple Scroll.* New York, 1985.

Yerushalmi, Yosef Hayim. *Zakhor: Jewish History and Jewish Memory.* Seattle, 1982.

Zlotnick, D. *The Tractate "Mourning" (Semaḥot)*. New Haven, 1966.

Zucker, Moshe. *Al Targum Rav Saadia Gaon la-Torah*. New York, 1959.

_____. "Toward the Solution of the Problem of the Thirty- Two Hermeneutic Rules and Mishnat R. Eliezer" (Hebrew). *PAAJR* 23 (1954): 1-39.

Zunz, Leopold/Albeck, H. *Ha-Derashot be-Yisrael*. Third ed. Jerusalem, 1974.

Index of Biblical and Postbiblical Sources

General Index